THE POETRY OF BROWNING
A CRITICAL INTRODUCTION

Robert Browning, taking tea with the Browning Society.

The Poetry of Browning

A CRITICAL INTRODUCTION

———◦◉◦———

PHILIP DREW

METHUEN & CO LTD · LONDON

First published 1970
by Methuen & Co Ltd
11 New Fetter Lane, London EC4
© *1970 Philip Drew*
Printed in Great Britain
by W & J Mackay & Co Ltd, Chatham
416 14470 5

Distributed in the U.S.A.
by Barnes and Noble Inc.

To my mother and
the memory of my father

CONTENTS

Contents

PREFATORY NOTE

I am grateful to William Heinemann Ltd and Dodd, Mead & Co. for permission to reproduce the drawing of Robert Browning from *The Poets' Corner* by Max Beerbohm.

Substantial parts of Chapters 1 and 8 have appeared in *Victorian Poetry*, part of Chapter 3 has appeared in *The Listener* and part of Chapter 11 in *Essays in Criticism*: I wish to thank the editors for their permission to reprint this material.

My thanks go also to Chatto and Windus Ltd and Random House Inc. for permission to quote from Robert Langbaum's *The Poetry of Experience*, and to University of Texas Press for permission to quote from *Dearest Isa: Robert Browning's Letters to Isabella Blagden*, edited by Edward C. McAleer. I should also like to thank John Murray (Publishers) Ltd for permission to quote fairly extensively from *Learned Lady, Letters from Robert Browning to Mrs Thomas FitzGerald 1876–1889*, edited by Edward C. McAleer and published by Harvard University Press, and to the Carl H. Pforzheimer Library which contains the manuscripts of the particular letters quoted.

Finally I wish to acknowledge three personal debts – the first to Irene Elsey for her inexhaustible patience and efficiency in preparing the final typescript; the second to my friends William and Joyce Thorne, who urged me to start this book and encouraged me to finish it; the last to my wife, *sine qua non*.

Glasgow, 1969.   PHILIP DREW

(The numbers in square brackets throughout the text refer to the author's notes collected at the back of the book.)

ABBREVIATIONS

BOOKS

Armstrong, *Reconsiderations*	Isobel Armstrong (ed.), *The Major Victorian Poets: Reconsiderations* (London, 1969)
Chesterton, *Browning* (EML)	G. K. Chesterton, *Robert Browning* (London, 1903) – English Men of Letters series
Cook, *Commentary*	A. K. Cook, *A Commentary upon Browning's 'The Ring and the Book'* (Oxford, 1920)
Curle	Richard Curle (ed.), *Robert Browning and Julia Wedgwood* (London, 1937)
DeVane, *Handbook*	William Clyde DeVane, *A Browning Handbook* 2nd ed. (New York, 1955)
DeVane, *Parleyings*	William Clyde DeVane, *Browning's Parleyings, the Autobiography of a Mind* (New Haven, 1927)
DeVane and Knickerbocker	W. C. DeVane and K. L. Knickerbocker (ed.), *New Letters of Robert Browning* (New Haven, 1950)
Griffin and Minchin, *Life*	W. H. Griffin and H. C. Minchin, *The Life of Robert Browning* 2nd ed. (London, 1938)
Hood/Wise	Thurman L. Hood (ed.), *Letters of Robert Browning collected by Thomas J. Wise* (New Haven, 1933)
Hudson	Gertrude Reese Hudson (ed.), *Browning to his American Friends* (New York, 1965)

Landis and Freeman	Paul Landis and Ronald Freeman (ed.), *Letters of the Brownings to George Barrett* (Urbana, 1958)
Lowry	H. F. Lowry (ed.), *The Letters of Matthew Arnold to Arthur Hugh Clough* (London, 1932)
McAleer, *Dearest Isa*	Edward C. McAleer (ed.), *Dearest Isa: Robert Browning's Letters to Isabella Blagden* (Austin, 1951)
McAleer, *Learned Lady*	Edward C. McAleer (ed.) *Learned Lady: Letters from Robert Browning to Mrs Thomas FitzGerald 1876–1889* (Cambridge, Mass., 1966)
B. Miller, *Portrait*	Betty Miller, *Robert Browning, A Portrait* (London, 1952)
J. H. Miller, *Disappearance*	J. Hillis Miller, *The Disappearance of God* (Cambridge, Mass., 1963)
Orr, *Handbook*	Mrs Sutherland Orr, *A Handbook to the Works of Robert Browning* 7th ed. (London, 1896)
Orr, *Life and Letters*	Mrs Sutherland Orr, *Life and Letters of Robert Browning*, revised by F. G. Kenyon (London, 1908)
Raymond, *Infinite Moment*	W. O. Raymond, *The Infinite Moment* (Toronto, 1950)
RB/EBB	*The Letters of Robert Browning and Elizabeth Barrett Barrett 1845–1846*, 2 vols. (London, 1899)
Sharp	William Sharp, *Life of Robert Browning* (London, 1890)
Sherwood	Margaret Sherwood, *Undercurrents of Influence in English Romantic Poetry* (Cambridge, Mass., 1934)
Worsfold, *Men and Women*	Basil Worsfold (ed.) *Men and Women* [1855] in *The King's Poets* (London, 1904), 2 vols.

PERIODICALS

ELH	*Journal of English Literary History*
JEGP	*Journal of English and Germanic Philology*
MLN	*Modern Language Notes*
MLQ	*Modern Language Quarterly*
MP	*Modern Philology*
PMLA	*Publications of the Modern Language Association of America*
PQ	*Philological Quarterly*
SEL	*Studies in English Literature*
SP	*Studies in Philology*
TLS	*The Times Literary Supplement*
UTQ	*University of Toronto Quarterly*
VNL	*Victorian Newsletter*
VP	*Victorian Poetry*
VS	*Victorian Studies*

INTRODUCTION

My object in this book is to show the distinctive qualities of Browning as a Victorian poet and to argue that these qualities are of value. I originally hoped to do this by providing a simple handbook which would enable those who were interested to read Browning for themselves, and would in particular equip a reader new to Browning with some knowledge of the technique required and of the kind of pleasure to be looked for. Having often quoted with approval the tag μέγα βιβλίον μέγα κακόν I intended it to be a short book. I encountered, however, what other writers on Browning have commented on, a deplorable lack of extended studies of individual poems to which the enquiring reader could be referred for guidance and example. I therefore found it necessary to supply these in the course of the discussion. They now form almost the largest part of the book, and certainly the most fundamental, since it is on them that the argument ultimately depends. The book thus stands or falls by its numerous accounts of single poems, such as *St. Martin's Summer, Rephan, Blougram, How It Strikes a Contemporary, Too Late, Red Cotton Night-Cap Country* and so on.

Then, as I wrote, it became plain that misapprehensions about Browning were seriously damaging the reception of his poetry. I was prepared to explain briefly why I thought it wrong to apply to Browning the popular labels of 'Romantic' and 'difficult' and 'optimistic'. What I was not prepared for was the amount of adverse or, to speak more plainly, hostile criticism which has been directed at Browning by writers of high academic reputation. It seemed necessary to show precisely where I found such criticism ill-founded, and thus I found myself writing what would more properly have found its place in another book, preferably not written by me.

In this way what began as a modest introduction to a major poet has become a much more presumptuous piece of work, an attempt to reverse the Browning criticism of the last seventy years, to supply what should have been written then but was not, and finally to suggest a possible line of advance for Browning studies.

The book is arranged according to the following scheme. In the first part of the book I examine certain widespread views of Browning which

I think mistaken. Thus Chapters 1–3 are designed explicitly to show that, far from being a Romantic poet by any generally accepted definition, Browning resisted or opposed many prevailing Romantic ideas of the nature of poetry and of the poet's responsibility, and is thus more accurately classified as anti-Romantic. The implicit argument is that this anti-Romanticism was a source of strength rather than of weakness in his poetry and that the modern reader should therefore, like Browning, examine carefully the claims made for the Romantic tradition after 1825 and reject a large part of them.

Next I deal in some detail with the most prevalent misconception of Browning's poetry – that it is wilfully difficult. I distinguish between surface difficulties (Chapters 4 and 5) and the more fundamental difficulties inherent in his complex presentation of his subjects (Chapters 6 and 7). These first seven chapters are designed to be read before Browning's poetry, to warn of the real dangers and difficulties and to show the imaginary ones for what they are.

In the second part of the book I examine one further popular idea of Browning, that he is dedicated to expressing a crude and heedless optimism which nobody can be expected to take seriously. I am not prepared to advance for Browning the sort of defence that is sometimes put forward, for example for the more esoteric poems of Yeats – that poetry is written with words, not with ideas, and it is therefore possible to enjoy the poetry even while one rejects the ideas as erroneous or nonsensical. On the contrary it is explicitly argued in the introduction to the second part of the book that Browning cannot be accepted as a great poet except by a critic who is prepared to read his poems as a whole; this entails understanding and paying attention to what Browning is saying. The critic must therefore come to terms with Browning's 'optimism'. Accordingly in Chapters 8 and 9 I try to suggest a way of reading his poems on philosophical and religious subjects and to show that they are very far from being based on a blind confidence in a benevolent Creator. Implicit in this part of the book is the argument that it is in general a defect of modern critics to accept, and indeed welcome, a definition of poetry which allows, and indeed encourages, them to confine their attention to the form of the poem, and that such a definition is too narrow.

The last chapters in Part Two lay more stress on Browning as a Victorian poet. In Chapter 10 I offer an account of the relation between the language of his poetry and that of familiar conversation, and in Chapter 11 an account of his choice and treatment of subjects drawn from the life of his time, especially in the longer poems of the 1870s. This part of the book assumes a knowledge of the poems discussed and designed to illuminate their qualities.

In Part Three I examine the opinions of the most influential critics of Browning from Arnold to Leavis, and try to indicate the major requirements in Browning studies today.

My principal object has been to secure a hearing for Browning and if possible to prepare the way for an informed reading of his works. I naturally hope that what I have written will encourage a number of readers to make a trial of his poetry, but it is no part of my business to try to form their opinions for them in advance. On the whole therefore I have avoided direct value judgements on individual poems: when people read Browning for themselves with an open mind my word of praise and blame will no longer be of any consequence.

Part One

Part One

✤ 1 ✤

Browning's *Essay on Shelley* and its relevance to his own poetry

Note,
In just such songs as Eglamor (say) wrote
With heart and soul and strength, for he believed
Himself achieving all to be achieved
By singer – in such songs you find alone
Completeness, judge the song and singer one,
And either purpose answered, his in it
Or its in him: while from true works (to wit
Sordello's dream-performances that will
Never be more than dreamed) escapes there still
Some proof, the singer's proper life was 'neath
The life his song exhibits, this a sheath
To that; a passion and a knowledge far
Transcending these, majestic as they are,
Smouldered; his lay was but an episode
In the bard's life . . . (*Sordello* III, 615–630)

Romantic, a word for which, in connexion with literature, there is no generally accepted definition. *The Oxford Companion to English Literature*, 3rd edition, p. 677

I

One of the most enduring impressions left by prolonged study of the poetry of Browning is of its uniqueness, a quality which is most easily characterized by pointing to Browning's radical difference from all other poets of the nineteenth century. This in turn is most briefly expressed by saying that the other poets were Romantics and Browning was not, but this deliberately naïve formulation will not take us much farther unless we can attach a definite meaning to the word 'Romantic'. On the simplest level we can collect a series of textbook attributes of Romanticism and set them out as follows:

(i) an interest in the magical, mysterious, exotic, and supernatural; (ii) an interest in, often amounting to a worship of, natural scenery; (iii) the use of a diction, often remote from ordinary speech, which is particularly rich in euphonious and evocative words and phrases; (iv) a tradition of detailed observation especially of natural objects (see (ii)); and (v) a belief in the supreme importance of the individual, and hence in the primacy of the personal will and intuition over the dictates of external authority. This often leads to an introspective melancholy, or to a mood of rebellion against established institutions. It is expressed in various other ways – as a regard for primitive rather than for civilized man, for Nature as opposed to Art, and for the Countryside as opposed to the City.

If we agree that these qualities characterize the work of nineteenth-century poets in general, we have only to test Browning's poetry for their presence. It is not difficult to decide that the first three qualities are not to be found, but rather their contraries, and that Browning thus differs remarkably on these issues from his contemporaries. It is possible to argue that he differs equally radically, though less conspicuously, in the way in which he manifests the fourth and fifth attributes: this will indeed be my contention in later chapters of this book.

Yet even if this last point were to be conceded at once a difficulty would remain, for it may well be objected that this collection of symptoms does not constitute a complete definition of a Romantic poet, since such a definition must take particular account of his idea of the nature of poetry and the function of the poet. In describing these ideas it is customary to make some use of the distinction between 'subjective' and 'objective', but these terms are themselves as protean as those they offer to explain. Their devious semantic history can be followed elsewhere [1]: by the 1850s, when Browning used the opposition between them as the organizing principle of his *Essay on Shelley*, they had been accepted as part of the vocabulary of criticism [2]. With their assistance Browning examines Romantic ideas of the poet's personality as an integral part of his poem and the consequent implication that the poet is in some sense personally committed to the opinions in the poem. The *Essay* is thus of considerable critical interest, not so much for what Browning has to say about Shelley as for the light it throws on Browning's own poetic practice and on his opinion of his contemporaries.

II

In 1851 Browning was asked by Moxon to write an introductory essay to a volume of letters thought to be by Shelley. They were discovered to be spurious, and the book was withdrawn early in 1852.[1] Since then Browning's *Essay* has been reprinted many times. It is the longest and most notable of his critical writings: indeed, apart from his *Essay on Chatterton*, it is his only considerable work in prose.

It has been subject to general misunderstanding. Even Professor W. C. DeVane, whose *Browning Handbook* is indispensable for a study of the poet, gives a rather inaccurate account of the argument. He refers to the influence on Browning of an article by Joseph Milsand in the *Revue des Deux Mondes* of August, 1851, and comments, following Griffin and Minchin's account in the *Life*: 'Milsand's analysis suggested Browning's contrast between the subjective and objective poets, Shelley and Shakespeare. Through Milsand's article Browning was able to see Shelley plain, and, more importantly, was able to formulate his own theory of poetry and see his own place as a poet, recognizing that in himself the subjective and objective elements were mixed' [3].

This is misleading in two ways. In the first place, Milsand's article bears almost no relation to the *Essay* and cannot have been a source for it. On the contrary Milsand himself in a later article [4] adopts with approval some of the ideas which

---

[1] One may suspect a connection with the successful prosecution of Moxon in 1841 for a libel on God by publishing Shelley's *Queen Mab*. Obviously it was necessary that any work that might restore Shelley's reputation should be published, especially by Moxon. It is also of interest to note that when the case against Moxon came to court Browning's friend Serjeant Talfourd, for the defence, insisted on the incompleteness of Shelley's achievement and his gradual development away from the crude atheism of *Queen Mab*, points which Browning emphasizes in his *Essay*.

Browning put forward in the *Essay*, clearly showing that he considers them to have originated with Browning.[1]

Secondly, Browning offers in the *Essay* an account of Shelley's poetic position and of his own which is quite different from that given in DeVane's summary. He begins by distinguishing what he calls the 'objective poet', who reproduces 'things external . . . with an immediate reference, in every case, to the common eye and apprehension of his fellow men. . . . Such a poet is properly the ποιητης, the fashioner; and the thing fashioned, his poetry, will of necessity be substantive, projected from himself and distinct.' We must not ask what it meant to its creator. We must take it as a fact, which each of us deals with as best he may. Shakespeare is cited as an example of this kind of poet. The biography of such a man is not without interest, but we can do without it. 'The work speaks for itself, as we say.'

On the other hand we have 'the subjective poet of modern classification'. He writes not for 'the many below' but for 'the One above him', who sees the absolute truth. Thus he writes about Platonic Ideas, thus he writes about 'the primal elements of humanity', thus he writes about his own soul. 'He does not paint pictures and hang them on the walls, but rather carries them on the retina of his own eyes: we must look deep into his human eyes, to see those pictures on them. He is rather a seer, accordingly, than a fashioner', and produces not so much a work as an effluence of his own personality. To know and understand his poetry we must know and understand the man himself.

It is natural to suppose that at this point in the essay Browning will hasten to classify Shelley as a subjective poet, thus justifying the publication of the letters he is introducing. But he proceeds to argue that when we are faced with a masterpiece we are entitled to believe without further scrutiny that it was inspired by a great moral purpose. 'Greatness in a work suggests

[1] The quotation from *Sordello* which stands at the head of this chapter indicates that the ideas underlying the *Essay* had been with Browning for some years. When Browning wrote to Carlyle (Hood/Wise, p. 36) that he had some of Carlyle's opinions in mind when he wrote the *Essay*, he did not necessarily mean it to be supposed that he agreed with them. In fact what he does is to take Carlyle's definition of a poet in 'The Death of Goethe' ('The true Poet is ever . . . the Seer; whose eye has been gifted to discern the godlike Mystery of God's Universe . . .; we can still call him a *Vates* and Seer . . .') and to treat it as a description of one kind of poet, insisting on the existence and the value of other kinds.

an adequate instrumentality.' He now applies this to the matter in hand by maintaining that we could, but for the special circumstances of the case, deduce Shelley's intellectual and moral stature from the quality of his verse alone, for in his surviving works he shows all the attributes of the 'whole poet', that is, a poet who combines the powers of the objective and the subjective poet. He sees the world as it is: he is not led to accept partial artistic successes as ultimate standards but looks higher than any previous writer: he realizes what he owes to his predecessors for their interpretation of the world and offers his own vision to the men of the future: finally, by means of this vision of the future and his knowledge of his own advanced nature he extends Man towards God. All this he does in language singularly in keeping with his lofty themes.

The argument to this point, at which Browning concludes his general observations on poetry, would lead the reader to suppose that, since Shelley's poetry is, like that of the objective poet, evidence enough by itself, there was no need of any biographical information. But Browning goes on to show that Shelley is a special case. He has said earlier that when a poet has died prematurely we may learn from his life whether he ever knew 'more than he spoke of', that is, than he was able to express in his poetry during his lifetime. Since Shelley was cut off in his youth we have at least one reason for wanting to know more about his life. In the second place, Shelley's life has been misconstrued, and this has led to a failure to appreciate his poetry. Therefore we must study his life.[1]

For the rest of the *Essay* Browning offers a defence of Shelley, which is of no immediate interest. It is intended to achieve the same object as the publication of material about Shelley's life, that is, to serve as a check to gossip which might lead one to suppose that Shelley was not of a moral stature high enough to produce a truly great work of art. He concludes with a discussion of Shelley's characteristic qualities as a poet. He takes Shelley's supreme ability to be that of connecting ideal Power

[1] Note that T. S. Eliot in 'The Use of Poetry and the Use of Criticism' says, 'The biographical interest which Shelley has always excited makes it difficult to read the poetry without remembering the man', an observation which confirms the soundness of Browning's feeling that it was vital to set in good order the record of Shelley's life.

and Love with real Beauty and Goodness. All his poetry has this high aim of reconciling the actual and the absolute. It would be easy to put forward *The Cenci*, for example, or *Julian and Maddalo*, or the *Ode to Naples* as successful objective poems, but it is more important to see that the body of work known as 'Shelley' – that is, the successful poems *and* the 'less organized matter' – is a product in its entirety of an even higher power.

The essay as a whole is ingeniously put together with frequent comings and goings, digressions and cross-linkings. It is not of great value as an introduction to the letters, since, as I have shown, much of its argument is devoted to showing that Shelley is not the type of poet whose works can be understood only through a study of his life. Apart from the measured grandeur of Browning's language when he pays homage to Shelley's transcendent gifts as a poet, the most interesting part of the essay is the beginning, when Browning makes one of his rare excursions into poetic theory. His remarks are given added relevance by their obvious connection with his own poetic practice. For instance, he writes, 'The objective poet, in his appeal to the aggregate human mind, chooses to deal with the doings of men (the result of which dealing, in its pure form, when even description, as suggesting a describer, is dispensed with, is what we call dramatic poetry).'

While it is clear that Browning would classify himself as an objective poet, he is far from conceding that this is an inferior order. He says quite unambiguously, 'It would be idle to inquire, of these two kinds of poetic faculty in operation, which is the higher or even rarer endowment', for they are equally necessary. There is no reason why a poet should not produce works of both kinds: in fact, we normally see a combination of both in any one poet: at best we may say that one poet is a comparatively pure example of one kind or the other. The point is that Browning certainly does not imply that objective poetry is of lesser value. Indeed, since he takes Shakespeare as his first example of this kind of poet it is evident that no such discrimination is in his mind.

Mrs Betty Miller is therefore wide of the mark when she writes, 'What emerges, nevertheless, is Browning's opinion, self-condemnatory, of the objective poet, or "artificer". Lacking the "self-sufficing central light" of a Shelley – or, more cul-

pably, shunning the "pure white light" of his own inspiration –
he is a mere "fashioner", a maker of "chains of cherry-stones";
not like Shelley, like the true poet, a prophet and a "seer" [5].
In this passage Mrs Miller assumes, in the face of Browning's
explicit statement to the contrary, that he considers the objective poet as having somehow failed to realize his potentialities.
To Browning the 'seer' and the 'fashioner' are equally poets: it
was Shelley's gift to combine both capacities. The phrase 'self-
sufficing central light' Browning uses to describe the power of
the works of Shelley to illuminate themselves: they are thus of
the same kind as those of the objective poets, and distinct from
those works which require biographical information to supple-
ment them. The contrasted phrases 'pure white light' and 'chains
of cherry-stones' I do not find in the *Essay*, the whole tenor of
which, as I have shown, resists any such opposition. When Mrs
Miller describes as 'self-condemnatory' Browning's classification of himself as predominantly an objective poet (that is, a
poet of the same kind as Shakespeare) she shows that she has
totally failed to follow the drift of the argument.

III

The relevance of the *Essay* to Browning must be established in
other ways than this. Three main points are to be made, all of
which mark Browning's sense of the difference between his own
poetry and that of the Romantic poets of the first half of the
nineteenth century.

First, Browning resisted throughout his career any attempt
to interpret his poems in the light of his life or, conversely, to
establish his personal opinions from those of the characters in his
poems. This has been criticized as showing a prudish, if not
morbid, love of privacy, but it is plain from the *Essay* that
Browning regarded the sort of poetry that he wrote as quite distinct from its creator. 'The biography of the worker is no more
necessary to an understanding or enjoyment of it, than is a
model or anatomy of some tropical tree, to the right tasting of
the fruit we are familiar with on the market-stall. . . .' In this
way Browning's inveterate dislike of those who drew parallels
between his poems and his life is given a theoretical justification in the *Essay*.

Secondly, Browning says, 'The objective poet . . . chooses to deal with the doings of men, . . . while the subjective poet, whose study has been himself, appealing through himself to the absolute Divine mind, prefers to dwell upon those external scenic appearances which strike out most abundantly and uninterruptedly his inner light and power, selects that silence of the earth and sea in which he can best hear the beating of his individual heart. . . .' Thus in the extreme case the objective poet fills his foreground with 'men and women' and offers merely 'occasional illustrations from scenic nature' subordinate to the human interest of his work, while the subjective poet is like a landscape painter who introduces only a few 'figures' into his composition of earth and sky. It is clear that Browning's own poetry illustrates his distinction between the subject matter of the two kinds of poet. He filled his poems with the doings of mankind, whereas almost all the other poets of the nineteenth century found their inspiration in solitude or in the countryside.

Finally, the *Essay* is of peculiar value since it is one of the few examples we have of comment by Browning on the course of poetic history. He describes what happens after a great surge of subjective poetry or a single great subjective poet has lifted up mankind 'by intensifying the import of details and rounding the universal meaning':

> A tribe of successors (Homerides) working more or less in the same spirit, dwell on his discoveries and reinforce his doctrine; till, at unawares, the world is found to be subsisting wholly on the shadow of a reality, on sentiments diluted from passions, on the tradition of a fact, the convention of a moral, the straw of last year's harvest. Then is the imperative call for the appearance of another sort of poet, who shall at once replace this intellectual rumination of food swallowed long ago, by a supply of the fresh and living swathe . . . prodigal of objects for men's outer and not inner sight, shaping for their uses a new and different creation from the last, which it displaces by the right of life over death.

The work of the objective poet endures until it is in turn superseded by that of the 'harmonizing' or subjective poet: thus poetry climbs one rung of the infinite ladder. That is the repeated pattern of poetic development – the objective poet providing the raw material of poetry, then the subjective poet combining and ordering this raw material, followed by a period of unreality until a new objective poet once more provides 'new substance'.

Since this is Browning's only account of poetic evolution it is of some interest to determine where in the cycle he placed the poetry of his own age. From the stress he lays on the importance of 'the silence of the earth and sea' to 'the subjective poet of modern classification' it seems likely that Browning has particularly in mind the Romantic poets of the early nineteenth century. If this is so his contemporaries are either the heirs of the great traditions of Wordsworth and Coleridge, or, equally possibly, they are even later in the great period of poetic change and merely chew the straw of last year's harvest. If Browning had wished to maintain the second position, it would have been open to him to argue that after more than fifty years the original Romantic impulse had begun to lose its vitality, not least because of its remoteness from the real world of men.

In either case, whether his contemporaries were working in a fruitful or in an exhausted tradition, Browning does not reckon himself of their number, for, unlike them, he is a predominantly objective poet, one whose task is to supply 'the fresh and living swathe'. That Browning was convinced of the importance of this task is clear from the *Essay*: one last quotation may stand as a fitting comment on his abiding concern with 'Man's thoughts, loves, hates':

> For it is with this world, as starting point and basis alike, that we shall always have to concern ourselves: the world is not to be learned and thrown aside, but reverted to and relearned. The spiritual comprehension may be infinitely subtilised, but the raw material it operates upon, must remain. [6]

How to read a
Dramatic Monologue

It is not in this sense that *Poesie* is said to be a kind of *Painting*; it is not the *Picture* of the *Poet*, but of *things* and *persons* imagined by him. He may be in his own practice and disposition a *Philosopher*, nay, a *Stoick*, and yet speak sometimes with the softness of an amorous *Sappho*. COWLEY, Preface to *Poems* (1656)

To maintain a complete and absolute impersonality in matter, and yet to develop and preserve a strong and unmistakable individuality in manner; to depict a wide variety of character without palpable bias, and yet to leave the moral bearings of the product not only uninvolved, but strongly self-evident; these are the two correlative aims with which every great dramatic poet, who cherishes the idea of benefiting his race, must labour. . . . With Browning these correlative aims seem never for a moment to have failed of their strong due influence. H. B. FORMAN [1]

> . . . A story I could body forth so well
> By making speak, myself kept out of view,
> The very man as he was wont to do,
> And leaving you to say the rest for him.
> (*Sordello* I, 14–17)

Browning's *Dramatic Lyrics*, his first collection of short poems, appeared in 1842. He prefaced it with an advertisement which read:

Such poems as the following come properly enough, I suppose, under the head of 'Dramatic Pieces'; being, though for the most part Lyric in expression, always Dramatic in principle, and so many utterances of so many imaginary persons, not mine.

He was to make similar claims throughout his life, especially in his letters. Sending a copy of Volume I of *Men and Women* to his friend Milsand on 10 August 1855 he wrote:

> My poems go under the distinctive title 'Men and Women' – they being really dramatic attempts and not a collection of miscellanies.

On 10 December in the same year he wrote to Ruskin

> The last charge I cannot answer, for you may be right in preferring it, however unwitting I am of the fact. I may put Robert Browning into Pippa and other men and maids. If so, *peccavi*: but I don't see myself in them, at all events.

Later in his life, in 1876, he was charged with having wrongly used the term High Priest, where Rabbi would have been more accurate. He replied:

> This comes of forgetting that one writes dramatically. The speaker, Baldinucci, is a typically ignorant Tuscan, and makes the gross mistake already noticed in Arbuthnot's *Martinus Scriblerus*.

In a similar way he explained that in *The Bishop Orders His Tomb at St Praxed's Church* 'the blunder as to the sermon is the result of the dying man's haziness; he would not reveal himself as he does but for that' [2]. Again he wrote with some indignation to Julia Wedgwood on 19 November 1868 after she had complained that he must be speaking in his own person when he referred to the *Pandects* in *The Ring and the Book* (V, 1781):

> Why is the allusion to Justinian *mine* and not the man's I give it to? The whole of his speech, as I premise, is untrue . . . but he was quite able to cant, and also know something of the Pandects, which are the basis of actual Italian law. (Curle, p. 161)

A final instance is to be found in his letter to Furnivall of 11 October 1881:

> Last, about my being 'strongly against Darwin, rejecting the truths of science and regretting its advance' – you only do as I should hope and expect in disbelieving *that*. It came, I suppose, of Hohenstiel-Schwangau's expressing the notion which was the popular one at the appearance of Darwin's book – and you might as well charge Shakespeare with holding that there were men whose heads grew beneath their shoulders, because Othello told Desdemona that he had seen such. (Hood/Wise p. 199)

In 1879 and 1880 Browning offered the public his two series of *Dramatic Idyls*, patiently explaining the title to Wilfred Meynell in his letter of 10 April 1879 – 'These [idyls] of mine are called "Dramatic" because the story is told by some actor in it, not by the poet himself.' While not all Browning's poems are dramatic in this sense, a large number of them are, and of these by far the most important are his dramatic monologues.

In this chapter I shall consider the implications of the word 'dramatic' in the term 'dramatic monologue', and the special technique which poems of this kind demand from the reader. In particular I want to establish the conditions, if any, under which we may claim to infer from a dramatic monologue Browning's own attitude to the speaker and hence to the topics under discussion in the poem.

I

The dramatic monologue, though it is often written about, is seldom described in detail. A simple straightforward account is that given by H. Buxton Forman in *The Fortnightly Review* in 1869:

> In each monologue some particular point of interest in the history of a human soul is taken up. The soul, whether historical or fictitious, generally speaks for itself all that is spoken – the artist invariably refraining from any appearance as a spokesman. In the course of the monologue all circumstances in the past development of the soul, which are available for illuminating the present point, are brought out, and the present or past action of other human beings on the speaker is indicated either by detail on the speaker's part, or by some such artifice as a sudden change in the tone of the monologue, from which we learn that the person addressed has said or done something; and sometimes the whole expression of the actual speaker is devoted to the analysis of another soul – the idealised reproduction of another character, or set of mental phenomena. This method, of course, affords a great compactness and symmetry to the series of circumstances relating to the particular mind under treatment; and the attention of the reader is to a large extent concentrated on that one soul, though it is quite possible to treat a plurality of souls ably in one monologue. [3]

Ina Beth Sessions offers a very rigid formal scheme of classification, specifying seven points which are to be found in the ideal monologue – (1) the speaker, (2) the audience, (3) the occasion, (4) interplay between (1) and (2), (5) revelation of character, (6) dramatic action, and (7) action taking place in the present [4]. Although Miss Sessions lays considerable stress on the last two points, (6) is not clearly defined and (7) is far from essential. It is not true that if a monologue refers to some exciting action simultaneously taking place it is necessarily more exciting than reminiscence or speculation. For Browning at least the important feature is point (5), but in his monologues the revelation of character is rarely simple.

To present the process as clearly as possible I suggest in this section an ideal basic pattern of the Browning monologue: in practice the monologues call for a fairly varied range of responses in the reader according to their deviations from the 'pure' form.

The typical form of one of Browning's dramatic monologues is a narrative (N) spoken by one person. From N we can infer one or more of the following:

   (i) the circumstances in which N is spoken,

  (ii) the preceding history of the speaker, especially the part that explains the occasion of N, and

 (iii) the character and motives of the speaker.

But these inferences are of two kinds:

  (A) those which the speaker realizes are apparent, and which he has presumably designed, and

  (B) those which the speaker has not designed, and which he presumably does not realize are apparent.

Thus the first step in reading a dramatic monologue is normally the drawing of inferences to complete the poem; the work the reader does, for example, in supplying inferences (i) and (ii) is equivalent to providing the context for the poem, as if it were a lyric in a play and the reader had to supply the play from the clues in the lyric. Sometimes this first stage is sufficient and the reader has no further action to take: some of Browning's shorter poems, for example, require only (i) and (ii) to be supplied in outline. The poem is then complete in the sense that there is no further revelation of the character of the speaker. Poems of this kind are more properly called dramatic lyrics than dramatic monologues.

In the body of major poems which call for a more complex response from the reader the next stage is normally one of comparison. These comparisons are of three possible kinds, sometimes mixed:

(i) When a monologue is spoken by a historical character or by an invented character set in a specific period of history we are normally required to compare what is presented as a contemporary account with our own fuller knowledge. *Karshish* is an obvious example.

(ii) More often the comparison is internal. That is, we compare $N+A$ with $N+A+B$; in this way we measure the speaker's version of the case against what we have learned *from his own words* to be the truth. This to my mind is the central characteristic of the dramatic monologue as Browning developed it, that without taking 'pointing-pole in hand' or chalking 'broadly on each vesture's hem/The wearer's quality' the poet provides in a single poem a man's version of reality and the standards by which that version is to be tested.

(iii) Occasionally we are required, as in *Caliban upon Setebos*, to compare the views put forward with our own. If there is no discrepancy then we must judge our own views as we judge those of the speaker: if there is a discrepancy then we must decide either that the speaker's arguments are false or that our own views are unsound. That is to say, the result of the monologue is to impose a fresh perspective on ideas which, for example, the reader has uncritically accepted.

This process of completion and comparison sounds, when analysed, mechanical, and not a possible response to *poetry*, but it is saved from being merely a logical exercise. In the first place the operations begin as soon as we start to read the poem and continue all the time we are reading it, often with unexpected revelations of fact or character. Further, when we have finished reading the poem and have carried out stage two (comparison) we are equipped with information to enable us to make fresh inferences and thus to modify stage one (completion) and thus perhaps prepare the way for a fresh stage two and so on. By these progressively closer approximations we arrive at a clearer understanding of the whole poem.

When these reactions have died down and we feel that we have the narrator and his poem in focus we are able to move on to the third stage, that of an assessment of the speaker and his views. (This assessment is always to some degree complicated by the fact that we have learned the story from the speaker and hence cannot be completely out of sympathy with him, although 'sympathy' is really too positive a word to use here. It is more accurate to say that we are acquainted with the speaker and that our judgement of him is influenced by this acquaintance, since we can no longer decide the question impersonally. In *The Bishop Orders his Tomb*, for example, our judgement of the worldliness and hypocrisy of the speaker is complicated by our sympathy for the speaker or, as I should prefer to say, by our acquaintance with him.) In *Andrea del Sarto* we must ultimately judge the speaker to be deficient in self-knowledge. He is pathetically incapable of deciding whether his painting or his wife is more important to him, he is conscious of falling short as an artist and as a husband, he senses that the two deficiencies are connected, and he blames one for the other in turn, never admitting that the same defect in his own personality is responsible for both.

This third stage can be summed up in one crucial question, the question we normally ask in order to determine our judgement – 'Why does the speaker represent this event to us in this *incomplete* way?' In poems like *Cleon* or *Karshish* we initially blame the narrator's lack of information on the fact that he stands too close to the events he is describing. Later of course we see that this lack of historical perspective is the equivalent of a similar defect in nineteenth-century man, and the individual importance of Cleon or Karshish is to that extent diminished. We have then a situation very like the third type of comparison I have distinguished, that is, we have to compare the speaker's position with our own. As usual in the third type, it is our own opinions which we are required to re-examine. We judge a certain character to be dishonest or superficial, only to realize that his opinions are a version of those we hold ourselves.

It must be repeated that these reactions to the monologue, which I have for convenience divided into successive stages, are not so divided when we read the poem. They overlap and continually modify one another. Thus the dramatic monologue normally requires from the reader a complex serial response. Naturally this is seen fully displayed only in the major pieces, such as *Bishop Blougram's Apology*, but it can be demonstrated on a small scale in a poem such as *Soliloquy of the Spanish Cloister* [5].

To begin with it is necessary to supply the setting of the poem: here the title tells us the minimum that is needed, but corroboration and expansion are eventually available from the poem itself (Stanzas IV and VI). As we read the narrative (N) we gradually learn the character of the speaker and of his principal subject, a fellow-monk called Brother Lawrence, who is gardening while the speaker watches him narrowly. (A) The Speaker wishes us to believe that Brother Lawrence is a bore (II), lecherous (IV), irreligious (V) and sycophantic (VI), whereas he is himself guiltless of these faults. But (B) the natural inference from the poem is that Brother Lawrence is an industrious and unselfish gardener who shows no sign of unmonastic desires for female company, whereas the speaker himself knows and thinks more than he should about the local women (IV), is superstitious (V), spiteful (lines 24, 47–48), given to reading pornographic books (VIII), and spends much of his time in devising diabolical but grotesque expedients for damning Brother Lawrence's soul. It is evident that his hatred of Lawrence springs from his own sense of inferiority and has warped his judgement: thus we can account for the discrepancy between N+A and N+A+B.

It requires no very austere moral standards to decide that the speaker is a hypocrite who conceals his malice and worldliness behind a façade of piety. However this judgement is, as usual, complicated by our acquaintance with the speaker who has, like Holy Willie, been entertaining us. Our provisional identification modifies the outright condemnation which would be the normal result of hearing about a monk such as the speaker, and our final verdict on him, though unfavourable, is not wholly without sympathy, or at least understanding. He is seen as the victim of the corrosive boredom of monastic life and of its pernicious effects on those who for one reason or another enter the cloister without any vocation. The fact that Brother Lawrence has such a vocation and is perfectly content with his monotonous and frugal existence only exacerbates the speaker, and not unnaturally leads him to focus all his resentment on the inoffensive gardener. We begin to judge the speaker as soon as we start reading the poem, so that in this example the three stages of assimilating the poem – completion, comparison and judgement – overlap.

II

So far I have been discussing Browning's dramatic monologues as though they were all cut from the same cloth. Now it is time to discriminate between them, and the basis on which I propose to make distinctions is that of the ease with which Browning's attitude can be separated from that of his speaker. The criterion will thus be the obviousness or obliquity of the presentation.

As an illustration of the point consider a work written for the theatre. In act one of *Pippa Passes* Pippa is given a short song:

> The year's at the spring
> And day's at the morn;
> Morning's at seven;
> The hillside's dew-pearled;
> The lark's on the wing;
> The snail's on the thorn:
> God's in his heaven –
> All's right with the world!

This lyric is carefully placed in the play. Its immediate purpose is by its freshness to bring home to Sebald, who overhears it, the oppressive weight of his illicit love for Ottima, 'magnificent in sin', a love which literally takes place in a hothouse. In the larger context the song is equally appropriate, for the 'Happiest Ones' of Asolo whom Pippa envies are far from happy, and before the day ends she will herself have narrowly escaped from a plot to decoy her to the brothels of Rome, where 'the courtesans perish off every three years'. A powerful element in the song is an ironic exploitation of Pippa's innocent trust in the world, which the rest of the play shows to be corrupt and guilty [6]. To quote the last two lines as though they expressed Browning's own optimism shows an obvious failure to understand what drama is.

This example illustrates in a crude form the basic point of the *separateness* of Browning and his speaker. Almost as unambiguous is *Up at a Villa – Down in the City* (1855), a poem in which the whole point is that the contrasts drawn by the speaker, with his exaggerated ideas of *savoir vivre*, are all reversed by the reader, so that the arguments advanced in favour of the town in fact discommend it, while the speaker's complaints about the countryside show only his own impercipience.

Most of Browning's dramatic monologues are of the type of which this is an extreme example. Few are equally short and simple, however; even a rather unsubtle poem like *Filippo Baldinucci on the Privilege of Burial* (1876) has rather more to it, and the best known monologues in *Men and Women* will not yield their meaning to a simple reversal of values. As I show in Chapter 6, *A Toccata of Galuppi's*, *Bishop Blougram's Apology* and *Mr. Sludge, 'The Medium'* require a complicated response from the reader and a most carefully qualified judgement of the speaker, while *Andrea del Sarto*, for example, is a good specimen of a monologue which arouses sympathy for the speaker far more strongly than censure.

So one might continue and construct a kind of spectrum – at one end the monologues in which Browning makes unmistakably clear his own attitude to the speaker, at the other the monologues which cannot be comprehended in the general scheme I have outlined. I have particularly in mind *Mr. Sludge, 'The Medium'*, *Prince Hohenstiel-Schwangau* [7] and *Fifine at the Fair* [7]. While we may infer something of Browning's own attitude to the matters under discussion we are not able to place the speaker with the same certainty as in many of the shorter poems. This does not invalidate my account of Browning's dramatic monologues in general. Most of his earlier and shorter monologues are to be read in the way I suggest, *Pictor Ignotus* being the main exception, but in his later longer monologues he is not offering such an easy judgement to the reader.

There are several possible explanations of this. One might suggest, for example, that as Browning grew older his opinions on many subjects, notably Christianity, became less assured. Again the length of the later poems encourages a more flexible approach. A simple right/wrong value judgement of the speaker exhausts the subject too quickly. We may compare the longer monologues with a novel, which exists by holding in tension differing sets of ideas, while the shorter monologues are more like short stories, which exist by virtue of expressing with sudden power a crucial glimpse of a single limited point of view. A third possible reason is to be found in *Prince Hohenstiel-Schwangau* itself. The Prince, after declaring that every man is free to choose for himself the way in which he will perform his allotted duties says

> To other men, to each and every one
> Another law! what likelier? . . .
> . . . I only know
> That varied modes of creatureship abound . . .
> What mode may yours be? I shall sympathise.

This accords so well with the speculations which Browning pursues in *La Saisiaz* that it suggests strongly that Browning was increasingly conscious of the subjective nature of his own judgements, and of the difficulty of finding justification for expecting other people to share his opinions. He is accordingly more ready to present a speaker without implying a single judgement of him, leaving the reader instead with the materials for a more tentative judgement. That is to say, after we have read a complex monologue we are not expected simply to condemn or sanctify the speaker. But the monologue itself has involved us so deeply in the speaker's subject that we can make up our own minds about that, and then compare our own position with the speaker's, according him more or less sympathy. This reader's response is far less under Browning's control than it was in the earlier monologues, but it is induced and to some extent conditioned by the poem.

In most of Browning's monologues careful reading allows the reader to perceive, although with varying degrees of certainty, Browning's own attitude towards his speaker. Generalizations about the whole range of Browning's monologues are misleading if they suggest that the mechanism is the same in them all. It is incorrect to say that we can *always* feel the strongly-indicated response which leads us to infer with confidence Browning's relation to the speaker: it is equally incorrect to say that we can *never* make such an inference.

III

It is in this sense that Browning's poetry is properly called 'dramatic' and it is these attributes of the drama and the dramatist's art which he prized. It should not be necessary to make this point at such length or to explain that it is a critical blunder to assume, in the teeth of the poet's own repeated statements and of the nature of the poems themselves, that Browning himself accepts at face value the opinions and doctrines which his characters are made to utter.

As I say, the point could be allowed to stand as self-evident were it not for statements such as Joseph E. Baker's that 'we are seldom safe in assuming that Browning disagrees with one of his characters' [8]. So far is this from being true that it could be more accurately phrased, 'We are never safe in assuming that Browning agrees with one of his characters.' The dramatic bent in Browning is so strong and his preference for ironic presentation so marked that a complete identity of view between the speaker and the poet is the exception rather than the rule, and should be admitted only after a most careful reading of the poem and never assumed *a priori*. In short, Browning's poetry should not be taken at its face value as a statement of his own attitude unless we can positively exclude the possibility of irony or dramatic obliquity. In practice it is necessary to relax this rule occasionally, but it remains nevertheless the ideal.

Does this lead us to the conclusion that we can never infer Browning's own views from a consideration of his dramatic monologues? Are we, that is to say, bound to accept each monologue as simply the utterance of an 'imaginary personage' which gives us no hint of how the poet expects us to regard it? It is at this point that I must reluctantly declare myself unable to accept the position of Robert Langbaum, whose book, *The Poetry of Experience* (London, 1957), is one of the most original and stimulating of recent works on Browning and indeed on all post-Wordsworthian poetry.

Langbaum's argument as far as it applies to Browning can be summarized as follows: After the Enlightenment there was a conflict between thought and emotion. The topographical poets attempted to 'heal the breach' by describing a landscape which gave rise at once to thought and emotion (pp. 38–39). Then

Wordsworth showed how such a poem could be brought to a dramatic climax with a sudden sharpening of the observer's apprehension of the landscape amounting to 'a revelation of his own sentience in nature'. (p. 42) 'The experience has validity just because it is dramatized as an event which we must accept as having taken place, rather than formulated as an idea with which we must agree or disagree.' (p. 43) *Tintern Abbey* and *Frost at Midnight* are expertly analysed from this point of view. For this 'way of meaning' Langbaum adopts Joyce's term *epiphany*, which, he says, 'grounds the statement of value in perception; it gives the idea with its genesis, establishing its validity not as conforming to a public order of values but as the genuine experience of an identifiable person'. (p. 46) The difficulty is 'to keep the poem located – to keep the dramatic situation from turning into a rhetorical device and the landscape from turning into a metaphor for an abstract idea'. The Romantic solution is to impose on the poem an extraordinary perspective which 'keeps the landscape intact by giving evidence of its being looked upon'. 'The authority of the perspective is, of course, reinforced by the autobiographical connection of romantic poetry, by the identification of the speaker as Wordsworth or Coleridge and of the location as places where they are known to have been.' (pp. 47–48)

Each poem is a step forward in the observer's knowledge of himself, a step taken by identifying himself in an aspect of the Other (the Other often being external Nature). 'For the observer does not so much learn as become something. Each discovery of the external world is a discovery of himself, and his identity with and difference from the external world.' (p. 49) 'The fact that meaning is evolved and is itself only an incident in the evolution of a soul explains the dynamic equilibrium of the poetry of experience', the name which Langbaum gives to all poetry of this type and which he uses as a generic term for all poetry after 1800. When we have read a poem of this kind 'the thing we are left with is the thing the observer is left with – a total movement of the soul, a step forward in self-articulation'. This is communicated 'not as truth but experience, making its circumstance ambiguously objective in order to make it emphatically someone's experience'. (p. 51) Hence the importance of the observer or narrator or central character. 'Because the observer has the same function whether or not he bears the poet's name, we should not – in those poems where he is Wordsworth or Keats or Shelley – think of him as the man his friends knew and his biographers write about; we should rather think of him as a character in a dramatic action.' (p. 52)

'The romantic lyric or poem of experience . . . is both subjective and objective. The poet talks about himself by talking about an object; and he talks about an object by talking about himself. . . . I know of no better way to describe the peculiar style of address of the distinctively romantic lyric than to compare it to one side of a dialogue, with the other side understood by its effect. The poet speaks through the observer of the romantic lyric the way a playwright speaks through one of his characters. . . . When we consider how dramatic the romantic lyric is . . . we can only wonder whether it can properly be called a lyric at all – whether the poetry of experience is not itself a new genre which abolishes the distinction between subjective and objective poetry.' (pp. 53–54) The same principles hold good for Romantic narrative poetry. '*Resolution and Independence* is not only a narrative about a meeting of two people, it is also a lyric about the evolution of an observer through his evolving vision of an old man. There is the same difference of actuality between the observer and the old man that there is between the observer of *Tintern Abbey* and the landscape.' (p. 54) The same movement of the narrator is to be observed in *Michael* and *Frost at Midnight*. (p. 55)

In this way Langbaum lays down his general case, (A) that the Romantic lyric is of the kind he has described. He next goes on to claim (B) that all dramatic monologues are particular examples of this general case. If he can prove (B) and his general position (A) is accepted, it will be readily conceded (C) that Browning wrote dramatic monologues and therefore (D) that the general description which Langbaum has given is true of Browning.

His argument for (B) is as follows. 'Wordsworth shows the connection between the dramatic lyric and the dramatic monologue, when he turns his visionary stare upon a solitary figure with the same transforming effect as when he turns it upon a natural object.' (p. 71) 'It is as the articulation of a meaning coming back from the *informed* object, that the dramatic monologue differs from other first-person utterances where the speaker is not the author.' (p. 72) 'The dramatic monologue, in other words, . . . must be a poem of experience. . . . The dramatic monologue [is], with its combination of dramatic and lyrical elements, an imitation of experience and the representative form of a poetry of experience.' (p. 73) '. . . To give facts from within, to derive meaning, that is, from the poetic material itself rather than from the external standard of judgment, is the specifically romantic contribution to literature.' Langbaum rejects the 'standard' account of the dramatic monologue as 'a reaction against the romantic confessional style' on the grounds that Browning and Tennyson both arrived at the same form independently. 'We must suspect that they inherited a form which required only one more step in its development to achieve the objectivity they desired.' (p. 79)

In support of this Langbaum quotes from Joseph Milsand's review of *Men and Women* [9], which suggests that Browning 'would have us conceive the inner significance of things by making us see their exteriors'. He concludes, 'Browning's innovations [are] part of a general change of sensibility – a demand that all literature yield much the same effect, an effect of lyrical intensity.'

Thus the argument so far runs:

  (i) Wordsworth's poetry is not simply autobiographical, but dramatic.

 (ii) There are connections between the dramatic lyric and the dramatic monologue.

(iii) Browning wrote dramatic monologues.

(iv) Therefore what is true of Wordsworth's poetry is true of Browning's.

But

  (i) Wordsworth's poetry is 'a poetry of experience'.

 (ii) In 'poetry of experience' the material exists apart from a moral judgement.

(iii) Therefore in Wordsworth the material exists apart from a moral judgement, and (from the preceding syllogism) the same is true of Browning's poetry.

It is easy to see how this argument leads Mr Langbaum to deny the moral implications of Browning's poetry.

I should like first of all to show why I disagree with this statement of the general case and then to explain why I cannot accept Langbaum's accounts of specific poems of Browning's.

The weakness of the general argument is clearly in the second premise of the first proposition. Langbaum uses the word 'dramatic' of Wordsworth's poetry, as the quotations show, in a very special sense. Even while he uses it he continually admits the autobiographical nature of Romantic poetry, as in the passage quoted from pp. 47–48. Further examples abound. For example, if the passage I have quoted from p. 43 is true then we can only accept the event as autobiographical; the use of the word 'genesis' in the passage from p. 46 must mean 'occurrence to the poet'; similarly 'the genuine experience of an identifiable person' calls unambiguously for a strong autobiographical element. Further 'the step forward in self-articulation', the end-product of a Romantic poem, is an affair not of the reader's 'self' but of the poet's. Indeed on p. 48 Langbaum says explicitly, 'The content and meaning of what [the poet] sees has existence and validity only within the limiting conditions of his gaze, which is why any idea we may abstract from the poem for general application is problematical. For not only is this a particular view of a particular landscape [sc. in *Tintern Abbey*]; but it is only Wordsworth, at that particular point in his life, with his particular problems and memories and with his sister beside him, who can see what he sees and find the meaning he finds.'

If then there is an element of objectivity in Wordsworth it is simply because he often bounces his poems back from some external object or incident, like a ship finding its position by radar. If his poems do not call for a moral judgement and have no application beyond themselves it is, on Langbaum's own showing, precisely because of their strong autobiographical element. Thus if Wordsworth's poems can be called 'dramatic' at all it is in a very different sense from that which the word bears in the phrase 'dramatic monologue'. Browning's objectivity consists not in offering a poem that exists in a moral vacuum but in his presentation of a character without reference to himself. As I have shown, this enables moral inferences to be drawn, apparently without the prompting of the poet, but at no stage does

Browning represent *himself* as evolving or stepping forward in self-knowledge. Browning in short is objective and dramatic as Shakespeare or Jonson were (see Chapter 1), not in the very unusual sense of the word which Langbaum employs to label Wordsworth and the Romantics.

I maintain then that Browning's poetry, though objectively presented, is essentially a poetry which demands judgements of the reader and normally provides him with fairly plain hints as to what that judgement is expected to be. Langbaum concedes that it is objectively presented, though he uses the word, as I have shown, in a novel sense, but denies that it has any general application.

His position can, I think, be fairly represented by two quotations. 'It [is] characteristically the style of the dramatic monologue to present its material empirically, as a fact existing before and apart from moral judgment which remains always secondary and problematical. Even where the speaker is specifically concerned with a moral question, he arrives at his answer empirically, as a necessary outcome of conditions within the poem and not through appeal to an outside moral code. Since these conditions are always psychological and sometimes historical as well . . . the moral meaning is of limited application but enjoys within the limiting conditions of the poem a validity which no subsequent differences in judgment can disturb.' (pp. 97–98) Langbaum concludes, 'Judgment is largely psychologized and historicized. We adopt a man's point of view and the point of view of his age in order to judge him – which makes the judgment relative, limited in applicability to the particular conditions of the case. This is the kind of judgment we get in the dramatic monologue, which is for this reason an appropriate form for an empiricist and relativist age.' (p. 107)

In other words we are never able to bring to bear on the speaker of a dramatic monologue those standards by which we judge the actions of men. Is this a true account of the position in which we find ourselves when we read a dramatic monologue ? I do not think that it is, and to make my reasons clear, I shall examine some of the evaluations of particular poems to which it leads Mr Langbaum and explain why I find these evaluations inadequate [10].

Langbaum begins by offering a very full and helpful account

of *My Last Duchess*, a poem on which he lays considerable stress [11]. He concludes by saying, 'We must be . . . concerned . . . to appreciate the triumphant transition by which (the duke) ignores clean out of existence any judgment of his story that the envoy has presumed to invent.' This is not, of course, the same as transcending the reader's moral sense. Even as the reader acknowledges what Langbaum calls the duke's 'immense attractiveness' he is conscious also of his heartlessness, his egotism and his greed. Indeed as Langbaum says 'The dramatic monologue relies on the tension between sympathy and moral judgment.' If this is so, it is important that when we suspend moral judgement for the sake of reading the poem, this should mean not an anaesthetizing of the moral sense for the duration of the poem but a recognition that our acquaintance with the speaker depends on a *provisional acceptance* of his point of view, an acceptance which is continually revised and qualified by our judgements as we read the poem. Sympathy with the speaker may therefore be the ultimate result of reading a dramatic monologue: it is not a necessary accompaniment or condition of our reading of it, and even if it were it would not preclude a moral judgement of the speaker, just as we are able to love people and judge them. Langbaum rightly says (p. 78) that we must stand in a sympathetic relation to the poem: clearly this is not the same thing as sympathizing with the speaker to the extent of subordinating to his our view of the situation he describes.[1]

For, as Langbaum again admits, 'There is at work in [the dramatic monologue] a consciousness, whether intellectual or historical, beyond what the speaker can lay claim to.' (p. 94) We know this, as I say, because we feel the version offered to us by the speaker is incomplete. For an understanding of the poem we must know *why* it is incomplete, and in answering that question we necessarily assess the speaker. Even in *Fra Lippo Lippi*, in which, since there is very little sense of Browning extending ironically beyond the speaker, our identification is almost com-

---

[1] Langbaum's account of *My Last Duchess* can be questioned on a fairly simple level. He says that 'the duke's motive [for speaking as he does] cannot be accounted for by the dramatic situation.' (p. 182.) It 'remains ultimately mysterious'. But we can provide him with a perfectly sound tactical motive if we take it that he is obliquely instructing the envoy about the behaviour he expects to find in his next duchess. See Laurence Perrine, 'Browning's Shrewd Duke', *PMLA*, LXXIV (1959), pp. 157-9.

plete and hence Langbaum's way of reading a dramatic monologue is more or less applicable, there is nevertheless the sense
that Browning's *historical* grasp is wider than Lippi's, that *he*
realizes, as Lippi could not, how pertinent to the arts of suc-
ceeding ages were the monk's comments on his own painting.
Indeed, it is because these parts of the monologue have this
additional significance that they seem to be, as it were, the
point of the poem.

In *Johannes Agricola* we have a clear example of a speaker
whose religious delusions have overpowered his reason and his
reverence. However splendid his language we must recognize the
pernicious effects of his doctrine. Yet Langbaum (pp. 87–88),
though he apparently realizes this, does not admit the poem as
calling for the exercise of the reader's judgement of the speaker.

Again in *Cleon* the speaker debates the question of immortality
of the soul and the inevitability of death, which, Cleon says,

> is so horrible,
> I dare at times imagine to my need
> Some future state revealed to us by Zeus,
> Unlimited in capability
> For joy, as this is in desire for joy.
> . . . But no!
> Zeus has not yet revealed it; and alas,
> He must have done so, were it possible!

Then in the last paragraph of the poem Cleon refers contemptuously to Protus' mention of Paul:

> . . . We have heard his fame
> Indeed, if Christus be not one with him –
> I know not, nor am troubled much to know.
> Thou canst not think a mere barbarian Jew,
> As Paulus proves to be, one circumcized,
> Hath access to a secret shut from us?
> Thou wrongest our philosophy, O king,
> In stooping to enquire of such an one,
> As if his answer could impose at all!
> He writeth, doth he? well, and he may write.
> Oh, the Jew findeth scholars! certain slaves
> Who touched on this same isle, preached him and Christ;
> And (as I gathered from a bystander)
> Their doctrine could be held by no sane man.

So the poem ends. Our acquaintance with Cleon should not blind us to the fact that he dismisses Christianity on hearsay evidence without any clear knowledge of its doctrines, simply because he cannot bring himself to admit that a barbarian can teach a Greek. The irony of the poem resides in this – that Cleon longs for a religion which offers the promise of personal immortality, yet when at last in his own lifetime he has the opportunity to hear Christian teaching he spurns it through pride. This is typical of the way in which in Browning's most highly organized dramatic monologues we are able to use the deficiencies of the speaker's version of the case to arrive at a judgement of him which is not one of simple moral approval or disapproval but an assessment of him and of his subject.

Similarly in *Karshish* the speaker, an Arab physician who has recently treated Lazarus, writes incredulously of his story, apologizing indeed for mentioning it at all. He observes that Lazarus is now impatient 'at ignorance and carelessness and sin', and is as unable to conceal this as Karshish himself would be when he listened to local doctors 'steeped in conceit sublimed by ignorance' talk about subjects of which he had himself certain knowledge. The inference is clear that Lazarus has in fact a profound knowledge denied to other men, but Karshish fails to make the inference. Instead he records, with great hesitation, as evidence of Lazarus' madness, his curious obsession with the 'learned leech' who brought him back from death:

> This man so cured regards the curer, then,
> As – God forgive me! who but God himself,
> Creator and sustainer of the world,
> That came and dwelt in flesh on it awhile!
> – 'Sayeth that such an one was born and lived,
> Taught, healed the sick, broke bread at his own house,
> Then died, with Lazarus by, for aught I know,
> And yet was . . . what I said, nor choose repeat,
> And must have so avouched himself, in fact,
> In hearing of this very Lazarus
> Who saith – but why all this of what he saith?
> Why write of trivial matters, things of price
> Calling at every moment for remark?
> I noticed on the margin of a pool
> Blue-flowering borage, the Aleppo sort,
> Aboundeth, very nitrous. It is strange!

He admits the awe with which Lazarus has touched him, and concludes:

> The very God! think, Abib; dost thou think?
> So the All-Great were the All-Loving too –
> So, through the thunder comes a human voice
> Saying, 'O heart I made, a heart beats here!
> Face, my hands fashioned, see it in myself!
> Thou hast no power nor mayst conceive of mine,
> But love I gave thee, with myself to love,
> And thou must love me who have died for thee!'
> The madman saith He said so: it is strange.

Here Karshish is debarred from an acceptance of Christianity not by pride, as Cleon was, but by his intellectual caution. Having diagnosed mania he is unable to admit that Lazarus is essentially sane, and so, ironically, he, like Cleon, fails to admit a truth which all his careful medical and psychological observation would confirm, and for whose acceptance he is imaginatively prepared.[1]

Thus in these two poems, although Browning maintains a strictly objective presentation, we do not rest content with the experiences that the poems describe. For these experiences, as Langbaum says in a passage I have already quoted, are limited. Indeed the speaker's limitations are in some ways the most important things in the poem,[2] for by forcing us to recognize them, Browning is able to control not only our attitude to the two speakers but to Christianity.

Moreover it is not simply an attitude to Christianity as it was in the days of the early church, but to Christianity in our own time. The pride which prevents Cleon from accepting the faith for which his heart is yearning and the intellectual scruples which prevent Karshish from recognizing the true nature of his

[1] The irony of the poem extends to the reference in the title to the 'strange medical experience' of Karshish the Arab physician: the point is that the poem describes not a medical but a spiritual experience. Further ironies in the poem are amply displayed by Wilfred L. Guerin, 'Irony and Tension in Browning's "Karshish"', *VP* I (April 1963), pp. 132–9. There is an interesting anticipation of the subject in Section XXXI of *In Memoriam*.

[2] These two poems are obvious examples to refute Langbaum's dictum that 'the meaning of the dramatic monologue is what the speaker comes to perceive' (p. 207), since the main interest of them lies in what the speaker is *unable* to perceive.

experience have their counterpart in the nineteenth century, and the twentieth.

Similarly when Langbaum writes, 'All dramatic monologues . . . end with the speaker's triumph over the conditions of the poem, with his acquisition of the poem as a new side of his own nature' (p. 208) one agrees perforce that the speaker has in some way changed between the beginning and the end of his poem. He has, simply by speaking the poem, acquired an experience which was not his before: so much is undeniable. But in poem after poem the vital point to observe is, as I have said, that the speaker understands himself and his own situation less thoroughly than the reader, who has nevertheless derived all his understanding from the poem. *Cleon* and *Karshish* are simply the most obvious of many refuting cases.

Langbaum is also quite right to say that there is an element of display in the dramatic monologue. The speaker *is* often trying to 'light up his own mind': this provides in some cases the motive for talking at all: the immediate tactical objectives of the performance become of secondary importance. But to agree with this point, important though it is, is not to agree that we are left with no standards by which to assess the mind so revealed to us.

When he talks of the speaker trying to impose his perspective on the poem Langbaum does not, as far as I can see, allow for the consequences of the fact that if we *notice* the speaker's idiosyncratic perspective (as opposed, that is, to accepting it unawares) then we are able, and obliged, to assess it. Langbaum seems to lose sight of the fact that *Browning* is writing the poems. If for example we forget Browning and think instead of 'The Song of Caliban', as Langbaum does on pp. 207–8, we necessarily ignore a complete layer of meaning, that which resides in Browning's ironic scrutiny of the arguments put forward by his own creature.

This is a further point of difference between the dramatic monologue as Browning handles it and the Romantic poem in which the poet himself is the chief character. On the latter kind of poetry I have already quoted the passage in which Langbaum says, '. . . The content and meaning of what (the poet) sees has existence and validity only within the limiting conditions of his gaze, which is why any idea we may abstract from the poem for general application is problematical.' In the dramatic monologue, by contrast, the ideas which the reader abstracts are of general application precisely because they are arrived at from observation of a limiting case and from an understanding of the distinction between 'a truth' and 'the truth'. A characteristic reaction to a dramatic monologue is the realization that the speaker's words, though not necessarily false, are nevertheless omitting or suppressing part of a larger truth. In other words, what we are given may well be a particular truth, but we are struck by its inadequacy, and from this move to an unrestricted position.

The limitations are often, by implication, those of Browning's own reader's – *Caliban* is again the obvious example – which makes it very difficult to accept Langbaum's contention that 'we adopt the point of view of [the speaker's] age in order to judge him'. I must admit that I am not altogether certain that I understand Langbaum's position here. The main tenor of his argument is as I have presented it, yet from time to time he seems to concede tacitly that the reader does in fact perceive and assess the *partiality* of the version of the truth that is put before him. I might mention p. 139 or p. 140 ('The general idea emerges as an inference only, and is never identical with what the speaker says') or p. 151 where he seems to admit that we understand Andrea 'in a way other than he understands [himself]'. The difficulty becomes manifest at the foot of p. 156, where he writes, 'The style of the address and the perspective both show the utterance as incomplete', a point that is not to be disputed, and then concludes the paragraph by saying, 'The final judgment, which is impossible where there is only one voice of a dialogue, corresponds to the reversal, which is impossible where there is only a single perspective. Without reversal or final judgment there can be no logical completeness, no *right* conclusion.' As I say, he makes no allowance for the significance of the incompleteness of the utterance.

Perhaps my main point can be expressed in brief compass by pointing out that a favourite mode of satire is the creation of a character speaking consistently in an assumed role. The satirist is in effect writing a dramatic monologue, yet everyone is familiar with his power to manipulate his *persona* to imply opinions and control judgements. Precisely the same resources are available to the writer of the verse monologue. If Langbaum's account of the operation of the dramatic monologue were correct it would be impossible to use the form, in verse or prose, for satiric ends [12].

IV

The relevance of this particular dispute to the main drift of my argument should now be plain. For if, following Langbaum, we accept every monologue as imposing its own perspective on the reader, we could never use one of Browning's monologues as evidence of Browning's own opinions. If, on the other hand, we are, as I have maintained, invited to observe the speaker with some care and to notice in particular where his opinions of the matters discussed are deficient, then we are in as good a position to infer Browning's own opinions as we are to infer the opinions of any writer of satire. We cannot establish beyond all possible objection from internal evidence that Swift disapproved of the measures suggested in *A Modest Proposal*, but we may make a reasonably convincing inference that he did. The question then to be considered in the remainder of the chapter is this; 'Assuming that we accept as generally true the poet's statement that his poems are essentially dramatic, when and under what safeguards can we use Browning's poetry as evidence of Browning's opinions?'

There is one special case where the general rule of assuming the impersonality of the poems may safely be broken. For, while Browning himself insisted on the necessary separation of the objective poet's life from his work, there are a number of poems in which he deliberately sets aside his mask to speak in his own person, in the way in which he has described so movingly in *One Word More* – 'Let me speak this once in my true person,/Not as Lippo, Roland or Andrea.' The most notable poems of this kind are first the prologues and epilogues to his volumes of poetry from *Men and Women* onwards, including Books I and XII of *The Ring and The Book* [13], secondly *La Saisiaz* [14], and thirdly the *Parleyings with Certain People*, in which as DeVane has ably shown, Browning speaks for himself and masks only the imaginary *listener* to his monologue. There are also a number of other places where Browning speaks with his own voice, but those I have mentioned are the most consistently revealing.

Secondly, I have tried to show that even in those poems where the objective presentation is absolute, one of Browning's strengths as a poet is his ability to manipulate for ironic ends the reader's attitude towards the arguments put forward by the speaker. We may therefore infer that when Browning contrives that the reader shall finish a certain poem with a particular attitude to the topics discussed, this attitude is one of which Browning approves, or of which he approved at the time when he wrote the poem. This is admittedly only an inference, but it is only an inference that when a man says something he means what he says. To establish this point we have to show that in the given poem there are signs that Browning is deliberately directing the reader's responses in a particular direction.

Further, we may observe the basic positions on which Browning relies for his ironic effects, those qualities which he assumes his reader will grant without question to be either laudable or reprehensible. From any poem then we may deduce some of Browning's basic assumptions about human values, or, granted that we share his basic assumptions, something of his particular views on the topics under discussion. From any given poem we infer in the first place only what is true of that poem. But if we find that several poems lead to similar conclusions our confidence in our inferences is strengthened, since we are doing no violence to our ideas of the human personality in crediting these harmonious views to a single person. We may say then that each inference has been in a way confirmed, since they might have contradicted one another but do not. Setting together these 'basic assumptions' and the consequent 'induced attitudes', we may compile a list of some of the positions Browning habitually adopts in his dramatic poems and, in a similar way, a list of the inadequacies in his speakers to which Browning most frequently calls attention.

The status of such lists is theoretically weak. They do not offer evidence of the same kind as the poems in which Browning speaks for himself. In some ways it is stronger: in others weaker. In any case, what Browning says in one poem is never *decisive* proof of what he means in another. At best, evidence of habitual opinions may be called in to corroborate a given reading, hardly ever to disprove one. Nevertheless if we want to make general statements about an entity called 'Browning's poetry' in the form 'Browning says A' we are forced to assume that the poems are not single self-subsistent works of art, each with its own values, but are part of an *oeuvre*, of which we can expect each part to be more or less consistent with the rest.[1]

Even further from the centre of Browning's poetic energy are the direct evidences of his life, of which the chief are the various volumes of his letters. They are not, on the whole, of great interest, nor are they very revealing. When he talks about Italian politics, or about his own poems or his contemporaries', or about literature in general, he has an interest and a professional authority which is not found elsewhere in his correspondence. On artistic and literary matters then (and perhaps on Italian affairs), the letters and the *Essay on Shelley* may be called in as confirmatory evidence for the existence of attitudes deduced from the poems. Similarly with various *obiter dicta* about poetry which have been preserved by his biographers. But all this, as I say, is second-order evidence. None of it can be used except, effectively, in the form of a general statement 'Robert Browning, the man, believed that A'. Even if we are able to set aside Browning's own indignant denial of the relevance of such observations, we can see that the general statement carries comparatively little weight in literary discussion against the specific statement 'In the poem before us Browning, the poet, says B'.

Finally I turn to an even less tangible point. We have to rely in our interpretation of the individual poems on a general knowledge of the period, which limits the attitudes we may plausibly ascribe to a prosperous, middle-class, much-travelled Liberal, brought up as a non-Conformist in nineteenth-century England. Thus while the other secondary sources I have mentioned might lead to a statement of the form 'Browning could not have meant A in this poem, because he says B elsewhere', a general familiarity with the period leads us to a statement of the form,

---

[1] J. Hillis Miller in his introduction to *The Disappearance of God*, pp. 15–16, makes the point explicitly. He writes, 'I have been guided by the assumption that each work by an author gives us a new glimpse of an underlying vital unity, a unity of the kind so eloquently defined by De Quincey in a passage from the "Suspiria de Profundis": "The fleeting accidents of a man's life, and its external shows, may indeed be irrelate and incongruous; but the organising principles which fuse into harmony, and gather about fixed predetermined centres, whatever heterogeneous elements life may have accumulated from without, will not permit the grandeur of human unity greatly to be violated . . ." '

'Browning could not have meant A in this poem because such a point of view would not have been possible at that time and place and level of society.' The second statement seems vaguer, but if it can be satisfactorily substantiated it proves in practice at least as valuable and enlightening as the first.

V

It is not difficult to see the attractions which the dramatic monologue held for Browning. The writer of dramatic verse has at his command certain technical resources: these Browning exploited throughout his life, and we may fairly assume that he recognized them and valued them.

For example, in the preceding sections I have shown that the response required from the reader is complex, involving him actively in the process of completely realizing the poem. Browning's use of this property of his form is further explored in Chapters 6 and 7.

Secondly the presence in the poem, besides the poet and the reader, of a third party, the speaker himself, adds to the narrative interest in a way now perfectly familiar to us from the novels of Conrad, to look no further[15].

Thirdly, the wide range of personae available to the poet means that he is not restricted to the one diction which would alone be appropriate to a series of poems all representing the poet's own experiences: instead he is stimulated to adopt a fresh way of writing with each new character.

Fourthly, although in a dramatic poem physical action is normally implied rather than described, and the dramatic poet is thus denied one kind of interest readily available to the narrative poet, he has nevertheless unrivalled opportunity for psychological exploration, just as a writer of fiction who uses the first person is able to describe the thoughts of his narrator with a minuteness which would strain the reader's credulity unacceptably if he met it in a story told in the third person.

Finally, the form offers the satirist's weapons of oblique statement and ironic attack.

These practical considerations seem to provide a completely adequate theoretical justification for the poet's choice of the dramatic monologue. But the form offers these advantages equally to any poet. It may then be asked why Browning is alone among the poets of his century in adopting a dramatic form for the bulk of his work.

Answers to this question are of two kinds – those beginning 'because' and those beginning 'in order to'. Many answers can be so phrased as to begin either way. The only answer that must begin with 'because' is Mrs Miller's. She suggests in effect that Browning wrote in this way because he was unable to write in any other, being, through fear or temperamental deficiencies, incapable of exposing his own personality in verse.[1] Apart from this conjecture of some irresistible inner compulsion all the other answers to the question can be more generously, and, I think, more accurately, presented as deliberate choices on Browning's part, as a preferred rather than as an enforced strategy, and thus properly begin 'in order to' [16].

There is no doubt that Browning valued the impersonality of the dramatic mode, and that the idea of the poet's appearing in his own person was not consonant with his ideas of his own poetry. This was because he felt that a great weakness of the poets of his own age was their commitment to their poems. Thus instead of answering the question, 'Why did Browning almost invariably choose an impersonal form of poetry?' with 'Because he dared not reveal himself', I should reply, 'In order to secure and reinforce, even to symbolize, the detachment which he valued so much in the poet: in order to avoid the subjectivity which he saw as vitiating so much Romantic verse.'

That Browning in fact held such opinions of the work of his contemporaries is the argument of the next chapter.

[1] Mrs Miller is repeating in a more elaborate and positive form the conjectures of F. R. G. Duckworth in the last chapter of his *Browning: Background and Conflict* (London, 1931). Her arguments are in turn expanded and set in a much fuller literary context in J. Hillis Miller's *Disappearance of God*. Professor Miller suggests that Browning writes dramatically and protects his private life because he has to conceal 'his secret failure', his 'shameful and reprehensible' indefinite self, which would affront his well-integrated contemporaries if he allowed it to appear. To disguise his uncertainty, therefore, he is obliged to commit himself to 'the life of the shape-changer, the life of the man who, nothing himself, borrows with the utmost irresponsibility the life of others'. The fourth section of Professor Miller's chapter on Browning is in effect an attempt to present dramatic poetry as a refuge for the poet who is unable to write 'confessional' poetry: the choice of the dramatic monologue can thus be held to be dictated by Browning's personal needs.

Browning and the rejection of the Romantic Tradition

Strafford. I shall make a sorry soldier, Lucy!
All knights begin their enterprise, we read,
Under the best of auspices; 'tis morn,
The Lady girds his sword upon the Youth
(He's always very young) – the trumpets sound,
Cups pledge him, and why, the King blesses him –
You need not turn a page of the romance
To learn the Dreadful Giant's fate. Indeed,
We've the fair Lady here; but she apart, –
A poor man, rarely having handled lance,
And rather old, weary, and far from sure
His Squires are not the Giant's friends. All's one:
Let us go forth!
Lady Carlisle. Go forth?
Strafford.   What matters it?
We shall die gloriously – as the book says.
                                   (*Strafford* II. ii)

In the rest of this book I shall point to various specific ways in which Browning's poetry lay outside the Romantic tradition, for example in his choice of subjects and in his diction. There is a substantial body of evidence that these differences were deliberately fostered by Browning in order to avoid what he saw as the deficiencies and errors of the other poets of his century. In this chapter I shall examine some of the places in his work where we may, under the conditions set out in Chapter 2, learn something of Browning's own opinions of the state of poetry in his own time, and something of that conscious reaction against his contemporaries and against the earlier Romantic writers which was such a powerful influence on his poetic career.

I

To say this is not to ignore Browning's youthful admiration for Shelley, to whom, as is well known, Browning pays generous tribute in *Pauline* (1833), freely acknowledging his poetic debts.[1] It is more difficult, however, to accept DeVane's judgement that 'the spirit of Shelley presides over *Sordello* (1840) almost as much as over *Pauline*' [1]. The opening of the poem includes the rather odd dismissive apostrophe to Shelley, but thereafter, while Browning frequently considers matters of poetic theory, there is little evidence that he has Shelley especially in mind while he is doing so.

The primary importance of *Sordello* lies in the fact that we may find in the poem the raw material, as it were, of many of Browning's later poems about poetry and the poet's responsibilities. In the first two books alone, he or his characters discuss *inter alia* the comparative virtues of narrative and dramatic poetry (i. 10–31), the objective and subjective perception of the beautiful (i.478–549), the power of the poetic imagination (i. 638–72), the relation of the poet to his audience (ii. 137–68), 'negative capability' (ii. 381–416), the use of the vernacular in poetry (ii. 569–79), the relation of the poet to his creations (ii. 621–35), and the relation of the poet's public and private lives (ii. 655–93, 784–801). The second half of the third book is entirely given over to a vast digression in which Browning speculates about such topics as the subjective and the objective poet, the poet's responsibility to suffering humanity (here the influence of Shelley is most apparent), the difference between his own 'awkward' poetry and the elegant verses that were in fashion, and the poet's ability to interpret experience. Although the later part of the poem is not so fertile in aesthetic ideas, it contains suggestive passages on, for example, the poet's social responsibilities (iv. 240–90), the all-commanding power of poetry (v. 505–665), and the folly of using natural images in order to diminish the status of man (vi. 1–7).

[1] H. B. Forman, writing in 1869, is rightly cautious of assuming that the addresses to 'the Sun-treader' represent Browning's own sentiments rather than those of the speaker. (See Chapter 12 for a further discussion of his interesting article.) I have suggested elsewhere that the speaker in *Pauline* is differentiated from the poet because he is placed in a specific dramatic situation, i.e. at the point of death.

Clearly we cannot use *Sordello* to discover exactly what Browning thought about poetry in 1840, partly because he expresses his ideas too Delphically for any very precise formulation, more importantly because he is not concerned in the poem to arrive at settled and clear-cut positions. What we have in the poem is, so to speak, the crude ore of his later writings about art and the artist, inconclusive, unworked, untransmuted. He is debating with himself the points at issue, staging a series of dialogues in which various opinions can be propounded without necessarily committing the author to the support of any of them. This disengaged play of opinion is one of the qualities that makes the poem 'difficult' [2].

The most interesting thing about *Sordello* is the plain evidence it provides that Browning had been thinking *for himself*, and thinking in a spirit of free inquiry, about the medium of poetry and the proper function of the poet. It is my contention, that because he investigated all these matters with an uncommitted mind at the beginning of his career he was never tempted thereafter to receive a tradition on trust, but was free to indulge the independence and originality of his own individual talent, not in thrall to the theories or to the example of the great Romantic poets but at liberty to criticize them if need be.[1]

For some fifteen years after *Sordello* Browning had comparatively little to say about his own art or about the duties and potentialities of the creative artist in general.[2] When he takes up the theme once more, in *Men and Women* (1855), he shows a strong tendency to explore the problems of the artist by writing

[1] Shelley is the obvious exception: even as late as 1855 (see *Memorabilia*) Browning's admiration for Shelley the man and the poet amounts to veneration, but before the end of his life his disapproval of Shelley's treatment of his first wife had become so strong that he refused the Presidency of the Shelley Society in the following terms: 'For myself, I painfully contrast my notions of Shelley the *man* and Shelley, well, even the poet, with what they were sixty years ago, when I only had his works, for a certainty, and took his character on trust.' (Letter to Furnivall, 8 December 1885.) Browning was not altogether true to his principles here, but when discussing subjective poets as a class and in the special case of Shelley he felt at liberty not to make a sharp distinction between the man and his work, while of course insisting on the distinction when considering objective poets.

[2] We may note in passing that in *Flight of the Duchess* V and X Browning satirizes the modish taste for the medieval, in precisely the same way as Peacock does in the character of Mr Chainmail in *Crotchet Castle* and as Thackeray does when he ridicules Barnes Newcome's choice of Anglo-Saxon christian names for his children.

about painters and musicians rather than directly about the
practice of poetry. In *Fra Lippo Lippi*, for example, a poem
which lies very close indeed to the centre of Browning's speculations about the nature and purpose of art, he draws the contrast
between two approaches to painting, exploring in some depth
a theme which he had earlier touched on briefly and from the
opposite point of view in *Pictor Ignotus* (1845). The speaker is
a painter who is chafing against the restrictions of conventional
religious art and longing for liberty to choose his own manner
and subjects. Lippi's patrons, 'the Prior and the learned', criticize
his realistic treatment of human figures and raise the stock
objections:

> How? What's here?
> Quite from the mark of painting, bless us all!
> Faces, arms, legs and bodies like the true
> As much as pea and pea! it's devil's-game!
> Your business is not to catch men with show,
> With homage to the perishable clay,
> But lift them over it, ignore it all,
> Make them forget there's such a thing as flesh.
> Your business is to paint the souls of men.

Lippi, later in the poem, makes his rejoinder to those who deny
value to an objective recording of reality. Addressing the
captain of the city-watch he says

> However, you're my man, you've seen the world
> – The beauty and the wonder and the power,
> The shapes of things, their colours, lights and shades,
> Changes, surprises, – and God made it all!
> – For what? Do you feel thankful, ay or no,
> For this fair town's face, yonder river's line,
> The mountain round it and the sky above,
> Much more the figures of man, woman, child,
> These are the frame to? What's it all about?
> To be passed over, despised? or dwelt upon,
> Wondered at? oh, this last of course! – you say.
> But why not do as well as say, – paint these
> Just as they are, careless what comes of it?
> God's works – paint anyone, and count it crime
> To let a truth slip. Don't object, 'His works
> Are here already; nature is complete;

> Suppose you reproduce her – (which you can't)
> There's no advantage! you must beat her, then.'
> For, don't you mark? we're made so that we love
> First when we see them painted, things we have passed
> Perhaps a hundred times nor cared to see;
> And so they are better, painted – better to us,
> Which is the same thing. Art was given for that;
> God uses us to help each other so,
> Lending our minds out. Have you noticed, now,
> Your cullion's hanging face? A bit of chalk,
> And trust me but you should, though! How much more,
> If I drew higher things with the same truth!
> That were to take the Prior's pulpit-place,
> Interpret God to all of you! Oh, oh,
> It makes me mad to see what men shall do
> And we in our graves! This world's no blot for us,
> Nor blank; it means intensely, and means good:
> To find its meaning is my meat and drink.

That the reader is intended to acknowledge the force of Lippi's observations on art is confirmed by the structure and circumstances of the monologue, in which the speaker expresses his abhorrence of the unnatural cloistered life of the monk and his love for the generous pleasures of the world. This parallels his impatience with the narrow conventions of devotional art and his desire to express freely and directly his love for 'the beauty and the wonder and the power'. The reader's sympathy is given to him as readily in the one case as in the other.

Although *Popularity*, one of the best-known poems in *Men and Women* (1855), is apparently a striking tribute to Keats, a careful study modifies this reading [3]. The first stanzas of the poem for instance clearly refer not to Keats himself but, as Basil Worsfold notes [4], to Browning's friend Domett, the subject of *Waring* and *The Guardian-Angel* and possibly of *Time's Revenges*, who went to New Zealand and was an unsuccessful poet. Stanza II sets the tone.

> My star, God's glow-worm! Why extend
>   That loving hand of his which leads you
> Yet locks you safe from end to end
>   Of this dark world, unless he needs you,
> Just saves your light to spend?

Browning prophesies that in time Domett's worth as a poet will be recognized. Meanwhile he offers him a parable in consolation. There follows the celebrated metaphor of the Tyrian dye, a blue tincture refined with great pains from the shells which a fisherman had brought from the depths of the ocean. It was so exquisite in colour that at last, when all the work was done, those who bought it were able to command the admiration of the public. Browning concludes

> Hobbs hints blue, – straight he turtle eats:
> Nobbs prints blue, – claret crowns his cup:
> Nokes outdares Stokes in azure feats, –
> Both gorge. Who fished the murex up?
> What porridge had John Keats?

It is plain from this that Browning puts Keats forward to Domett as an instance of the irrelevance of popular appeal. Keats, who was the originator and pioneer of a style of writing, was unrecognized and unrewarded. His vulgar imitators, however, enjoy the world's esteem. Thus while the poem implies that Browning appreciated the originality of Keats' poetry, it is not this but Keats' *unpopularity* which is the vital point of comparison. Browning once more expresses his contempt for those of his contemporaries whose stock in trade was a diluted Romanticism.

When Browning redistributed his works in 1863 he placed '*Transcendentalism: A Poem in Twelve Books*' first among the poems still called *Men and Women*: poems standing in this position often express Browning's own views on some aspect of his art, and this is no exception. He begins by upbraiding a brother poet for speaking rather than singing. What the poet says is admirable, but why, Browning asks, does he make such a business of putting it into verse when the result is as dry as prose. The poet replies 'Grown men want more from verse than images and melody: they require reason and analysis.' Browning rejoins that this is not true. In youth we live, he admits, among objects whose meaning we do not understand. After a little we find that we have lost our youth. Which then is more use to us – an account of the significance of experience or a book which actually creates new material and new experiences? Clearly the latter, which makes us young once more by enabling us to contemplate the living objects themselves, not merely an abstract account of their inner meanings.

This poem is in the same territory as the *Essay on Shelley*, for it distinguishes two types of writer – the first, like Boehme, offers to synthesize and interpret experience in terms of its mystical meaning: this roughly corresponds to the subjective poet in the *Essay*. The second, like John of Halberstadt, actually creates phenomena, and thus corresponds to the objective poet – 'John, who made things Boehme wrote thoughts about'. Browning says that even grown men (or perhaps *especially* grown men) prefer the second kind of poet, since he restores to them some of the powerful sensations of youth. The first kind of poet has thus an inaccurate conception of the real business of poetry. Far from criticizing his own poetry, as John Bryson suggests [5], Browning is protesting here against the contemporary fashion for writing long expository poems which, instead of recreating experience, treat philosophical ideas abstractly [6].

Of *One Word More*, the last poem in *Men and Women*, it need only be remarked at the moment that it is explicitly designed by Browning as a comment on his own art, thus conforming with the normal pattern of opening and closing poems, and that in it Browning is at pains to emphasize that he is for once forsaking his normal manner, the oblique or dramatic, for the sake of addressing himself as a man, not as a poet, to E.B.B. It is clear that Browning considers the separation between the poet, who writes for the public, and the man, who has a right to a private life, to be as distinct as that between the two sides of the moon. The differences between this and many of the more extreme Romantic attitudes towards poetry need not be stressed [7].

If corroboration is needed of Browning's independence from the Romantic tradition throughout his career, it can be found in his letters; perhaps the best-known passages are those in which he speaks critically of Hugo – 'he gives you *panforte* for the sacramental wafer', – of Swinburne – 'the *minimum* of thought and idea in the *maximum* of words and phraseology', – and of Rossetti – '*scented* with poetry, as it were – like trifles of various sorts you take out of a cedar or sandal-wood box' [8]. The most celebrated passage of all is in a letter of 1846:

I would at any time have gone to Finchley to see a curl of [Byron's] hair or one of his gloves, I am sure – while Heaven knows that I could not get up enthusiasm enough to cross the room if at the other end of it all Wordsworth, Coleridge and Southey were condensed into the little China bottle yonder, after the Rosicrucian fashion . . . they seem to 'have their reward' and want nobody's love or faith. [9]

II

Byron did not always command Browning's unqualified admiration. A passage in *Prince Hohenstiel-Schwangau* (1871) is the most familiar of many in which a speaker, with Browning's apparent sympathy, rejects the attitudes of Byron towards Man and Nature, in particular the celebrated passage at the close of *Childe Harold* in which Byron apostrophizes the 'deep and dark blue Ocean' and contrasts the abiding might of the sea with the transience and pettiness of Mankind [10]. The Prince's comment is as follows:

> However did the foolish pass for wise
> By calling life a burden, man a fly
> Or worm or what's most insignificant?
> 'O littleness of man!' deplores the bard;
> And then, for fear the Powers should punish him,
> 'O grandeur of the visible universe
> Our human littleness contrasts withal!
> O sun, O moon, ye mountains and thou sea,
> Thou emblem of immensity, thou this,
> That and the other, – what impertinence
> In man to eat and drink and walk about
> And have his little notions of his own,
> The while some wave sheds foam upon the shore!'
> First of all, 't is a lie some three-times thick:
> The bard, – this sort of speech being poetry, –
> The bard puts mankind well outside himself
> And then begins instructing them: 'This way
> I and my friend the sea conceive of you!
> What would you give to think such thoughts as ours
> Of you and the sea together?' Down they go
> On the humbled knees of them: at once they draw
> Distinction, recognize no mate of theirs
> In one, despite his mock humility,

> So plain a match for what he plays with. Next,
> The turn of the great ocean-play-fellow,
> When the bard, leaving Bond Street very far
> From ear-shot, cares not to ventriloquize,
> But tells the sea its home-truths: 'You, my match?
> You, all this terror and immensity
> And what not? Shall I tell you what you are?
> Just fit to hitch into a stanza, so
> Wake up and set in motion who's asleep
> O' the other side of you, in England, else
> Unaware, as folk pace their Bond Street now,
> Somebody here despises them so much!
> Between us, – they are the ultimate! to them
> And their perception go these lordly thoughts:
> Since what were ocean – mane and tail, to boot
> Mused I not here, how make thoughts thinkable?
> Start forth my stanza and astound the world!
> Back, billows, to your insignificance!
> Deep, you are done with!' [11]

The Prince's rejection of 'the bard's' pseudo-philosophy is complete and simple, resolving itself into the proposition 'All else but what man feels is nought.'

Similarly in Browning's next long poem, *Fifine at the Fair* (1872), the speaker makes fun of Byron's philosophy and grammar alike.

> Man, outcast, 'howls,' – at rods? –
> If 'sent in playful spray a-shivering to his gods!'
> Childishest childe, man makes thereby no bad exchange.
> Stay with the flat-fish, thou! We like the upper range
> Where the 'gods' live, perchance the dæmons also dwell,
> Where operates a Power, which every throb and swell
> Of human heart invites that human soul approach,
> 'Sent' near and nearer still, however 'spray' encroach
> On 'shivering' flesh below, to altitudes, which gained,
> Evil proves good, wrong right, obscurity explained,
> And 'howling' childishness. Whose howl have we to thank,
> If all the dogs 'gan bark and puppies whine, till sank
> Each yelper's tail 'twixt legs? for Huntsman Commonsense
> Came to the rescue, caused prompt thwack of thong dispense
> Quiet i' the kennel; taught that ocean might be blue,
> And rolling and much more, and yet the soul have, too,
> Its touch of God's own flame, which He may so expand

'Who measuréd the waters i' the hollow of His hand'
That ocean's self shall dry, turn dew-drop in respect
Of all-triumphant fire, matter with intellect
Once fairly matched; bade him who egged on hounds to bay,
Go curse, i' the poultry yard, his kind: 'there let him lay'
The swan's one addled egg: which yet shall put to use,
Rub breast-bone warm against, so many a sterile goose![1]

These two passages, each of considerable length, sit rather
uneasily in their context, more as if the opinions were gratui-
tously offered by Browning because he himself felt them strongly
than as if they were dramatically appropriate. Moreover their
similarity of tone argues that it is Browning rather than the two
very different speakers who feels so strongly about Byron's
apparent wish to exalt Nature in order to exaggerate the little-
ness of man.[2]

This theme, and in particular the attack on Byron, is continued in the volume *Pacchiarotto* (1876). *At the Mermaid* is a
dramatic lyric, written in the character of Shakespeare, that is to
say, an objective poet. He makes the point to which Browning
so often recurs – the essential distinction between the poet's life
and his work:

> Here's my work: does work discover –
>   What was rest from work – my life? . . .   (III)

> Blank of such a record, truly
>   Here's the work I hand, this scroll,
> Yours to take or leave; as duly,
>   Mine remains the unproffered soul. . . .   (IV)

---

[1] *Fifine*, Section 67. Note also that in the same poem Browning makes Don Juan
quote ironically a half-line from Macaulay's *Ivry* – 'Oh pleasant land of France'.
The resemblance in metre between the two poems is, I think, coincidental.

[2] Cf. Browning's letter to Miss Egerton Smith, 16 August 1873: 'In the Spectator
which came yesterday, somebody repeated that foolish lie that I called Lord Byron
"a Flatfish". Those are the practices of your more lively article-mongers, who tell
these lies, like Austin, for the malice rather than the fun of the thing. I never said
nor wrote a word against or about Byron's poetry or power in my life; but I did
say, that, if he were in earnest and preferred being with the sea to associating with
mankind, he would do well to stay with the sea's population; thereby simply taking
him at his word, had it been honest – whereas it was altogether dishonest, seeing
that nobody cared so much about the opinions of mankind, and deferred to them,
as he who was thus posturing and pretending to despise them.'

> Which of you did I enable
>   Once to slip inside my breast,
> There to catalogue and label
>   What I like least, what love best,
> Hope and fear, believe and doubt of,
>   Seek and shun, respect – deride?
> Who has right to make a rout of
>   Rarities he found inside?   (V)

'Shakespeare' goes on to say that the 'last king' of poets had been known for his lack of self-control, and that he himself is now expected to be equally ready to reveal his own personality. It is not clear who is meant by the 'last king'. DeVane suggests that Browning has Wordsworth in mind here; while lines 57–58 admittedly imply that the poet referred to had become Poet Laureate, the rest of the stanza seems far more appropriate to Byron than to Wordsworth, who is not especially given to making an exaggerated display of his own feelings in verse. Certainly in Stanza XI, as DeVane notes, the sarcastic reference to the last king as 'your Pilgrim' shows that the Byron of *Childe Harold's Pilgrimage* is there intended. Shakespeare ironically regrets that he cannot live up to such pessimism, nor has he cause to rail at the fickleness of women (XIV). If he is told that 'at centre Song should reach *Welt-schmerz*, world-smart!' he must 'waive the present time'. The last stanza hints at a hope that some future age will appreciate his work.

While we must not make the error of supposing that the Shakespeare of the poem is Browning himself, the poem is clearly not restricted in its application to Elizabethan literature, for Shakespeare is speaking of the perennial problem of the objective poet confronted by an audience that expects or demands subjective poetry.

House continues the theme of *At the Mermaid*. It is not, as far as I can see, a dramatic monologue in any sense. There seems no reason, apart from our knowledge of Browning's normal practice in this matter, why we should not take it that Browning is expressing in this poem his own feelings about inquisitive critics. It may be objected, 'In the poem before us Browning explicitly refuses to make poetry out of his personal feelings: how then can you put forward the poem as evidence of what he actually thought?' But in the poem Browning is concerned to make the distinction between the public and the private lives of the poet – the one is fair game for critics: the other is not their affair and they have no right to object if the poet keeps it out of his poetry. The poem is about Browning's opinions on the true grounds and province of criticism: it is concerned not with details of his private life but with his relation as a poet to his readers. It may thus be taken as an expression of his own opinions without violating the privacy on which he insists in the poem. The last stanza is the most significant:

> 'Hoity toity! A street to explore,
>   Your house the exception! "*With this same key*
> *Shakespeare unlocked his heart.*" ' once more!
>   Did Shakespeare? If so, the less Shakespeare he! [12]

Here Wordsworth is satirically quoted and indignantly contradicted [13].

Although the next poem in *Pacchiarotto* is clearly connected in mood with *House* it is an over-simplification to take it as merely a rather more cumbrous statement of the same position. Whereas *House* is designed to rebuff those who wish a poet to express his own deepest emotions in verse so that they may satisfy their curiosity about what these emotions are, in *Shop* Browning asks himself what the proper relationship should be between an artist and his work and his public. To answer this question he first describes two shopkeepers. The first has a window full of startling gewgaws. Browning tries to imagine what a glorious house such a shopkeeper must have, far from his place of business. But in fact he found that the owner's home was merely a hole in the wall behind his shop, since he had no interest in life beyond driving a roaring trade. Thus he worried not about the worth of what he sold, but only about its popularity. Browning imagines the true shopkeeper as living a very different kind of life: his shop would be bare and comfortless to show off the goods on sale, he would not be very interested in his customers or in whether or not they bought anything, he would be eager to close the shop, and when it was closed he would go as far away from it as he could. A man has to appear in public and face the world in order to make a living, but it does not follow that he should have no private life. For example, butchers should paint, bakers write verse, candlestick makers play the flute. This would be infinitely better than 'shop each day and all day long', for such a life values the wrong kind of achievement.

The application to Browning's personal situation is quite clear – all men should, as he often insisted, have a private as well as a public life. The reference to his poetry is less clear, since there is no warrant in the poem for supposing, as is usually assumed, that Browning is 'really' describing two kinds of poet. Stanzas I–XII have a certain affinity with Browning's descriptions elsewhere of the subjective poet, whose life and work are inseparable. Here for the first time, I think, Browning sees this as something to be deplored. Stanzas XIII–XIX are closely related in tone to *One Word More*, Browning's most deeply personal reflection on life and art:

> God be thanked, the meanest of his creatures
> Boasts two soul-sides, one to face the world with,
> One to show a woman when he loves her!   (XVII)

To that extent *Shop* has particular reference to his own poetic situation. But the poem's main interest to the student of nineteenth-century poetry lies in the attitude that it rejects, for its informing idea is completely contrary to influential contemporary ideas about the poet's function, and about the place of the poet's personality in his poem.

The *Epilogue* to the *Pacchiarotto* volume is of first importance for an understanding of Browning's view of the place of his own work in the poetry of the Victorian age. In it Browning talks first about poetry in general and then meets specific criticisms which have been made of his own poetry. He uses a sustained set of parallels throughout, by which 'wine' stands for poetry. 'Strong harsh wine' thus stands for powerful poetry, 'sweet wine' for melodious poetry, and 'nettle broth' for satirical poetry, while 'cowslips' becomes a term for 'pleasing fancies or happy memories' as opposed to 'grapes' which denotes 'real experiences'. This continued use of correspondences as poetic euphemisms or code-words rather than as symbols is strained to the utmost, robbing the poem of all aesthetic appeal and sometimes obscuring the meaning of particular passages.

The general sense, however, is clear enough. The public cry for wine (= poetry) that shall be both sweet and strong. When they are given poetry which is only one or the other they dispraise it for its deficiency, failing to recognize its positive quality (Stanzas I–IV, Stanza II affording a fair description of Browning's own verse). Some people maintain that it is possible to have both qualities together, but Browning says that to ask for such poetry is to show an ignorance of the way in which poetry is written – no practising poet or conscientious critic, for example, would make such an unreasonable demand. The public, on the other hand, insists that the poet should make his work at once powerful and palatable to his audience, and cites Shakespeare, Milton, Pindar and Aeschylus as examples of poets who have done this (V–IX). Browning replies by alleging that the people who praise these dead poets never read them. If they did he would take some notice of their opinions, but they look at a few plays of Shakespeare's and neglect the rest, a few lines of Milton and no more (X–XII; XIII and XIV anticipate a later section of the argument). And what they do read is either what a critic tells them they ought to like or scraps of somebody else's reading. Such then are the people who claim to find the old poets superior to the new. Browning agrees that if they find new verse unsatisfying they are quite right to regale themselves on the old, but he scoffs contemptuously at the idea that they in fact regale themselves on anything, especially if it requires any labour to discover it (XV–XVIII).

Still retaining the 'wine' metaphor Browning turns to his own poetry – ''Tis said I brew stiff drink.' People complain that instead of being flowery and springlike Browning's verse is autumnal and 'stiff' (as a Frenchman will describe a brandy as *dur* rather than *souple*). Browning replies that strong wine seldom seems sweet when it is new, but has to be laid away to become mellow (XIII–XIV). He adds that even if his poetry is never to mature into something that will gladden the heart of man he must still write it, and he undertakes that it shall at least never lack strength. It will be wine made of grapes – that is, the subject of his poetry will be real human experiences, 'Man's thoughts and loves and hates'. He scorns those who prefer poetry, like Byron's, about 'the Dark Blue Sea', for his province is man (XIX–XX).

It may be suggested by an ingenious adviser that Browning could sweeten his poetry with 'cowslips' (here apparently a metaphor for fanciful images of a pleasing kind) which are plentiful and easily gathered. Indeed, using these 'cowslips' one can make some kind of miniature poetry. Thus instead of man's thoughts and loves and hates one can have first the typical Romantic pseudo-idea, 'Man is insignificant compared with the works of Nature', secondly sentimental poems about sweet-hearts parted, and thirdly, playfully ironic pieces such as Pope's letters to Martha Blount. Thus a poet could, as it were, make cowslip wine, that is concoct a kind of mock-poetry full of frolic fancy, suitable for children if not for men (XXI–XXIII). Browning replies that he knows of the existence of 'cowslips', but he has no intention of using his store of agreeable fancies to make a juvenile poetry. Indeed, he implies, even cowslips are too good to waste on those who have never appreciated the genuine wine he offered them. He may be called ungrateful for not amusing his critics, but, he concludes, if they cannot enjoy the true grape he will offer them instead, not cowslip-wine but nettle-broth, which is supposed to purge the blood; that is, he will write astringent verse, hoping that it will have a whole-some effect on his ill-humoured readers (XXIV–end).

As I say, the general sense of the poem is not in doubt. The digression (VIII–XII, XV–XVIII) about the merits of old authors is pointed, but not entirely relevant. The chief ambi-guity of the poem is latent in the metaphor Browning uses. He does not make it plain whether it is possible for wine to be both strong and sweet, whether this is possible only with the passage of time, or whether strong wine necessarily matures into a less harsh drink. Thus at first he says to his critics, 'You can have strong poetry or sweet poetry. No poetry is both at once.' But when his critics point to the ancient poets as being both strong and sweet he shifts his ground slightly and says, 'Ah, but that has come with the passage of time. My own poetry may (will?) grow less harsh one day.' It is in the passages in which he dis-cusses his own work that the real interest of the poem lies (XIII–XIV, XIX–XX).

III

In Browning's later years we may still find poems such as *Tray* (1879), which burlesques the exaggerated and artificial heroics

of Morris and Byron, *Gerousios Oinos* (1883) [14], which mocks
the complacent pride of the moderns in their own insipid verses,
Round us the Wild Creatures . . . (1884), which reiterates
Browning's preference for the stir and bustle of life 'up and
down amid men',[1] and *Poetics* (1889), in which Browning
expresses unambiguously his own opinions of the unreality of
much Romantic nature imagery. In the main, however, when he
refers directly to poetry he is not concerned, as he was earlier,
with the immediate indignant rejection of specific Romantic
poems and writers. Instead he dwells increasingly on the great
theoretical questions, especially the question of the proper business of the poet; even here his conclusions are strikingly at
variance with prevalent Romantic doctrines.

The *Parleyings With Certain People of Importance in Their
Day* (1887) has been thoroughly treated by W. C. DeVane [15].
The work represents, as DeVane has shown, Browning's own
commentary, characteristically oblique, on many problems of
contemporary interest. Naturally the theory and practice of
writing poetry figure prominently in the discussions. In the
Parleying with Christopher Smart Browning wonders why
Smart, after his superb revelation of the glories of the creation
in the *Song to David*, in which he 'pierced the screen/'Twixt
thing and word, lit language straight from soul', reverted to
'a drab-clothed decent proseman'. He conjectures that Smart
realized that it was not enough merely to enable mankind to
perceive the beauties of Nature: it was the poet's task also to
teach men what use to make of the world:

> Nature was made to be by Man enjoyed
> First; followed duly by enjoyment's fruit,
> Instruction. . . .   (IX)

Therefore once the poet has by the 'word's flash' brought man
to realize the strength and beauty of the world it is pointless for
him to continue and 'particularize/All, each and every appari-
tion'.

With the comment, 'Oh, yes –/The other method's favoured

---

[1] DeVane comments (*Handbook*, p. 479), 'It is of course the choice which Browning
has made throughout his life as poet. . . . This major characteristic of Browning's
art is the more notable in a century so devoted to the appreciation of nature.'

in our day!' Browning turns the poem into an attack on certain of his contemporaries, who, far from describing the world too vividly or curiously, do not condescend to scrutinize the details of creation at all: they claim nevertheless to be able to explain the secrets of the Universe. Browning observes that this is to arrive at the conclusion without examining the premises. 'If you cannot discover Will, Power, and Love by your observations on Earth, it is no use trying to deduce them from some fanciful laws about the behaviour of the Universe as a whole. This leads first to disappointment when things as they are do not correspond with things as you think they should be, and ultimately to pessimism.' Which modern poet Browning is hitting at in these lines is not clear. DeVane suggests Rossetti, Morris and Swinburne as targets, especially the latter, but the case would be much more convincing if it could be shown that Browning had some specific poem in mind. It is clear, however, that Browning is repudiating two distinct types of poetry. The first is the kind that merely entertains, which does no more than particularize the wonders of the world. This is inadequate because it offers no guidance to mankind: it 'pleases simply', whereas the poet's 'function is to rule'. He rejects also the kind of poetry, at present even more popular, which offers 'the end ere the beginning', that is, pretends to teach the inmost secrets of the Universe without having studied things as they are. In between lies the recommended middle way, which is to proceed from a limited but adequate observation of the earth step by step to such general conclusions about universal laws as are possible in a man's lifetime.[1]

The argument is continued from a slightly different point of view in the *Parleying with de Lairesse*. This is not an easy poem, first because de Lairesse is set up as a stalking-horse, whereas the person with whom Browning is really arguing is Matthew Arnold [16]; secondly because Browning's favourite parallel

---

[1] Cf. the following passage from a letter of Browning's to Mrs Thomas FitzGerald of 19 September 1880: 'Before attempting to imagine an angel, one ought to be able to express a stone or a flower. . . . I know a sad instance of a young man, a friend of mine, who took the contrary course. He had great imagination and at once tried to draw things much above angels when he was unable really to properly draw apes: and I gave him introductions to Leighton, Millais, Rossetti & Watts: I remember Millais said of his specimen-drawings "He begins where Michelagnolo never arrived".' (McAleer, *Learned Lady*, pp. 93–94)

between poetry and painting is exploited throughout the poem, and remarks about one art have continually to be translated into terms of the other [17]; and thirdly because, as so often, Browning writes satirically in many places.

He begins by making it clear that de Lairesse was blind. Then in Sections II, III and IV he offers his version of de Lairesse's advice to his pupils, ironically commending it:

> But – oh, your piece of sober sound advice
> That artists should descry abundant worth
> In trivial commonplace, nor groan at dearth
> If fortune bade the painter's craft be plied
> In vulgar town and country! Why despond
> Because hemmed round by Dutch canals? Beyond
> The ugly actual, lo, on every side
> Imagination's limitless domain
> Displayed a wealth of wondrous sounds and sights
> Ripe to be realized by poet's brain
> Acting on painter's brush!   (II)

Being blind, de Lairesse was able to disregard actual appearances and to remove from his imaginary paintings everything mean and base, so that he is able to describe Holland as if it were ancient Greece.[1]

Section V is crucial to the poem. Browning puts the following case. Suppose he could combine with the things that he actually sees on 'Earth's common surface' de Lairesse's power of changing them imaginatively, especially by associating them with Greek legend. Would this mean that he lost the 'hard fast wide-awake/Having and holding nature for the sake/Of nature only'? If he could imagine the nymph of the apple-tree, in short, would this mean that he lost the apples themselves? To elucidate this 'moot point' Browning agrees that simple observation of the world is not enough of itself:

[1] The whole of *De Lairesse* exhibits a curious relationship with Whistler's 'Ten O'Clock Lecture' (1885). On the subjects of art Browning and Whistler agree: on the function of art they are almost totally opposed. The following sentence shows the extent of the agreement and the opposition – 'Art is occupied with her own perfection only – having no desire to teach – seeking and finding the beautiful in all conditions and in all times, as did her high priest Rembrandt, when he saw the picturesque grandeur and noble dignity in the Jews' quarter of Amsterdam, and lamented not that its inhabitants were not Greeks.'

> . . . for sense, my De Lairesse,
> Cannot content itself with outward things,
> Mere beauty.   (V)

Thus the primitive stage of simply recording beauty as an end in itself is demonstrably inadequate. Hence the Greek habit of animating Nature 'Until the solitary world grew rife/With Joves and Junos, nymphs and satyrs.' It was a way of satisfying the soul's craving for some sort of interpretation of experience. Thus men used always to link earthly things to heavenly, real things to ideas, and de Lairesse, since he was blind, had the same faculty. The modern mind, though still active, produces only *factual* hypotheses to explain the mysteries of the world. Why has man lost his imaginative powers? Would it in fact be possible still to take the animistic view of the world, viewing all nature in some anthropomorphic guise?

In Section VII Browning replies that it would of course be possible to do this, but retrograde. Man is naturally progressive: where Present differs from Past, Past must be less than Present. To demonstrate the modern method Browning offers to go over the scenes of a day with de Lairesse, finding in each of them a more profound significance.

In the next four sections (VIII–XI) Browning describes four different times of day – daybreak, morning, noon and sunset. To each of them he attaches a scene from Classical legend or history. Finally he shows how even the old symbolic or mythical figures of Greece are to be explained much more fully in modern terms. For instance, Browning, like Shelley, sees Prometheus as symbolizing Man's defiance of tyranny: Artemis he sees as the death-dealer: in the Satyr he finds qualities of pathos, while the encounter of Darius III and Alexander the Great impresses him by its momentousness. Finally Browning depicts nightfall (Section XII). The sun goes down, the mountains turn black, the clouds grow grey and threatening instead of pink: all is dark and hostile, daunting him who must travel. Clearly there is no road back for the spirit of man into mythology or the heroic age. Even the so-called 'spirit of Hellenism' is really a phantom. The whole of this section brings to mind such *loci classici* of Victorian poetry as *Ulysses*, *Thyrsis*, and the end of *Sohrab and Rustum*. Browning says that it is folly to lament the passage of time: one should rather rejoice, for if life were static it would not be worth living. He expresses

> Heart's satisfaction that the Past indeed
> Is past, gives way before Life's best and last,
> The all-including Future. . . . .
> . . . . Soul,
> Nothing has been which shall not bettered be
> Hereafter. (XIII)

It is wrong to keep delving back into Man's past, when his present state is so much more important. It is equally mistaken to concentrate *solely* on man's present achievements and ignore the past. We should neither despise man's history nor allow our study of it to cut us off from what exists in the present. Some poets, and here Browning undoubtedly has Arnold in mind, say that we must take the retrograde course of redevising a Classical mythology,

> Push back reality, repeople earth
> With vanished falseness,

and deny any value to the facts of modern life unless they are made insipid by fanciful treatment.

In the concluding sections (XIV–XVI) Browning rejects this attitude, declaring that he prefers reality to illusion.

> The dead Greek lore lies buried in the urn
> Where who seeks fire finds ashes.

As he did in *Cleon* he argues that Greek philosophy, which was the highest truth the Greeks had to offer, was at best comfortless, offering no hope: even if death comes to him, as it did to the Greeks, as the last and worst of man's misfortunes, he is nevertheless confident that 'what once lives never dies'. God will certainly not fail his creatures just at the point 'There where the heart breaks bond and outruns time'. Thus when spring comes, instead of musing sadly on man's mortality, like the Greeks or like Arnold, it is possible to welcome the season with a cheerful song of hope. The modern method, then, is to accept reality, and to interpret it not by some fanciful correspondence with a false mythology but in terms of a much profounder insight into the essential qualities of a scene or situation. Those who have failed to realize that man has developed and who refuse to welcome the progress of humanity are limiting themselves to a barren field of poetry, just as the art of the Greeks was ultimately limited by their sterile philosophy. As for the Christian the life of the individual moves towards its consummation, so the life of mankind as a whole moves towards perfection, and the poet's place is in the vanguard.

Thus in this poem Browning links his trust in God and faith in human destiny with his chosen subject of man in the modern world. 'I who myself contentedly abide/Awake, nor want the wings of dream, who tramp/Earth's common surface, rough, smooth, dry or damp.' (V) Even if his argument, particularly this association, depends on assertion rather than logic, he nevertheless points to two distinctive features of English poetry in the nineteenth century. First, its generally pessimistic and elegiac tone: secondly, the poets' reluctance to write about contemporary life. In the closing sections Browning connects these two features with some adroitness and repudiates them both.

The arguments which Browning puts forward in *de Lairesse* are set in a rather different light in his *Parleying with Charles Avison*, in which he discusses the transience of the arts. Although each musician is admittedly superseded by his successors this does not mean that his work goes for nothing. Similarly we must not feel that what was once thought to be true is of no value now that another truth has taken its place. It was the bud that was essential for the fruit.

> Soon shall fade and fall
> Myth after myth – the husk-like lies I call
> New truth's corolla-safeguard: Autumn comes,
> So much the better! (XIII)

There is no contradiction here with *de Lairesse*. In *Avison* Browning is explaining the value of the art of the past in general as a necessary early stage in man's interpretation of the world. In *de Lairesse*, talking of Greek legends in particular, he points out that, great though their value and power in the past, they are inappropriate for the present, which must, as he says in the first part of *Avison*, continually find new forms of expression [18].

Asolando (1889), the harvest of his last years, is as a whole more personal than Browning's other collections of verse. In it Browning frequently reflects on poetry and on the vision of the world which he has expressed in his poems. The *Prologue* is, as often, directly concerned with Browning's own art. The first two stanzas are supposed to be spoken by an unnamed poet, who laments that in his old age he has lost the power of investing common objects with an unearthly glory: the reference to Wordsworth is unmistakable, although the poem is almost equally applicable to the Coleridge of *Dejection*. Browning retorts that it is better to see 'the naked very thing' and to know it for what it is than to drape objects in 'falsehood's fancy-haze'. He admits that in his own youth 'natural objects seemed to stand/Palpably fire-clothed!' whereas now

> the lambent flame is – where?
> Lost from the naked world: earth, sky,
> Hill, vale, tree, flower, – Italia's rare
> O'er-running beauty crowds the eye –
> But flame? The Bush is bare.

Nevertheless, Browning concludes, in this new clarity of vision he can understand 'Earth's import' more clearly: he realizes that it is not Nature which is to be marvelled at, but God. DeVane aptly comments 'Not only, then, does the poem concern itself with the main subject of the volume, but it illustrates also the sub-title, *Fancies and Facts*. The preference for facts is of course a part of Browning's poetic creed' [19].

Development is a poem whose understanding is vital for a balanced assessment of Browning's views of truth and false-hood, myth and reality, faith and doubt; for it suggests a possible way of reconciling the apparently divergent doctrines of *Christopher Smart* and *de Lairesse* on the one hand and *Fra Lippo Lippi* and '*Transcendentalism*' on the other. There is no difficulty about taking the poem personally, since Browning expressly indicates in line 84 that he is discussing his own views and their development. Yet although it is apparently written in a mood of simple reminiscence the reasoning behind the poem is typically complicated and oblique.

The paradox which Browning exploits in this poem is that while truth is better than dreams it can sometimes only be grasped by first accepting what is not true. His conclusion is that the young are best encouraged to accept stories such as Homer's in the light of simple faith in their historical truth, for at that stage they need some such imaginative realization of ethical values. Later they will 'by slow and sure degrees/ . . . sift the grain from chaff,/Get truth and falsehood known and named as such,' and understand that truth is a complex thing. Moreover the essence of Homer's teaching will be implanted in their hearts 'freed and fixed/From accidental fancy's guardian sheath' [20]. When they encounter ethical teachings they will approach them with more respect and understanding. Myths play a similar part in human development.[1] Browning insists that pure reason, though it is ultimately superior to fancy and fable, would not have been serviceable in the earliest stages of the evolution of the human race. The specifically religious implications of this are discussed in detail in Chapter 9, pp. 237–39.

While the various parallel themes are given varying emphasis Browning's general position is clear. That fanciful, or even false views of the world, if they are appropriate to their audience and implant in a simple heart their underlying truth, are of great value. But, and this is where Browning, as in *de Lairesse*, declares himself a realist rather than a Romantic, 'no dream's worth waking'. 'Dreams' were once an essential stage in development but man grows older and wiser. Similarly, Browning in his old age sees the dreams for what they are, and devotes himself to a study of what is real and permanent, what he calls in *Dubiety* 'Truth ever, truth only the excellent'.[2]

---

[1] Cf. *Reverie*:

> As the record from youth to age
>   Of my own, the single soul –
> So the world's wide book: one page
>   Deciphered explains the whole
> Of our common heritage.
>
> How but from near to far
>   Should knowledge proceed, increase?
> Try the clod ere test the star!
>   Bring our inside strife to peace
> Ere we wage, on the outside, war!   (31–40)

[2] It is instructive to compare Browning's arguments here with those he provides for Bishop Blougram. His own predilection for illustrations of this kind made it easy

Perhaps the finest epitome of Browning's views on poetry is to be found in one of the intercalary poems in *Ferishtah's Fancies*, which runs as follows:

> Fire is in the flint: true, once a spark escapes,
> Fire forgets the kinship, soars till fancy shapes
> Some befitting cradle where the babe had birth –
> Wholly heaven's the product, unallied to earth.
> Splendours recognized as perfect in the star! –
> In our flint their home was, housed as now they are.

DeVane says that this poem 'compares the mystery of fire, struck from flint but forgetful of its birth, to the child in the cradle, come from heaven but now housed on earth,' and suggests that this idea is connected with that of the preceding poem, *The Sun* [21]. But the comparison DeVane suggests does not hold good, since the things compared are opposite processes. Nor is the poem's connection with *The Sun* at all easy to demonstrate, for if the poem in fact refers, as *The Sun* does, to man's idea of the deity, it bears the unlikely interpretation that even the most elevated of our ideas about the nature of God are in origin merely human.

It seems more probable that the poem is a comment on the Poet's speech in *Timon of Athens*:

> Our poesy is as a gum, which oozes
> From whence 'tis nourish'd: the fire i' the flint
> Shows not till it be struck; our gentle flame
> Provokes itself, and, like the current, flies
> Each bound it chafes.   (I. ii.22)

Browning gives a slightly different turn to the image, making the point that poetry, which seems so heavenly in its perfection that we are tempted to imagine for it a correspondingly god-like genesis (such as the divine spark of inspiration), has

---

for him to sympathize with Blougram and render even his spurious arguments convincing. Fundamentally, however, Blougram's position and Browning's are worlds apart, for Browning really believes that the Gospels contain an important truth, however difficult it is to disentangle it from what is false or misleading. Browning moreover is not in the end prepared to say that anything is better than truth: the *Ethics* have to be studied at last. Blougram on the other hand simply makes play with man's weaknesses in youth to justify his own present lack of belief. For more on *Blougram* see Chapter 6.

nevertheless its origin in the life of man and human experience.[1] This unexalted, humble notion of poetry is, of course, consonant with Browning's habitual view of his own writing.

I have been concerned to show that Browning's rejection of many central Romantic positions persisted to the end of his life. In addition to the examples given I might mention his contemptuous reference in *Waring* to contemporary men of letters and his deliberate attack on *Omar Khayyám* in *Rabbi Ben Ezra* [22], or more dubious instances such as his writing of *Fifine at the Fair* as an ironic commentary on Rossetti's *Jenny*. Further evidence could be produced abundantly from his own conversations and letters. Far more important, however, is the great body of his poems in which, even when he does not explicitly comment on his art, he bears testimony, by his choice of subject, tone and diction, to his devotion to his own way of poetry.

IV

If we try to abstract from his poems and from his *Essay on Shelley* a summary of Browning's poetic theory we find that his opinions on the nature of poetry are by no means fixed. In the *Essay on Shelley* he deals, as I have said, with the distinction between subjective and objective poetry, classifying himself as an objective poet, that is, one who looks outwards rather than inwards for the ultimate standards which determine his poem, and measures the poem against some independently-existing reality. His truth, that is to say, is a truth of correspondence rather than of coherence. However great and subtle the poet's transformation of the external world he is ultimately dependent on it as simultaneously the origin of his work and the standard by which it must be judged, 'at once the source, and end, and test of Art'.[2] To this extent the objective poet is, by definition, mimetic, a label which does not exclude the processes of the creative imagination. As a dramatic poet, moreover, Browning

[1] Cf. the *Epilogue* to the Second Series of *Dramatic Idyls*: 'Rock's the song-soil rather, surface hard and bare.'

[2] Cf. the *Essay on Shelley*: 'For it is with this world, as starting point and basis alike, that we shall always have to concern ourselves: the world is not to be learned and thrown aside, but reverted to and relearned. The spiritual comprehension may be infinitely subtilized, but the raw material it operates upon, must remain.'

is in a particularly obvious way a notable exponent of mimesis, for he tries to counterfeit in the words of his poem the words of a man speaking in a given situation. He is almost an illusioinst, working in a kind of verbal *trompe l'oeil*. Imagination is required of him, but observation must precede imagination. His object, in short, is to convince the reader of the 'realness' of his situations by a profusion of accurately observed detail, imaginatively selected and combined.

Since it is his contention that the subjective poet is also, though in a different way, 'impelled to embody the thing he perceives', Browning may be said to hold a generally mimetic theory of poetry. In confirmation of this we may observe that his favourite figure for the discussion of the nature and purpose of the poet's art is the parallel between the poet and the artist, a parallel which is most revealing. In *Abt Vogler* the extemporizer makes the point very plainly that in poetry and painting

> effect proceeds from cause,
> Ye know why the forms are fair, ye hear how the tale is told;
> It is all triumphant art, but art in obedience to laws. (VI)

In contrast to this we have the unique gift of the musician 'that out of three sounds he frame, not a fourth sound, but a star'. It is a commonplace that Browning's poetry does not depend on that magical laying together of words to produce a fresh and unpredictable thing which is one of the special powers of the Romantic poet. This is not his métier, and indeed it seems to lie outside his conception of what poetry can be. He sees the poet as doing very much the same thing as the representational painter, and constantly, almost obsessively, draws the parallel between the two arts.[1]

It is not, I think, possible to harmonize in the same way all Browning's ideas of the poet's function and obligations. The contradictions must simply be accepted: we may say, if we wish, that they are the product of different dramatic viewpoints, or that Browning's opinions changed as he grew older, or that he

---

[1] Cf. *Avison* VI–VIII, where Browning makes the point that even music is not essentially different from the other arts. As the poet is armed with his 'word-mesh' and the painter with his 'swift colour-and-line-throw' so the musician has his 'master-net', with which he strives to capture 'truth's very heart of truth', for on him too is laid the duty of expressing a truth about mankind.

never really made up his mind about the difficult theoretical questions lying behind his discussions of the practice of poetry and the duties of the poet.

The chief problem which exercises his mind is, 'How far is it sufficient for an artist simply to *present* a picture of the world, whether derived from observation or intuitively? Is it incumbent on him also to explain what is to be learned from his picture?' As I have said, in *'Transcendentalism'* and in *Fra Lippo Lippi* he not only praises the artist who simply creates reality, but rebukes in the persons of Boehme and the Prior, those who wish a work of art to carry an explicit moral lesson. In the *Parleyings*, however, he presents the opposite point of view, praising Smart's superb intuitive picture of the creation in *The Song of David*, but praising even more highly his decision to follow 'enjoyment' with 'instruction'. Similarly in *de Lairesse* Browning repudiates 'mere beauty' in favour of the poet's explanation of the essential qualities of a scene or situation. He has moved a long way from Fra Lippo Lippi's 'If you get simple beauty and naught else,/You get about the best thing God invents.'[1]

Thus we may fairly say that in so far as we can construct a coherent theory from Browning's works his idea of poetry is consistently mimetic (and towards the end of his life more or less explicitly didactic) [23]. In practical terms this means that Browning always insists that true poetry is grounded in experience of real life. The poet may explain the application of the reality he has perceived or he may not: either way is possible. But what he must not do is to fail in the vital task of the poet, that of placing his readers in touch with a real world. The cardinal sin of the poet is to allow abstractions or conventions to become a substitute for experiences. It may seem odd to say that for Browning poetry was never abstract, when so many of his poems consist of adventures in the realm of ideas. The point is that Browning is forced into an exploration of the metaphysical world by his experience of the human situation, by his desire to understand why he is as he is. His method is on the whole empirical. 'Let us start from what we know for certain and see whether or not we can base any conclusions on it.' What

[1] The contradiction is softened by a line of argument such as Browning offers in *Development*, that 'delight' is a necessary preliminary to the truth, that in youth Homer is a better teacher than Aristotle.

he is opposed to is any attempt to make experience conform to an *a priori* theory of how things should behave. 'Live and learn,/Not first learn and then live, is our concern.'

Although Browning's poems about the arts cannot be reduced to a completely consistent aesthetic system I do not think that this need trouble the reader unduly. In the first place the poems stand or fall as poems, not as contributions to a theory. The viewpoint that Browning adopts for each poem is the interesting thing: the correspondences and contradictions of these viewpoints are of minor importance. Secondly, it is a fair judgement that, sympathetically viewed, Browning's ideas about his art are reasonably coherent compared with those of most poets. At least one may justly say of Browning that he was always fairly sure what he wanted of poetry, that his ideas about poetry are his own and owe little to fashion or tradition, and that his practice did not vary too widely from his theory.

V

This brief survey of Browning's views has been designed to show that he not only tacitly made certain essentially un-Romantic assumptions about the nature of poetry, but was more or less explicitly opposed to what he saw as the deficiencies of the Romantic poets of his own century. We may express these for the most part as perversions or excesses of the qualities set out at the beginning of Chapter 1:

(i) the exaltation of the exotic over the familiar; (ii) an exaggerated interest in natural scenery, indeed any interest in Nature which tended to diminish by comparison the stature of men and women; (iii) the use of 'poetic' language, especially if this tended to diminish the reality of the subject of the poem;[1] (iv) the theory that the poet and his poem were necessarily inseparable, that the poet's life could be called in to explain the poem and that the poem represented as statement the opinions

---

[1] Cf. Browning's letter of 30 June 1887 to Henry G. Spaulding:

All this will show that I have given much attention to music *proper* – I believe to the detriment of what people take for 'music' in poetry, when I had to consider that quality. For the first effect of apprehending real musicality was to make me abjure the sing-song which, in my early days, was taken for it.

of the poet; and (v) the inescapable sense of the imperfection and mutability of all institutions, leading to an expression of loneliness, world-weariness, pessimism and despair.

Although his profound distaste for current poetic attitudes suggests that Browning was not a Romantic, it is nevertheless true that other criteria might give a different verdict. We might, for example, choose a deliberately unsophisticated definition and say that a Romantic is a man who believes in the supreme value of passionate love, and that Browning is therefore a Romantic. But the results of any subtler tests, if they indicate that Browning was a Romantic at all, will only, I think, do so with considerable qualifications. Two examples must suffice.

First we may take as our standard the position put forward in Coleridge's *Dejection*:

> O Lady! we receive but what we give,
> And in our life alone does Nature live:
> Ours is her wedding garment, ours her shroud!
>   And would we aught behold, of higher worth,
> Than that inanimate cold world allowed
> To the poor loveless ever-anxious crowd,
>   Ah! from the soul itself must issue forth
> A light, a glory, a fair luminous cloud
>   Enveloping the Earth —
> And from the soul itself must there be sent
>   A sweet and potent voice, of its own birth,
> Of all sweet sounds the life and element!   (47–58)

that is the idea, common to Romantic poets and philosophers alike, that the creation is without significance except in so far as the mind of man endows it with meaning. Such a belief would hardly be possible to one who considered himself an objective poet, and indeed we find that far from accepting the Coleridgean or Kantian point of view Browning continually questions it and returns to it as a fruitful paradox. Ultimately, I think his own opinion was that the external world existed and was significant, even though such a belief entailed apparently insuperable epistemological difficulties.

The second 'test' can be put in the form of a syllogism as follows: 'It is a universal characteristic of the great Romantic poets (and of them alone among poets) that they celebrate the supremacy of the individual, the single unique self-responsible human soul, whereas, for example, the Augustans dwelt on the beauty of an ordered universe in which the individual was subordinate to the religious or social structure of which he was a part. Now Browning is supremely the poet of the individual. Therefore he is a Romantic.'

If this account corresponds to what people actually feel when they are reading Browning, then there is no room, or need, for debate. But it is worth noting that as an argument it is far from watertight. For it is possible to object that concern with the primacy of the individual may be considered a historical accident, or universal nineteenth-century phenomenon. Such an accident, affecting an entire age, though it may differentiate the poets of that age from those of earlier and later ages, does not necessarily constitute a valid differentiating feature within the age itself, since, to take the present case, concern for the individual would in the nineteenth century be common to Romantics and anti-Romantics alike and thus would not serve to distinguish between them. I don't think that this altogether applies to Browning, for on the whole his passionate interest in the nature of individual man is so strong that in spite of all other differences it ultimately forms a powerful bond between his poetry and that of, say, Shelley or Byron or Victor Hugo. Whether this is a historical accident or not, it is *felt* when the poems are read.

In any case, as I shall show later, Browning is often concerned with the individual in a distinctively undogmatic way. He accepts knowledge of the existence of the self as a certainty, but this is not simply made the occasion for a triumphant self-assertion. Especially in his later poems, such as *Fifine at the Fair* and *La Saisiaz* and *Ferishtah's Fancies*, he takes the idea of the individual man, who creates the world from his own perceptions and derives the root of morality from his own experiences, and questions its implications. His mistrust of laws and standards which may prove purely subjective and his constant attempts to establish some absolute, no matter what, that should have a sounder base than the flux of the individual consciousness, are impressively persistent. They are, moreover, not by any simple definition Romantic. Browning asks the difficult question, 'If man is free to act as he wishes, deriving his standards only from his own inmost being, is there any way of showing that one way of life is preferable to another? If not, does it follow that there is no motive for action but simple gratification of the senses?'

It is true to say that all the poems in which Browning scrutinizes the springs of conduct are, at least in part, anti-Romantic since, instead of glorifying the primal impulse, they offer a scrupulous examination of the value of particular human motives. Although Browning was sure of 'the holiness of the heart's affections' he realized that this was not a sufficient guide to social conduct, for example. One of the preoccupations of his poetic maturity was to consider how to advance beyond the simple Romantic truths – 'from a given point evolve the infinite'.

VI

I am aware that I have not answered the large question 'Was Browning a Romantic?' for here defining the question, if any definition is in fact possible, will itself provide an answer. The purpose of this chapter and of Chapter 1 has been to show that, whether or not he was fundamentally a Romantic, Browning saw himself as proceeding contrary to the main course of nineteenth-century poetry, and indeed as consciously opposed to it. It was not perhaps possible for anyone living at that time not to be in some sense a Romantic, but I think that it was possible for a poet to fight against being a Romantic poet and that Browning did so with some success. It will be one of the arguments of the rest of this book that Browning's reaction was not backwards into Augustanism (the imagination boggles, not unpleasantly, at the idea of Johnson's *Life of Browning*), but, if the oxymoron is permitted, forward to the twentieth century.

❖ 4 ❖

The surface difficulties of
Browning's poetry – I

'My God! I'm an idiot. My health is restored, but my mind's gone. I can't understand two consecutive lines of an English poem.'

DOUGLAS JERROLD on Sordello

Tennyson said that there were only two lines in it [*Sordello*] he could understand, the first and the last, and that neither of these was true. They were

> Who will may hear Sordello's story told;

and

> Who would has heard Sordello's story told.

D. C. SOMERVELL, 'The Reputation of Robert Browning'

After dinner tried – another attempt – utterly desperate – on Sordello; it is *not* readable. MACREADY, *Diary* (17 July, 1840)

I was so wholly unable to understand it [*Sordello*] that I supposed myself ill. HARRIET MARTINEAU, *Autobiography*

Mrs. Carlyle said that she had read the book through without being able to make out whether Sordello was a man, a city, or a book.

DEVANE, Handbook, p. 85

She talked about poetry, Tennyson, and Wordsworth; asked me if I understood Browning's 'Sordello'; and she comforted me, after my stammering confession that I did not, by telling me that she was delighted to hear that; for she did not understand it either and it was pleasant to have a companion in ignorance.

CHARLES KINGSLEY, Alton Locke

Read Browning's play [*The Return of the Druses*], and with the deepest concern I yield to the belief that he will *never write again* – to any purpose. I fear his intellect is not quite clear.

MACREADY, Diary (3 August, 1840)

Browning came before I had finished my bath and really *wearied* me with his obstinate faith in his poem of *Sordello*, and of his eventual celebrity, and also with his self-opinionated persuasions upon his *Return of the Druses*. I fear he is for ever gone.

MACREADY, *Diary* (27 August, 1840)

Do you know, I have been told that *I* have written things harder to interpret than Browning himself? – only I can not, can not believe it – he is so very hard.

ELIZABETH BARRETT, letter to Mr Westwood

I object a little to your tendency . . . of making lines difficult for the reader to read. . . . Not that music is required everywhere . . . but that the uncertainty of rhythm throws the reader's mind off the rail . . . and interrupts his progress with you and your influence with him.

ELIZABETH BARRETT, letter to Browning (21 July, 1845)

'I hope that these young people will make themselves intelligible to each other, for neither of them will ever be intelligible to anybody else.' WORDSWORTH, on Browning's marriage

We may as well say bluntly it [*Sordello*] is totally incomprehensible as a connected whole.

LOWELL, *North American Review* (April 1848)

. . . I verily believe his school of poetry to be the most grotesque conceivable. With the exception of the *Blot on the Scutcheon*, through which you may possibly grope your way without the aid of an Ariadne, the rest appear to me to be Chinese puzzles, track-less labyrinths, unapproachable nebulosities.

FREDERICK TENNYSON (1854)

There is no getting through the confused crowd of Mr. Browning's Men and Women. *Blackwood's*, LXXIX (February 1856), p. 135

Who will not grieve over energy wasted and power misspent, – over fancies chaste and noble, so overhung by the 'seven veils' of obscurity, that we can oftentimes be only sure that fancies exist?

Athenaeum, November (1855)

The most cursory perusal [of *Men and Women*] can hardly escape a conviction that the poet's *penchant* for elliptical diction, interjec-tional dark sayings, *multum in parvo* (and, sometimes, seemingly

minimum in multo) 'deliverances', flighty fancies, unkempt simili-
tudes, quaintest conceits, slipshod familiarities, and grotesque
exaggerations is unhealthily on the increase.

Bentley's Miscellany, XXXIX (1856)

Obscurity is the evil genius that is working the ruin of this poet:
Browning is, pre-eminently, the King of Darkness.

Irish Quarterly Review, VI (1856)

We do not believe that they [Browning's works] will survive,
except as a curiosity and a puzzle. *Edinburgh Review*, CXX (1864)

I have tried to read him, but without much success. I wish the poets
now-a-days would not sing in such devilish queer measures. It
bothers me horribly; and as regards these poems, I cannot understand
a tenth part of them. There is something in the English atmosphere
and diet that unfits a man for the comprehension and enjoyment
of all transcendentalism and of whatever passes a certain limit
of common sense. In America, very probably, I might have enjoyed
these poems. HAWTHORNE, *Notebooks*

Poor Mr. Browning is both muddy and unmusical to the last degree.
In fact, his style may fairly be described as the very incarnation of
discordant obscurity.

ALFRED AUSTIN, *The Poetry of the Period* (1870)

'Well, Browning, you have taught the English people one thing
any way – you have taught them the value of punctuation.'

CARLYLE

I remarked, however, upon the large demands Browning makes in
this book [*Aristophanes' Apology*] on his readers' knowledge, and
said that I believed no one would be able to understand all the
allusions without referring over and over again to the Comedies:
and he thus wilfully restricted the number of his readers to the
comparatively few. He would not hear of explanatory notes; said it
could not be helped, but that he was not likely to try anything of
the kind again. ALFRED DOMETT, *Diary*

He was at that time engaged in revising the proof-sheets of
'Dramatic Idylls', and after luncheon, to which he very kindly bade
me remain, he read aloud certain selected passages. . . . I would
give much to live that hour over again. But it was vouchsafed in

days before the Browning Society came and made everything so simple for us all. I am afraid that after a few minutes I sat enraptured by the sound rather than by the sense of the lines. I find, in the notes I made of the occasion, that I figured myself as plunging through some enchanted thicket on the back of an inspired bull. A Recollection by Edm*nd G*sse (in *A Christmas Garland* by MAX BEERBOHM)

'Take 'em back; bewilderments I hate; and predicaments I can't abear!' A housekeeper on Browning, quoted by THEODORE WATTS, *Athenaeum* (10 May, 1879)

He [Browning] has got a great deal of what came in with Kingsley and the Broad Church school, a way of talking (and making his people talk) with the air and spirit of a man bouncing up from the table with his mouth full of bread and cheese and saying that he meant to stand no blasted nonsense.
HOPKINS, letter to R. W. Dixon (1881)

> Browning is – what?
> Riddle redundant,
> Baldness abundant,
> Sense, who can spot?
>> H. W. HANCOCK

It is questionable whether the poet would not have gained more admiration as well as given more pleasure had he condescended to attract the vast numbers his obscurity repels, by 'completing his incompletion' and letting his meaning 'pant through' the beauty of his poem a little more decidedly and distinctly.
DOMETT *Diary* (1883)

Meredith is a prose Browning and so is Browning. He used poetry as a medium for writing in prose.
WILDE, *The Critic as Artist*, part 1

Mr. Browning, who often amuses himself by writing in a cipher to which he alone has the key, has seldom propounded to his disciples a more hopeless puzzle.
Review of the *Parleyings*, *Saturday Review* (26 February, 1887)

He [Browning] is a very extraordinary man, very generous and truthful, and quite incapable of correcting his literary faults, which at first sprang from carelessness and an uncritical habit, and are now born and bred in him. He has no form, or has it only by accident when the subject is limited. His thought and feeling and knowledge are generally out of all proportion to his powers of expression.

BENJAMIN JOWETT, letter to Lady Tennyson

I have a fine tale of Althea Gyles. She brought a prosperous love-affair to an end by reading Browning to the poor man in the middle of the night. She collects the necessities of life from her friends and spends her own money on flowers.

W. B. YEATS, letter to Florence Farr

And did you once find Browning plain?
And did he really seem quite clear?
And did you read the book again?
How strange it seems and queer.   C. W. STUBBS

I cling to the dear old tradition that Browning is 'difficult' – which we were all brought up on and which I think we should . . . feel it a shock to see break down in too many places at once.

HENRY JAMES, 'The Novel in *The Ring and the Book*'

At the beginning of Chapter 2 I pointed out that Browning's dramatic poems, especially the long monologues, demanded an acquired reading technique: one result of this is to give them a particular kind of complexity, which is illustrated in Chapters 6 and 7. Of course, not all Browning's poems have this dramatic concentration and complexity: some, for example, have a simple narrative form. Yet even these poems may present obstacles to the reader who expects to be able to understand them as rapidly as he absorbs Tennyson, say, or Byron or Gay. In this Chapter and in Chapter 5 I shall examine the surface difficulties which arise from unfamiliar syntax, accidence, vocabulary and allusion rather than those which arise from structural intricacy or from eccentricity or profundity of thought. They are in short the difficulties which prevent us from answering the question 'What is the poet saying?' rather than 'What does the poet mean by what he says?' In general my argument will be that the reader's estimate of the importance of such difficulties depends on how far he is prepared to agree that these are in fact two different questions.

I

The quotations at the head of this chapter illustrate Browning's reputation for obscurity of manner: as many again could be collected without trouble. Whether or not they are all genuine expressions of bewilderment, there is no doubt that popular report of Browning's inaccessibility, exaggerated almost to the point of legend, seriously affected his relations with the public in his lifetime, and even today deters many prospective readers. Without in any way trying to deny the existence of the difficulties in his work I want to discover first how widespread they are, secondly, where they do exist, *what* they are, thirdly how important they are (i.e. how easy it is to ignore or overcome them and whether it matters which we do), and fourthly, if they are important, what effect they have, for good or bad, on the poems. Finally I shall look at Browning's own comments on his reputation for crabbedness and incoherence.

First of all it must be emphasized that the difficulties are not universal. There are unnumbered passages and indeed complete poems of Browning's in which the simple sense of the words presents no more difficulty even to a reader of today than, say, one of Wordsworth's Lyrical Ballads or a poem by John Betjeman. I may instance 'How They Brought the Good News from Ghent to Aix', or The Pied Piper, or The Laboratory, or The Confessional, or Evelyn Hope, or Home-Thoughts, from Abroad, or Memorabilia, or Prospice, and there are many others. They are not usually of very great length, and are often uncomplicated also in structure and theme. Their language is simple in the sense that we can construe them quite satisfactorily by the normal standards of Victorian prose, the vocabulary makes no special demands on our knowledge, and there are no allusions too recondite or subtle for the ordinary reader. We are conscious that we are being addressed by someone with a distinctive style, but the language he is using is recognizably that of ordinary writing or conversation between men with no special knowledge. The effects which Browning obtains with this style are described in Chapter 10.

Nevertheless in other poems Browning makes demands on his readers far more taxing than those of any other poet of his time except Hopkins. They are of two kinds: first, he requires his reader to bring to the poem an extensive vocabulary and a correspondingly wide knowledge in many fields; secondly, the reader thus equipped is required to display great agility in following the extraordinary swiftness of the poet's mind.

The range of Browning's vocabulary is enormous, embracing a variety of technical terms, as for instance those of music; a variety of foreign words, especially in the poems set abroad, as for instance Italian in *Old Pictures in Florence* and *The Ring and the Book*, or French in *Fifine at the Fair*; a similar variety of classical words in the poems with Greek and Roman settings; and a surprising number of words of so characteristically Victorian usage that they already present problems or traps to the reader of today, as for instance in *Mr. Sludge, 'The Medium'* or *Pacchiarotto*. In addition, when he is writing on historical subjects he uses English words no longer current in his day. The meanings of all these words can be discovered, fairly readily in most instances, from works of reference, although there is no doubt that a fully-glossed edition of Browning would encourage many people to read him who are at present deterred by not knowing the meaning of all the words he uses.

It is less easy to settle the meaning of many of his coinages – often nonce-words, often having no possible life outside the poem they were created for. This new-minted vocabulary is characteristic of Browning, but does not present any difficulty to the experienced reader. The significance of the new word is normally evident from its use in the poem. For example, 'hand-impulsion' (*Prince Hohenstiel-Schwangau*), 'self-acquainting' (*Old Pictures in Florence*), 'linden-flower-time-long' (*Sordello*), 'fawn-skin-dappled hair' (*A Pretty Woman*).

Almost the severest difficulty with which Browning's vocabulary confronts the reader is its sheer size. It is so varied and so enormous that Browning demands always the full extent of his reader's knowledge of the language, and keeps his faculties always at full stretch. Browning's utter avoidance of the conventional word never allows the reader to relax into the comfortable circuit of a limited number of familiar terms. Even the common words which Browning uses are given a new interest by a slightly changed sense. A simple example comes from *Old Pictures in Florence*:

> Happier the thrifty blind-folk labour,
> With upturned eye while the hand is busy,
> Not *sidling a glance* at the coin of their neighbour.   (X)

i.e. 'casting a sidelong glance at'. Again from *The Englishman in Italy*:

> Red-ripe as could be
> Pomegranates were *chapping* and splitting
> In halves on the tree.   (22–24)

'Chapping' is unexpected here, but it is precisely the right word to describe the first small fissures in the skin.

This unsparing use of uncommon words or of common words in an uncommon sense presents the reader with, what is always an obstacle, a sense of *oddity*, a feeling of language pushed to the borders of what is idiomatically possible. Sometimes this is of course the essential part of the poet's work and the result is a triumphant new addition to the language: sometimes the result is at best one of excessive clumsiness and contrivance, at worst of temporary or permanent unintelligibility [1].

As well as making unprecedented demands on his reader's knowledge of words Browning places a similar strain on his reader's knowledge in general. Breadth of vocabulary is matched by breadth of allusion. This is perhaps most noticeable in Browning's poems on Italian art, where he assumes as a minimum the reader's acquaintance with the names and schools of all the chief Italian painters. His shorter poems on Greek and Roman themes require little more than an ordinary acquaintance with Classical history, literature and mythology, although the translations naturally call for a more thorough understanding, and *Aristophanes' Apology* depends for its effect on the reader's complete familiarity with the works of Euripides and Aristophanes. *Sordello* notoriously demands a detailed knowledge of an obscure period of Italian history, but this is an early poem, and Browning thereafter rarely makes the mistake of over-estimating so crudely the reader's power to grasp allusion. Nevertheless he writes always for an educated reader, one, for instance, who knows or can readily discover what the Wairoa is [2], where Vishnu-land is [3], who Guillim was [4], what *Rinaldo* is [5], what breccia is [6], who Ebion [7], St Scholastica [8], Boehme [9], and Escobar [10] were, what an arch-genethliac is [11], what the Promachos was and why it was especially associated with the Rocky Ones [12], and what Justinian's *Pandects* were [13].

So far the allusions I have mentioned would have presented to Browning's original readers much the same degree of difficulty as they do to us. There is however in Browning a substantial body of references which his original readers would have found perfectly plain, since they were to matters of common knowledge at the time, but which we do not pick up so readily. All the allusions to the liberation of Italy, for example, which are to us references to the history book, were to Browning's contemporary audiences references to the newspaper. Similarly names once current – like Radetzky (*Old Pictures in Florence*), Colenso (*Gold Hair*), Sir Edwin (*The Inn Album*), Ess or Psidium (*The Inn Album*), Alfred Austin (*Pacchiarotto*), Guizot and Montalembert (*Respectability*), Renan (*Epilogue to Dramatis Personae*), Pradier (*Prince Hohenstiel-Schwangau*), Jenny Lind and the Benicia Boy (*Mr. Sludge, 'The Medium'*) or Quicherat (*Parleying with Francis Furini*) are now in varying degrees mysterious and make Browning's poetry appear remote and inaccessible instead of topical and fresh.

II

So much then for the demands Browning makes on the supply of information which the reader brings to his poetry. The remaining difficulties are to be resolved not by anterior knowledge but by imaginative and intellectual agility. It is not part of my concern to offer explanations of Browning's poetry in terms of the events of his life, but the following passage from Mrs Orr's *Handbook* may help to characterize the nature of his obscurity:

> 'Paracelsus' had recently been published, and declared 'unintelligible'; and Mr. Browning was pondering this fact and concluding that he had failed to be intelligible because he had been too concise, when an extract from a letter of Miss Caroline Fox was forwarded to him by the lady to whom it had been addressed. The writer stated that John Sterling had tried to read the poem and been repelled by its verbosity; and she ended with this question: *'doth he know that Wordsworth will devote a fortnight or more to the discovery of the single word that is the one fit for his sonnet?'* [Mrs Orr's italics]

Mr. Browning was not personally acquainted with either John Sterling or Caroline Fox, and what he knew of the former as a poet did not, to his mind, bear out this marked objection to wordiness. Still, he gave the joint criticism all the weight it deserved: and much more than it deserved in the case of Miss Fox, whom he imagined, from her self-confident manner, to be a woman of a certain age, instead of a girl some years younger than himself; and often, he tells us, during the period immediately following, he contented himself with two words where he would rather have used ten. The harsh and involved passages in 'Sordello', which add so much to the remoteness of its thought, were the first consequences of this lesson. 'Pauline' and 'Paracelsus' had been deeply musical, and the music came back to their author's verse with the dramas, lyrics, and romances by which 'Sordello' was followed. But the dread of being diffuse had doubly rooted itself in his mind, and was to bear fruit again as soon as the more historical or argumentative mood should prevail.

The determination never to sacrifice sense to sound is the secret of whatever repels us in Mr. Browning's verse, and also of whatever attracts. [14]

Of *Sordello* itself Mrs Orr says:

The poem was written under the dread of diffuseness which had just then taken possession of Mr. Browning's mind, and we have sometimes to struggle through a group of sentences out of which he has so laboured to squeeze every unnecessary word, that their grammatical connection is broken up, and they present a compact mass of meaning which without previous knowledge it is almost impossible to construe. We are also puzzled by an abridged, interjectional, way of carrying on the historical part of the narrative; by the author's habit of alluding to imaginary or typical personages in the same tone as to real ones; and by misprints, including errors in punctuation, which will be easily corrected in a later edition, but which mar the present one. [15]

The first effect of this 'dread of diffuseness' was to lead Browning to take liberties with syntax in the interests of concision, using words in a way sanctioned neither by written nor by spoken prose usage. Some of these constructions are widely used by other poets; others are distinctively Browning's own. For example, inversion, a device which every English poet has used at some time and which is acceptable even in prose, Browning at times employs ruthlessly, not to say insensitively.

This is especially obvious in poems where the rhymes present a definite challenge. For example:

> That, had not fear sent Pacchiarotto
>   2   3 1
> Off tramping, as fast as could trot toe . . .
>
>   behold, Pacchiarotto,
> 1 2   3   4   5   13 14 15
> The pass which thy project has got to,
> 6   7   9   10 11 12   8
> Of trusting, nigh ashes still hot – tow! (*Pacchiarotto* XVI)

In such poems the variations on normal prose order which are traditionally permitted to poets as an occasional licence Browning takes as completely equivalent alternative constructions. The reader of Browning must therefore be prepared for full, or excessive, advantage to be taken of all the liberties allowed to the poet.

Sometimes the eccentric order of words is combined with a succession of metaphors, each used to illustrate a point briefly. When Browning writes like this the unwieldiness of a prose paraphrase becomes a revealing index of the compression of the verse. An instructive example is to be found in Stanzas IX and X of *A Pretty Woman* (1855):

> As, – why must one, for the love forgone,
>   Scout mere liking?
>   Thunder-striking
> Earth, – the heaven, we looked above for, gone!
>
> Why with beauty, needs there money be –
>   Love with liking?
>   Crush the fly-king
> In his gauze, because no honey-bee?

A paraphrase would read 'Why, simply because we cannot love a girl, must we reject merely liking her? [To do this is like] blasting earth out of existence simply because we find we cannot have the heaven we were looking for. Why must we ask for money when we can have beauty? [Why must we] ask for love when we can have affection? [Why must we] crush a fly, whose gauzy wings have their own quality, simply because he is not a honey-bee?'

The rhetorical questions, each inviting the response, 'There is no need to do that,' are characteristic of what Mrs Orr calls Browning's 'abridged, interjectional way' of carrying on a narrative or an argument. This is not simply a matter of omitting words, of using elliptical constructions, or of placing undue reliance on apposition as a means of relating similar ideas. Such devices do indeed give rapidity and compression to the surface of Browning's poetry, but the real reason why Browning's poetry is so much denser than say Arnold's or Rossetti's is the speed with which thoughts move,[1] a speed generated almost entirely by omission (e.g. of a step in an argument), or by an unheralded shift of tone (e.g. a sudden change from narrative to imperative, or to a rhetorical question or to a parenthesis), or by the surprising treatment of a metaphor (e.g. prolonging its activity in the poem after its initial impact by treating it as an agreed analogy which is available to the speaker for use in the conduct of his argument).

To illustrate this compression it may be helpful to describe three short poems of Browning's, running them through in slow

---

[1] Cf. here Swinburne's defence of Browning in *George Chapman: A Critical Essay* (1875): 'If there is any great quality more perceptible than another in Mr. Browning's intellect it is his decisive and incisive faculty of thought, his sureness and intensity of perception, his rapid and trenchant resolution of aim. To charge him with obscurity is about as accurate as to call Lynceus purblind or complain of the sluggish action of the telegraphic wire. He is something too much the reverse of obscure; he is too brilliant and subtle for the ready reader of a ready writer to follow with any certainty the track of an intelligence which moves with such incessant rapidity, or even to realise with what spider-like swiftness and sagacity his building spirit leaps and lightens to and fro and backward and forward, as it lives along the animated line of its labour, springs from thread to thread and darts from centre to circumference of the glittering and quivering web of living thought woven from inexhaustible stores of his perception and kindled from the inexhaustible fire of his imagination. He never thinks but at full speed; and the rate of his thought is to that of another man's as the speed of a railway to that of a waggon or the speed of a telegraph to that of a railway. It is hopeless to enjoy the charm or apprehend the gist of his writings except with a mind thoroughly alert, an attention awake at all points, a spirit open and ready to be kindled by the contact of the writer's.' Cf. also Robert Langbaum, 'Browning and the Question of Myth', *PMLA*, LXXXI (1966), pp. 575–84, esp. pp. 579–80.

motion, as it were. Consider first the opening stanzas of the poem *Before*:

I

Let them fight it out, friend! things have gone too far.
God must judge the couple: leave them as they are
— Whichever one's the guiltless, to his glory,
And whichever one the guilt's with, to my story!

II

Why, you would not bid men, sunk in such a slough,
Strike no arm out further, stick and stink as now,
Leaving right and wrong to settle the embroilment,
Heaven with snaky hell, in torture and entoilment?

III

Who's the culprit of them? How must he conceive
God — the queen he caps to, laughing in his sleeve,
' — 'Tis but decent to profess oneself beneath her:
Still one must not be too much in earnest, either!'

In the first stanza Browning indicates with extreme brevity that the speaker is a neutral spectator or referee at a duel and is addressing another spectator, that one of the duellists is innocent and that the other is guilty. The guiltless one is left to his glory, the guilty one to the verdict of the present narrative. The last three words are also to be taken as an abrupt interjection — 'to my story!'

The speaker then asks rhetorically, referring to an implied question by his hearer, 'Surely you would not tell men who are as deeply involved as this in an unsavoury quarrel to stay so for ever, leaving the matter to settle itself, right meanwhile being entangled with wrong and contaminated by it?' The metaphor of a 'slough' for an intolerable situation between two men suggests the picture of them both jammed together in a stinking swamp. Unless they make this present effort to release themselves, right and wrong, heaven and hell will also remain in the same unnatural juxtaposition, each tangled with and torturing the other.

The third stanza begins with another question of a kind exceedingly common in Browning. It is not a rhetorical question, since it does not imply that the answer is so obvious that it does not need to be stated. It is partly an intuition by the speaker of a question that his listener has in mind, or, occasionally, a repetition of a question which the listener has actually asked. It is equivalent to the invitation 'Consider for a moment the question of which of these men is the culprit', and has its reply later in the poem when the speaker says 'So much for the culprit. Who's the martyred man?' The status of the next sentence in stanza three is difficult to determine: it is in effect an exclamation, 'How low an opinion he must have of God, estimating Him as he does a lady to whom he pays reverence while thinking to himself, "It's only decent to make professions of inferiority, but it doesn't do to intend them too seriously." '

So the poem continues, using, in almost equal numbers, simple statements, exhortations and questions of various types.

VIII

> All or nothing, stake it! Trusts he God or no?
> Thus far and no farther? farther? be it so!
> Now, enough of your chicane of prudent pauses,
> Sage provisos, sub-intents and saving-clauses!

IX

> Ah, 'forgive' you bid him? While God's champion lives,
> Wrong shall be resisted: dead, why, he forgives.

A paraphrase of this would read, 'Let him (i.e. the man whose cause is just) risk everything. Does he trust God or not? Or does he trust Him, but not enough to fight? I understand him to say that he trusts God enough to fight now. Very well. Now the time is past for any devices for delay and compromise. Ah do you (i.e. the listener primarily, but a more general sense is implied, cf. "your" two lines before) maintain that the wronged man should forgive his enemy? (I will reply to you on his behalf that) he will resist wrong in God's name as long as he lives. Not until he is dead will he accept forgiveness as a substitute for fighting for what is right.' The poem concludes with the speaker addressing the two combatants directly, telling them to prepare to fight.

The 'difficulty' of the poem clearly lies in following the rapid transitions of mood (in the grammatical sense) and giving each change its proper significance in the context of the story which emerges as lying behind the poem, but which is alluded to throughout as if it were known to the listener.

A more extreme example of the same effect is to be found in the last stanza of *Popularity*, a passage well known through its exposition by G. K. Chesterton [16]. But the beginning of the poem offers almost as many problems to the inexperienced reader.

I

Stand still, true poet that you are!
    I know you; let me try and draw you.
Some night you'll fail us: when afar
    You rise, remember one man saw you,
Knew you, and named a star!

II

My star, God's glow-worm! Why extend
    That loving hand of his which leads you
Yet locks you safe from end to end
    Of this dark world, unless he needs you,
Just saves your light to spend?

III

His clenched hand shall unclose at last,
    I know, and let out all the beauty:
My poet holds the future fast,
    Accepts the coming ages' duty,
Their present for this past.

IV

That day, the earth's feast-master's brow
    Shall clear, to God the chalice raising;
'Others give best at first, but thou
    Forever set'st our table praising,
Keep'st the good wine till now!'

The general drift of the passage is clear enough. Browning is addressing a poet who has not achieved fame and assuring him that one day his work will be recognized. The difficulty is to discover exactly what Browning is saying and who he is talking about. In the first stanza he 'fixes' the poet for us as a painter might pose a model whom he is going to use in a picture which will show the model's true nature. 'I know you,' Browning says, meaning that he knows his model to be a true poet. 'The time will come when you will no longer be with us. When you rise afar (i.e. when you achieve fame in a far country *or* in a distant time)[1] remember that there was one man (i.e. Browning) who recognized you for what you were and hailed you as a new star in the firmament of poetry.' The last lines of this stanza contain an obvious allusion to Keats's sonnet *On First Looking Into Chapman's Homer*, where the poet speaks of his excitement at discovering the world of Homer – 'Then felt I like some watcher of the skies/When a new planet swims into his ken.'

Browning continues, 'To me you are a star: to God a glow-worm (i.e. a small but beautiful light which He has put into the world for a purpose). Unless He has need of you and is preserving your light now so that it can be revealed even more brightly later on, why does He extend His loving hand which leads you from one end of this dark world to the other yet keeps you safe from harm?' Here Browning is I think referring to his friend Domett, who had gone to New Zealand (see *Waring*) and was also a poet of little reputation. The difficulty in the stanza is the abrupt change of scale. The image shifts from that of Browning on earth looking up at the light of a star to that of God carefully shielding the minute light of a glow-worm in his hand, conveying it safely through the dark world and yet preventing men from seeing it.

'God's hand will unclose one day, I know, and show men the beauty of your light. My poet' (note sudden change to third person) 'is sure of his hold over the future and accepts the homage of ages yet to come, a time which will be the present day when our own age has passed away (i.e. the homage of future generations is something which will be perpetually renewed, whereas popularity with one's contemporaries is soon past).' The appositions in the last three lines of this stanza compress the ideas.

'When God does reveal you as a poet it will be as if He set fresh wine before His guests at a banquet, his guests being all mankind. The feast-master (i.e. the spokesman of humanity at large) will lift his cup to God and say, "Other hosts give their best wine at first, but you by always offering us a wine better

---

[1] Cf. *Waring*, 'Oh, never star/Was lost here but it rose afar!' Possibly William Sharp had these lines in mind when he wrote 'On the night of Browning's death a new star suddenly appeared in Orion.' (*Life*, p. 198.) The Astronomer Royal thought otherwise.

than the one before, keep us always praising you, and you have kept your good wine until this late time." ' The argument, of course, is that Domett need not worry about the slow growth of his fame. First, fame in the future is more enduring than fame in the present (Stanza III). Secondly, a late revelation of an excellence is always welcome, and is a sign of God's providence. The allusion is to John II, 10.

Thus in these twenty lines Browning has managed to pack a great deal, partly by grammatical economies, but even more by rapid transitions from metaphor to metaphor – the artist and his model, the star, the glow-worm clenched in the hand, the wine at the feast – each one developed or exploited in the interests of close compression of meaning but at the cost of ready comprehensibility. With the beginning of Stanza V the texture at once becomes more open, with a recapitulation of the metaphor of the artist and his model:

> Meantime, I'll draw you as you stand,
>   With few or none to watch and wonder:
> I'll say – a fisher, on the sand
>   By Tyre . . .

And then begins the celebrated, extended image of the blue dye of the Tyrian shellfish, only to be obtained by labour and cunning. This dye comes to stand for the quintessence of poetic excellence. Browning concludes his poem, in the passage to which Chesterton calls attention:

> And there's the extract, flasked and fine,
>   And priced and saleable at last!
> And Hobbs, Nobbs, Stokes and Nokes combine
>   To paint the future from the past,
>   Put blue into their line.
>
> Hobbs hints blue, – straight he turtle eats:
>   Nobbs prints blue, – claret crowns his cup:
> Nokes outdares Stokes in azure feats, –
>   Both gorge. Who fished the murex up?
>   What porridge had John Keats?

Provided that the reader knows that the murex is the whelk from which the dye is obtained and that Hobbs, Nobbs, Stokes and Nokes are fictitious names signifying the rag tag and bobtail of the world of literature, no special demands are made on his knowledge. But the metaphor of the Tyrian dye as the essence of poetry shifts abruptly into another of high living as a measure of popular esteem, and the poem finishes with two rhetorical questions. The first demands the answer 'Not Hobbs, Nobbs, Stokes or Nokes, who are merely imitators. The real pioneering work is done by the true poets, of whom Keats is one, and so is the poet I am addressing.' The second expects the answer, 'None, or at best only plain porridge (i.e. little worldly success).' The consolation that the poem offers to the unsuccessful poet such as Domett (or, it is tempting to add, Browning himself) is therefore that the 'world's good word' is not a necessary reward of poetic originality: indeed it almost implies that the contrary is true, that good poets are never recognized by their contemporaries, and that poets so recognized are never good.

It is plain that Browning exploits metaphors here to give succinctness to his poem by supplying symbols for ideas. Thus 'blue' becomes a brief label for a particular kind of poetic excellence.[1] These symbols are then treated familiarly as if they were objects within the reader's experience, and are manipulated as if they were real. The original equivalence is not usually in doubt; what is not clear is what development of the tenor is implied by a development of the vehicle.

My third example is *St. Martin's Summer* (1876). K. L. Knickerbocker, in a sympathetic study of the poem [17], has suggested that it was occasioned by Browning's proposal to Lady Ashburton in 1869 and his subsequent feelings that he had tarnished his wife's memory. It seems to me that this experience and its aftermath may well lie behind the poem, but even if this is true it tells us nothing about the poem and nothing that we did not already know about Browning, except perhaps that there are parallels closer than he would have admitted between his work and the occasions of his own life.

[1] This trick of picking up a phrase of the poet's own and alluding to it familiarly is found in much of Browning's verse. In *Bishop Blougram's Apology*, for example, the metaphor of the ship's cabin is introduced near the beginning and later invoked by the Bishop as an idea with a status of its own. An extreme instance of this internal allusiveness is to be seen when Browning nicknames a character in one of his own poems, perhaps on the strength of an earlier reference, perhaps not, and then uses the nickname as a substitute for the character's proper name (e.g. 'Sister Cherry-cheeks', *Two Poets of Croisic*, CXXV, CXLVI).

The poem itself is a monologue spoken by a young man to an even younger woman, and proceeds by the familiar means of interjections, questions, and imagined interruptions or expostulations; syntactically it is orthodox enough, except Stanzas IV and VII. The real difficulty comes with what Knickerbocker calls its 'fantastic, elliptical metaphors'. In the first stanza the speaker tells the woman not to protest at what he has just been saying, hardly even to kiss him. They both have experience of the way love develops, of how the greenest leaf turns most withered, of how the clearest burst of blue turns to the most overcast sky, in short of how love (which is the most glorious relationship) turns to friendship (which is the drabbest). Each of them, that is to say, has learned that the more intense an experience is the more dismal its termination will be.

Since this is so the speaker opposes the woman. She 'would build a mansion': he 'would weave a bower'. Throughout the poem these two expressions are used as metaphors (almost as euphemisms) for different kinds of relationship possible to them. The woman's 'mansion' stands first for a permanent, definite, householding, ratepaying relationship, as for instance marriage and an establishment and an acceptance of the full obligations of husband and wife. It is an ambitious relationship since it depends on the strength of their love for each other, so that the second meaning of 'mansion' is 'deeply committed love'. The speaker's 'bower' is tentative, experimental, empirical, changeable, above all living and flexible. It is 'timid', since it allows each of them to hold back from full commitment. These two terms assumed, the speaker can then use them in argument, as though the point of disagreement between him and the woman were a purely domestic one about the kind of dwelling they were going to choose. He puts, as it seems, a practical point – 'Walls admit of no expansion': this can be elaborated into 'Once we have built a mansion we shall be unable to make it larger', and, on the real level of argument, into 'If we define too closely what we expect of each other then we are committed to what we announce. We shall be unable to change our relationship, even to a more intimate one.' On the other hand 'Trellis-work may haply flower/ Twice the size.' That is, 'If we have a bower made of living parts it is capable of growing', and on the deeper level, 'If we don't commit ourselves too deeply or precisely then we allow our relationship room to develop: it will be a living, not a static, thing.'

In the third stanza the speaker asks what it is that brings cheer to the winter, and answers that it is the sight of new buds taking the place of the dead flowers. Similarly the end of their life will be gladdened by the sight of the new buds around the speaker's 'bower', whereas it would bring only sadness to see the woman's 'mansion' wrecked before the middle of autumn. In personal terms this means that a relationship such as the speaker desires is one that continually renews itself and will bring them pleasure until they die, whereas the woman may find that her more rigid relationship collapses quite soon, with no hope of renewal. The speaker is here clearly glancing back at the unhappy experience he has referred to in the first stanza – presumably he and another woman had committed themselves some time before to building a 'mansion' of complete love, only to see it wrecked.

Continuing this theme in Stanza IV the speaker says that although he is still young, as she is (not, by the way, a point of resemblance to Lady Ashburton and Browning himself), he has in his past reason for his timidity, and in Stanza V he explains this by introducing the second main metaphor of the poem. Written out, in translation as it were, this stanza would read, 'Surely a graveyard casts its gloomy shadow over the spot where we plan to build our dwelling. Moss may drape each headstone and footstone, violets may hide names and dates from being spelled out, but, although the bodies rot thus in obscurity, the ghosts of the dead escape.' Of course, like the 'mansion' and the 'bower', the 'graveyard' has no actual existence. It is a figure for the past lives of the speaker and the woman. Although this past is now far behind them, so that even the details are no longer clear, memories are still with them both – the 'ghosts' of the past.

At this point it is important to notice that we are still moving in the world of metaphor: it is not a necessary inference that the speaker is talking about people who are actually dead, any more than he is talking about an actual graveyard. In the poem's terms 'dead' means simply 'in the past': it may also mean 'physically dead'. Compare the term 'dead love', which is similarly ambiguous. The danger is of assuming that the speaker is Browning, the woman Lady Ashburton, and the 'dead' love Mrs Browning,

which at once limits our reading of the poem. The graveyard
imagery certainly has overtones of mortality, but not so strongly
as to entitle us to regard the question as settled. Indeed when
we look back at lines 3–6 of Stanza I we may be encouraged to
feel that the speaker's past includes experience of the way love
dies by turning into something less, not by the physical death of
the beloved.

In Stanza VI the speaker apologizes for admitting so frankly
that he is haunted by memories of his past life. He asks 'Am I to
be blamed if I pledged my soul to endless duty many times?
Will you be hard on Love, now that it is in the grave (i.e. now
that it is simply a thing of the past)?' She would, he says (VII),
be fairer to blame not Love, or his first love, who is no longer
responsible, but rather Grief, which is fickle, Time, which
proves treacherous, Chance, Change, and all things that deflect a
man from his purpose, and even Death, who refuses to thrust the
sickle (which laid love low) through the flowers which later
shroud Love's corpse. Having extracted this from its syntactic
snares, we can now 'translate' the metaphors. 'Do not blame me
for having once been in love with someone else', the speaker says.
'Rather blame my timidity and apparent reluctance on the unpredictable way in which grief still visits me, on Time which
ought to obliterate the past but treacherously refuses to do so,
on anything at all which weakens human resolve, even on the
fact that what killed my love has not killed my memories of it.'

In the next stanza he challenges the woman to deny that she
too has similar memories, not necessarily of a dead husband: the
poem need not be retitled *Any Widower to Any Widow*. He says
(IX) that nobody blames her for the death of her previous love.
Similarly he has nothing, or very little, to reproach himself
with. Love, after all, is a mortal emotion and therefore cannot be
expected to last for ever. Nothing could be more absurd than to
expect the pair of them to feel remorse. It is enough that when
they lost love they felt its loss severely. There is a marked
change of tone in this stanza. The casuistry of earlier stanzas is
underlined as the speaker tries to assume a reasonable, slightly
callous, man-of-the-world air, but he finishes with a sigh,
'Though now – alas!'

This is merely an interjection and he resumes his argument in
the tenth stanza, reverting to the metaphor of the 'bower' and

the 'mansion'. He says that the 'corpse' of Love, that is the actual love of someone else, does not trouble them any more – only its 'ghost', that is the memories of it. It is because this ghost is a warning to them of the dangers of placing trust in 'durable mansionry' that the speaker weaves his bower, making his life conform to what seems to be a law of nature. The ghost's warning is simply the speaker's memory of his previous love-affair, when he swore 'vows of endless duty' yet all ended in disaster. This memory, he says, warns him of the danger of supposing love to be immutable: he therefore plans a shifting, contingent relationship, and thus tries to make his life conform to what he has learned from experience. 'Law' is used here in the sense of 'scientific law' rather than 'law of the land'.

In Stanza XI he says that the solid mansion (or the hope that love will prove durable) attracts disaster, whereas if the bower (or less binding tie) surpasses their expectations and endures until the winter of their lives then it will be nothing to marvel at since boughs are resilient (that is, light things are flexible). If on the other hand it falls flat, it is such a temporary structure that they will hardly need to wonder at its ever having existed at all. That is, whatever happens to the less elaborate dwelling they will feel no violent emotions of surprise. So, he says (XII), let her stop protesting and coaxing him with kisses, for they must both recognize that genuine joy is a sober thing, a matter of common sense and compromise. This is not a joke. If she does not believe him let her ask Penelope or Ulysses, who were old in their youth (i.e. who even when young had enough sense not to expect too much of love).

Therefore (XIII) there is no reason for ghosts to feel angered, that is for memories of past loves to come between them. He tells the woman to treat all the interference of the ghosts as merely 'faint march-music in the air', urging them to join the great band of lovers instead of hanging back: far from daunting them the memories of their previous loves should encourage them to love again. So far the speaker has, we feel,[1] been arguing at least as much to convince himself that deep love is inevitably dangerous as to convince the woman, and at this point he seems to have succeeded. Yet even while they embrace one another (XIV) and congratulate themselves on having

[1] The speaker's voice has faint overtones of Don Juan in *Fifine at the Fair*.

cheated their first loves, there comes a sudden terror to the speaker (XV). He calls out on the woman, since he suddenly sees that what he has loved in her has really been a memory. It was his first love whom he had been embracing and who had deceived him. It is past loves that are really powerful (XVI). They had simply used the woman to make themselves palpable: she was the illusion, they were the reality. Now that he has realized this, the speaker and the woman can come together in no sort of union, ambitious or tentative, for she is simply a vehicle. Everything about her that had attracted him came from his memories of past love (XVII), each low word that won him, each soft look that observed him to be a victim of love. All that is left to the woman as her own contribution are the tears which she is now shedding and the noise she is now making.

> Undone me –
> Ghost-bereft!

The woman is lamenting, but it is really the speaker who is utterly undone, since he is now finally bereaved, having lost even his ghosts: he has no longer even the unspoiled memory of his former love.

The speaker, then, begins by defending a temporary non-committal relationship and justifies this by referring to a previous love with whom he had attempted a more ambitious union. The memory of this is the 'ghost' which warns him not to make the same mistake again. He therefore tries to encourage the woman to accept him on his own terms, but even as he does so he realizes that the 'ghosts' are more potent than he had supposed, since he has all the time been in love not with the woman but with his own memories: now not even these are left to him. The 'bower' which he has so powerfully recommended on grounds of expediency is desirable only because he has once tried to build a 'mansion' and failed. The reader is left in no doubt at the end of the poem that the 'bower' stands for a cowardly, makeshift kind of love and that the 'mansion' is infinitely preferable, even though its destruction has been infinitely painful to the speaker.

This is simply an explanation of what the words say – the tactics of the poet: I leave aside all questions of structure and major variations of tone – his strategy – and of course any kind of

evaluative comment. But just to explain fully (and I have tried
to leave no difficult point without comment) what Browning
said has taken me well over three times as many words as he
needed. But *St. Martin's Summer* is, I think, as difficult to un-
ravel as any poem of Browning's; it does yield to patience and
an acquaintance with Browning's way of handling words; and
once the general method is seen it can be applied to many other
poems.

III

So much then for the 'compression' of Browning. The last category in this analysis of the difficulties he presents to a reader is
that of simple failure to communicate, those places where a
knowledge of syntactical habit, a familiarity with words and
allusions and a readiness to pursue a metaphor through all its
shifts and condensations are still not enough to assure the reader
that he has followed Browning's mind, or, even worse, those
places where the only way to construe a passage yields contradictions or nonsense. Examples of complete impenetrability are
not easy to come by, even in *Sordello*, but Stanzas 4 and 5 of
By the Fire-side, in spite of recent commentary [18], continue
to puzzle me. In the first edition (1855) the poem begins as
follows:

1

How well I know what I mean to do
  When the long dark Autumn evenings come,
And where, my soul, is thy pleasant hue?
  With the music of all thy voices, dumb
In life's November too!

2

I shall be found by the fire, suppose,
  O'er a great wise book as beseemeth age,
While the shutters flap as the cross-wind blows,
  And I turn the page, and I turn the page,
Not verse now, only prose!

3

Till the young ones whisper, finger on lip,
  'There he is at it, deep in Greek –
Now or never, then, out we slip
  To cut from the hazels by the creek
A mainmast for our ship.'

4

I shall be at it indeed, my friends!
  Greek puts already on either side
Such a branch-work forth, as soon extends
  To a vista opening far and wide,
And I pass out where it ends.

5

The outside-frame like your hazel-trees –
  But the inside-archway narrows fast,
And a rarer sort succeeds to these,
  And we slope to Italy at last
And youth, by green degrees.

A general interpretation of this passage is not difficult to arrive
at. For example, 'The person of the monologue . . . is a man
who is old enough to picture what he will do in the "long dark
evenings" of the autumn of his life. He will read Greek – no
longer verse but only prose – by the fireside, but his thoughts
will drift away from the book into a long retrospect. (In this
retrospect the incidents of the past are merged and blended with
the physical environment in which they occurred.) He will think
of Italy . . .' [19]. But precisely how does the speaker get from
Greek by the fire to Italy in youth? The study of Greek proli-
ferates, or ramifies into day-dreams, no doubt, and this suggests the metaphor of 'branch-work' in which the 'branches' are
seen as (?) actual branches composing a kind of pergola leading
like a corridor back into time. Is this the 'vista'? If so, how does
it open 'far and wide'? And does the speaker when he 'passes
out where it ends' emerge from it, or, as Stanza 5 implies, enter
it? The 'outside-frame' of this walk is like the hazel-trees the
children cut from the creek, that is presumably slight, or close
together, or possibly far apart, but the 'inside-archway' (and I
do not see what this signifies) narrows fast,[1] and a rarer sort
(less common? thinner on the ground?) succeeds to these
(hazel-trees?) and we slope to Italy at last, and youth by green
degrees. The difficulty does not lie in understanding why a man

[1] Most subsequent editions have 'widens' here, which does not really help. I think
that this is one of the instances described by Mrs Orr (*Life and Letters*), when she
says, 'I think he often tried to remedy by mere verbal correction, what was a defect
in the logical arrangement of his ideas.'

whose attention wanders from his book should feel insensibly led
to think about his youth, but in seeing how this idea is to be
derived from an extended metaphor about branches and even
more in visualizing exactly what sort of physical structure
Browning is trying to indicate for the material level of his
metaphor. The whole exercise seems pointless if the general
underlying idea is in fact a great deal clearer than the metaphor
which purports to convey it. The uneasy combination of the
physical and the abstract, compounded here by an uncharac-
teristic imprecision in the use of words, produces a passage
which it is not, I think, possible to understand as poetry should
be understood. The poem suffers accordingly [20]. A similar uncertainty clouds the end of *The Two Poets of Croisic* (e.g.
Stanzas CLIV, CLVII–CLIX). Again the general sense of the
passage is clear, but the precise development of the argument
and the final placing of the elements of the poem are thrown into
doubt by syntactical abruptness, extraordinary condensation,
and an agitated series of unconvincing metaphors. This unresolved obscurity impairs the poem.

In the last resort then we must be prepared for Browning not
to make sense and for the poem to be seriously damaged by the
failure. This rarely happens in the poems later than *Sordello*.[1]
Far more often the reader encounters situations such as I described earlier, where difficulties exist but can be with more or
less effort resolved or, failing this, ignored, without noticeably
impairing the reader's progress through the poem.

Does it matter which we do? And what effect on us as readers
has the existence of such difficulties? In the following chapter I
suggest some answers to these questions.

[1] There are parts of *Prince Hohenstiel-Schwangau* (e.g. pp. 123–4) and *Fifine at the
Fair* (e.g. 125, 128) of which I have not seen any completely convincing detailed
interpretation. *Bad Dreams* II and III are equally puzzling.

❧ 5 ❧

The surface difficulties of
Browning's poetry – II

Was it 'grammar' wherein you would coach me –
You, – pacing in even that paddock
Of language allotted you *ad hoc*,
With a clog at your fetlocks, – you – scorners
Of me free of all its four corners?
Was it 'clearness of words which convey thought?'
Ay, if words never needed enswathe aught
But ignorance, impudence, envy
And malice – what word-swathe would then vie
With yours for a clearness crystalline?
But had you to put in one small line
Some thought big and bouncing – as noddle
Of goose, born to cackle and waddle
And bite at man's heel as goose-wont is,
Never felt plague its puny *os frontis* –
You'd know, as you hissed, spat and sputtered,
Clear cackle is easily uttered! (*Pacchiarotto, XXVIII*)

I

It seems reasonable to argue from general principles that to
ignore through laziness any part of any poem because it is not
immediately intelligible, or alternatively to accept through
ignorance a passage as intelligible which is not in fact thoroughly
understood is to fail in one's duty as a reader of the complete
poem. In practice, however, a failure to grasp all the possible
meanings of a poem or even to grasp any meaning at all is by
no means always a barrier to enjoyment.[1] For instance, Orsino's

[1] Cf. Coleridge's celebrated remark, 'Poetry gives most pleasure when only
generally and not perfectly understood.' (*Anima Poetae*)

introduction to *Come away*, *death* is extraordinarily difficult to render completely into a prose paraphrase:

> Mark it, Cesario; it is old and plain:
> The spinsters and the knitters in the sun,
> And the free maids that weave their thread with bones,
> Do use to chant it: it is silly sooth,
> And dallies with the innocence of love,
> Like the old age.

Yet a reader, and still more a spectator in the theatre, can accept this speech quite happily without inquiring into the meaning of every word.

Similarly Milton's sonnet on his blindness is still perfectly acceptable as a poem even to a reader who fails to notice the sequence of commercial images *spent*, *talent* (two senses), *lodg'd* 'deposited', *useless* 'without interest or increase', *account*.

Again in Gray's *Elegy* it is easy to surmount the awkwardness in

> The boast of heraldry, the pomp of pow'r,
> And all that beauty, all that wealth e'er gave,
> Awaits alike th' inevitable hour.

The apparent lack of concord can be explained by taking 'awaits' as a singular verb after the multiple subject of the preceding lines, although Gray certainly intended 'th' inevitable hour', that hour which lies in wait and which nothing can escape, to be taken as the subject of the sentence.

> In the beginning was the Word.
> Superfetation of τὸ ἕν,
> And at the mensual turn of time
> Produced enervate Origen.
> (*Mr. Eliot's Sunday Morning Service*)

How easy it is to make some sort of sense of this passage by assuming that τὸ ἕν means The One (τὸ ἕν) [1]. Or in Dylan Thomas's 'The force that through the green fuse drives the flower' how much more satisfactory to suppose that when Thomas wrote 'fuse' he really meant 'flex'.

These and similar difficulties in other poets the reader may skate over, secure in the speed of his passage. Though the inferior way of dealing with a poet's difficulty it is the easier and often the pleasanter. It is, however, a pleasure which Browning seldom allows his readers. The combination of different kinds of obstruction in his verse virtually forbids rapid reading, however rapidly the poet may be hurrying forward with the story or argument. Thus when confronted with a difficult place in his verse it is not only unfair on general grounds to turn a blind eye to it but very hard to do so in any particular instance. If then the obstacles are not to be ignored how are they to be overcome?

In the words of one early explicator, Browning 'has the curiosities of all dictionaries at his fingers' ends' [2], and he thus requires his readers to show an equal familiarity with the dictionary. His eye is always on his poem, never on his reader, when he is choosing a word: appropriateness, not familiarity, is rightly his criterion, and appropriateness often calls for a word which is right precisely because it is unusual, a foreign word for instance, or for a word which is unusual precisely because it is right, a technical term for instance [3]. Annotated editions of the poems would save the reader the trouble of consulting a dictionary, but they are by no means easy to find [4].

Were they readily available they would, of course, help to elucidate the historical allusions with which the poems are sprinkled. In default, most problems can be solved by the use of standard works of reference or works of specifically Browning scholarship [5]. Particular subjects on which Browning had wider knowledge than is now common are painting and music. Much of his information about painters comes from three books – Vasari's *Le Vite dei Pittori* (1572–4), Baldinucci's *Delle Notizie dei Professori del disegno da Cimabue* . . . (1681–1728), and Pilkington's *Dictionary of Painters*, revised by Henry Fuseli (1805). A slight acquaintance with these clarifies many of Browning's references to painting, but the poet spent much of his life in Italy, and was often writing from his own knowledge of the masterpieces of Italian art.

His knowledge of music was also soundly based. He had been instructed in harmony by the celebrated John Relfe, and had set to music some poems of Donne, among them *Goe and Catch a Falling Star*. A number of articles deal with his poems about music [6]: also of interest is a book by Charles Avison himself, *Essays on Musical Expression* (1752), which Browning read and used.

Finally, in a less specific way, DeVane's excellent book on

Browning's *Parleyings* (1927) gives an unequalled insight into the resources of Browning's knowledge. DeVane gave his book the subtitle *The Autobiography of a Mind*, and commented, '. . . The seven men represent seven major interests of Browning's life – philosophy, history, poetry, politics, painting, the Classics (Greek), and music. Moreover, the men chosen to be parleyed with had in some way been influential, usually in Browning's youth, in shaping his ideas upon their respective subjects.' DeVane's commentary throws much light upon the extent of Browning's knowledge of these subjects and on the general direction of his interest in each.

Most of Browning's major poems are thus by now provided with some sort of apparatus for the unlearned, or are at least greatly simplified if the reader is even superficially acquainted with the sources of Browning's own knowledge. The chief exceptions are the early *Paracelsus* [7], and the long poems of the 1870s from *Prince Hohenstiel-Schwangau* to *La Saisiaz* [8], notably *Aristophanes' Apology*, which is the most erudite of Browning's poems and probably the most truly difficult. Mrs Orr offers an exceptionally helpful commentary, but the reader who feels that he has understood the whole poem is either extraordinarily learned or very easily satisfied [9]. In this poem, as in all his poems on historical subjects, Browning assumes that the reader knows what he is talking about, knows who Pym was, what Clive did, and why Pheidippides ran from place to place. Very often indeed the poems depend on a fresh insight into their subject, or a subtle playing off of a historical incident against a Victorian theme. A reader who is not equipped with the historical information which Browning assumes is not equipped to read the poem fully. Even casual references to the past or to historical figures are not made by Browning without design: their elucidation almost invariably sharpens the poem's effect. While they may sometimes be ignored without disaster the effort of discovering their import is seldom without reward.

The allusions to events of Browning's own time form a special case. Their topicality, once no doubt a source of particular interest, has gone. Is there any way of recapturing their immediate appeal to Browning's original readers, and, if there is, is the effort to do it worth making? The problem is one familiar to all who have studied, for example, Shakespearean comedy, or

The Dunciad. The reasonable answer is that we shall not appreciate the poet's work fully unless we put our knowledge on a level with that of the poet's original audience, so that we do not falsify the assumptions he is constantly making about what is so familiar as to need no explanation; but to put this forward as an attainable state is only to delude. We can never so familiarize ourselves with Shakespeare's world that a pun on two senses of a word, both now obsolete, moves us to spontaneous laughter. We can never know Pope's Grub Street intimately enough to appreciate instantaneously the relative obscurities of the various sons of Dulness. It is intellectually conceivable that an assiduous scholar might by a sustained course of reading in nineteenth-century newspapers, periodicals and reviews become as well acquainted with the identity of each eminent or humble Victorian and with prevailing beliefs and superstitions as, say, Jowett or perhaps Delane. But this is not a practical demand.[1] What used to be called an educated acquaintance with Victorian history will do much, and a taste for Victorian biography, autobiography, letters, memoirs and novels will do more to provide a necessary background, but for almost every reader it is inevitable that knowledge will come only as a deliberate act of discovery after meeting a specific reference. When we encounter the name 'Rouher' in *Fifine at the Fair*, or read of 'Rarey drumming on Cruiser' in *A Likeness*, we are, unlike the readers of 1872 or 1864, forced outside the poem to cure our ignorance: having discovered who Rouher, Rarey and Cruiser were we must take our new knowledge back to the poem and try to bring the two together.

On the local level this is quite hard enough. Small allusions to passing events either escape our notice or, if they are noticed, defy solution. The problem is even more pressing when the interpretation of the poem depends on understanding the full implications of what is said, as for example the references in *Bishop Blougram's Apology* to Pugin, Count d'Orsay, Verdi and Rossini, Schelling, Strauss, Newman, King Bomba and Antonelli, Fichte and so on. The reader can often do no more than sigh and wait for the great annotated edition which a number of American scholars are at present preparing.

[1] Joyce is reported to have said of *Finnegans Wake*, 'The demand I make on my readers is no less than the application of a lifetime.'

Browning was almost alone among Victorian poets in choosing Victorian life as the subject of many of his major poems, and in understanding these extended presentations of the nineteenth-century world the reader's difficulty is less, as it happens, than in placing incidental allusions. Reading *The Inn Album*, for example, which is all about Victorian England, is no more difficult than reading a Victorian novel. Like Trollope or Surtees or Henry James or Thackeray, Browning explains his world to his readers: the work of art becomes an extraordinarily powerful illumination of its own milieu. The positive results of this are indicated in Chapter 11.

We have finally to decide how closely it is necessary for the reader to follow Browning's compressed, rapid and metaphorical habits of mind. These are not simply affectations of style which can be disregarded if they do not give pleasure, but are part of the language in which Browning expresses himself. To read a poem of Browning's is to expose ourselves to the poet's characteristic way with words; clearly the attempt to pretend that he is writing like anybody else must fail, and even if it could succeed, would do so only by distorting the poem. But to explain to somebody precisely how to understand a poem by Browning is no easy matter. His personal interpretation of the licence allowed to the poet to impose his own syntax on the language is something to be discovered only by experience.

It is not altogether easy to understand why so many readers of poetry today are prepared to tolerate or welcome in contemporary poets a degree of obscurity and abruptness which they find unacceptable in Browning. It is perhaps unkind to suggest that a change in the general idea of what poetry is and of what poets are trying to do has encouraged a more charitable attitude to obliquity of statement in poetry, but that this charity is extended only if the poet is in turn prepared to accept a definition of poetry which makes it a more trivial activity. If we take a poem as nothing more than an inexplicably pleasure-giving arrangement of words, we can, whenever we are confronted with a check, murmur contentedly, 'A poem should not mean but be', and surrender ourselves to the familiar pleasures of imperfect comprehension. But Browning, as I suggest in this chapter, constantly resists any attempts by the reader to use his poetry in this way: his voice is insistently heard, saying, 'It is the glory and the good of Art,/That Art remains the one way possible/Of speaking Truth.'

It is ironic that today, when lucidity is not counted a particular merit in a poem and Browning might reasonably expect to rank as a not unduly difficult poet, he has again fallen foul of the critics because the surface of his work is held to be of little intrinsic interest and to play a subordinate part in the poem, a failure which it is hopeless to try to palliate by pointing to qualities which lie deeper than the surface. Indeed the fact that such irrelevant and unliterary motives as the desire to write what is true have determined the language of the poem is taken as a further proof that Browning is not a poet.[1]

Doubtless the critics are right according to their lights, just as Browning's contemporaries were right to criticize him because the meaning of his poems was hard to come by: it is true that the challenge of his poetry can neither be easily overcome nor comfortably declined. He demands, as he has always done, informed alert reading. His poetry cannot be understood except by a willing reader, prepared to follow the poet's thought, to understand arguments and to evaluate them, and to respond not simply to the pattern but to the pressures of a poem. I am suggesting in short that we should read Browning not with the easy-going collaboration which is all that many contemporary poets get, and all they appear to expect, but with the scrupulous respect that we extend to the Metaphysicals. I should emphasize in particular the necessity of paying to Browning's treatment of metaphor the kind of attention that we habitually pay to the extended conceits in a Metaphysical poem.

This seems to me a crucial test of ways of reading poetry,

[1] Cf. Hardy's Apology prefixed to *Late Lyrics and Earlier*: 'The thoughts of any man of letters concerned to keep poetry alive cannot but run uncomfortably on the precarious prospects of English verse at the present day [1922] . . . We seem threatened with a new Dark Age.

I formerly thought, like other much exercised writers, that so far as literature was concerned a partial cause might be impotent or mischievous criticism; the satirizing of individuality, the lack of whole-seeing in contemporary estimates of poetry and kindred work, the knowingness affected by junior reviewers, the overgrowth of meticulousness in their peerings for an opinion, as if it were a cultivated habit in them to scrutinize the tool-marks and be blind to the building, to hearken for the key-creaks and be deaf to the diapason, to judge the landscape by a nocturnal exploration with a flash-lantern. In other words, to carry on the old game of sampling the poem or drama by quoting the worst line or worst passage only . . .'

since the developed metaphor, which is not used simply for decorative effect, demands for success a willingness on the part of the reader to accept the parallel which the poet implies, and this acceptance has to be not simply a matter of suspension of disbelief but an act of co-operative response, such as we make when we assent to an illustrative comparison in debate. The initial metaphor and its subsequent development form a standard 'unit' of Browning's poetry. It is in this that his similarity to the Metaphysicals is to be most clearly seen: this likeness should not, however, be exaggerated, since there are also fundamental divergences of technique. In particular Browning does not exploit the paralogical uses of metaphor.[1]

Most readers, however, will be reminded of the Metaphysicals by the way in which Browning expands and explores a metaphor, as in the poems I analysed in the previous chapter, or uses it simply as a succinct expression of a complex idea or relationship. The metaphor of the bower and the mansion in *St. Martin's Summer* is a case in point. Until the reader has accepted the aptness of the comparison Browning is unable to develop his metaphor and show its multiple application. The first step then towards understanding this important unit in Browning's verse is to recognize that, as in a Metaphysical poem, metaphors will be used constructively rather than illustratively or decoratively. The second step is to be prepared for Browning to build rapidly on the initial premise. He reifies the metaphor, so to speak, almost as if he were saying, 'Now that we have agreed that poetry is a blue dye there's no need for me to say "poetry" any more, so I shall just talk about "blue" or "blue dye", and, notice, what I say about "blue dye" will make sense for both

[1] A common sequence in a Metaphysical poem is (i) equivalence of object and metaphor $(A = B)$; (ii) expansion of metaphor $(B \rightarrow B1)$; (iii) conclusion that the original object can be similarly expanded $(\therefore A \rightarrow A1)$. The introduction of the metaphor is thus the first term in a pseudosyllogistic conceit. A simple example is Herbert's *The Windows*, which is built up of two of these sequences as follows: (i) Man is (like) brittle glass $(A = B)$; (ii) But glass is useful for windows $(B \rightarrow B1)$; (iii) Therefore Man can let light into the temple of the Lord $(A \rightarrow A1)$. Although Man can let in light by his speech alone this is an ineffective way to preach God's eternal word. (i) Thus Man is (like) plain glass, which lets through a 'watrish, bleak, and thin' light $(A = B)$; (ii) But we can improve plain glass by annealing colour into it $(B \rightarrow B1)$; (iii) Therefore Man's preaching is improved if his life, not just his doctrine, shows the Word's light $(A \rightarrow A1)$. This compact argumentative use is not found very frequently in Browning.

our meanings of the phrase.' In short, much of the apparent impenetrability of Browning's verse vanishes once the reason for it is understood, or, to put it another way, once the reader realizes what positive effects Browning achieves by being difficult. As a practical step towards this and towards acquiring an ability to read Browning's verse fluently and with a sufficiently capacious grasp of its meanings, nothing is more helpful than studying thorough and sympathetic analyses of single poems. These are not easy to find, but a few can be recommended [10].

II

It is plain that the word 'difficulty' when it is used in criticism of Browning occupies a whole range of meanings. At one extreme it refers to minor or local uncertainties and ambiguities, or to occasional unexpected or unconventional words or constructions, or even to a general uncouthness or unfamiliarity of diction. At the other it implies the inaccessibility or incomprehensibility of an entire poem, or even Browning's total inability to articulate his meaning. That the poetry can in some sense be called difficult is not of itself a condemnation, but each degree of difficulty holds its own hazards for the poet.

The disjointed syntax and the omission of the lubricating particles produce on occasion lines of a harshness and downright ugliness not to be matched outside Hopkins or Empson. Passages like the notorious

> Irks care the crop-full bird ? Frets doubt the maw-crammed beast ?

or

> 　　　　　　the kindled eye,
> Split beak, crook'd claw o' the creature, cormorant
> Or ossifrage . . .

though fortunately uncommon in Browning, are not without parallels. Even when the result is not positively grating there is a pervasive activity of the surface – rather like atmospherics on the wireless – which disturbs and abrades the reader continually, and, like a disagreeable accent, or, as Henry James said, like a speech impediment, distracts attention from what is being said to the manner in which it is put.

It is tempting to think of this as a specifically Victorian weakness and to point to comparable failures in the worst

Victorian buildings, with their abundance of fussy, irrelevant detail, or in the worst Victorian design, with its cardinal fault of excessive applied decoration. Closer, perhaps, is the resemblance to the worst of Wagner, with its characteristic defects of excessive length and over-emphasis, which ultimately detract from the interest of the subject and force the personality of the artist himself insistently before the audience. It is perhaps fairest to find a parallel with the more ornate kinds of Victorian lettering, original and striking, but so elaborately Gothicized or rustic-fantasticated that it is hardly possible to read the words. A typical example comes from *Aristophanes' Apology*:

> Still – since Phrunicos
> Offended, by too premature a touch
> Of that Milesian smart-place freshly frayed –
> (Ah, my poor people, whose prompt remedy
> Was – fine the poet, not reform thyself!)
> Beware precipitate approach! Rehearse
> Rather the prologue, well a year away,
> Than the main misery, a sunset old.

The third line is especially revealing. The allusion is to the defeat of the Athenians at Miletus: Browning's typically over-weighted circumlocution attracts attention to this passing reference, detaining the reader in an unimportant parenthesis and forcing on his consciousness the irrelevant message, 'Only Browning writes like this.'

From such phrases it is but a short step to a more serious poetic fault, the use of a complex form of words when this is not necessary or appropriate. This is not merely irritating, but has the effect of pitching the reader's expectations rather high. What in another writer, Wordsworth say, might reasonably serve as the central theme of a short poem seems faintly bathetic in Browning, since the intricacy of the language has encouraged us to expect a less superficial analysis of the situation than we in fact find. The two series of *Dramatic Idyls* both seem to me to endanger their reception by the unfulfilled promise of their verbal 'busyness'.

When Browning is dealing with matters of more profundity, exploring metaphysical paradoxes or the tortuous recesses of men's minds, his difficulty is more understandable, but its ill effects are hardly more acceptable. In *La Saisiaz* [11], or in the *Parleyings*, the last section of *Bernard de Mandeville* for example, or in *Mr. Sludge, 'The Medium'*, or in *Abt Vogler*, while it is true that the subject is of sufficient importance to justify language more than ordinarily wrought, there is nevertheless a linguistic barrier between the reader and the theological or psychological point that Browning wishes his speaker to make. To the necessary difficulty of the ideas is added an indirectness of expression for which no immediate poetic necessity can be seen. Thus in those poems of Browning's which depend for their effect on the intellectual understanding by the reader of an idea, the poet's failure to express this idea clearly enough represents *prima facie* a failure in communication.

The final adverse effect of Browning's 'difficulty' in both senses is not upon his poems but upon his public. By a familiar process, a reputation for impenetrability deters all but a minority of readers, while the poet, even as he feels acutely the lack of a large popular audience, is hardened in his determination not to dilute his poetry. The gulf widens: at last licences freely permitted to other poets are sufficient to strike terror into the reader. I have suggested some practical ways of overcoming the difficulties, but when a person is afraid of the water it is no good telling him that he won't be afraid once he has learned to swim. Browning is still unpopular partly because the reputation for being unintelligible still clings to him.

It might be thought that it was only in his own time that the 'lack of melody' in his verse was used as a convenient excuse by those who were reluctant to grapple with the real difficulty which he presented in his metaphysically or psychologically involved poems, but even today the voices of critics echo the phrases of their Victorian ancestors.[1] The case is seldom argued

[1] E.g. L. G. Salingar, 'Robert Browning', in *The Pelican Guide to English Literature* (ed. B. Ford) Vol. 6, (Harmondsworth, 1958): 'No doubt his failure to "speak out" must have been responsible for much of the obscurity of his verse, for its mystifying digressions, tortuous reasoning, and abnormally involved syntax. At its best his poetry has the courage of its defects' (p. 246); David Page, 'And So is Browning', *Essays in Criticism*, XIII (1963), pp. 146–54: 'The Browning worth bothering about is not the man who wrote hectoring uplift and a jungle of turgid argument. Under this rubbish there is a tough but honest doubter struggling to get out'; K. W. Gransden, *Tennyson: In Memoriam* (London, 1964): '. . . Browning will usually be found to be wrapping up quite simple ideas in layers of verbal

in sufficient detail to make even a brief examination of it worth while; an exception is S. W. Holmes's attempt to apply modern psychoanalytic theories to Browning's verse [12]. He suggests that Browning suffered from a lack of organization of his thoughts, notably a failure to distinguish between objects, sense-impressions, and words. This kind of confusion is said to be responsible for the defective speech of stutterers. Mr Holmes suggests that Browning's obscurity is an analogous condition. The fallacy here is plain. Mr Holmes says that in stutterers mental confusion is reflected in an inability to speak clearly. He notices that Browning's poetry is sometimes difficult to understand, and unwarrantably concludes from this that Browning suffered from a similar personality disorder.

Mr Holmes makes one useful point, that in *Sordello* Browning's failure to define clearly such vital tools of his argument as the words *soul* and *mind* makes it difficult for him to write precisely and difficult for the reader to understand him. But Mr Holmes's point is limited to *Sordello* – he hardly refers to another poem – and proves unhelpful when we deal with the poems of Browning's maturity. The whole apparatus of the causes of stuttering which Mr Holmes erects proves misleading, since it suggests a mechanical model without providing one. The true grounds for criticism of Browning's diction in *Sordello* and his more metaphysical long poems can be stated without employing Mr Holmes's speculative psycho-biographical argument – they are simply that to a discussion of subjects already complex Browning adds a complexity of language which obscures his thought without adequate compensating enrichment, even though he is writing a kind of poetry which requires the reader's full understanding at every level.

III

The prescription for the ideal reader who is to attain this ideal understanding is, I realize, daunting. It is true that many of

---

cotton wool, multiplying examples or analogies and repeating the same idea in different ways, thereby spoiling even his more lyrical poems.' (p. 43)

See also *A Literary History of England*, ed. A. C. Baugh (London, 1950), where Samuel C. Chew writes of 'The confused energy of his style, the reposelessness, the persistent allusiveness, and the quality that an unsympathetic critic [F. R. G. Duckworth] has described as "garrulous pedantry" and "lumpy and gritty erudition".'

the critical exercises and disciplines which I have recommended are no more strenuous than those necessary for the conscientious reading of any verse. It is a commonplace (or perhaps I should say that it used to be so) that we must learn the poet's language before we can read his poetry, that what time has dimmed the critical reader can only with an effort make clear, that to read a poet who writes for educated men one must educate oneself. But the task is obviously much more taxing for the reader of Browning than for, say, the reader of Tennyson. Why then should anybody choose to read a 'difficult' poet? Or, to put the question in another way, what effects for good does Browning's 'difficulty' have on his verse?

First a word of caution. As I noted when discussing Browning's choice of the dramatic monologue it is extremely difficult to distinguish between cause and effect in these matters; answers might begin indifferently 'because' or 'in order to', so that to explain the results of his way of writing is often to assume that the wish to obtain these results constitutes his reasons for writing in this way, whereas strictly speaking the reasons for his difficulty are a matter for historical rather than critical conjecture. It seems however that they must be represented by one or more of the following overlapping statements:

   (i) Browning did not know whether he was difficult or not;
  (ii) Browning was trying to write clearly and failing;
 (iii) Browning was deliberately difficult for the sake of writing obscure poetry;
 (iv) Browning could not help being difficult because he was writing about difficult subjects;
  (v) Browning was deliberately difficult because there were compensating advantages;
 (vi) Browning did not care whether he was difficult or not.

An examination of these may at least eliminate some of them, leaving the reader free to make his choice of the rest.

(i) At the beginning of Chapter 4 I have printed a selection of the more celebrated comments on Browning's style: it is not conceivable that in the face of this barrage of complaint and abuse the poet did not know that some readers found his verse hard to follow. Throughout his life his friends, admirers and enemies reproached him with every fault from lack of smoothness to downright incomprehensibility. In his letters, his poems and his reported conversations he referred to these charges frequently and made his own defence, which I consider under (vi) below.

(ii) If (ii) is true, the failure is either through inability to write clearly in verse or, as Mr Holmes suggests, through an inability to formulate his ideas clearly in the first place. That Browning was unable to write lucidly in verse is clearly not universally true, since many of his poems are clear and cogent. Plainly the man who wrote Section II of *The Flight of the Duchess* is, as Browning would say, 'free of all the four corners' of English verse:

> Ours in a great wild country:
>> If you climb to our castle's top,
>> I don't see where your eye can stop;
> For when you've passed the cornfield country,
> Where vineyards leave off, flocks are packed,
> And sheep-range leads to cattle-tract,
> And cattle-tract to open-chase,
> And open-chase to the very base
> Of the mountain where, at a funeral pace,
> Round about, solemn and slow,
> One by one, row after row,
> Up and up the pine-trees go,
> So, like black priests up, and so
> Down the other side again
>> To another greater, wilder country,
> That's one vast red drear burnt-up plain,
> Branched through and through with many a vein
> Whence iron's dug, and copper's dealt;
>> Look right, look left, look straight before, –
> Beneath they mine, above they smelt,
>> Copper-ore and iron-ore,
> And forge and furnace mould and melt,
> And so on, more and ever more,
> Till at the last, for a bounding belt,
> Comes the salt sand hoar of the great sea-shore
> – And the whole is our Duke's country.

Similar examples abound. It is conceivable that the statement is true of specific poems, but improbable, since Browning's technical resources were extraordinary, and there is no reason to

suppose that, had he wished to express himself more perspicu-
ously, he would have been unable to do so. Is it true that
Browning was using his poem as the place where he sorted out
the doubts and uncertainties in his own mind, that what he offers
us in his ratiocinative poems, which are the ones which may truly
be called difficult, is the raw material of speculation or the discordant hammerings of the workshop? I do not think that this is
a fair account of most of Browning's poetry. He does not as a
rule reckon to find the poem appearing in the act of writing:
on the contrary he often had a shrewd idea before he began
writing of what he intended to do.[1] It would be fairer to say that
the difficulties arose because he was determined to realize a
specific idea and not to allow it to be modified by the pressures
of composition (see point (iv)). If point (ii) is true of any of his
poems it is true of *Sordello*.

(iii) The third suggestion, that Browning wrote obscurely
for the sake of being obscure, what Domett called being 'difficult
on system', is one which does not bear close examination. For
there are in fact few impenetrable thickets in his work, which
removes as a possible motive his desire to conceal the emptiness
of a particular passage behind a screen of apparently meaningful
words. In any case in the nineteenth century no special prestige
attached to the reputation of being Delphic: it did Browning
incalculable   damage   without   bringing   any   compensating
advantage.

(iv) Is it true then to say that the subjects on which Browning
wrote could only be treated in verse which is hard to understand?
This seems unlikely, since what is complained of in Browning is
rather that he uses involved languages to express what are
conceptually not very ambitious ideas. Nor does it follow that
the verse gets thornier as the level of abstraction grows higher,
for some of his poems which give most trouble in exegesis are
concerned with simple everyday matters. It is nevertheless fair
to say that Browning's poems are often concerned with the
essential paradoxes of the human situation, such as the existence
of evil and pain, or with ethical questions, such as whether the

[1] Robert Preyer 'Two Styles in the Verse of Robert Browning', *ELH*, XXXII
(1965), pp. 62–84, cites the *PRB Journal* of 28 February 1850 as authority for the
fact that Browning used to write down on a slate a prose outline of the argument
of his poems.

end justifies the means. In these matters certainty is impossible, and definiteness imprudent or dishonest. Very often the point of the poem is to sharpen the paradox by maintaining both parts as evenly as possible, like the paradoxical 'truths' of Christianity which lead only to heresy if one wing is emphasized at the expense of the other. Unless the paradox in the poem is preserved the result is artistic imbalance. Thus the themes which Browning favours often prohibit complete clarity and encourage a use of language which keeps the reader aware of all the possibilities of the situation [13].

(v) If we continue to consider Browning's poetry from this point of view it is plain that there are certain positively beneficial effects which accrue even from this apparent defect of diction, and which he may be presumed to have intended. What is under discussion here is, of course, 'difficulty' in the sense of 'asperity' or 'crabbedness' or 'rapidity' rather than in the sense of 'impenetrability'. First, his poetry has always a surface interest. He seems seldom to drift into the 'intelligibly laid down path' of effortless but predictable writing which Hopkins labels *Parnassian*, but rather to fall in the category of *Olympian*, 'the language of strange masculine genius which suddenly, as it were, forces its way into the domain of poetry, without naturally having a right there' [14]. Secondly, intricate sentences whose meaning is not immediately perceptible are often particularly appropriate to characters who are being less than frank with their audience: Browning's style is dramatically in keeping with the tortuous nature of the argument. Again, in his explorations of the recesses of human motive Browning is moving in a world where finality is not to be looked for: the elusiveness of the personality under examination is matched by the impression that the language of the poem has not been exhaustively apprehended. Generalizing this point, one may say that Browning claimed to offer a picture of life as it was, and that roughness and unevenness will always be the mark of the realist rather than blandness and 'finish'. Finally, though as I say it is difficult here to separate results and motives, Browning's disregard of normal prose syntax and order and deliberate use of the whole of his wide vocabulary enables him to display his great ingenuity in the handling of stanza-form, metre and rhyme. This opportunity is clearly an advantage to the poet, even though it

may be misused to the point of becoming grotesque. But
Browning's occasional over-exuberant exhibitions of agility do
not affect the point that, by sacrificing a degree of clarity, he
can display a corresponding degree of technical freedom.

The suggestion that Browning was deliberately difficult for
the sake of these advantages must be accepted with reserve. It
would be more accurate to say that he consciously accepted the
drawbacks of a certain way of writing because this alone enabled
him to write the sort of poems he wanted to write. But this is
not to say that he ever had the ambition to be a difficult poet. His
intricacy is a thing accepted, not chosen.

(vi) If he knew what he was doing, is it true to say that he
did not care whether he was difficult or not? Once again the
answer is that he knew and cared (and even regretted) that he
was alienating some readers, but nevertheless held his course,
since clarity and ease of communication were not his primary
objects. 'I desire to write out certain things which are in me and
so save my soul.' The extent to which he was concerned at the
bewilderment of many readers is to be seen from the following
selection of the statements he made at different times in reply to
charges of obscurity.

On the specific issue of *Sordello* his preface to the second
edition (1863) remains the poem's best defence:

> I wrote it twenty-five years ago for only a few, counting even in these
> on somewhat more care about its subject than they really had. My
> own faults of expression were many; but with care for a man or book
> such would be surmounted, and without it what avails the faultless-
> ness of either? I blame nobody, least of all myself, who did my best
> then and since; for I lately gave time and pains to turn my work into
> what the many might, – instead of what the few must, – like: but
> after all I imagined another thing at first, and therefore leave as I
> find it.[1] The historical decoration was purposely of no more im-
> portance than a background requires; and my stress lay on the
> incidents in the development of a soul: little else is worth study. I,

[1] There is an interesting parallel between this decision of Browning's and an
observation of Bishop Butler's, quoted by A. Symons in his *Introduction to the Study
of Browning* (1886), p. 18. Butler says that the only people he will allow to judge
whether or not his sermons are obscure are those 'who will be at the trouble to
understand what is here said, and to see how far *the things here insisted upon, and not
other things*, might have been put in a plainer manner.' (*Works* 1847, Preface to
Sermons viii–ix; my italics.) Symons' book has some useful critical comments.

at least, always thought so – you, [Milsand], with many known and unknown to me, think so – others may one day think so . . .

Men and Women gave rise to a more general discussion of the difficulty of his verse. Some time before its publication in 1855 Browning wrote to Milsand, 'I am writing – a first step towards popularity for me – lyrics with more music and painting than before, so as to get people to hear and see', and a little later he wrote to Forster of the same volumes, 'I hope to be listened to, this time . . .' However, the reception of the work was not favourable [15]. Ruskin wrote to the poet, expressing his bewilderment with certain passages. Browning replied in a letter which is so revealing that it must be quoted at length.

My dear Ruskin, – for so you let me begin, with the honest friend-liness that befits, – You never were more in the wrong than when you professed to say 'your unpleasant things' to me. This is pleasant and proper at all points, over-liberal of praise here and there, kindly and sympathetic everywhere, and with enough of yourself in even – what I fancy – the misjudging, to make the whole letter precious in-deed. . . . For the deepnesses you think you discern, may they be more than mere blacknesses! For the hopes you entertain of what may come of subsequent readings, – all success to them! For your bewilderment more especially noted – how shall I help *that*? We don't read poetry the same way, by the same law; it is too clear. I cannot begin writing poetry until my imaginary reader has con-ceded licences to me which you demur at altogether. I *know* that I don't make out my conception by my language; all poetry being a putting the infinite within the finite. You would have me paint it all plain out, which can't be; but by various artifices I try to make shift with touches and bits of outlines which *succeed* if they bear the con-ception from me to you. You ought, I think to keep pace with the thought tripping from ledge to ledge of my 'glaciers', as you call them; not stand poking your alpenstock into the holes, and demon-strating that no foot could have stood there; suppose it sprang over there? In prose you may criticise so – because that is the absolute representation of portions of truth, what chronicling is to history – but in asking for more *ultimates* you must accept less *mediates*, not expect that a Druid stone-circle will be traced for you with as few breaks to the eye as the North Crescent and South Crescent that go together so cleverly in many a suburb. Why, you look at my little song as if it were Hobbs' or Nobbs' lease of his house or testament of his devisings. . . .

Browning next deals with some of Ruskin's detailed criticisms. There follows the passage already quoted at the beginning of Chapter 2 about the dramatic character of Browning's writing. Browning continues

> Do you think poetry was ever generally understood – or can be? Is the business of it to tell people what they know already, as they know it, and so precisely that they shall be able to cry out – 'Here you should supply *this* – *that*, you evidently pass over, and I'll help you from my own stock'? It is all teaching, on the contrary, and people hate to be taught. They say otherwise, – make foolish fables about Orpheus enchanting stocks and stones, poets standing up and being worshipped, – all nonsense and impossible dreaming. A poet's affair is with God, to whom he is accountable, and of whom is his reward: look elsewhere and you find misery enough.

Browning mentions the noble passages which were normally cut from a performance of *Hamlet*. 'Are these wasted, therefore? No – they act upon a very few, who react upon the rest: as Goldsmith says, "Some lords, my acquaintance, that settle the nation, are pleased to be kind." '

> Don't let me lose *my* lord by any seeming self-sufficiency or petulance: I look on my own shortcomings too sorrowfully, try to remedy them too earnestly: but I shall never change my point of sight, or feel other than disconcerted and apprehensive when the public, critics and all, begin to understand and approve me. But what right have *you* to disconcert me in the other way? [16]

In 1868 Browning wrote in somewhat similar terms to his friend William Kingsland. The most celebrated passage from this letter is the following:

> I can have but little doubt but that my writing has been, in the main, too hard for many I should have been pleased to communicate with; but I never designedly tried to puzzle people, as some of my critics have supposed. On the other hand, I never pretended to offer such literature as should be a substitute for a cigar, or a game at dominoes, to an idle man. [17]

Not long afterwards Browning came to feel that he had at last a body of sympathetic readers, and for his preface to the First Series (1872) of *Selections* from his verse he wrote a final paragraph as follows:

A few years ago, had such an opportunity presented itself, I might have been tempted to say a word in reply to the objections my poetry was used to encounter. Time has kindly co-operated with my disinclination to write the poetry and the criticism besides. The readers I am at last privileged to expect, meet me fully half-way; and if, from their fitting standpoint, they must still 'censure me in their wisdom,' they have previously 'awakened their senses that they may the better judge.' Nor do I apprehend any more charges of being wilfully obscure, unconscientiously careless, or perversely harsh. Having done my utmost in the art to which my life is a devotion, I cannot engage to increase the effort; but I conceive there may be helpful light, as well as reassuring warmth, in the attention and sympathy I gratefully acknowledge.

Finally I quote a revealing series of passages from two letters which Browning wrote in 1883 to Mrs Thomas FitzGerald. She had been puzzled by some of the poems in *Jocoseria* and had consulted a learned young lady of her acquaintance,[1] sending the young lady's observations on to Browning. He replied

I return you the young lady's letter. In the former of the two letters I got this week, you vexed me by speaking disparagingly of your 'brain-pace' &c. May I venture to say that all its fault is in the exercise of industry in a wrong direction – so far as regards my poems, at least. If you would – when you please to give them your attention – to confine it to the poems and nothing else, no extraneous matter at all, – I cannot but think you would find little difficulty: but your first business seems to be an inquiry into what will give no sort of help.

Browning gives Mrs FitzGerald practical advice on how to read the poem *Adam, Lilith, and Eve,* and then continues:

So with *Jochanan* [*Hakkadosh*]: there was no need to 'know *d'avance* all the Talmudic stories' – which, – such of them as I referred to, are all sufficiently explained in the poem itself – indeed every allusion needing explanation is explained. But you begin by asking of a friend 'Who Jochanan was': why, *nobody*. 'John' (as the name is in English) was no more the 'John' mentioned by your friend than he was St. John of the Gospels: the poem *tells* you *who* he was, what he was,

---

[1] No doubt Emily Harris, of whom Browning wrote to Mrs FitzGerald on 8 November 1883, 'Tell dear Miss Harris that I hear of every one of her actions with great interest, and shall be delighted to read her paper on the Jewish trumpet.' (McAleer, *Learned Lady*, p. 174)

where he lived, and why he was about to die: what more do you want? . . . Years of study of dictionaries and the like would make the student learned enough in another direction but not one bit more in the limited direction of the poem itself. I say all this because you imagine that with more learning you would 'understand' more about my poetry – and as if you would somewhere find it already written – only waiting to be translated into English and my verses: whereas I should consider such an use of learning to be absolutely contemptible: for poetry, if it is to deserve the name, ought to create – or re-animate something – not merely reproduce *raw* fact taken from somebody else's book. If you will only concern yourself with what is set down, – regarding a name as a name that explains itself, and a passing allusion <as> just an allusion and no more, you will find no difficulty but what is a fault *in the writer* . . . I am so anxious to stand well in your eyes that I talk thus plainly.

Browning's next letter to Mrs FitzGerald begins:

> *Dear Friend*, – all is well, then, and, once directing your intelligence the simple straight way – to the substance of whatever poem you do me the honor to read, and not the quite extraneous matter of what – besides the substance – may be found touching upon it elsewhere, – I shall be sure of your understanding – however I may be uncertain of your liking what I write: my faults, as a writer, are many, I well know: but, as a poet, I do not let my imagination lie so idle as to versify what other writers have already invented. [18]

It is no longer possible to share Browning's confidence that a reader who approaches his poems without assistance and without preparation will understand them with 'little difficulty'. As I have suggested in this chapter, the inexperienced reader will find the going considerably easier if he uses what help is available. But the two letters are a salutary reminder that the primary quality which the reader must bring to Browning, as to every other poet, is a willingness to read with attention and an open mind. 'My own faults of expression were many; but with care for a man or book, such would be surmounted, and without it what avails the faultlessness of either?'

IV

To what conclusion does all this point? Simply that Browning claimed throughout his life to write as clearly as he could, and this claim it seems right to accept as true. We can then exempt

Browning from the charge, sometimes formulated, more often implicit, that he deliberately constructed 'bewilderments and predicaments' because he thought that he could trade on his readers' incomprehension. We may also, I think, exempt him from the charge of sheer incompetence, using as evidence the abundant examples of brilliantly sustained metrical skill. We are brought to the conclusion, which with almost any other poet we might have taken for granted in the first place, that he wrote as he did because it was natural for him to write so, that he accepted the disadvantages of his method for the sake of its positive virtues, but that, like every other poet, he depended on his readers to bring to his poetry sufficient goodwill to overcome its unfamiliarity and reveal its qualities. One bitter little comment shows how sharply he felt the lack of this goodwill:

> As to my own poems [*Men and Women*] – they must be left to Pro-
> vidence and that fine sense of discrimination which I never cease to
> meditate upon and admire in the public: they cry out for new things
> and when you furnish them with what they cried for, 'it's *so* new,'
> they grunt. [19]

More is needed now, however, than goodwill. One argument of this book is that to grasp Browning's achievement we must think again about what we mean by poetry. If, for example, we think of the poet's task as mainly the patterning of words so that they react unpredictably and produce infinitely receding reverberations we shall find it hard to think of Browning as a poet at all, for he takes comparatively little pains to secure effects of this kind. But if we concede that poetry has great areas in common with prose, if with Keats we think that Invention is the Polar Star of poetry, if we found our definition of what a poem is on Homer, Virgil and Dante, as well as on Hopkins and Eliot and Emily Dickinson and 'H.D.' and E. E. Cummings, we can place Browning's insensitivity to surface in the right perspective.

What I have said in this chapter, though chiefly directed to the issue of verbal difficulty, is of course not without application to the other and more profound sources of complication in his work. Two of these – the complexity Browning achieves by the satiric use of the dramatic monologue and the use he makes of philosophical or pseudo-philosophical ideas – are examined in Chapters 6 and 7.

❖ 6 ❖

Other difficulties – I

'The best part of an author will always be found in his writings'
JOHNSON, quoted by Hawkins

Having mastered the idiom, what further obstacles does the reader find to a full understanding of Browning's poetry? In Chapter 7 I examine some poems which are hard to read simply because Browning is exploring concepts which are in themselves difficult to follow: in this chapter I shall illustrate some of the complexities which are inherent in his choice of form, even when he is not handling particularly abstruse ideas.

I

It has been suggested in Chapter 2 that an essential quality of the dramatic monologue is the demand that it makes on the reader to complete the poem, by drawing, for example, the necessary inferences about the circumstances in which the speaker comes to deliver his story. Reading Browning's poetry is thus from the beginning normally an active, concreative process, and therefore offers difficulties to those who are not used to making this kind of response to a poem.

Another characteristic of Browning's monologues is the apparently loose ordering of the parts. The plan of the poem is rarely straightforward: there are digressions, parentheses, trains of thought broken and resumed later, sometimes a seemingly random succession of arguments and illustrations, possibly even an abrupt change of direction in the last few lines, as in *The Englishman in Italy*, or a sudden startling shift of focus 'from the microscopic to the transcendental'. This informality of construction is of course essential to Browning's success in counterfeiting the untidy workings of the human mind. His monologues do not in fact proceed by free association, and do not pretend to offer an approximation, as Joyce, for example, does, to the stream of consciousness of the speaker, but the order of ideas in the poems is determined by dramatic appropriateness and not by considerations of clarity or cogency. The reader must therefore be prepared to follow a tortuous and repetitive series of observations and reflections rather than a logically connected series of propositions.

Above all he must be prepared for the major demand made by Browning on the reader of his dramatic monologues – that he shall be continually vigilant to distinguish between truth and sophistry, between deception and self-deception, between clear sight and the limitations of the speaker.

These crucial discriminations can be made with confidence only as a result of a scrupulous reading of the individual poem. It is not enough to nurse in the mind a rigid, but necessarily ill-defined, construct labelled 'Browning's Position', and to refer all cases to this, concluding without uneasiness that if what the speaker says corresponds with what we have already decided Browning 'really' thinks then Browning cannot be writing ironically, whereas if the speaker puts forward opinions at variance with our idea of Browning's own they can be dismissed as satirical. The fallacies of this position must be obvious. In the first place, such a proceeding is totally opposed to any way of reading his poetry of which he himself approved. If one thing is certain about Browning it is that he emphatically rejected any interpretation of his poetry which relied on relating it to the private opinions of Browning the man. In the second place, if we exclude our knowledge of Browning's private sentiments how are we to learn Browning's mind except from his poems? And if the touchstone 'Browning's Position' is to be derived from the poems then it is logically inadmissible to use it in the antecedent process of deciding what the poems mean. In the third place, implicit in the method is the assumption that all Browning's poems must agree one with the other. Taken to its logical conclusion this is easily seen to be unacceptable, for it implies, rigorously construed, that Browning *always* said the same thing, for if he did not it would follow that we could not rely on one poem as an index of his sympathies in another. Of course it is reassuring if we notice a correspondence between two poems: it suggests to us that we are not going to finish up with a number of poems so diverse in direction that it will be psychologically impossible for us to accept that they are all the work of a single author. The relation of one of Browning's poems to another is of importance only in so far as it corroborates or casts doubt on the infinitely more important conclusions which are derived from the individual poems.

My position then is that each poem is a unique and complete work of art requiring no private knowledge of the poet's mind for its interpretation. To rely on external rather than internal evidence is to blur the sharp edges on which Browning expended infinite pains. By careful reading all Browning's poems, even the most bewildering, can be understood and enjoyed, because each carries within itself a carefully devised system of values. Thus if we wish, for example, to claim that a particular passage in a particular poem is ironically intended, the only evidence of weight is evidence derived from the poem itself, not from analogous situations in other poems. Since Browning is almost always writing dramatically and thus presenting the situation obliquely, such evidence can in practice be obtained only by a slow and concentrated reading of the text. Naturally it is harder to read a poem in this way than by calibrating a general impression of the poem against a general impression of what Browning personally believed, and construing the poem accordingly.

To show how taxing it may be to look consistently at the poems themselves I give a fairly full analysis of two pieces – *A Toccata of Galuppi's* and *Bishop Blougram's Apology*, and follow this with a shorter account of *Mr Sludge, 'The Medium'*.

II

The most casual reading of *A Toccata* is enough to show that it is an extremely moving poem, powerfully evoking the spirit of eighteenth-century Venice, and written in a metre and stanza form that Browning handles with quite magnificent assurance. It gives great satisfaction at a first reading: the question 'What is it all about?' is one which many readers will be content not to ask.[1]

---

[1] For instance Mrs Orr says, 'This sense is created by the sounds, as Mr Browning describes them: and their directly expressive power must stand for what it is worth. Still, the supposed effect is mainly that of association; and the listener's fancy the medium through which it acts.' (*Handbook*, p. 247)

But if we do ask what the poem means the reply is not
simple.

First we may learn that the speaker is an Englishman, clearly
not Browning himself, for he says in Stanza III 'I was never out
of England.' His audience is the spirit of the fashionable
eighteenth-century composer Galuppi. The Englishman clearly
has very little notion of Venice or Venetian life, but sees it as a
compound of St Mark's, the Doges, Shylock's bridge and the
Carnival, and solemnly tells Galuppi that 'the sea's the street
there'. At first he addresses Galuppi rather condescendingly,
picturing him as playing his music to deaf ears. In fact the
Englishman patronisingly imagines that Galuppi admits to him
that his plaintive music, instead of touching the hearts of the
Venetians, simply inspired them to live for the day. The way in
which the Englishman by the use of the phrase 'do you say?'
(line 12) proceeds to impute a series of descriptions to Galuppi
is typical of Browning's method in his monologues. A certain
vigilance is called for even to decide whose sentiments are being
put forward at any point. Here Stanzas IV, V, and VI are clearly
what the Englishman imagines that Galuppi is trying to tell
him about life in Venice. Stanzas VII, VIII, IX, and X are the
Englishman's own comments or speculations.

Up to Stanza X the Englishman is perfectly content with the
account he has given himself of Galuppi's music and of the frivo-
lous young people of Venice. The *volta* comes with Stanza XI.
The Englishman is a scientist (Stanza XIII) or at least well
versed in science [1], and feels very secure in his own insular
ideas and in the power of reason, yet he is disconcerted to find
that Galuppi's music affects him inexplicably. (Hence presumably his attempt in the earlier stanzas to diminish the power
of the music by showing that the fashionable world of Venice
ignored or misinterpreted it.) He now figures Galuppi as speaking to him in a voice of sombre irony: the ability to speak ironically establishes the musician as the superior character in the
dialogue. Galuppi's message to the Englishman is once more
that all things are transient; this is reinforced by the power of the
music to call up in the listener's mind all the glory of Venice that
has passed away – the young people, the lovers, the dances, the
composer himself. Only the music has survived 'like a ghostly
cricket, creaking where a house was burned'. Galuppi was in fact

right about the Venetians (Stanza XIV): might he not also be right about the Englishman for all his pride in his scientific knowledge? Galuppi's music, which brings to mind the transience of wordly things, shows the weakness of both kinds of materialism – the hedonistic materialism of eighteenth-century Venice and the scientific materialism of nineteenth-century England. In the last stanza the Englishman makes the obvious application to his own case, but before he does so he swings for a moment into imaginative sympathy with the 'dear dead women' of Venice. Then he completes the parallel.

The poem is thus complex, and a complex response is demanded if the reader is to appreciate the whole poem. The speaker's version of the case has not to be accepted at its face value; first of all his personality and his limitations as an observer must be deduced from the poem and his judgements assessed accordingly. His complacency at the beginning of the poem must be set against his sobered mood at the end.

Finally of course we must not forget that the poem is not in fact a dialogue between two people in different countries and centuries, between a live Englishman and a dead Venetian. Neither of them speaks: what Browning gives us is a dramatic and verbal realization of one man listening to the music of another.[1] The poem is a dialogue between a composer and his audience.

III

A more complex example of the difficulty of deciding the status of arguments dramatically presented is provided by *Bishop Blougram's Apology*, which I shall examine at length. For help in understanding this poem Browning's readers are indebted to two articles which have appeared in the *University of Toronto Quarterly*, 'Blougram's Apologetics' by F. E. L. Priestley and 'Browning the Simple-Hearted Casuist' by Hoxie N. Fairchild [2]. Professor Fairchild's article is the more general. He argues that while Browning was interested in casuistry and delighted in the manifold complexity of a person or a situation, he nevertheless felt that 'it was necessary "to save the soul beside" and his simple heart could not extract sufficiently clear

---

[1] The Englishman may in fact be playing Galuppi's music to himself: 'blind' (line 2) conveys the slightest hint that he is using his eyes as well as his ears.

didactic principles from the complexities in which his subtle brain delighted. Hence his too frequent reliance, in ostensibly dramatic writing, on the essentially undramatic giveway.' In considering this important article it is necessary to make the distinction, which Professor Fairchild obscures, between the explicit statements of Browning *in propria persona* at the end of the poem and the tailpieces spoken by the monologuist himself and designed to complete the 'placing' of the speaker. It seems unreasonable to object to the second category as 'simplifications', especially as, when talking of *Cleon*, Professor Fairchild refers to 'the ironic giveaway'. If the 'giveaway' is itself ironic it is hard to see why it is any less dramatic than the rest of the poem. In no poem mentioned by Professor Fairchild is the speaker consciously giving himself away. Thus the dramatic characterization is maintained. In all his dramatic monologues Browning, as I have tried to demonstrate in Chapter 2, implies his attitude to the speaker through the speaker's own words. This point is obvious in *My Last Duchess*, which Professor Fairchild praises for its delicacy, but it is no less true of the other dramatic monologues. What Professor Fairchild holds against Browning is that in order to indicate his own opinion of the speaker Browning relies on certain expected reactions in his readers. Professor Fairchild apparently feels that this destroys any possibility of complexity or of ambiguity. One may doubt whether this is even theoretically sound. In practice it is certainly not true, as may be seen from *Mr Sludge, 'the Medium'*.

Professor Fairchild writes 'Browning will not permit such casuistry to pass without more obvious exposure. Sludge himself is made to show us the "real" truth. . . . Having had his fun, Browning does his duty. We are left in no doubt as to what to think of Sludge.' Yet clearly Professor Fairchild's opinion of Sludge is very different from that of, say, G. K. Chesterton, who writes, 'The simple truth . . . is that *Mr Sludge, 'the Medium'* is not an attack upon spiritualism. It would be a great deal nearer the truth, though not entirely the truth, to call it a justification of spiritualism. . . . Sludge is a witness to his faith as the old martyrs were witnesses to their faith, but even more impressively. . . . It may be repeated that it is truly extraordinary that any one should have failed to notice that this avowal on behalf of spiritualism is the pivot of the poem.' [3]

When, however, we come to consider those poems at the end of which Browning speaks with his own voice, as, for example, *Bishop Blougram's Apology*, it may appear that Professor Fairchild has a stronger case. In theory it is certainly destructive of the dramatic balance of a monologue if the author finds it necessary to tell us how to regard the speaker. In fact, however, as Professor Fairchild admits, widely divergent views of Blougram are entertained, Professor Priestley's, for example, being entirely opposed to that of many other readers, notably that of Chesterton, who describes Blougram as 'a vulgar, fashionable priest, justifying his own cowardice over the comfortable wine and cigars' [4]. Ambiguity, it seems, has managed to survive even Browning's explicit 'giveaway'.

A more recent article takes a position somewhere between Priestley and Fairchild [5]. Professor Palmer holds that 'contradictory interpretations of Blougram's character have arisen because the poem actually makes no judgement of that character and that the poem's central meaning is not dependent upon such a judgement'. (p. 109) Again he says '. . . we should permit the poem to do what it actually does – leave the speaker's moral character ambiguous – and if we must judge Blougram, recognize that we, not the poet, are judging him.'

The purpose of the present account is to show the Chesterton's view of Blougram, Professor Priestley's view of Blougram, Professor Fairchild's view of Blougram and Professor Palmer's view of Blougram have all elements of truth in them, but they are all incomplete since they take the poem for a much simpler thing than it really is.

Since its publication Professor Priestley's article has won wide acceptance [6]. His general position may for the moment be represented by its conclusion: 'The victory, unexpected to be sure in its scope, is Blougram's.' He offers an account of Blougram's arguments which represents the Bishop as completely successful in routing Gigadibs and defending his own position. Certainly he demonstrates beyond doubt that the Bishop not only scores a series of debating points but establishes against Gigadibs a number of logically valid positions and, what is more, does so with Browning's evident sympathy. This fact makes it very difficult to regard Blougram simply as Browning's portrait of 'a cold-hearted, worldly sceptic'. On the other hand, in the course of his arguments the Bishop is guilty of many fallacies and professes to adopt standards which it is impossible to ascribe to any honest man, much less to Browning himself.

The divergent opinions about the direction of the poem's ironic attack arise because of this apparent duality in Browning's attitude to Blougram, since different critics are able to found their position on different parts of the poem, passing over in silence those passages which tell against their argument. To offer a comprehensive interpretation we must begin, I think, with a detailed examination of the circumstances of the monologue. The Bishop is entertaining Gigadibs, a journalist. It seems probable that Gigadibs has written an article attacking Blougram and that this is referred to in lines 40 and 47. Gigadibs has apparently argued from an atheist or at least strongly agnostic position. The Bishop's first task therefore is to demonstrate that this position is untenable, and this, as Professor Priestley shows, he does with some skill. But to succeed completely he has also to convince Gigadibs that his own position is the best remaining. It is here that he commits his fallacies, and here that Browning's satiric purpose is most evident. The total result therefore of the monologue is first to establish by argument that the unbeliever is unable to prove that his way of life is any more honest than that of the sceptic who conforms for material benefit, and secondly, since Blougram's justification of the conforming sceptic depends on a series of fallacies, to imply the unsoundness of his position. This effect is illustrated in the conclusion. Gigadibs is routed from his original atheism, sees however that the compromise recommended by Blougram is even less attractive, and embraces the third possibility which has been implied throughout the monologue – that of simple belief in the light of the Gospels.

I am well aware that my argument depends on establishing that Browning's method in the poem is that of satire and that a satiric intention is notoriously difficult to prove beyond all possible objection. There are three sorts of evidence which can be brought forward here. First, and far and away the most important, is the evidence of the direction of Browning's sympathies to be found from a close reading of the poem itself, that is, not from any of Browning's other poems or from any *a priori* idea of what he ought to think. I take it as an axiom that when Blougram offers a fallacious or specious argument, or founds his case on an absurd example, or simply talks nonsense Browning knows that he is doing so and permits him to do so because he is at this point writing ironically and allowing the Bishop to expose the flaws in his own defence. In addition certain nuances of expression may be pointed to. Secondly, in order to corroborate conclusions derived from the poem itself, I mention also certain passages from other poems which show Browning dealing with related topics or which help to define a particular word in Browning's vocabulary. Thirdly, I have from time to time drawn attention in footnotes to some parallels between Blougram's arguments and those of well-known ironic defences of Christian thought and practice, such as Swift's *Argument against Abolishing Christianity* and Samuel Butler's *The Fair Haven* (1873). While these parallels are far from conclusive they do at least suggest that not all Blougram's arguments are to be accepted at their face value.

The first point to notice is that it is only Blougram who speaks. This means that as he has, so to say, to make Gigadibs' moves for him, none of his arguments need be conceded as conclusive unless we are prepared to concede also that he has in fact, in all relevant instances, chosen the strongest possible move for his opponent. However the basic position from which Gigadibs begins his attack is not in doubt. His criticism is directed not against religion as such but against those who accept the rewards of faith while they are still full of doubt: thus the ground is prepared for his conduct at the end. To him no halfway house is possible. If the Bishop drives him from his unbelief his only alternative is the life of faith. Lines 84–85 confirm this view of Gigadibs' position and recall a similar situation in *A Grammarian's Funeral*.

> That low man goes on adding one to one,
> > His hundred's soon hit:
> This high man aiming at a million,
> > Misses an unit.
> That, has the world here – should he need the next,
> > Let the world mind him!
> This, throws himself on God, and unperplext
> > Seeking shall find him. (117–24)

Here Browning's sympathy is clearly with the man who, like

Gigadibs, demands all or nothing.[1] Blougram continues to attack the position he imputes to Gigadibs and does so by means of the 'cabin' metaphor (line 100). This seems very convincing, but in fact it assumes what it is trying to establish. If faith can be won and retained piecemeal it is reasonable to compare it to a number of separate material objects and to conclude that just as a sensible man has only as many physical possessions as he can comfortably accommodate so it is sensible to go through life with only as much faith as one finds convenient. But of course this rests precisely on the point which Gigadibs denies. This is made clear in line 150, where Gigadibs is said by Blougram to insist that for him belief must be something fixed, absolute, and exclusive.

In line 173 Blougram proceeds to the real matter of the poem. His argument is to be as follows. 'Assume that belief is impossible. I now say that two positions remain – complete unbelief, which you say is the more honest, and partial belief, which I say is just as honest and far more agreeable in the world.' When Blougram's arguments convince Gigadibs that unbelief is barren and Blougram's life convinces Gigadibs that compromise is odious, the only course left will be to examine the first assumption.

In what follows, the attack on unbelief and the demonstration of the impossibility of a life of consistent denial of God are conducted, as Professor Priestley shows, with considerable finesse and poetic force. Lines 176–197 exemplify this. The irony of the monologue however lies in Blougram's failure to see that his arguments drive Gigadibs (and the reader) not towards his own worldly compromise but towards a position of affirmation of belief. Lines 197–212 have this double-edged property.

At the same time Blougram's efforts to put a good face on his

---

[1] Cf. *Red Cotton Night-Cap Country* IV, 353–9; *The Inn Album* 1833–5.

There are also echoes of Bunyan's Mr By-ends, e.g., 'Why they [Christian and Hopeful] after their head-strong manner, conclude that it is duty to rush on their journey all weathers, and I am for waiting for wind and tide. They are for hazarding all for God at a clap, and I am for taking all advantages to secure my life and estate. They are for holding their notions, though all other men are against them; but I am for religion in what, and so far as the times and my safety will bear it. They are for religion when in rags and contempt; but I am for him when he walks in his golden slippers in the sun-shine, and with applause.' (*The Pilgrim's Progress* Part I). At this period Browning's Christianity is not unlike Bunyan's.

own way of life depend on fallacious arguments. For instance in lines 270–300 he makes a distinction between matters like love and religion and the other affairs of a man's life, but he does not substantiate this distinction nor, even if he had, would it follow, as he implies, that no man was free to change his religious beliefs. Blougram says that wishing to declare himself among the believers he decided to do so in the most unequivocal way, by embracing the Catholic faith, which is 'the most pronounced moreover, fixed, precise/And absolute form of faith in the whole world' (306–307). There is little irony in his description of the benefits it brings him and he himself expects that Gigadibs will criticise him for his gross standards of success. To this Blougram would say first that, assuming full faith to be impossible, he is making the best use he can of his life, and secondly that even by the highest standards he cannot be judged a failure. It is interesting to see how Browning develops this second point. Blougram assumes that Gigadibs will reply, 'You may succeed in the general estimation but "one wise man's verdict outweighs all the fools". Men of sense know that either you believe in the most patently false tenets of the Church, in which case you are a fool, or else you see their falseness but still pretend to believe, in which case you are a knave.' They

> approve in neither case,
> Withhold their voices though I look their way:
> Like Verdi when, at his worst opera's end
> (The thing they gave at Florence, – what's its name?)
> While the mad houseful's plaudits near out-bang
> His orchestra of salt-box, tongs and bones,
> He looks through all the roaring and the wreaths
> Where sits Rossini patient in his stall. (379–386)

This is one of the most telling images in the poem, but Bougram meets it with a front of sophistical levity.

He says that as long as the wise do not know whether he is a fool or a knave they are unable to make up their minds about him. His learning saves him from being thought simply a fool: presumably his position in the Church saves him from being thought simply a hypocrite. Thus as long as he can hold the balance between the two he will attract attention without being finally judged one or the other, since wise men are just the sort

of people to shrink from labelling a person completely fool or
completely knave.

> Fool or knave?
> Why needs a bishop be a fool or knave
> When there's a thousand diamond weights between? (404–406)

This is a fallacious argument. If Blougram is a compound of foily
and knavery the wise man knows enough to condemn him, even
though he cannot analyse the compound. In these lines Blougram exposes the whole weakness of his position of compromise.
Professor Priestley's account of this important passage ignores
the obvious element of sophistry. He reduces it to the question
'Why may not the simple truth be that Blougram actually
believes what he professes to believe?' This cannot be taken
from the text.

There follows an episode of typical sleight-of-hand, in which
Blougram challenges Gigadibs to say whom he admires, under-
taking to show that he is himself at least as worthy of approbation. He assumes, without justification, that Napoleon will be
Gigadibs' first choice. Now even if we allow that Gigadibs might
reasonably profess admiration for someone who achieved
secular power by secular means, it is illegitimate for Blougram
to refute this general position by refuting a particular instance of
it, especially one that he has himself selected. In fact his attack,
for such it is, on Napoleon, while it makes the valid point that
Napoleon was himself actuated by a burning faith and is thus an
odd object of admiration for a rationalist, is of no assistance to
Blougram in dislodging Gigadibs, much less in recommending
his own middle position.

Shakespeare is next considered (485–554), and the Bishop's
argument is similarly fallacious. Indeed it is so typical of his
method that it repays analysis in some detail. First of all he
again moves from the general position to attack a particular
instance. He then says that he could not write *Hamlet* or *Othello*.
But this is irrelevant, since they are discussing only Gigadibs'
standards of human achievement, not whether it is possible for
Blougram to *be* himself Gigadibs' ideal man. Blougram then says
it is not for him to choose to be a great artist. Either he is an
artist or he is not. If he is he has no need to try to be one. But
this is a fallacy, for Blougram should have said 'Either I have the

capacity to be an artist or not.' Then of course it does not follow that if he has the capacity he need make no further effort. Blougram says that he and Shakespeare had one end in common – to obtain pleasant and artistic surroundings to live in.

> We want the same things, Shakespeare and myself,
> And what I want, I have. (539–540)

Blougram is able to obtain far more of the things he wants than Shakespeare could. The fallacy here lies in Blougram's considering only those areas where his material tastes and Shakespeare's coincide and making the satisfaction of those tastes the sole criterion of success.[1] In any case success or failure is not the issue. Gigadibs' supposed argument would turn on the worthiness of the life lived. Blougram implies (line 524) that Shakespeare is no very elevated ideal, since he spent his whole life trying to reach a state which the Bishop has already surpassed. An embezzler might just as well say when rebuked by the example of an honest shopkeeper, 'But all he is trying to do is to win for himself and his family the affluence that I already have.' The point of the whole passage is that Gigadibs' real quarrel with Blougram is about means, not about ends, about the *value* of a particular way of life, not about its *rewards*. Blougram consistently refuses to meet Gigadibs on this ground.

The discussion of Luther (555–591) is a central part of the poem. It begins

> Believe – and our whole argument breaks up.
> Enthusiasm's the best thing, I repeat;
> Only, we can't command it.

Blougram goes on to extol, in words in which I can detect no trace of irony, the incandescent power of an active faith. But to the challenge to live his own life in the light of such faith the Bishop can reply only with prudential maxims. It was all very well for Luther: he happened to be born at a time when passionate affirmation of faith was practicable. 'Such Luther's luck was – how shall such be mine ?/If he succeeded, nothing's left to do.' This is a simple wrong statement. Blougram goes on to say that the other way of bringing a new revelation to mankind is

---

[1] Cf. *Rabbi Ben Ezra* XXIII, 'Not on the vulgar mass/Called "work" must sentence pass,/Things done, that took the eye and had the price.'

that of Strauss, that is by examining Christianity as a historical phenomenon with a view to stripping it of its mythical accretions. From this course prudence again restrains the Bishop. Moreover a congregation freed by Blougram's teachings from all moral obligations would hardly feel obliged to reward him. Finally

> there's still that plaguey hundredth chance
> Strauss may be wrong. And so a risk is run –
> For what gain?

Here, as in line 477, the faint possibility that Christian teaching may be true is seriously advanced by the Bishop as an argument in favour of a line of conduct.[1]

I do not feel that Professor Priestley offers an adequate account of this vital passage. He says that 'Gigadibs, having granted the value of enthusiasm, is inclined to restrict his approval to enthusiasm like Luther's, enthusiasm "on the denying side." ' This misrepresents even Blougram's twisting of Gigadibs' position and obscures the calculation which lies behind Blougram's consideration of enthusiasm.

In lines 599–646 Blougram discusses the uses of faith, assuming that Gigadibs puts forward the arguments in lines 592–598. This is another difficult passage, partly because the transitions are abrupt, and partly because the Bishop is typically dislodging Gigadibs from one position while at the same time offering a disingenuous defence of his own – disingenuous because he does not meet Gigadibs' main objection that it is dishonest to combine an imperfect faith with professions of complete belief. All the arguments that Blougram brings forward in this passage try to justify 'as much faith as one can muster'. Some of them are fallacious, as 608–609, but some are of real force, especially 626–636, which firmly place on the unbeliever the onus of justifying his disbelief, thus materially helping to strengthen the case against scepticism and laying the way open for a *complete* acceptance of the Christian faith. Lines 636–646 are likewise efficacious in showing that mere intellectual doubts need be no

---

[1] Paul F. Mattheisen ('Gosse's Candid "Snapshots" ', *VS*, VIII (1965), pp. 329–54,) prints a revealing anecdote from the Gosse MS. in Rutgers University Library: 'Locker defended and praised Croker, to Browning's long-suppressed but finally-outbursting indignation; B. told a story of Croker's saying, when a young man, "Now what side would you advise me to take up in politics? Liberalism is pushing ahead, but then, you know, it might pay to head a reaction!" ' (pp. 345–6)

obstacle to belief and thus making it easier for Gigadibs to abandon his scepticism.

From line 647 onwards Blougram seems aware that the real danger is not that Gigadibs will remain entrenched in his atheism but that he will attack Blougram from the point of view of a believer. He thereupon deploys a great gallery of arguments, which are designed to show that Christianity as Christ taught it is impracticable.[1] As one would expect his arguments are all fallible. He begins by taking for granted a position which not everyone would be prepared to concede, when he asserts in lines 648–657 that pure faith is too fierce for humanity to bear. He develops this in lines which can only be read as ironically intended by Browning

> Some think, Creation's meant to show him forth:
> I say, it's meant to hide him all it can,
> And that's what all the blessed Evil's for.
> Its use in time is to environ us . . .
> . . . time and earth case-harden us to live (652–62)[2]

[1] Cf. Swift, *Argument against Abolishing Christianity*: 'I hope no Reader imagines me so weak to stand up in the Defence of Real Christianity, such as used in Primitive Times (if we may believe the Authors of those Ages) to have an Influence upon Mens Belief and Actions: To offer at the restoring of That would indeed be a wild Project; It would be to dig up Foundations, to destroy at one Blow all the Wit, and half the Learning of the Kingdom; to break the entire Frame and Constitution of Things, to ruin Trade, extinguish Arts and Sciences with the Professors of them; In short, to turn our Courts, Exchanges, and shops into Deserts . . . Therefore I think this Caution was in itself altogether unnecessary (which I have inserted only to prevent all Possibility of Caviling) since every candid Reader will easily understand my Discourse to be intended only in Defence of Nominal Christianity, the other having been for some time wholly laid aside by general Consent, as utterly inconsistent with all our present Schemes of Wealth and Power.'

Cf. also *The Fair Haven*, Ch. III: 'It is only conventional Christianity which will stand a man in good stead to live by; true Christianity will never do so . . . And what if some unhappy wretch, with a serious turn of mind and no sense of the ridiculous, takes all this talk about Christianity in sober earnest, and tries to act upon it? Into what misery may he not easily fall, and with what life-long errors may he not embitter the lives of his children.'

[2] Cf. *The Fair Haven*, Ch. IV: 'He saw the Divine presence in everything – the evil as well as the good.' The Bishop's argument here is very like that of Don Juan (*Fifine* 101), where Browning also uses the word 'case-hardened', referring to 'the soul's case, distinct from the soul's self'. That Browning does not usually consider 'case-hardening' a desirable process we may see from *Paracelsus* I, 746 ('And men have oft grown old among their books/To die case-hardened in their ignorance')

Similarly in line 663 Blougram says 'The feeblest sense is trusted most', again without any attempt to prove or exemplify. This cannot be taken as a contribution to a serious discussion; it is consistent only with a satiric presentation of Blougram's argument. He continues

> the child
> Feels God a moment, ichors o'er the place,
> Plays on and grows to be a man like us.

Blougram, unlike Wordsworth, apparently approves of the process by which the child gets rid of his clouds of glory, forgets that imperial palace whence he came, moves away from the master-light of all our seeing, and grows up normal. Admittedly Browning did not share the prevalent Romantic tendency to idealise childhood, but it is not, I think, possible to conceive of his using this line of argument in any spirit but that of irony. In lines 666–668 Blougram in fact gives a very revealing account of his own position, comparing it to that of Michael, who must keep calm because he feels underfoot a snake which can be kept quiet only if he stands still. This parallel would hardly tempt Gigadibs to the life of the sceptic who maintains a resolute appearance of belief.

Again, as if offering a more homely illustration of the preceding point, Blougram says that he needs snuff to stir his torpid nostrils almost to the point of sneezing. Just as snuff encourages in the nose an awareness of the pleasures of not actually sneezing, so, Blougram implies, doubt encourages an awareness of the pleasures of faith. An itching nose is better than a tranquil one, he asserts: thus, by implication, a continually agitated faith is better than a settled one. The faultiness of this analogy is readily seen in the conclusion Blougram draws from it: 'Say I – let doubt occasion still more faith!' If this were a true conclusion it would also be true, and not merely absurd, to say 'Let snuff occasion still more not sneezing.' We may notice also the difficulty of reconciling Blougram's description of faith as 'a vertical sun' with 'the torpor of the inside-nose', and secondly the irresponsibility with which he discusses doubt as if it were an agreeable stimulant (see lines 229–230).

---

and *Balaustion's Adventure* 1591 ('So, the selfish Pheres went his way,/Case-hardened as he came.')

Next, like a cardsharper forcing a card, Blougram foists another line of argument on Gigadibs, that before the Reformation everybody had faith. Blougram replies that in that credulous age people believed happily in every traveller's tale and yet lived their life like beasts. Belief in itself, especially if it comes without an effort, is, he implies, worthless as a guide to conduct. To Blougram belief has no consequences. He sees that it is possible to entertain belief of a kind because of a credulous disposition and still act wickedly, but he does not meet the argument that an active faith is possible now, as it was in the Middle Ages. He fallaciously narrows down the argument to the kind of belief that is possible 'with soul more blank than this decanter's knob'.

Blougram then goes on to argue that the testing-time for a man comes when he fights within himself. We must admit that doubt is valuable if, by overcoming it, we arrive at a faith based on a firm conviction rather than one grounded in mere credulity. But it does not follow from this that doubt is to be regarded as a good in itself, much less that we should value doubt above faith.[1] Thus when Blougram adds, 'Prolong that battle through his life', he is clearly in the realm of nonsense. Once committed to this line Blougram continues in patent absurdity:

> Here, we've got callous to the Virgin's winks
> That used to puzzle people wholesomely –
> Men have outgrown the shame of being fools.
> What are the laws of Nature, not to bend
> If the Church bid them, brother Newman asks.
> Up with the Immaculate Conception, then –
> On to the rack with faith – is my advice!
> Will not that hurry us upon our knees
> Knocking our breasts, 'It can't be – yet it shall!
> Who am I, the worm, to argue with my Pope?
> Low things confound the high things!' and so forth. (699–709)

[1] It is tempting to cite *Rabbi Ben Ezra* III: 'Rather I prize the doubt/Low kinds exist without', and to argue that this shows that Browning also valued doubt as a good in itself. But even if we grant the questionable assumption that Rabbi Ben Ezra here voices Browning's own thoughts, it is clear that his comment refers specifically to the hopes and fears of youth, without which men would be no better than the birds and the beasts, 'finished and finite clods, untroubled by a spark'. The Rabbi later expresses his conviction that his youthful doubt will be dispelled in old age – 'Young all lay in dispute: I shall know being old.'

I do not think that even Professor Prestley can take seriously the argument that, since the struggle for faith is worth more than faith itself we should continually keep ourselves at full stretch by trying to believe ever more incredible dogmas. The whole passage must be read as Blougram's defence of his own protestations of complete conformity, which Browning here satirises with great comic vigour.[1] Isobel Armstrong (*Reconsiderations*, pp. 116–18) has some penetrating comments on the tone Blougram adopts at this point in the poem. She observes acutely, 'It is not so much that the Bishop's position is implausible . . . but the coarsening undergone in this thin and facile formulation makes it impossible to accept what the words create of it. This is what the poem is about.'

713–723 is an odd little passage, which reads almost as if it ought to come before line 693. Blougram offers a typically fallacious refutation of the general position that there are still men of faith by forcing a particular example on Gigadibs and then asking rhetorically how real and active this faith is. If Browning really wishes to provide Blougram with serious arguments the example he chooses here is a singularly poor one for his purposes. Can it conceivably be maintained that Browning is writing without satiric intent when he makes Blougram put forward as an example of 'faith' the regime of King Bomba, which Gladstone, in his 'Public Letter to Lord Aberdeen', described in

---

[1] Cf. Hume, *Natural History of Religion*, Sect. xi: '(Popular theology) has a kind of appetite for absurdity and contradiction. If that theology went not beyond reason and common sense, her doctrines would appear too easy and familiar. Amazement must of necessity be raised: Mystery affected: Darkness and obscurity sought after: And a foundation of merit afforded to the devout votaries, who desire an opportunity of subduing their rebellious reason, by the belief of the most unintelligible sophisms.'

Cf. also Byron's account of how successive attacks of illness have made him increasingly orthodox:

> The first attack at once proved the Divinity
> (But *that* I never doubted, nor the Devil);
> The next, the Virgin's mystical virginity;
> The third, the usual Origin of Evil;
> The fourth at once establish'd the whole Trinity
> On so uncontrovertible a level,
> That I devoutly wish'd the three were four
> On purpose to believe so much the more.
> (*Don Juan*, XI, 6)

a celebrated phrase as 'the negation of God erected into a system of government'?

Blougram now offers to summarise his conclusions. He says first

> my doubt is great,
> My faith's the greater – then my faith's enough.

This is the only real argument with which he is provided, and even this is no defence against the charge that he professes complete freedom from doubt and indeed offers to instruct others in matters of faith. That he is conscious of his weakness here is shown by his otherwise illogical switch to a justification of his own acceptance of the more brazen frauds of the Catholic Church. Blougram offers two defences of this. First he alleges that he is unable to distinguish between the essential and inessential dogmas of his church and must therefore accept all lest he should lose all. This deliberate decision of Blougram's to accept even the patent absurdities of Catholicism and to profess belief in them should be carefully distinguished from Gigadibs' refusal to be satisfied with anything less than complete faith. Secondly he pleads that his influence over 'the rough purblind mass we seek to rule' depends on his readiness to grasp the extremities of faith. If he ceased to proclaim his belief in the more extravagant superstitions he would to that extent lose his control over the more ignorant members of his church. It is not hard to see the worth of such an argument. Even granted that it is a true account of the practices to which Blougram is obliged to resort in order to maintain his personal influence, it cannot stand as a contribution to a general discussion.

The Bishop admits that his standards are material – 'I act for, talk for, live for this world now' (770), and suggests ingeniously that the surest way to lose 'true life' is to try to live in the next world, instead of this.[1]

> I'm at ease now, friend – worldly in this world
> I take and like its way of life . . .
> And God, if He pronounce upon it all,
> Approves my service, which is better still.

[1] Cf. *The Ring and the Book,* X. 1930–41, where the Pope imagines the Abate putting forward with similar casuistry a defence of his own hypocrisy. Cf. also *Easter-Day*, XI, where one of the speakers, a man of easy faith, says 'Here I live/In trusting ease.'

> If He keep silence, – why for you or me
> Or that brute-beast pulled-up in to-day's 'Times',
> What odds is't, save to ourselves, what life we lead? (797–805)

This does not take account of the possibility, which is the Christian belief, that God notices man's conduct in this world but does not at once pronounce on it, so that the wicked may appear to flourish. But of course if this is so it does not follow that what a man does with his life is of no importance except to himself.[1] Blougram now abandons defence, and once again, where he attacks disbelief, has the victory. He supposes that at this point Gigadibs will say that if a man is in fact a sceptic he should 'act up to' his principles. But, Blougram asks, how can sceptics live completely consistent lives? If they really behaved according to their principles there would be nothing to stop them from indulging every desire, for when a sceptic has traced morality back to its foundations he finds only 'certain instincts, blind, unreasoned-out'. These instincts, however, he dare not set aside. He is thus, as Blougram says,

> as much a slave as I,
> A liar, conscious coward and hypocrite,
> Without the good the slave expects to get,
> Suppose he has a master after all! (841–844)

This is one of the arguments which finally dislodges Gigadibs from his scepticism, since it convinces him that atheism does not bring freedom to the atheist.

From line 845 to line 852 we traverse one of the most difficult passages in the poem. Although it is loosely expressed, and the precise meaning is hard to establish, the general sense is clear enough. Blougram puts forward a claim to feel a need for God and to find that need satisfied. If we assume that he is not simply lying in this matter, how can his claim be reconciled with an interpretation of the poem which maintains that Blougram is satirized when he defends his own position and can be regarded

---

[1] Two other characters come to mind with these words of the Bishop, and may suggest where Browning's own sympathies lay. First Porphyria's lover sitting by her body, 'and yet God has not said a word!' Secondly the poet in *How It Strikes A Contemporary* 'doing the King's work all the dim day long'. 'But never word or sign, that I could hear,/Notified to this man about the streets/The King's approval of those letters conned/The last thing duly at the dead of night.'

as arguing honestly only when he attacks the atheist position?
Mrs Orr suggests a possible approach. Her comment on the
passage is: 'The Bishop's instincts . . . demand for him a living,
self-proving God (here the doctrine of expediency reasserts
itself)'[7]. A 'self-proving' God is a God who makes no demands on faith. Blougram dismisses faith in God's existence as
belief in a 'mere name': he asks for a material, indeed a physical
relationship between his God and himself, and, claiming to feel
some such tangible proof of God's presence, in spite of what he
has said earlier about the impossibility of certainty and the value
of constant doubt, treats this 'knowledge' as a justification for
centring his main interests in this world. Clearly it is a crude and
easy kind of religious satisfaction.[1] Nevertheless Blougram can
truly say 'I live my life here; yours you dare not live,' since he at
least enjoys his life in this world: Gigadibs the atheist has, as
Blougram has shown, neither happiness in this world nor hope
of happiness in the next. Once again the Bishop's arguments rout
Gigadibs while at the same time they expose the weakness of his
own position.

    In the following section (853–891) Blougram gives his own
satirical version of Gigadibs' present way of life. The whole of
the passage, even lines 865–871, is what the Bishop assumes
Gigadibs would say for himself, while the imagery, which de-
bases the whole picture, is Blougram's own contribution. Gigadibs, according to Blougram, would argue as follows 'You are
distorting the truth, since ordinary people have open to them
another way of life. Knowledge and power (like yours) have
rights, but so have ignorance and weakness. We are not called
on to make a crucial effort to find truth as long as we make an
honest attempt to do so, and thus show our right to live in the
world. After all, men are, strictly speaking, animals, with an
animal's limited powers of vision. What then is the point of
pretending to see what we cannot, as you do? I admit that the
world would be a richer place if we could see the truth about
everything, especially if we could really see God in the world, but
nevertheless I am bound to say only what I think true.' At this
point Blougram with great skill identifies Gigadibs' account of
his way of life with the sort of argument that might be put for-

---

[1] Cf. *Easter-Day*, XXXIII: 'Thank God, no paradise stands barred/To
entry, and I find it hard/To be a Christian, as I said.'

ward by an intelligent sheep. Gigadibs says, according to Blougram, that he finds many things which he does happily, many things which he has no inclination to do, and many things he would do but for the disapproval of his fellow-men (although he sometimes strikes a balance between his inclinations and his fear of displeasing his fellows). Thus, alternately indulging his desires and checking them through fear, Gigadibs claims to go through the world 'with not one lie'. In this passage Blougram puts the case for Gigadibs' agnostic way of life at its strongest, and allows his imagery to establish that it is at best as limited as the way of life of an animal. This is really the final stroke in Blougram's argument against Gigadibs, as opposed to his defence of his own position; it is intended to contrast Gigadibs' sheeplike existence with is own highly civilized life. However, the contrast appears to Gigadibs 'another way than Blougram's purpose was', between the full life of faith and the restricted life that Blougram has shown Gigadibs' to be.

Blougram devotes the last section of the monologue to a contemptuous comparison of his own position in the world with Gigadibs':

> In truth's name, don't you want my bishopric,
> My daily bread, my influence and my state? (903–904)

He virtually challenges Gigadibs to try to publish the 'interview', confident that it would not be believed. He is quite certain that he has not only vanquished Gigadibs' atheism but also successfully defended his own compromise between faith and the world. In this last passage he states with great condescension and complacency his conviction that the only possible alternative to Gigadibs' mean way of life is one of luxury and worldly influence. For evidence that Browning is unlikely to put forward these arguments sympathetically we need look no further than Section X of *Easter-Day*. Blougram places himself on the level of the collectors of snuffboxes and unusual beetles, and he is condemned by the words of the Lord in Section XX of the same poem:

> Thy choice was earth: thou didst attest
> 'Twas fitter spirit should subserve
> The flesh, than flesh refine to nerve
> Beneath the spirit's play.

Browning's whole purpose in *Easter-Day*, to which *Bishop Blou-gram's Apology* stands in a singularly close relationship, is to show the inadequacy of life on earth as an end in itself.

Browning now talks in his own person, making, Professor Fairchild says, 'a rather awkward effort to extract the simple wholesome truth.' It must be noted that Browning does not make a direct statement of his own view of the issues discussed (this would be awkwardly done indeed to judge by the varying inter-pretations) but simply narrates, without comment, the effect of the monologue on Gigadibs. First, however, he deals with the Bishop.

> For Blougram, he believed, say, half he spoke. (979)

This, I suggest, is the half of his speech which expresses the inadequacy of the life of the sceptic and the impossibility of Blougram's ever agreeing to live such a life, with its spiritual and material poverty. The rest of his speech, Browning says, was half *ad hoc*, half suppression, designed 'for argumentatory pur-poses', and represented not his beliefs, but what appeared to him the best line of defence. He took up positions for convenience, but pretended that they were invariable convictions, and indeed, compared with Gigadibs' ideas 'flung daily down' in his news-paper articles, such they seemed. On the other hand he left out of account certain fundamental instincts since they were not easy to manipulate in argument. One must agree with Professor Fair-child here that the reader might be expected to grasp these facts from the poem itself.

> He said true things, but called them by wrong names. (995)

This is a difficult line of which I have not seen a satisfactory explanation[8]: it means, I think, that many of the points Blou-gram made in his defence, for instance those about the difficulty of belief, were reasonable taken by themselves. Blougram, how-ever, fallaciously claimed that they represented valid steps in his argument. Similarly his arguments against atheism, which are perfectly sound, he attempted to construe into a defence of his own position.

Thereafter the poem is straightforward. In his last nine lines of silent meditation Blougram professes himself quite satisfied with the arguments he has put forward, and reveals that the topics discussed mean nothing to him. His only concern is with whether he has successfully justified himself against the present attack on his position.

Gigadibs on the other hand has given close attention to everything that the Bishop has said. Routed from his position of complete unbelief and convinced by Blougram's blatant dishonesty of the falsity of any midway position, he is seized with 'a sudden healthy vehemence', renounces his life in Britain, and decides to lead, with his family, a simple life in Australia.

> there, I hope
> By this time he has tested his first plough,
> And studied his last chapter of St. John.

The significance of the last line is first general – that in future he will draw his faith from the Gospels, and secondly particular – since the last chapter of John's gospel suggests an answer to the question which Blougram had asked earlier, and which is to be found in Matthew – 'What think ye of Christ?'

The final contrast is pointed when Gigadibs buys 'not cabin-furniture/But settler's-implements.' In other words he faces the world not as a place to be made comfortable and then passively accepted, which is Blougram's way, but as a place which challenges man to make his home and fashion his destiny by courage and industry.

Thus the whole *effect* of the Bishop's monologue is clearly to convert Gigadibs from disbelief to Christianity. It is not hard to see why the reviewer in *The Rambler*, generally taken to be Cardinal Wiseman himself, although protesting against Browning's 'most unworthy notions of the work of a Catholic bishop', nevertheless detected 'an undercurrent of thought that is by no means inconsistent with our religion'. Similarly one can see why Browning objected to the description of the poem as a personal satire on Wiseman.

In short, I cannot accept Professor Priestley's arguments in favour of Blougram, since they cover only half the poem. In reply to Professor Fairchild I would maintain that the poem's mechanism is a great deal more complex than he shows it to be. I agree with Professor Palmer that Browning does not *judge* Blougram, but he *places* him so precisely that the reader can, without ambiguity, distinguish between the truth and sophistry of his

arguments and, if he wishes, arrive at his own judgement of
Blougram's moral character.

This judgement is not a simple one, for Blougram is not
presented as an entirely unsympathetic figure. Gigadibs is a person of little consequence, and the Bishop ironically diminishes
even his slight importance (920–970). In a sense the whole
monologue is too ample for Gigadibs: after a time the Bishop is
speaking for himself, partly to paper over the thin places in his
own conscience, partly as a journey of discovery in a realm which
he did not often enter, his own mind. Browning made one significant change in the poem. In the edition of 1855 line 978 read
'While the great bishop rolled him out his mind'. For later
editions Browning altered this to

> While the great bishop rolled him out a mind
> Long crumpled, till creased consciousness lay smooth.

This sense that Blougram is talking largely for the sake of exploring his own mind is powerful in the poem. It is perhaps not
too much to say that he realises the fallacies of his own arguments
but dare not face the implications of his reliance on these fallacies.
If he achieves, as some critics have suggested, a tragic status, it is
because he is no longer able to take his arguments to their logical
conclusion. Gigadibs can go to Australia and begin a new life:
Blougram cannot, and therefore must content himself with parad-
ing in his own justification arguments in which he cannot believe,
although at times he has painful glimpses of a world of faith he
can never reach (e.g. lines 165–167, 182–197, 555–569, 934–
942). At the very end of the poem, however, Browning perhaps
wishes to suggest that even for Blougram there is hope:

> if the ground should break away
> I take my stand on, there's a firmer yet
> Beneath it, both of us may sink and reach. (1000–02) [9]

It is in his self-frustrated desire for faith that the reader, even
while he observes the sophistry of his arguments, sympathises
with Blougram, just as he sympathizes with Karshish and Cleon.
But to say that we sympathize with the speaker and at the same
time condemn his disingenuousness is not to say that the two
impulses cancel out, leaving us with a neutral poem. On the
contrary the poem is a powerful affirmation of the Christian faith,

made even more powerful by being put into the mouth of one who is not himself able to sustain the demands of Christianity.

IV

The mechanism of *Bishop Blougram's Apology* is not precisely copied in any of the later monologues. In *Mr. Sludge, 'The Medium'*, however, the same basic method can be observed, with slight but interesting variations.

The scene is set, very rapidly, and we learn that the speaker is one Sludge, who has been detected in fraud by his patron, Hiram H. Horsefall, to whom he is now making his defence. The first half of the poem is devoted to Sludge's explanation of how he came to set up as a medium, and how he was led to cheat those who believed in his powers. Broadly speaking the substance of this part of the poem is an attack on his audiences. At first they were too credulous, then too eager for spectacular manifestations. Because they despised the medium and expected him to be unstable and erratic they accepted his frauds. At the same time they required him to swear that they were true, thus corrupting him further. Sludge describes their prurience, their appetite for lies, their consequent lack of logic in examining evidences, and the various unworthy motives which led individual members to 'take up' spritualism. In this part of the poem Sludge, like Blougram, when he attacks has the victory and carries complete conviction.

Two short passages should be noted which look forward to the second part of the poem. In the first Sludge mentions in passing that although he was tempted into a life of deceit because it profited him, nevertheless 'There's something in real truth (explain who can!)/One casts a wistful eye at.' This passage gives Sludge a certain moral superiority over Horsefall and his friends. Although he is the cheat and they are the gulls, at least he realizes that he is being corrupted, whereas it never occurs to them that they are degrading their medium. In the second passage Sludge argues that his lies helped the cause of religion. The irony here cannot be missed, and prepares us for the equivocal nature of the second part of the poem.

This second part consists of Sludge's defence of his own actions, and here, again like Blougram, Sludge argues far less cogently. First he claims that his naïve belief in the reality of communication between the dead and the living has scriptural warrant and that it is therefore a truly religious belief. But he at once casts doubt on this by saying that when Providence communicates with him it tells him when to have his hair cut, which strangers to cheat, when to sell his dog and how to win small bets. To the obvious question 'Shall the Heaven of Heavens/ Stoop to such child's play ?' Sludge replies that Science has shown the mysteries of the Universe in the most minute particles or organic life. This, even if true, is not an answer to the objection.

Sludge offers an alternative line of argument, saying that if man really is the heir to all the ages then everything in this world and the next should be at his service. But the conclusion that Sludge draws from this is that he will be told when to trump at whist. This is absurd. If we take Browning to be a serious poet we must assume that he knows when he is writing nonsense, and that if he does so he has a serious purpose. His purpose here can only be to expose the absurdity of the initial postulate that all the works of Nature are designed to minister to man.

Sludge next claims that he has not only the power to perceive inexplicable phenomena but the ability to synthesize such phenomena into a system universally true:

> I see gold, all gold and only gold,
> Truth questionless though unexplainable,
> And the miraculous proved the commonplace.

This claim to the incredibly rare gift of seeing the supernatural at work everywhere in the world Sludge does not substantiate except by saying

> '. . . Was that so strange?
> Are all men born to play Bach's fiddle-fugues,
> 'Time' with the foil in carte, jump their own height,
> Cut the mutton with the broadsword, skate a five,
> Make the red hazard with the cue, clip nails
> While swimming, in five minutes row a mile,
> Pull themselves three feet up with the left arm,
> Do sums of fifty figures in their head,
> And so on by the scores of instances?
> The Sludge with luck, who sees the spiritual facts
> His fellows strive and fail to see, may rank
> With these . . .'

Doubt is at once cast on the validity of Sludge's boast of such a transcendent gift by his equating it with a series of more or less trivial accomplishments: in the following lines there is more than a suggestion that he merely pretends to this gift out of vanity in order to compensate for his defects, especially his cowardice, deceitfulness, vanity and indulgence in debilitating fantasy.

Finally Sludge executes a brilliant series of variations on a theme dear to all Browning's casuists – the argument that the end justifies the means, and that therefore a lie is justified if it leads to truth or makes truth more acceptable. Clearly this line, if established, would go a long way to justify a fraudulent medium. What is to prevent the reader from accepting Sludge's arguments at their face value? First of all, there is the memory of Sludge's own words at the beginning of the poem – 'there's something in real truth . . ./One casts a wistful eye at.' If his patrons are in fact guilty of having corrupted Sludge, as he has so powerfully maintained, it is because they have forced him into a world of lies. If Sludge now justifies lying he weakens the whole tenor of the first part of the poem. Secondly the reader remembers Sludge's obviously specious defence of the use of fraudulently produced manifestations in the service of religion. The two arguments are identical, except that the second is more discreetly presented than the first. Thirdly, Sludge does not show at any point that truth has in fact followed from his lies. He says that things happen at his séances which he cannot altogether explain: this is as far as he is prepared to go.

His real defence is the other wing of his argument: that his lies have helped to make the real world more tolerable. Here as W. O. Raymond has well observed [10], Sludge's arguments are those of Francis Bacon. He says that nobody can enjoy the world as it is, but that, in Bacon's phrase, 'the admixture of a lie doth ever add pleasure . . .'

> 'I cheat, and what's the happy consequence? . . .
> [*My audience finds*]
> Each want supplied, each ignorance set at ease,
> Each folly fooled . . .
> You're supplemented, made a whole at last.'

It may be all illusion, but it is at least an illusion you veritably do share with a large number of distinguished people.

I think that the reader is intended to see that this reasoning is not good, and that what Sludge purports to offer is not in fact the 'happy consequence' of his deception. While it is hard, if not impossible, to establish whether or not Browning intended this passage to be read ironically, it is worth noting that the fantasy world that Sludge offers is described in phrases which are, to say the least, equivocal. It is a world in which 'each folly' is 'fooled'; it is one 'not quite like life', for it is 'all half-real,/And you, to suit it, less than real beside,/In a dream, lethargic kind of death in life'; those who inhabit it 'banish doubt,/And reticence and modesty alike!' To corroborate this indication that Browning is in fact writing ironically we may observe that the view of the real world as a place where no fulfilment is possible is not one which we should expect Browning to endorse.

Sludge's final point is that if, to achieve this desirable end, he has lied, he has done no more than many writers do. The powers of imaginative fiction, he suggests, are counted as a virtue, as 'creativeness and godlike craft' in the poet, historian or story-teller, but if a medium is once detected fabricating the evidence he is abused and assaulted. Sludge himself goes far to expose the weakness of this particular line of defence when he remarks that the writer is always proud to admit that his work is 'fancy all: no particle of fact'. Once this point is conceded it is easy to see that the argument as a whole need not be taken seriously, since it depends on a faulty analogy. On the one hand we have the creative artist, always prepared to acknowledge his own inventiveness and writing for an audience which is fully aware of the status of his activity and indeed derives its pleasure from what Johnson calls 'the consciousness of fiction': on the other hand we have the medium who denies his inventions and profits from his audience's belief that fraud is fact. I find it hard to believe that Browning failed to see the speciousness or obtuseness of arguments like these: if he did realize their hollowness, it follows that he put them into Sludge's mouth for ironical ends.

Sludge's arguments in his own defence thus fail to convince. On analysis each of them is seen to turn on a weakness in his audience, who are disposed to credit the hand of Providence in the trivial affairs of man, prepared to believe anyone who claims to have systematized isolated phenomena, and eager to listen to anyone who offers them a world of pleasant illusion in exchange for the world of hard reality.

The difficulties in the poem are three. First, Sludge among all his lies, half-truths, evasions and sophisms makes one or two remarks which seem to show that he has a genuine regard for truth: this makes it hard to see him as a figure portrayed with consistent irony, as for example when he says 'Really, I want to light up my own mind.' Secondly, some of the arguments which Sludge uses to recommend his case are very close to those which Browning puts forward non-ironically elsewhere, in *Development*, for example, or in the celebrated image of the gold and the alloy at the beginning of *The Ring and the Book*. Thirdly, much of what Sludge says about spiritualism and the way in which mediums are led to sacrifice their own personalities and pander to the taste of their audience is recognizably close to Browning's own opinions of the right relation of the poet to *his* audience. As I have said, we need not regard either of these last two difficulties as insuperable, since there is no reason why we should expect Browning always to say the same thing, but there is no denying that the existence of discrepancies of this kind is disconcerting.[1]

They are perhaps less worrying if it is agreed that Sludge, like Blougram, is not an entirely unsympathetic character. The pattern of the two poems is essentially the same. Each of the speakers attacks his listener and does so with good arguments: each of them defends his own practice and does so with plausible but specious arguments, but neither of them is satirized in such a way as to rob him of all the reader's sympathy. Both of them are learning more about themselves as they speak. The difference between the two poems, a difference which makes *Sludge* a more difficult poem to evaluate than *Blougram*, is this. Our sympathy with Blougram is slight. He is talking to a social inferior whom he despises, and attempting to justify his deception of his 'million imbeciles' in the name of Christ. He is secure in his position. Sludge on the other hand has much stronger claims on our sympathy. He is a detected cheat, brought to the point of confession by his patron, who is in part responsible for corrupting him. He shows that those whom he deceived were poor creatures, and that he did little harm by his deception. Moreover,

[1] They are not, strictly speaking, difficulties in the poem, but difficulties that arise if we try to make the poem accord with the rest of Browning.

as I have said, the grain and the chaff in his defence are not to be winnowed apart so easily as in Blougram's.

As Professor Fairchild has pointed out, the tailpiece to the poem does much to qualify our sympathy for Sludge, and thus ensures that we are not misled into taking all his arguments at face value. Even so, the poem is not simple, and it is a critical task of some intricacy to describe precisely the variation in Browning's sympathies in the course of the monologue [11].

V

The three poems which I have dealt with in this chapter show in different degrees the element of 'difficulty' in Browning which arises from his ironic handling of an argument. To show this as clearly as possible I have treated them more or less as if they were statements in plain prose. When it is remembered that all the speakers have a quick wit, great fecundity in illustrative similes and metaphors, and the power to speak at times with a poet's tongue, all qualities which modify and complicate our judgements, and when, finally, it is remembered that all these monologues have also the aesthetic appeal of, to put it at its lowest, unfailingly competent metrical discourse, it will be realized that it is no simple response which Browning demands from his readers.

When the ideas from which his poems are made are themselves hard to grasp, a further set of demands is made on the reader. In the following chapter I shall examine some of the poems in which Browning explores intellectual or metaphysical concepts of some intrinsic difficulty.

Other difficulties – II

PHILO: Why is there any misery at all in the world? Not by chance surely. From some cause then. Is it from the intention of the Deity? But he is perfectly benevolent. Is it contrary to his intention? But he is almighty. Nothing can shake the solidity of his reasoning, so short, so clear, so decisive; except we assert, that these subjects exceed all human capacity, and that our common measures of truth and falsehood are not applicable to them; a topic, which I have all along insisted on.   HUME, *Dialogues Concerning Natural Religion*

The question [of perception] is one in which it is peculiarly difficult to make out what another man means and even *what one means one's self*. Professor CLIFFORD, quoted in Domett's notes to *Ranolf and Amohia*

I

Something to see, by Bacchus, something to hear, at least!
There, the whole day long, one's life is a perfect feast;
While up at a villa one lives, I maintain it, no more than a beast.

In *Up at A Villa – Down in the City* the speaker, an Italian person of quality, disparaging the Tuscan countryside, where there is 'nothing to see', and expressing his desire to live in the town, which is always full of gossip, noise and motion, shows in every line his inability to value the beauty of the country in face of the garish pleasures of urban life. The reader who has enjoyed this poem may suppose that it is always possible to arrive at Browning's own opinions by simply inverting the values of the speaker – what he calls bad is really good, what he calls clever is really dishonest, and so on. Of course the process is by no means as simple as this. As I have shown in the previous chapter, what is required of the reader of *Sludge* or *Blougram* is a continuous and subtle discrimination and assessment of tone and argument. Some of Browning's monologues are even more complex: *Prince Hohenstiel-Schwangau* and *Fifine at the Fair* will be examined in their place.

The essential features of the problem of interpreting such a poem may be illustrated in brief compass by an account of *Caliban upon Setebos*. As we read this poem we have, as is not uncommon in Browning's monologues, moments when we sympathize with the speaker, notably lines 150–169, where Caliban pathetically tries to imitate Prospero. But it is clear that in general his attitude to the world about him is one of complete callousness: he is ready to stone a crab to death or twist off its pincer, to pluck the feathers from a live jay or to burn a young kid. All creatures weaker than he is are subject to his power, and when he uses this power he is conscious only of his own emotions: the imaginative effort of conceiving the pain or terror which his actions bring to his victims is beyond him. His is not simply a world in which there is no love, but a world in which there is no feeling possible towards an inferior except a jealous anger. Accordingly Caliban has constructed a God who created the world through envy and torments it through pride, manifesting himself only in malice. Setebos can be known only in his wrath and in the infliction of pain: all pleasures must be taken in spite of him or when he is unaware.

The inadequacy of this conception of the creator is immediately obvious. It is also obvious that it derives from Caliban's deficiencies. Thinking only of his own immediate selfish gratification he creates a selfish God precisely in his own image. 'Thou thoughtest that I was altogether such a one as thyself.' What is the effect of this dramatic presentation of Caliban? It is clear that we are to reject the way his mind works and his home-made Godhead, but in favour of what? Is the poem directed against 'natural religion'? Or against the doctrines of evolution? Or against Calvinism? Or against orthodox theology? Or against anthropomorphism in religion? Or against the Higher Critics of the Bible?

It is sometimes suggested that the poem is a satire on the theories of evolution which were so much in people's minds in the 1860s. This seems unlikely. None of the cardinal doctrines, such as spontaneous genetic change or natural selection, is mentioned, and none of the obvious implications of evolution, such

as the wastefulness of nature, the improbability of special creation, or the erroneousness of Genesis is exploited at all. The
poem deals essentially with an older problem, the evidences for
the existence of God.

There seems to be no objection taken to anthropomorphism as
such. For instance Sycorax has transmitted to her son (line 170)
the idea that above Setebos is a greater power, the Quiet. 'This
Quiet, all it hath a mind to, doth.' This power stands in the same
relation to Setebos as Prospero does to Caliban. By contemplating these relationships Caliban is able to conceive of another
world infinitely superior to this. The apprehension of God in
human terms is a primitive but essential stage in the religious
development of man. Caliban, however, clearly makes for himself
a God with none of the attributes of deity except power, which
suggests that in 1864 Browning thought that such religious ideas
as might be evolved naturally by unaided man would necessarily
be limited.[1] Most obviously of course he represents Caliban as
unable to conceive of the love of God.

The anti-Calvinism in the poem is more obvious. For example,
when Caliban says

> Let twenty pass, and stone the twenty-first,
> Loving not, hating not, just choosing so

or

> He hath a spite against me, that I know,
> Just as He favours Prosper, who knows why?

he is clearly hitting at the doctrines of election and reprobation.
But the range of the poem is wider than simple Calvinism. Any
view of God which sees Him as limited by the moral inadequacies
of man comes under attack.

Many arguments of the poem are, not surprisingly, reminiscent
of Hume's *Natural History of Religion*, especially of the celebrated passage in which he makes the point that although the
contemplation of the world affords an irresistible argument for the
existence of an intelligent God, this is not to say that primitive

---

[1] The idea that a man's religious beliefs develop in sophistication and abstraction
as he grows older and that the general religious beliefs of mankind do the same thing
as the world grows older is one that recurs in Browning's poems from 1864 onwards, cf. *A Death in the Desert*, 453 ff.

man formed his conception of the deity in such a rational way:

> Even at this day, and in Europe, ask any of the vulgar, why he believes in an omnipotent creator of the world; he will never mention the beauty of final causes, of which he is wholly ignorant: He will not hold out his hand, and bid you contemplate the suppleness and variety of joints in his fingers, their bending all one way, the counterpoise which they receive from the thumb, the softness and fleshy parts of the inside of his hand, with all the other circumstances, which render that member fit for the use, to which it was destined. To these he has been long accustomed; and he beholds them with listlessness and unconcern. He will tell you of the sudden and unexpected death of such a one: The fall and bruise of such another: The excessive drought of this season: The cold and rains of another. These he ascribes to the immediate operation of providence: And such events, as, with good reasoners, are the chief difficulties in admitting a supreme intelligence, are with him the sole arguments for it.

Caliban goes a stage further and speculates about the nature of Setebos, but the parallel is close enough to suggest that at least part of Browning's implied criticism is like Hume's, directed against those whose anthropomorphism leads them to a debased view of God. Caliban's transference of his own cruelty and envy to Setebos leads him to create a vindictive, jealous God; the reader having observed this and perceived Caliban's error, is required to examine afresh his own conception of God and to see how far he is himself guilty of worshipping a deity without love or compassion for his creation. Again a comment of Hume's is to the point, this time through the mouth of Philo in the *Dialogues Concerning Natural Religion*:

> *To know God*, says Seneca, *is to worship him*. All other worship is indeed absurd, superstitious, and even impious. It degrades him to the low condition of mankind, who are delighted with entreaty, solicitation, presents, and flattery. Yet is this impiety the smallest of which superstition is guilty. Commonly, it depresses the Deity far below the condition of mankind; and represents him as a capricious Daemon, who exercises his power without reason and without humanity! And were that divine Being disposed to be offended at the vices and follies of silly mortals, who are his own workmanship; ill would it surely fare with the votaries of most popular superstitions.
>
> (Part XII)[1]

[1] Cf. the following passages from Hume's *Natural History of Religion*:
  Barbarity, caprice; these qualities, however nominally disguised, we may

The question of how far the poem is a satire has been extensively canvassed [1], and I have no intention of contributing to the argument, except to point out that Browning's letter to Furnivall makes quite clear, what should in any case be sufficiently obvious from the poem, that *Caliban* is to be read dramatically [2]. Browning's 'targets' in the poem so to speak, are defined by the different roles which Caliban assumes. Sometimes he prefigures a dogmatic self-centred Calvinist. Sometimes he offers a *reductio ad absurdum* of Rousseauism. Sometimes he represents those who found their religious beliefs on the Old Testament without taking account of the teachings of Christ.[1]

If the poem is a satire then it is a rather advanced kind of satire. It suggests that what is important in man's conception of God is precisely the quality which is conspicuously omitted from the poem, that is, love. It suggests that the crude theology at which Caliban has arrived is not particularly easy to distinguish from the doctrines of many people who would call themselves good Christians. And at the same time it suggests that Caliban's creed is not much different from what would be left of religion if disintegrators like Renan and Strauss had their way. After all, if, instead of the Gospels, we had to rely only on Man's experience of a hostile or indifferent natural world and of the workings of his own cruel heart, might we not conceive of a God very like Setebos?

---

universally observe, from the ruling character of the deity in popular religions. (Ch. XIV)

What a noble privilege is it of human reason to attain the knowledge of the supreme Being; and, from the visible works of nature, be enabled to infer so sublime a principle as its supreme creator? But turn the reverse of the medal. Survey most nations and most ages. Examine the religious principles, which have in fact, prevailed in the world. You will scarcely be persuaded, that they are anything but sick men's dreams. (Ch. XV)

[1] Perhaps nothing makes so plain the way in which Browning was perpetually harassed by the task of preventing Christian paradoxes from turning into philosophical dilemmas as a study of the religious writings of John Stuart Mill, notably the *Three Essays on Religion* (1874), e.g. 'The Author of the Sermon on the Mount is assuredly a far more benignant Being than the author of Nature. But unfortunately, the believer in the Christian revelation is obliged to believe that the same being is the author of both.' Although their upbringing and early religious experiences were vastly different Browning and Mill reached not dissimilar states of belief at the end of their lives.

The difficulty of the poem is twofold. First of all, the many-sided satirical impulses are hard to reconcile with the belief that Browning shared with Hume that 'the cause or causes of order in the universe probably bear some remote analogy to human intelligence'. If man in fact forms his idea of God from whatever materials are to hand and progressively improves and refines it, what is Caliban doing wrong? The answer, I think, is that Caliban is behaving properly, that is according to his nature. But the ideas which are natural in a primitive creature are reprehensible in nineteenth-century man, who should have advanced to an altogether more elevated idea of the relation of God and mankind.

The second kind of difficulty is also indicated by Hume, when he says, at the very end of his *Natural History of Religion*

> The whole is a riddle, an aenigma, an inexplicable mystery. Doubt, uncertainty, suspence of judgment appear the only result of our most accurate scrutiny, concerning this subject.

This passage, and the other parallels with Hume, may be taken to indicate that the difficulty resides in the subject, not in Browning's unskilful handling of it.

The criticism of *Caliban* that seems to me to carry most weight is that the poet's targets are widely dispersed, too widely in fact for the complete success of the poem. We learn unmistakably that the relation of Caliban to Setebos, that of a vicious dog to an arbitrary master, is wrong, but the positive side of the satire, which would indicate the right relationship, is insufficiently defined. The initial choice of Caliban as speaker made such definition additionally hard to present. Browning brilliantly recreates a primitive and therefore limited view of the world and man's place in the world, but this is by definition incompatible with a sophisticated and comprehensive account of the issues at stake, and particularly of their implications for modern man.

II

The consideration of *Caliban* can be generalized into a very simple proposition about Browning, that his poetry is often difficult because he has chosen to write about subjects which are intrinsically difficult to understand. The concepts he is handling are elusive, and no certainty is to be looked for at the end of the argument. Often indeed the most that is to be expected is the clearer recognition of a paradox. Such topics as the problem of evil and pain, the right way to govern a kingdom, the conditions under which a man can proceed from a particular observation to a general statement, the relationship between experience, knowledge and belief, the question of whether in a given situation the end in view can justify the means adopted, and the interaction of myth and revelation in Christianity are among those he or his characters discuss. The issues raised are not easy to grasp even in the cool unhurried prose of a work of philosophy, much less in the active shifting verse of Browning. Nor are these matters used simply as sources of imagery or poetic ideas, as for example Tennyson uses the theories of evolution in *In Memoriam*, but their metaphysical and theological implications are argued out, obliquely and directly, from different points of view.

As an example consider *A Death in the Desert* [3] where there is patently considerable sympathy between Browning and his speaker, St John, and yet the poem is not easy to read.[1] This is partly due to the awkward arrangement of the conflicting arguments, partly to the abstruse nature of the subject and its direct reference to contemporary theological disputes. The frame of the poem is typically ingenious. Browning imagines a manuscript with a history of direct transmission from its author to Cerinthus, a sceptic, who reads it and presumably comments on it in the poem's last lines. Cerinthus is chosen because his opinions seem to offer a parallel to the speculations of the German critics who, like Cerinthus and the Ebionites, were suggesting that Christ was no more than a good, but deluded, man. The body of the poem is devoted to giving the last words of St John, as he wonders about the future of Christian teaching and the status of the Gospels in future time. He tries to imagine what arguments might then be brought forward against the truth of what he has

[1] This bears on my disagreement with Langbaum in Chapter 2. Browning doesn't *satirize* John, and clearly feels warmly towards him, but he necessarily represents John as confronting a different, and really easier problem. Browning doesn't know what John knows at first-hand, but equally John doesn't know what Browning knows about the later history of Christianity. Even though Browning is not using John's ignorance ironically, an absolutely essential part of the poem resides in the consciousness that the speaker is represented as not having access to all the information available to the poet and the reader. John is almost as much a prisoner of his age as Cleon or Karshish.

written. Of course, having seen Christ, he has certain knowledge, but he sets this aside and tries to meet the sceptics on their own ground.

For the sceptics' two main arguments Browning turns to opinions current in his own day. The first argument is the stronger, and John presents it, if not with sympathy, at least with evident respect. It is agreed that Love is vital to mankind, and Christ, according to the Christians, was Love incarnate. But this, the sceptic says, does not prove the existence of Christ: it rather provides evidence for the contrary, since the fact that we recognize this quality in Christ shows that Love is part of Man's own nature. ''Tis mere projection from man's inmost mind.' Similarly Man is the source of the Will and the Intelligence which he attributes to God, just as he once created the anthropomorphic gods of Greece. This argument is put with extraordinary force, and is not answered directly.

The second line of argument which John puts into the mouth of his imaginary sceptic is concerned with Christian evidences. It raises such questions as whether the Gospels are true records, and if so how we are to explain the miracles. If miracles were possible to God then, why are there no miracles now? Alternatively if the Gospels are not literally true, why is man left to depend on such imperfect supports in his quest for certainty? Ultimately the argument turns on the nature of faith. Browning's observations on these notorious cruces in divinity are interwoven with his much less confident replies to the first argument.

The poem as a whole then takes as its subject matter a series of speculative theological and critical problems: in discussing them Browning deploys a series of ideas current at the time when the poem was written. Even when they are encountered in prose these ideas are of some complexity: Browning makes them no easier to follow by manipulating for his own purposes the normal logical order of objection and response, and offering instead, as more appropriate dramatically, a loose, conversational flow of the mind from one position to another.[1] In

---

[1] If we wish to take the arguments and counter-arguments in a logical sequence it is necessary to read the poem in a revised order such as the following: 1–365; First argument: 366–421, 474–513, 549–570; Second argument: 514–539, 540–548, 274–365, 424–473, 571–688. (See Chapter IX, p. 213) This radical shifting about of parts of a debate is not without parallel elsewhere in Browning. See, for example,

addition, for reasons which are set out in Chapter 9, his final position in the poem is one which ultimately depends on a complex amalgam of faith and logical argument.

The difficulty of the poem is real, and springs from Browning's endeavour to employ abstract ideas and the terms of philosophical discourse in a medium where few modern readers are prepared to encounter them and on terms which finally set at naught rational conclusions. Although *A Death in the Desert* has its admirers, it must, I think, be accounted a less than completely convincing attempt to use as the matter of poetry the clash of opposed speculations on subjects of intrinsic complexity and importance.

III

In *Caliban* and *A Death in the Desert* Browning was to some extent making extra difficulties for himself because they are both written from a nominally Christian point of view. Reading them one has a continual feeling that the answer Browning wants to arrive at is a Christian answer, but that anti-Christian arguments are exerting a strong intellectual and imaginative appeal. Hence the ambivalence which makes them so interesting. The poems I want to consider in the remainder of this chapter, beginning with *La Saisiaz* (1878), are difficult in a different way, precisely because Browning rules out the possibility that our doubts can be set at rest by Christian revelation, and tries to evolve an advanced form of religious belief from first principles.

The occasion of *La Saisiaz* was the sudden death of a old friend of Browning's, Miss Anne Egerton Smith, while she was staying with Browning and his sister near Geneva in a villa called 'La Saisiaz', which is Savoyard for 'the sun'. During the

---

Bishop Blougram's Apology, where lines 713–723 would come more logically before 693, or the *Epilogue* to *Pacchiarotto*, where Stanzas XIII and XIV interrupt the argument of Stanzas X–XVIII and are not replied to until Stanza XIX. A more debatable example is to be found in *Rabbi Ben Ezra*, where lines 49–72 present obvious difficulties of interpretation (see David Fleisher, '*Rabbi Ben Ezra, 49–72*: A New Key to an Old Crux', *VP*, I (1963), pp. 46–52). They read quite easily if Stanzas XI and XII are transposed. Of course I am not suggesting that there is any textual warrant for this, simply that the poem at this point offers us colloquial inconsequence at the expense of logical coherence. In the same way it is simpler to take Stanza 25 of *Reverie* in between Stanzas 19 and 20.

summer of 1877 Miss Smith and Browning had read with great
interest a two-part article by Frederic Harrison in *The Nineteenth
Century* called 'The Soul and Future Life' (see *La Saisiaz*, lines
163–164). Later in the same year this was adopted as the first
article in a symposium on the subject in which 'sundry minds of
mark' discussed the question of the immortality of the soul, for
the most part without appeal to Christian revelation or authority. As DeVane puts it, '*La Saisiaz* may be said to be Browning's
contribution to this debate' [4].

Most readers of the poem will value it for its opening (1–216)
in which Browning tenderly addresses Miss Smith, evoking the
pleasures of their holidays together and the charm and splendour
of the country around Mt Salève, or the end (525–618), where
Browning, in his most brilliant vein, calls upon all the celebrated authors associated with the district to contribute to the
force of his message. Certainly these passages have an immediate
appeal. My concern at the moment, however, is to examine the
central parts of the poem, in which Browning, speaking for once
in his own person, meditates on the possibility of life after death
and on the moral implications of the conclusions he reaches.

Throughout the poem Browning, like the contributors to the
symposium, accepts the implied prior conditions of the debate
and does not introduce Christian evidences. He determines to
start with brute facts, that is with facts which we know certainly but which we are incapable of proving. The two facts
from which he begins are the thing perceiving and 'the thing
perceived outside itself'.

> I have questioned and am answered. Question, answer presuppose
> Two points: that the thing itself which questions, answers, – is,
> it knows;
> As it also knows the thing perceived outside itself, – a force
> Actual ere its own beginning, operative through its course,
> Unaffected by its end, – that this thing likewise needs must be;
> Call this – God, then, call that – soul, and both – the only facts
> for me.
> Prove them facts? that they o'erpass my power of proving,
> proves them such:
> Fact it is I know I know not something which is fact as much.
>
> (217–224)

Browning says that there are only two things he knows for

certain – his own existence as a being capable of distinguishing pleasure and pain (262), and a something else which is independent of his existence. These two entities he calls soul and God: he wishes to discover whether or not the immortality of the soul can be proved or disproved simply from a consideration of these two facts. He *knows* that the self exists and that the not-self exists: his problem is to move from *is* to *shall be* (235).[1] Various possible methods of proceeding are canvassed and rejected, some with scorn, some with regret (255). Since Browning wishes to rest his argument solely on what he knows to be certain fact he will not pretend to speak for other people, only for himself. This is the first of many warnings in the poem that Browning claims no objective validity for his conclusions: they are grounded, he says repeatedly, on his own experience and on his own perceptions of what is painful or pleasurable: he therefore refuses to assert them as generally true. In the middle of a sentence for example he suddenly interjects, 'If – (to my own sense, remember! though none other feel the same!) – ' (268).

Being given simply his own experiences in this world his task is to use them to evolve a scheme of values: this necessarily entails a judgement of the power, wisdom and benevolence of the Creator, or, to state the matter less theologically, a judgement of whether man is happy or not.

> Solve the problem:
> 'From thine apprehended scheme of things, deduce
> Praise or blame of its contriver, shown a niggard or profuse
> In each good or evil issue! nor miscalculate alike
> Counting one the other in the final balance, which to strike,
> Soul was born and life allotted: ay, the show of things unfurled
> For thy summing-up and judgment, – thine, no other mortal's
> world!'
> (287–292)

His own experience has taught him one fact – that absolute

---

[1] Cf. Richard Jefferies, *The Story of My Heart*: 'Three things only have been discovered of that which concerns the inner consciousness since before written history began. Three things only in twelve thousand written, or sculptured, years, and in the dumb, dim time before then. Three ideas the Caveman primeval wrested from the unknown, the night which is round us still in daylight – the existence of the soul, immortality, the deity.' (Ch. III)

wisdom, goodness and power are not to be reconciled with the
state of the world as he finds it, and he is at once led to the
classic theological dilemma:

> . . . Did he [God] lack power or was the will in fault
> When he let blue heaven be shrouded o'er by vapours of the vault,
> Gay earth drop her garlands shrivelled at the first infecting breath
> Of the serpent pains which herald, swarming in, the dragon death?
>   (303–306)

Browning rejects the suggestion that misery has been deliberately introduced into the world in order that man shall value
happiness more, for this is too petty a motive for the mind which
framed the Universe:

> Can we love but on condition, that the thing we love must die?
> Needs there groan a world in anguish just to teach us sympathy –
> Multitudinously wretched that we, wretched too, may guess
> What a preferable state were universal happiness?   (311–314)

Suppose one assumes that the Universe has been created simply
to serve as an enormous teaching-machine (320), with the sole
purpose of instructing one man how to make the appropriate
responses. Then, Browning says, if the lessons he learns are
never to be put to use elsewhere, if, in short, he saw no future
life at all (not even a life in Hell) and could discern nothing
beyond his own immediate sensations of pleasure and pain, he
would have to say that *whatever happened* the sorrows of such an
existence outweighed the joys.

> I must say – or choke in silence – 'Howsoever came my fate,
> Sorrow did and joy did nowise, – life well weighed, – preponderate.'
>   (333–334)

This is clearly not, as it is sometimes taken to be, a straightforward declaration that Browning's life was on the whole more
unhappy than not.

An existence of the kind Browning has imagined he will, he
says, endure if he must, but he cannot admit that it is the work of
'a cause all-good, all-wise, all-potent', since God's qualities,
judged purely on the evidences of this world, must seem as
limited as man's (348). The function of this passage in the poem
is in effect to terminate the first line of reasoning; for if exclud-

ing the conjecture that there may be a life after death leads us to an impasse of this kind, it appears that the next step in the argument must be to allow the conjecture and examine the consequences.

Browning acknowledges the suffering of the world – indeed it is notable that, here as elsewhere, the recognition of the imperfections of the human condition is vital to his thought – but his reaction is to say, 'As long as I am assured of a second life I am content to accept the pains of this life, because they make the life to come all the more glorious. Just as knowledge, beauty and truth are most precious in the presence of their opposites, so love is most keenly felt and thoroughly understood when it is lost. If only we live after death, all the pain of loss is distilled into the quintessence of love.'

> Grant me (once again) assurance we shall each meet each some day,
> Walk – but with how bold a footstep! on a way – but what a way!
> – Worst were best, defeat were triumph, utter loss were utmost gain.
> Can it be, and must, and will it? (387–390)

It is to be observed that in this section of the poem Browning's language becomes much more vivid and passionate, just as his propositions become less rigorously formulated and more dependent on metaphor. He recognizes that there is a strong element of hopeful surmise in his refusal to believe that an omnipotent God can merely have created this world without an after-life, and determines to abjure 'the ready "Man were wronged else"', and 'the rash "and God unjust".' (400) He will derive his conclusions, that is, not from an *a priori* idea of what man is entitled to expect, but from what he declares to be inherent in 'fact's self', the basic premises of the existence of God and the soul.

In the second half of the poem Browning stages a colloquium between Fancy and Reason, reverting for the sake of clarity and interest to his favourite dramatic mode. 'Fancy' really means 'the right to make assumptions which can be shown to be necessary to the debate'. Since they are 'necessary' they have the status of certainties, or 'facts'. Fancy, that is, is allowed to indulge in the kind of surmise from which Browning had explicitly barred himself earlier in the poem. The first necessary assumption is, of course, 'that after body dies soul lives again', since the whole of the first part of the poem has demonstrated that unless this is conceded the argument cannot proceed. The purpose of the debate is to elicit, by propounding and demolishing various hypotheses, the conditions under which man could be allowed to know that his soul is immortal, how, in short, we should have to act in this world if we knew certainly that there was a life to come. Fancy and Reason reach the point where they agree that in order to proceed at all one must postulate not only life after death, but that suicide shall be forbidden and that it shall be known beyond doubt to all men that this life is the crucial testing-ground for their future life. At once Reason draws the conclusion that if this last postulate is granted then man's moral nature is at once destroyed.

He uses a familiar argument. If we knew as certainly as we know the elementary propositions of geometry that heaven or hell depended on our 'earthly deed', then the meaning of good and evil would be obliterated, since if you decree that a man will go to Heaven only if he behaves virtuously, he will behave virtuously only because he must, just as he is breathing only because he wants to keep alive, and can claim no credit for it:

> Prior to this last announcement, earth was man's probation-place:
> Liberty of doing evil gave his doing good a grace.   (491–492)[1]

The position now is that Browning, in the debate of Fancy and Reason, has explored the second wing of the argument (i.e. that in which it *is* permissible to assume a future life) and has reached an equally unacceptable terminus. It seems that *either* one admits that a future life is not provable from first premises, in which case it is impossible to reconcile the imperfections of

---

[1] Cf. RB's letter of 25 September 1845 to EBB:

The partial indulgence, the proper exercise of one's faculties, there is the difficulty and problem for solution, set by that Providence which might have made the laws of Religion as indubitable as those of vitality, and revealed the articles of belief as certainly as that condition, for instance, by which we breathe so many times a minute to support life. But there is no reward proposed for the feat of breathing, and a great one for that of believing – consequently there must go a great deal more of voluntary effort to this latter than is implied in the getting absolutely rid of it at once, by adopting the direction of an infallible church, or private judgment of another – for all our life is some form of religion, and all our action some belief, and there is but one law, however modified, for the greater and the less.

this world with its creation by an omnipotent omnibenevolent God, *or* one admits that if a future life must therefore be assumed it cannot be known to man except on terms that (i) make man's behaviour in this world of no significance, or (ii) make it so crucial that man's freedom of moral action is extinguished. All these are unacceptable, and the inquirer is left with no certainties, but also with the moderately cheerful conclusion that as it would be unreasonable to expect certainty in these matters its absence need not be a cause of despair. All man's soul can do on earth is

> pass probation, prove its powers, and exercise
> Sense and thought on fact, and then, from fact educing fit surmise,
> Ask itself, and of itself have solely answer, 'Does the scope
> Earth affords of fact to judge by warrant future fear or hope?'
> (521–524)

The argument here hinted at has Browning's characteristic ingenuity. It runs, 'Only if we have limited knowledge can we view this life as a life of probation: but only if we view this life as one of probation can we postulate a future life.' Thus the imperfection of man's knowledge becomes a necessary condition for the immortality of the soul. Browning does not bring this argument to the surface, insisting rather on the duty of man to exercise his 'sense and thought' on the problem of life after death.

He then addresses Miss Egerton Smith again, making the familiar point that, although she was now able to resolve his doubts, such an assurance as she might give him would utterly change his life, since it would come in place of hope. As we have seen at the conclusion of the debate between Fancy and Reason, Browning maintains that certainty cannot supersede hope without abrogating the moral laws of life and destroying the value of goodness. But, as things are, at least he is not left entirely without consolation in his darkness:

> Hope the arrowy, just as constant, comes to pierce its gloom,
> compelled
> By a power and by a purpose which, if no one else beheld,
> I behold in life, so – hope!
> Sad summing-up of all to say!
> *Athanasius contra mundum*, why should he hope more than they?
> (543–546)

The answer, of course, is that Browning's hope is stronger than a mere disposition to look on the bright side. It has almost the status of a rational belief, since it appears in the poem only after all the alternative positions have been systematically scrutinized and found unacceptable.

At this point Browning considers the nature of literary fame and influence. Thinking of Rousseau and Byron, who had both lived near by, he reflects that, because they were famous, their message of despair was readily accepted by their readers. The reason then for desiring fame [5], for desiring the learning of Gibbon, the wit of Voltaire (also distinguished local authors), the eloquence of Rousseau and the poetic power of Byron, is to make a single statement which will carry conviction to the multitude, even if the 'man of sense' deplores its crudeness.[1] This statement is that Browning 'at least believed in Soul, was very sure of God!' which, as the reader will remember, were the two 'brute facts' on which the whole structure of the poem was originally grounded. Browning says with rueful humour, 'Well, the debate may have been inconclusive, and no doubt I have failed to prove the immortality of the soul, but at least my basic assumptions were religious ones and were compatible with the dignity of man. If these notable pessimists could "witch the world" simply because of their literary gifts and not because of their irresistible reasoning, there is no reason why I should not also carry conviction by a sufficiently conspicuous declaration of my own not altogether unhopeful conclusion.'

At this point we can understand the reason for the apparently

---

[1] Note that Byron himself (*Childe Harold* III, lxxvii–lxxxi, civ–cvii) associates Rousseau, Gibbon and Voltaire with the Swiss landscape:

> Lausanne! and Ferney! ye have been the abodes
> Of names which unto you bequeath'd a name;
> Mortals, who sought and found, by dangerous roads,
> A path to perpetuity of fame:
> They were gigantic minds, and their steep aim
> Was, Titan-like, on daring doubts to pile
> Thoughts which should call down thunder, and the flame
> Of Heaven again assail'd, if Heaven the while
> On man and man's research could deign do more than smile.
>
> (cv)

Browning asks that the literary gifts of these celebrated sceptics, mockers and infidels may aid him to make his own simple statement of positive belief.

excessive protestations earlier in the poem that Browning is speaking only for himself. The doctrine of 'His own world for every mortal' is now utilized to show that if Browning elects to hope he has as good a right to do so as other men have to choose despair. 'Knowledge stands on my experience.' (272)

The last lines of *La Saisiaz* refer to the actual writing of the poem, in London in November. They repay fairly detailed examination, especially since Professor Priestley has raised a number of interesting questions about them [6].

Browning speaks of his reasoning in the poem as a chain, not a very dashing image, and says that he seemed to forge it one evening as he descended from Salève – 'seemed to forge' because the chain is only a metaphor. He found that it led him without a break to Miss Smith's grave, meaning, I think, that the grave is the boundary at which all such reasonings must break off and yield to speculation. Although he has admitted that the links in his reasoning are slight and the whole argument inconclusive his thoughts were not so loosely linked, nor the texture of his argument so tenuous, but what he was able to remember the different steps and carry it back to London. Since that time he has felt the need to examine the argument and clarify any ambiguities. This he has done, for what it is worth. At the time he could not have set down his argument and examined it: instead he kept his memory of the time when he fashioned it, like a root that is only to be planted out in a favourable season.[1] The idea of memories as the seeds of poetry leads Browning to reflect on those memories which he deliberately refuses to bring to life again for fear of their power. Here he is thinking not only of Miss Smith but also of his dead wife, with whom Miss Smith has already been explicitly associated (211–216). This feeling that throughout the debate Browning's real concern is with his wife's immortality no less than with Miss Smith's gives his conscientious grapplings with the conditions of existence a personal poignancy rare in his work. There is present also the idea not uncommon in his later poems that his love for his wife is his only guarantee of permanence in a world of relative values. Hence the importance of assuring himself that her death has not

---

[1] 'Reinterment' (614) means 'planting out' in order that it may grow, not, as Professor Priestley suggests, 'burying again' so that it may be hidden from public view.

essentially changed the nature of this love. The last words of the poem – 'Least part this: then what the whole?' – mean first, 'This poem represents only the smallest part of what I remember of Miss Smith; how great then must my total store of such memories be?' and secondly, 'My memory of Miss Smith is in turn only the smallest part of the sad yet sweet memories which I dare not bring to life again: how great then must the rest be?'

The major critical difficulty with which the poem confronts the reader is that of holding in focus simultaneously the parts in which Browning is describing the occasion of the poem (1–216, 373–404, 525–618) and those in which he is pursuing a chain of speculative reasoning. As I say, the sense that his love for his wife animates his speculations does much to hold the two parts together, but hardly enough. The framework, which is vivid, interesting, and full of immediate impressions, gives a most agreeable picture of people of leisure and culture enjoying a long holiday in pleasantly varied scenery. For all this the figure of Miss Smith is an adequate symbol. But in the rest of the poem the terrain Browning traverses is all interior, metaphysical, and difficult to understand in the absence of the familiar sense of contact with a physical world which we have come to consider characteristic of poetry. These parts of the poem depend for their arrangement not on the poet's aesthetic sense but on the developing demands of a logical argument, and depend for their appreciation more on the intellectual powers than on the sensitivity of the reader, and even here he is apt to encounter frustration since many of the arguments lead nowhere except to a pre-arranged dead-end. Yet, when all this is said, reading *La Saisiaz* gives a pleasure and excitement not often given by English verse after 1830. To deny that this is a poetic pleasure is to cling to a very narrow definition of poetry.

IV

It is usual to dismiss as 'mere gray argument' any of Browning's later poems which present difficulties of the same kind as *La Saisiaz*, but this is not altogether fair. The poems are speculations, imaginative attempts to actualize a philosophical position or dilemma, to embody it in the diagram-drama of a fable, precisely the sort of thing that happens in *Ferishtah's Fancies*. A

useful insight into Browning's methods and into his favourite
lines of thought is to be had by looking at three late poems,
Jochanan Hakkadosh from *Jocoseria* (1883), and *Rephan* and
Reverie from *Asolando* (1889). Each of them approaches by a
different route the problem which had exercised Browning in *La
Saisiaz*, the nature of the next world, and, more immediately,
the consequences for our understanding of this world of the
knowledge that there is or is not to be a life after death.

The story of *Jochanan Hakkadosh* is derived from Rabbinical
lore. The Rabbi Jochanan, old, wise, and on the point of death,
is privileged to extend his life by four periods of three months
each, the gifts of a married lover, a soldier, a poet, and a states-
man. At the end of each three months he declares what he has
learned from his experience of another way of life. Each time he
can report only utter disillusion and the complete disparity
between the ideal and the actual. 'Love, war, song, statesman-
ship – no gain, all loss.' By chance Jochanan is granted a further
reprieve of three months, this time the gift of a 'certain game-
some boy'. At the end of this period he declares that he has
arrived at 'utter acquiescence in my past,/Present and future
life.' He has attained to a 'calm struck by encountering opposites,/Each nullifying either!' Thus he finds that in the world

> hopes which dive,
> And fears which soar – faith, ruined through and through
> By doubt, and doubt, faith treads to dust – revive

> In some surprising sort.   (721–724)

Jochanan announces to his disciple Tsaddik his 'strange and
new/Discovery! – this life proves a wine-press – blends/Evil and
good.' The source of his new happiness is his perception that
apparent opposites are not after all incompatible:

> how seem
> Then, the intricacies of shade and shine,
> Oppugnant natures – Right and Wrong, we deem

> Irreconcilable?   (745–748)

Tsaddik concludes that as a special dispensation the spirit of
Jochanan is being allowed to linger half-way between life and
death,

> and, as a fine
> Interval shows where waters pure have met
>
> Waves brackish, in a mixture, sweet with brine,
> That's neither sea nor river but a taste
> Of both – so meet the earthly and divine
>
> And each is either.   (788–793)

The poem ends,

> Thus was brought about
>
> The sepulture of Rabbi Jochanan
> Thou hast him, – sinner-saint, live-dead, boy-man, –
> Schiphaz, on Bendimir, in Farzistan!

Thus the last part of the poem mirrors the reconciliation of opposites which has brought Jochanan his final happiness in a fusion of his own wisdom and the urchin's innocence. The climax of the poem is his vision of the ultimate knowledge, the beyond-earthly perspective which reconciles all contraries, shows the vanity of all striving, and presents the fusion of the actual and the ideal.

Rephan offers a fable whose implications are quite different. In a note Browning refers to a story by Jane Taylor called 'How it Strikes a Stranger'. The stranger in the story is a dweller on another planet who becomes an inhabitant of Earth. Learning that 'the alternative of happiness or misery in a future state' depends on his conduct on Earth he devotes himself with extreme earnestness to his religious duties, the consciousness of death being always before his eyes. Browning takes very little from the story except the idea of an inhabitant of another planet conceiving the wish to visit Earth. His poem, which is a dramatic monologue, is in fact entirely devoted to an account by the stranger of his previous life on the star which Browning calls Rephan. The stranger tells of a state of absolute perfection, where there was 'nowhere deficiency or excess', 'no want' and 'no growth', since all was already complete. There was no better or worse, no spring, no winter, no hope, no fear, nothing but happiness and serenity. Clearly Rephan possessed the tranquil freedom from conflict which Jochanan Hakkadosh welcomed as the ultimate gift of heaven. Yet the stranger speaks of 'the prison-gate of Rephan my Star,' and says

> How long
> I stagnated there where weak and strong,
> The wise and the foolish, right and wrong,
>
> Are merged alike in a neutral Best,
> Can I tell? (76–80)

He says that he longed for 'no sameness but difference/In thing
and thing,' for the possibility of improvement, for the chance to
'aspire yet never attain/To the object aimed at!' even for suffering, for doubts, hopes, fears and aspirations. The poem ends,

> When the trouble grew in my pregnant breast
> A voice said 'So wouldst thou strive, not rest?
>
> 'Burn and not smoulder, win by worth,
> Not rest content with a wealth that's dearth?
> Thou art past Rephan, thy place be Earth!'

At first reading this poem seems totally inconsistent with
Jochanan Hakkadosh. Some of the incompatibility is softened
when we remember that both poems represent the point of view
of an imaginary character. Each character has been empowered
by supernatural means to experience two ways of life and to
assess them both from his experience. Jochanan and the stranger
agree in describing an earthly life that is one of striving and incomplete realization of the ideal, and a life elsewhere that is one
of harmony and the complete resolution of contraries. Each
despises the world he lives in and longs for the qualities of the
other world. Jochanan attains to 'ignorance confirmed/By
knowledge': the stranger in *Rephan* longs to 'wring knowledge
from ignorance'. There is an obvious consistency in Browning's
definition of the human condition: what changes is the vantage-
point on human life which he adopts. From *Jochanan* the inference is that the imperfections of this world will be harmonized
only after death: from *Rephan* one may take the more obviously
bracing message that the imperfections of this world, rightly
viewed, are positively desirable.

Of course there is no reason why Browning should always say
the same thing, but the desire to abstract a coherent doctrine
from those poems in which he is clearly offering the fruits of his
speculations about human life is a very natural one, and constitutes a further source of difficulty.

If we go even further, and demand to know what Browning himself thought in his old age, as death came closer, *Reverie*, the last poem except for the *Epilogue* in his last volume of poems, is perhaps the place to look. It is also a poem which presents most of the different kinds of difficulty I have discussed in this chapter. Like *Jochanan* and *Rephan* it deals with the human lot, with the problem of evil, with the difficulty of arriving at certain knowledge, and with the proper faith for a man to have. None of these questions is easy, and Browning's handling of them makes them no easier. *Jochanan* and *Rephan* are comparatively comprehensible because Browning embodies the two contrasted ways of life in the experience of his imagined characters. In *Reverie* on the other hand he treats similar questions conceptually, offering us the attempts of a mind limited by its own restricted experience to break through by sheer speculative energy into a world differently organized. Instead of defined details of experience Browning is handling terms which resist definition, such as Power, Love, Good, Knowledge and Life. The difficulty of the poem, as one would expect, is that Browning is elucidating his own ideas of these key terms as he goes along, yet the elucidation cannot be followed by the reader without an understanding of the poem, which in turn depends on knowing the meaning of the key terms.

A prose summary is the clearest way of displaying the underlying structure of the poem, although it arrests the fluidity of idea which is the poem's most interesting feature. The first point to note is that we have no warrant for assuming that Browning is writing dramatically here, while there are various details, such as the title, which suggest that he is recording the play of his own thoughts.[1] In particular Stanza 7

> As the record from youth to age
> Of my own, the single soul –
> So the world's wide book: one page
> Deciphered explains the whole
> Of our common heritage.

picks up a favourite idea of Browning's, and one which is at the

---

[1] Cf. 'The evidence of divine power is everywhere about us; not so the evidence of divine love.' Browning, quoted by Mrs Orr, 'The Religious Opinions of Robert Browning', *Contemporary Review*, LX (1891), pp. 876–91.

centre of *Development*, the poem immediately before *Rephan* and *Reverie* in the *Asolando* volume. *Development* is certainly about Browning's own experience of life.

Browning begins with a simple declaration of trust ('I know') that 'Power' will one day 'come full in play' either on earth or in some other world (Stanzas 1–3). When this happens the imperfections of human knowledge will be overcome and he will know the truth certainly, not just about his own life, but about the whole of 'the legend of man', for one is a microcosm of the other (4–7). Thus if we want to know more about the development of the world we must first know ourselves. Browning, in his youth, surveyed the whole world of Nature, everything that forms the mind, and found complete intellectual satisfaction, since everything moved according to natural law. His mind therefore paid tribute to the 'Omnipotence' that had formed the world.[1] ('Omnipotence' is a crucial term in the poem. It shows how close 'Power' is to being simply a synonym for the Almighty.) (8–12) But his heart had reservations, being unable to ignore the evil in the world. Yet since what is good on Earth *is* good and indisputably deserves to be loved, Browning was able to understand how, if the mind could analyse how Power would complete its work, evil would seem unreal, a mere temporary veiling of the good. Mind therefore would be able, like an alchemist, to refine away the dross (evil) from the gold of Life (good) (13–15).

The Omnipotent is by definition unlimited, while Good is plainly limited and imperfect. Thus Man's desires do not concern Power, which is unchangeable. Rather his perpetual prayer is that Power will make Good equally omnipresent and unlimited. Man can then respond in his turn by paying the final tribute of unlimited Love (16–19). At present everything but Man seems self-sufficient, operating with an instinctive sense of its own part in the Universe. But if Man asks for Knowledge about the origins of the Earth he meets with the answer, 'Be ignorant ever!' (20–22, 26) But if on the other hand Browning looks for some solution to human problems he, like everybody else, knows what answer to make. Anybody can see that there is

[1] Cf. Hume once again: 'But as men farther exalt their idea of their divinity; it is their notion of his power and knowledge only, not of his goodness, which is improved.' (*Natural History of Religion*, Ch. XIII.)

one thing which could at a stroke end the suffering of mankind
and set to rest the anxieties of the inquiring mind. All that is
needed is for power to exert itself and all natural laws could be
suspended. Power could prevent chance, change and death, and
could clearly (since even the human mind can conceive this
idea) invent a new law of nature simply abolishing everything
which vexes or hampers mankind (22, 24, 27–28). Of course
this cannot be, yet to the human mind it seems that it would be so
easy if only unlimited universal Power were matched by unlimited universal Love. As it is, all man can do is speculate about
the possibility: if only he could be confident that Love, when
made fully manifest, would be equal in scope to the Power that is
evident everywhere in the world (29–31).[1] This at any rate,
Browning interjects, has been the pattern of his own development and changing views of the world (cf. Stanza 7). How does
it compare with that of mankind in general?

He assumes that the world would reply, 'If only we could
fathom the reason for God's creation of the world. At the
moment of creation Knowledge flooded the earth, doubt was
banished, and there was universal praise of God's Power. If only
Good had been equally unrepressed then nothing but praise
would have greeted a perfect Creation. If Good had displayed
itself as amply as Power there would be a single chorus of
praise.' (That is, just as Browning's mind was early able to
grasp the might of the creator but was unable to reconcile it

---

[1] With the whole of *Reverie*, but especially with this passage, cf. Richard Jefferies,
The Story of My Heart, Ch. III e.g. 'It is matter which is the supernatural, and
difficult of understanding. Why this clod of earth I hold in my hand? Why this
water which drops sparkling from my fingers dipped in the brook? Why are they at
all? When? How? What for? Matter is beyond understanding, mysterious, impenetrable; I touch it easily, comprehend it, no. Soul, mind – the thought, the idea –
is easily understood, it understands itself and is conscious . . . I can see nothing
astonishing in what are called miracles. Only those who are mesmerised by matter
can find a difficulty in such events. I am aware that the evidence for miracles is
logically and historically untrustworthy; I am not defending recorded miracles.
My point is that in principle I see no reason at all why they should not take place
this day. I do not even say that there are or ever have been miracles, but I maintain
that they would be perfectly natural. The wonder rather is that they do not happen
frequently. Consider the limitless conceptions of the soul: let it possess but the
power to realise those conceptions for one hour, and how little, how trifling, would
be the helping of the injured or the sick to regain health and happiness – merely to
think it. A soul-work would require but a thought.'

with the presence of evil, so mankind as a whole had rapidly
understood and praised the Power of the Creation but was unable to give equal praise to Good (31–34).) Indeed Browning
has found in the span of his own life what the world has found
in the span of history, that Power seems actually to be at war
with Love. His only recourse has been to evolve a faith that
there would some day be a reconciliation of opposites. This faith
is all that can give hope to man, overwhelmed by resistless
fact and the knowledge that 'all is effect of cause'.[1] Even this
knowledge he owes to the agency of the loveless Power he is
struggling against (35–38). Although Man in this situation
sometimes seems as passive as clay in the hand of the potter, has
even the most perfect moulded shape the pangs which are the
essential life of man? No, nor has it his ability to project his
thoughts towards the future and towards Heaven (39–40).

If this is so, then life for Man must mean waking, not sleeping,
rising, not resting, aspiring from the barren completeness of
Earth to the difficult steep of Heaven, where alone Power is
Love and rewards those who have aspired to a higher life than
the Earth offers. Browning has faith that this will be. He has
always known that Power existed. He has learned from his own
experience that, with an effort, Love can be as clearly discerned.
One day he will apprehend life's law for himself and for mankind, perhaps not on Earth, but if not, then 'yonder, worlds
away' (41–44).

The bearing of this poem on the topics discussed in *La Saisiaz*,
Jochanan Hakkadosh, *Development* and *Rephan* does not need
stressing, but one small point is perhaps worth attention. At the
end of *Reverie* Browning says that the true end of man is to

> press
> From earth's level where blindly creep
> Things perfected, more or less,
> To the heaven's height, far and steep,
>
> Where, amid what strifes and storms
> May wait the adventurous quest,
> Power is Love. (41–42)

[1] Cf. 'It is impossible to wrest the mind down to the same laws that rule pieces of
timber, water, or earth. They do not control the soul, however rigidly they may bind
matter.' *The Story of My Heart*, Ch. III.

It is interesting to note that the Earth is now characterized by 'Things perfected'. Power has operated with extraordinary efficiency, but the world that has resulted is blind and servile, whereas Browning is careful to stipulate that even in Heaven, where Power and Love are conjoined, 'strifes and storms' await 'the adventurous quest'. Jochanan's heaven of oppugnant natures fused into harmony is given its final amenity, the promise that man's spirit will not be obliterated in a world of universal perfection, but will still aspire.

(In passing, I might draw attention here to *Never the Time and the Place*, the short poem that follows *Jochanan Hakkadosh* in *Jocoseria*. It deals with the question of life and love after death with a more direct technique and from an entirely different point of view. The last lines –

> Or narrow if needs the house must be,
> Outside are the storms and strangers: we –
> Oh, close, safe, warm sleep I and she,
> – I and she!

present the grave as the final place of rest and reunion, narrow but not uncosy, in fact very much the same image as Hardy was later to exploit so expertly and so often.)

V

My account of *Reverie* is, I think, generally on the right lines, but there are several passages where I cannot be certain of the meaning: even if I were, an assessment of the poem would still not be easy. *Reverie* illustrates very clearly the senses in which Browning may truly be said to be a difficult poet. First, the field of ideas into which he takes the reader in this and similar poems – perception, the nature of inductive reasoning, the arguments in favour of natural religion, the existence of evil and pain, the sources of moral values, and so on – are notoriously treacherous ground for the philosopher and the Christian apologist alike. Yet very often Browning requires us not merely to grasp but to evaluate the arguments he is pursuing or presenting. He does not use a philosophical position, that is to say, simply as a starting-point from which he can write, or as an asserted 'given' which he will assume as true and will proceed to make real in his poetry, as Wordsworth, for example, does not argue the case for pantheism in *The Prelude*, nor Shelley the case for liberty in *Prometheus Unbound*. Browning, on the other hand, is much of the time conducting a seminar in verse, relying not on the power of his language nor on the force of his imagery to compel the reader's belief and attention but on the cogency of his dialectic, and on the excitement of the pursuit of an elusive idea, the excitement of the exploration of his own mind. Thus while compared with most later poets Browning's difficulties of diction and syntax are negligible, he is more difficult than they are in a different way – because he is writing about mental experiences of more subtlety and complexity than those they are writing about.

This leads to a further source of critical difficulty in reading Browning, the necessity of keeping two modes of expression in a constant relation. The reader of *La Saisiaz*, for example, is required to exert concentration to prevent the poem from separating into two parts, one primarily imaginative and evocative, the other primarily ratiocinative and speculative, and each appealing to the reader for a different, if not a mutually exclusive, kind of conviction. The most frequent form of despair in reading Browning comes from the feeling that the two modes have either separated completely or are both present but in conflict, either the demands of forensic necessity impeding the free exercise of the imagination, or the poet irresponsibly fantasticating and complicating the patient work of the metaphysician. This despair is aggravated when, as often, Browning seems to be depreciating the value of the intellect while appealing to the reasoning faculties of the reader.

These habits are in practice frequently found to be obstacles to the full enjoyment of the poems, but it is important to note that they are not *necessarily* so. It is not valid to complain, 'Browning distresses me because he is trying to do something that poetry is not supposed to do', for this assumes that there are agreed *a priori* limits to what poetry can and cannot do. Browning plainly does not accept any such assumption. In rejecting it he is implicitly asserting the right of the poet to write about whatever he likes. In particular he is trying to win back territory once held by poetry and now lost to prose. If this enterprise is worthwhile, as I believe it to be, then it is so irrespective of the success or failure of individual poems.

VI

I conclude this discussion of Browning's 'difficulty' conscious that the term itself is not helpful and is indeed in one sense actively misleading. It suggests a lapse on the poet's part, and that his friends should either clear him of the charge or at least enter a reasonably plausible plea in mitigation. But in writing these last four chapters it has been plain to me that I have been describing not an accidental blemish of style, or a regrettable disparity between conception and execution, but Browning's whole way of looking at the world and expressing what he sees, which calls neither for defence nor apology. The fairest verdict seems to be very close to Coleridge's celebrated comment on Milton:

> The reader of Milton must be always on his duty: he is surrounded with sense; it rises in every line; every word is to the purpose. There are no lazy intervals; all has been considered, and demands and merits observation. If this be called obscurity, let it be remembered that it is such an obscurity as is a compliment to the reader; not that vicious obscurity, which proceeds from a muddled head. [7]

Part Two

Part Two

Introduction

On the nineteenth century I offer no general chapter. The chapters on Wordsworth, Shelley and Keats (together with the relevant notes) do with regard to the Victorian age all that seems to me necessary to complete the account given in *New Bearings in English Poetry*. There seemed little point in going on to deal with Tennyson and the pre-Raphaelites in detail. They do not, in fact, lend themselves readily to the critical method of this book; and that it should be so is, I will risk suggesting, a reflection upon them rather than upon the method: their verse doesn't offer, characteristically, any very interesting local life for inspection. F. R. LEAVIS, *Revaluation*

It is convenient to gather together at this point and restate explicitly a number of ideas which are expressed in a less systematic way elsewhere in the book.

In the discussion of Browning's difficulties I found it necessary, for the sake of clarity, to discuss separately those difficulties which are encountered on the surface of his poetry and those which are due to his dramatic technique or to the complexity of the ideas he is handling. I was obliged, to borrow two disagreeable but useful words from art criticism, to consider in isolation the microstructure and the macrostructure of the poems [1]. At first sight it appears that the defender of Browning's poetry is in a cleft stick. For if he defines poetry in such a way as to justify concentration on the microstructure it is perfectly plain that Browning does not offer or try to offer the sort of cortical interest which would qualify as poetry under such a definition. To put it baldly, Browning's chief concern was normally for what he had to say rather than for the words he had to use to say it. 'Look through the sign', he says in the *Parleying with de Mandeville*, 'to the thing signified.' Yet if his advocates rely on the macrostructure it appears that such critics as Henry Jones and George Santayana have effectively disposed of Browning's pretensions to have anything worthwhile to say.

In the remainder of this book I shall consider this dilemma and the possible ways of resolving it.

I shall suggest for example in Chapter 10 that a careful examination of Browning's microstructure is not altogether unrewarding. In Chapter 8 and in the last section of Chapter 12 my object is to show that Jones and Santayana have not said the last word about Browning's religious and philosophical ideas. In particular I wish to show that Browning's poetry cannot be adequately described or assessed by a critic who considers any feature of it in isolation from the others.

It should be noticed that this is not a difficulty peculiar to Browning, but lies at the heart of every critical discussion of any work of art. It is all very well to proclaim the identity of Form and Content, but it is a very different thing to write criticism which considers both simultaneously and accords each its due importance. In literary criticism certain conventions are tacitly accepted – thus, in discussing poetry the microstructure is all that the serious critic need concern himself with: if he gets that right then what he says about it will be an adequate criticism of the poem as a whole. In discussing the novel, on the other hand, the actual language is not the critic's primary interest, although the more conscientious will draw attention to isolated verbal felicities or idiosyncrasies [2]. By good fortune our greatest author wrote in verse, which ensures that his microstructure is adequately attended to, and wrote plays, which forces the critic to think in terms of dramatic structure. Accordingly there is a considerable amount of Shakespearean criticism which performs the astonishingly difficult feat of discussing a work as a whole. But even with this example of what can be done critics have not surprisingly taken the easier path and preferred works which can be in some sense criticized from one point of view or the other but not both.

Most people would agree that no poet can be completely apprehended by such a partial approach, but some poets suffer more than others, and the Victorians, I think, at present suffer worst of all, simply because their major works are long poems which a modern reader must reject if he approaches them with any *exclusive* set of critical demands [3]. In Chapter 11 I offer my own attempts to discuss some of Browning's longer poems in rather more comprehensive terms than is usual.

✣ 8 ✣

Browning's optimism

MRS KNOWLES : Must we then go by implicit faith?
JOHNSON :   Why, Madam, the greatest part of our know-
             ledge is implicit faith.
                        BOSWELL, *Life of Johnson*, 15 April 1778

All human knowledge is uncertain, inexact, and partial.
                        BERTRAND RUSSELL, *Human Knowledge*, p. 507

Browning's fame as a poet, as Professor Boyd Litzinger has
shown [1], was closely involved with his reputation as an
optimistic philosopher. When the philosophy was discredited the
poetry suffered also, with the result that critics today seldom
offer to explore, much less to defend, those areas of Browning's
work that border on the religious or metaphysical. In this
chapter I shall consider in what sense Browning may be
correctly termed an optimist and suggest that his optimism is not
of a kind which necessarily damages his poetry.

I

There are two prevalent misconceptions of the nature of Browning's optimism, one simple, the other sophisticated. It might be
thought unnecessary to deal with the crude misjudgement which
ascribes to Browning himself opinions which he has put into the
mouth of his characters for dramatic purposes. Yet even such
eminent scholars as Wellek and Warren can allow themselves to
pronounce, 'The oracular sayings of Victorian poets such as
Browning, which have struck many readers as revelatory, often
turn out mere portable versions of primeval truths.' They illustrate this in a footnote, 'E.g. "God's in his Heaven; all's right
with the world" is an assertion that God has necessarily created

the best of all possible worlds' [2]. The inadequacy of this
reading can be demonstrated very easily in two ways. First,
simply by looking at the end of *Pippa Passes* as well as at the
beginning. Pippa's songs have throughout the play been used as
instruments of dramatic irony. At the beginning of her last
speech she has returned at nightfall to her room – 'Day's turn is
over, now arrives the night's' – and reflects on the events of the
day in terms deliberately designed to call in question the imagery
of her earlier carefree song:

> The bee with his comb,
> The mouse at her dray,
> The grub in his tomb,
> Wile winter away;
> But the fire-fly and hedge-shrew and lob-worm, I pray,
> How fare they? . . .
> The summer of life so easy to spend,
> And care for tomorrow so soon put away!
> But winter hastens at summer's end,
> And fire-fly, hedge-shrew, lob-worm, pray,
> How fare they?
>
> (IV, 239–244, 247–251)

In Chapter 2 I have shown also why Wellek and Warren's procedure is generally invalid: my conclusions may be summed up
by pointing out that if their method was justifiable it could be
used equally well to establish Browning's misanthropy by
attributing to him the sentiments of the closing lines of Fra
Celestino's sermon:

> But, for one prize, best meed of mightiest man,
> Arch-object of ambition, – earthly praise,
> Repute o' the world, the flourish of loud trump,
> The softer social fluting, – Oh, for these,
> – No, my friends! Fame, – that bubble which, world-wide
> Each blows and bids his neighbour lend a breath,
> That so he haply may behold thereon
> One more enlarged distorted false fool's-face,
> Until some glassy nothing grown as big
> Send by a touch the imperishable to suds, –
> No, in renouncing fame, my loss was light,
> Choosing obscurity, my chance was well.
>
> (*The Ring and the Book*, XII, 635–646)

Even when the speaker appears to be little more than a formal disguise for Browning himself it is dangerous to conclude that the opinions he expresses are in fact Browning's own. *Rabbi Ben Ezra*, for example, is at first sight completely without the characteristic refraction of vision which normally distinguishes the speaker's views from the poet's. The Rabbi appears to be simply a very holy, very old man, the apotheosis of mature wisdom, who is made the mouthpiece of Browning's profoundest reflections on the human condition. Yet the simple assumption that every statement made by the Rabbi is a statement of Browning's own opinions is without warrant: it would be more accurate to say that what the Rabbi confidently affirms is an expression of what Browning earnestly hopes may be true. The poem is an imaginative exercise, an attempt to express an ideal by a dramatic presentation of a man who has reached extreme old age without finding it necessary to despair [3].

Rabbi Ben Ezra begins by praising 'doubt' (16–18); by this he does not mean scepticism in matters of religion, but the quality of not being satisfied, of being uncertain how best to use the great gift of life. Man is distinct from the mere *consumers*, to whom satiety is an end in itself: he is more akin to God the provider. From this follows the Rabbi's whole argument – that man is a being with higher duties than the rest of creation but with correspondingly higher rewards. Browning, who was a man of fifty when he wrote the poem, imagines that a very old man who had led a holy life might have the conviction that he could recognize the perfection of the world. At the end of his life he would be able to look back and assess the world and his own achievements with an eye of complete comprehension, almost with the eye of God.

> All I could never be,
> All, men ignored in me,
> This, I was worth to God, whose wheel the pitcher shaped.
> Ay, note that Potter's wheel,
> That metaphor!
>
> (148–152)

In the last six stanzas of the poem Rabbi Ben Ezra examines the appropriateness of the metaphor of God as Potter and man as clay. It has often been observed that the immediate source of the

metaphor was FitzGerald's *Omar Khayyám*, which appeared in
1859; it appears certain to me that the entire poem is designed
as a direct counter to the *Rubáiyát*, one Eastern sage being employed to confute another. But this does not mean that all that
Rabbi Ben Ezra says is to be attributed directly to Browning,
any more than we can identify Omar with FitzGerald.

The significant feature of the poem is that Browning's
persona, having borrowed a metaphor for human experience,
sees that it can be interpreted in two contrary ways. One can
say either, 'Man is simply a pot on Time's wheel: the wheel
spins so fast that we must live for the moment', or 'Man is
simply a pot on Time's wheel: but the whole function of the
wheel is to shape a pot with a worthy use.' Characteristically
Rabbi Ben Ezra says 'Look not thou down but up' (175): that is,
when there is a choice of two alternatives choose the more hopeful. It is in this that we recognize his optimism, with which
there is no reason to suppose that Browning lacks sympathy.

Now while it is a fallacy to conclude from this and similar
monologues that Browning's was a poetry of unalloyed optimism and to condemn or praise it accordingly, it is true that in
general his satire is seldom directed against characters who take
a sanguine view of man's place in the universe, of God's providence, and of the ability of the ordinary man to live a life
pleasing to God and humanity by the exercise of a few simple
positive virtues. *Per contra* he seldom depicts without irony a
character who takes refuge in scepticism or casuistry.

II

If the arguments that I have put forward in earlier chapters are
accepted, it follows that many accounts of Browning as a Victorian Soame Jenyns can be set aside on the grounds that they
fail to take account of the dramatic element in his poems. It is
less easy to counter the suggestion that Browning's optimism
depends on his persistent undervaluing of the intellect in order
to justify his wilful refusal to see the world as it is. This is the
direction of attack encouraged by Sir Henry Jones, although
he offers also some elegant variations on the main line. His
book, *Browning as a Philosophical and Religious Teacher*,
appeared in 1891, just over a year after the poet's death. Its

influence on the assessment of Browning as a poet has been incalculable.[1] It is a long book, and apparently very thorough and detailed, but, as A. C. Bradley noticed, it is diffuse and repetitive. The main argument which Jones is concerned to establish runs on these lines. 'Browning tries to demonstrate that there is an utter severance between the intellect and the emotions, between the heart and the head: that the heart is an infallible guide to conduct and the intellect worthless. Logically his contempt for the intellect should lead him to complete agnosticism and pessimism: in fact he arbitrarily asserts an optimistic view of the world, holding that ignorance of God's purposes is essential to our moral growth.' Having set this up as Browning's position, Jones attempts to demolish it, and claims to have done so. His final chapter begins:

> I have tried to show that Browning's theory of life, in so far as it is expressed in his philosophical poems, rests on agnosticism; and that such a theory is inconsistent with the moral and religious interests of men. The idea that truth is unattainable was represented by Browning as a bulwark of the faith, but it proved on examination to be treacherous. His optimism was found to have no better foundation than personal conviction, which any one was free to deny, and which the poet could in no wise prove. The evidence of the heart, to which he appealed, was the evidence of an emotion severed from intelligence, and therefore, without any content whatsoever. 'The faith,' which he professed, was not the faith that anticipates and invites proof, but a faith which is incapable of proof. In casting doubt upon the validity of knowledge, he degraded the whole spiritual nature of man; for a love that is ignorant of its object is a blind impulse, and a moral consciousness that does not know the law is an impossible phantom – a self-contradiction. [4]
>
> (p. 342)

This severe indictment has been generally accepted as satis-

---

[1] The world's leading Browning scholars speak of the book in terms of unstinted praise: 'The most detailed, sympathetic, and yet judicious treatment of Browning's ideas upon philosophy and theology.' (DeVane, *Handbook*, p. 478); 'the most profound and excellent of books of this kind on Browning.' (ibid. p. 587); 'brilliant and profound'. (H. B. Charlton, 'Browning's Ethical Poetry', *Bulletin of the John Rylands Library*, XXVIII (1942–3), p. 43); '. . . a masterpiece of exposition'. (H. B. Charlton, 'Browning as a Poet of Religion', ibid. p. 272); '. . . a classic of literary criticism'. (Raymond, *Infinite Moment*, p. 38). See also C. R. Tracy, 'Browning's Heresies', *SP*, XXXIII (1936), p. 611.

factorily proved. In addition many critics have accepted the further implication that, since his optimism is valueless and his poetry is optimistic, his poetry is flawed by this central deficiency.

The first step in a defence of Browning against such a charge must be to indicate briefly the unsoundness of any argument which treats poems as if they were no more than prose essays, and takes as its only criterion logical or metaphysical consistency. Professor Jones himself admits the fallacy of ignoring Browning's imaginative presentation of ideas:

> Art is not a process, but a result: truth for it is immediate, and it neither admits nor demands any logical connection of ideas. . . . [Browning's] doctrine is offered in terms of art, and it cannot have any demonstrative force without violating the limits of art. . . . Still, it is not when he argues that Browning proves: it is when he sees, as a poet sees. . . . Browning's proofs are least convincing when he is most aware of his philosophical presuppositions; and a philosophical critic could well afford to agree with the critic of art, in relegating the demonstrating portions of his poems to the chaotic limbo lying between philosophy and poetry. (Chapter IV, pp. 89–90)

Now this is a statement of the case with the first part of which few people would disagree. Similarly when Jones says in his introductory remarks, 'The interpretation of a poet from first principles carries us beyond the limits of art; and by insisting on the unity of his work, more may be attributed to him, or demanded from him, than he properly owns', one can only agree again. Yet he continues, 'Nevertheless, among English poets there is no one who lends himself so easily, or so justly, to this way of treatment as Browning.' (p. 10) He does not offer to explain why it is just to treat Browning in this way, completely ignoring the admirable sentiments he expresses later in the book.

But even if we allow Professor Jones the right to treat the poems as essays in metaphysics, there are many unsatisfactory features in his book. I should like to mention two points especially, first the evidence which he offers in support of his case and secondly his treatment of that evidence.

III

Perhaps his most serious deficiency is that he makes no attempt to consider the whole of Browning's 'teachings' on religion and philosophy. He doesn't, for example, comment on Browning's distinctive views on such subjects as the historical evidences for Christianity, the relationship between the Church and the Christian, love between human beings, the relationship of ends and means, the importance of choice in the life of the individual and the allied problem of free will. Nor does he have much to say about such a characteristic tenet of Browning's as personal immortality. Indeed the innocent reader of Jones's book would reasonably but erroneously conclude that the only philosophical and religious topics that the poet treated with any seriousness were questions of perception and knowledge and the problem of evil.

The reason for this eccentric view of Browning's thought is that Jones limits his attention to a very small number of poems, a sample far too small to establish any general point whatever. The crucial steps of his argument are in effect drawn from the following poems: *Christmas-Eve and Easter-Day, La Saisiaz,* the *Parleying with Francis Furini, A Pillar at Sebzevar* and *A Bean-Stripe* (both from *Ferishtah's Fancies*), and *Reverie* (from *Asolando*). He ignores or hardly considers such important poems as *Caliban upon Setebos,* the *Epilogue* to *Dramatis Personae, Bishop Blougram's Apology, Fifine,* most of the *Parleyings,* and *Mr. Sludge, 'The Medium',* to name only a few. It will be noticed that the poems which he does choose are in an obvious sense not typical of Browning, since they are not dramatic in form.[1]

Jones's avoidance of these important poems not only leads him to ignore large tracts of Browning's more metaphysical poetry, but sends him astray in his treatment of the poems he does choose to deal with. While it is true that each of Browning's poems is self-sufficient, it is also true that in the later poems, such as those in *Ferishtah's Fancies,* Browning is using a vocabulary which he has forged in his major poems. To take only the most obvious examples, 'love' in Browning is not simply a mindless instinct, ignorant of its object: it comes almost to stand for everything that is valuable in human life. Similarly, we have learned from Browning's great gallery of sophists and

---

[1] This at least saves Jones from the elementary error of ascribing the speaker's sentiments directly to the poet, although he twice quotes 'God's in his heaven' etc. as if it were a simple statement of a cheering truth.

casuists that by 'knowledge' he means particularly the kind of
unreal ratiocination which tries to replace the experience of the
individual by an abstract generalization. If we have read and
comprehended the whole body of Browning's work and appreciated his constant efforts to *animate* his terms, we shall not misunderstand Browning's exaltation of love at the expense of
knowledge. Although the whole of his last chapter implicitly
admits the need of a broader approach, Jones attempts hardly
any interpretation of this kind. The only poems he uses with
any consistency for the purpose of explaining Browning's life-
long attempts to supply a full definition of these crucial elements
in his vocabulary are *A Death in the Desert* and the Pope's
monologue from *The Ring and the Book*.

Jones, then, limits himself to a small fraction of Browning's
work, but even in the poems which he considers with some care
he leaves out of account passages which do not accord with the
main lines of his argument [5]. He is not concerned to interpret
Browning's speculations, much less to illuminate the poems. His
continual labour is to sift through a few pieces and to extract
from them those passages which suit his purposes. Upon this
material he imposes a rigid pattern, forcing a definite opposition
where Browning is content to indicate a disharmony. As I have
indicated, his basic fallacy is to treat the poet as a rival philosopher. Jones says (p. 275), 'He offers a definite theory to
which he claims attention . . . on the ground that it is a true
exposition of the moral nature of man. . . . Browning definitely
states, and endeavours to demonstrate a theory of knowledge, a
theory of the relation of knowledge to morality, and a theory of
the nature of evil.' But this is not so. Browning has written a
number of poems for which part of his raw material was arguments about these subjects. They were written at various times
and in varying tones, some in his own person, some not, and in
each poem Browning made use of the ideas which suited the
poem best. What the poems have to say about life they say, not
by making a series of flat theoretical statements about ethical
problems, but by presenting an enactment of a complex and
fluid situation. They were not intended to be literally consistent with each other, much less to form an ordered philosophic
system. The fact that Jones can produce a logical dilemma by
setting a snippet from one poem against a snippet from another

shows not the confusion of Browning's thought but the un-soundness of Jones's method. His book, *The Philosophy of Lotze* (1895), a thorough and penetrating critique, covers very much the same ground as his *Browning*, and repeats some of his earlier arguments. In each work he is in effect defending Hegel by attacking those who found Idealism simply a collection of 'pale and vacant general ideas': his fallacy is to suppose that the poet and the philosopher can be answered by the same arguments.

IV

So much for Professor Jones's presentation of Browning's 'philosophy': I turn now to his attempts to refute it. It is notable that even when he has simplified the poet's ideas and erected them into a suitable argument he is often unable to show their error. For example, in a central passage of the book (pp. 237–41), Jones deals with Browning's theories of the imperfection of human knowledge. Browning emphasizes the difficulty of being certain of more than one's own existence, and of maintaining that one's own judgement is more accurate than another's or that the laws that govern one's own life govern anybody else's. These are valid questions, and Browning raises them to show how difficult it is for the intellect to arrive at general truths. In short he points out a celebrated metaphysical dilemma. Jones's comment on this is that if Browning carries this line of reasoning to a logical conclusion he will find himself in a celebrated metaphysical dilemma.

Similarly on pp. 310–11, Jones reverts to a consideration of Browning's difficulty in reconciling perfect knowledge with moral responsibility. He says, 'It is impossible to conceive how the conduct of a being who is moral, would be affected by absolute knowledge; or, indeed, to conceive the existence of such a being. . . . A being so constituted would be an agglomerate of utterly disparate elements, the interaction of which, in a single character, it would be impossible to make intelligible.' But this is precisely the point Browning is making – that we cannot conceive moral responsibility co-existing with complete knowledge and must therefore suppose that lack of certain knowledge is a necessary condition of moral development and thus not irreconcilable with the idea of a just God. On this line of speculation

Jones comments in a favourite phrase [6], 'I do not stay here to inquire whether sure knowledge would really have this disastrous effect of destroying morality, or whether its failure does not rather imply the possibility of a moral life.' Nowhere in the book does he show directly that Browning is at fault in supposing that, if retribution followed Sin as certainly as pain followed fire and it were as certainly known that this was so, then avoiding Sin would be of as little moral worth as avoiding fire is now.

Again, after his inaccurate summary of *A Bean-Stripe* Jones says, 'I shall not pause at present to examine the value of this new form of the old argument, "*Ex contingentia mundi*".' In fact he never resolves the paradox which Browning deals with in the poem. His reply is always that rightly viewed the paradox vanishes, but his own explanations of the correct point of view cause more confusion than they remove. For instance, one of Browning's great problems is how to argue from his own experience to a truth which will hold good for other people, that is, how to develop a generally valid argument on the basis of subjective knowledge. In Chapter IX Jones attempts a criticism of Browning's view of knowledge, apparently including the poet among the 'relativists, phenomenalists, agnostics, sceptics, Kantians [7] or neo-Kantians – all the crowd of thinkers who cry down the human intellect.' Here Jones seems to be considering Browning as a subjective idealist, whose work will result in reducing all Idealism to the absurdity of solipsism.

He sees the difficulty which confronted Browning and which eventually led him to doubt the infallibility of intellectual processes, but, declaring that 'the method of fixed alternatives' is 'inapplicable', refuses to offer any direct refutation of Browning's main point that human knowledge is conditioned and relative. Instead he first asserts that 'our thought is essentially connected with reality' (p. 297) and then (p. 299) embarks on a long parallel between thought and the moral consciousness:

> In morality (as also is the case in knowledge) the moral ideal, or the objective law of goodness, grows in richness and fulness of content with the individual who apprehends it. *His* moral world is the counterpart of *his* moral growth as a character. Goodness *for him* directly depends upon his recognition of it. . . . In morals, as in knowledge, the mind of man constructs its own world. And yet . . . *the moral law does not vanish and reappear with its recognition by*

> *mankind.* . . . With the extinction of self-consciousness all moral goodness is extinguished. The same holds true of reality.

This seems to me indistinguishable from the subjectivism which Jones criticized in Browning, although it will be observed that the sentence I have italicized runs counter to the rest of the argument. Jones proceeds to enlarge at considerable length on his basic premise that 'the negative has no meaning, except as the expression of a deeper affirmative.' He makes the application to Browning by saying,

> If he acknowledges that the highest revealed itself to man, on the practical side, as love; he does not see that it has also manifested itself to man on the theoretical side, as reason. The self-communication of the Infinite is incomplete; love is a quality of God, intelligence a quality of man; hence, on one side, there is no limit to achievement, but on the other there is impotence. Human nature is absolutely divided against itself; and the division, as we have already seen, is not between flesh and spirit, but between a love which is God's own and perfect, and an intelligence which is merely man's and altogether weak and deceptive. (p. 307)

These last two sentences, which are presumably Jones's version of what Browning thinks, are not refuted by the first sentence which Jones offers as a solution of the dilemma, for it evades the precise difficulties which Browning continually confronts – 'If both love and the intelligence are manifestations of the Infinite how is it that they so often prompt a man in different directions? And while they can theoretically be reconciled as aspects of the same harmonious whole, if in practice a man is forced to choose between them, as in fact often happens, which is he to choose?' In short Jones's concern is with the soundness of a metaphysical theory: Browning's concern is with life, which he sees as a succession of extraordinarily difficult ethical choices.[1]

Jones, in the course of a brief but entertaining summary of European thought [8], says that with the new light of the philosopher-poets of Germany 'the antagonism of hard alternatives was at an end'. To Jones this meant the reconciliation of opposites in statements such as, 'The negative implies the affirmative and is its effect' (p. 141), and, 'The process towards

---

[1] Cf. 'Duty and love, one broad way, were the best –
    Who doubts? But one or other was to choose'
    (*Bifurcation*, 17–18)

truth by man is the process of truth *in* man: the movement of knowledge towards reality is the movement of reality into knowledge.' (p. 304) Browning, although usually classified as an Idealist, is not content with vapid formulas of this kind for reconciling individual responsibility with Divine omnipresence. To Jones's affirmation 'The individual does not institute the moral law; he finds it to be written both within and without him' (p. 142), Browning opposes simply a series of instances of conflict between the 'law within' and the 'law without'.[1]

Browning then, as indeed is a commonplace of criticism, is concerned with men as individuals and with their relationships to their fellow men. Jones, on the contrary, is always concerned to avoid recognition of men as individuals. In Chapter III he offers a typically disingenuous evasion of a central difficulty of Hegelianism, that it diminishes the status of the individual. He writes 'Thus, when spirit is spiritually discerned, it is seen that man is bound to man in a union closer than any physical organism can show; while "the individual," in the old sense of a being *opposed* to society and *opposed* to the world, is found to be a fiction of abstract thought, not discoverable anywhere, because not real.' A few pages later he says, 'Individualism is now detected as scepticism and moral chaos in disguise.'[2]

From such a point of view Browning is clearly in error, since he insists on the reality of the individual as the very foundation stone of all knowledge. His skill in philosophical argument may be called in question, but his grasp of life as it is never falters. His poetry is grounded in his own experience; if therefore he encounters a paradox in his own nature or in his picture of the world or in his apprehension of God, he does not attempt to resolve it in the interests of the tidiness of a metaphysical theory, but gives it full expression.

For example, he constantly makes the distinction between certain knowledge and religious faith, which he finds in his own

[1] Cf.

> White shall not neutralize the black, nor good
> Compensate bad in man, absolve him so:
> Life's business being just the terrible choice.
> (*The Ring and the Book*, X, 1236–38)

[2] It is only fair to say that Jones's attack on individualism at this point apparently has its origin in his conviction that individualism is necessarily incompatible with social responsibility.

experience to be a unique order of belief. Jones as persistently affects to misunderstand this vital distinction. I have already quoted the passage in which he says of Browning, ' "The faith," which he professed, was not the faith that anticipates and invites proof, but a faith which is incapable of proof.' But Browning, like most people, would deny that any faith was required to believe that which could be demonstrated.[1] For him an act of trust was an essential element in faith: this meant believing even when the reason withheld its assent. When his poetry has a design upon the reader, that design is very often to convince him of the contingent nature of the reason and thus to make it easier for him to perform the decisive act of trust.

In the same way Jones complains about Browning's optimism that it 'was found to have no better foundation than personal conviction, which any one was free to deny, and which the poet could in no wise prove.' Jones does not, of course, show that there is any proof of an optimistic view of the world. In default of this, what better foundation could a man have than personal conviction, or, indeed, without personal conviction, what foundation at all?

V

I should not, however, like to suggest that nothing is to be learned from the book, especially in view of the generosity of the heading to Chapter XI.[2] Jones establishes the following useful points. First that *A Bean-Stripe*,[3] *A Pillar at Sebzevar*, and the

---

[1] In this connection it is interesting to compare Coleridge (*Biographia Literaria*, Ch. X), as quoted in Chapter 9, p. 219. See also *Christmas-Eve*, Section V:

> [God's plan was] To create man and then leave him
> Able, His own word saith, to grieve Him,
> But able to glorify Him too,
> As a mere machine could never do,
> That prayed or praised, all unaware
> Of its fitness for aught but praise and prayer,
> Made perfect as a thing of course.

Jones quotes this passage with approval in his concluding chapter.

[2] Jones quotes *Andrea del Sarto*: 'Well, I can fancy how he did it all. . . . He means right – that, a child may understand.'

[3] Browning's metaphor of the beans which are partly white and partly black has come in for particularly severe handling. It is perhaps worth noting here that Melville, who is not usually accused of a facile optimism, uses a similar image in 'The Encantadas': '. . . Even the tortoise, dark and melancholy as it is upon the back,

Parleying with Francis Furini are not the best of Browning. Jones has, as I say, treated the poems unfairly, but even so most readers will agree that his unfavourable verdict on them has some critical justification. Secondly, he stresses the irrationality of Browning's optimism, indeed of all his ethical and metaphysical speculations. As I have said, Browning would not have denied this, arguing that faith transcends logic: this is a position which he has reached with open eyes and by diligent self-searching, and with continual insistence on the need for each individual to discover its truth for himself. Nevertheless Jones properly draws attention to the *voulu* element in Browning's cheerfulness, which brings it at times close to heartiness. It is true to say that a quality in which Browning is deficient is the determination to follow his reason steadfastly even when it is in conflict with all he most values. But to say this, of course, is simply to describe the converse of one of his most striking gifts.

Thirdly, Jones's book is valuable if it encourages or provokes readers to look on Browning's works not as metrical tracts from which stray sentences are to be selected as ethical mottoes but as poems which happen to take a metaphysical dilemma as their starting-point.

Finally Jones rightly emphasizes, as every critic has done, the importance of love in Browning's poetry, and the remarkable way in which Browning continually suggests the correspondence between human love and divine love, which is the *raison d'être* of the Universe, a correspondence which at once ennobles human love and makes divine love more intelligible. Indeed in Chapter VI and in most of Chapter XI Jones offers a substantially accurate summary of the ideas in many of Browning's important poems: it is hard to understand how he reconciles his generous tributes

---

still possesses a bright side; its calipee or breast-plate being sometimes of a faint yellowish or golden tinge. Moreover, everyone knows that tortoises as well as turtle are of such a make, that if you but put them on their backs you thereby expose their bright sides without the possibility of their recovering themselves, and turning into view the other. But after you have done this, and because you have done this, you should not swear that the tortoise has no dark side. Enjoy the bright, keep it turned up perpetually if you can, but be honest, and don't deny the black. Neither should he, who cannot turn the tortoise from its natural position so as to hide the darker and expose its livelier aspect, like a great October pumpkin in the sun, for that cause declare the creature to be one total inky blot. The tortoise is both black and bright.' (Sketch Second)

to the poet's insight in these chapters with his general condemnations elsewhere in the book.

VI

With every allowance made for its good points Jones's book still stands condemned as fundamentally defective in method and infinitely mischievous in effect. Its claim to enlighten the reader on Browning as a philosophical and religious teacher is weakest precisely where expert assistance would be most helpful, on the extremely difficult point of the relation of Browning's metaphysical and epistemological theories to his religious beliefs. Not only does Jones fail to see the distinction which, in some poems, Browning makes between logical conviction and an act of faith, but he apparently does not realize the bearing of the attacks which, in other poems, Browning makes upon the reason in the interests of faith. Browning makes one point repeatedly, that all our intellectual processes are incapable of proof [9] – we cannot *prove* that the external world exists; we cannot *prove* the law of cause and effect, we cannot *prove* that other people even see the world as we do, much less that they ought to agree with our moral and religious conclusions; we cannot *prove* that our wills are free; we cannot even *prove* that we are awake. But we know that it is unthinkable to live as if all these points were open questions, and so we bridge the gap by an act of faith.

Browning is prepared to concede that to live at all one must accept certain basic assumptions unproved, but he does not allow the reader to forget the existence of these initial acts of faith. If then religion is attacked in the name of reason, he points out that reason itself is based on an act of trust, and argues that if everyone accepts unprovable intellectual postulates because life would be meaningless unless one did, then he is himself justified in accepting unprovable postulates about religion and the nature of man because his life would be meaningless unless he did.

Thus at the core of Browning's philosophical and speculative poems we find not an impulsive and emotional denial of man's intellectual responsibilities but a constant awareness of his intellectual limitations.[1] This, together with a mind incapable of

[1] Cf. Coleridge again: 'Wherever the forms of reasoning appropriate only to the *natural* world are applied to *spiritual* realities, it may be truly said, that the more

drawing comfort from dogma, forces Browning always into a position of questioning and doubting. He characteristically finds himself in a situation where he must choose between hope and utter despair.

The argument, then, of Browning's metaphysical poetry is not, as Jones represents it, a simple Panglossian optimism, accompanied by a deliberate smothering of the reason lest it should inconveniently draw attention to certain deficiencies of the Creation. On the contrary its origin is very often in a mood of grief or anxiety, doubt or distress, caused perhaps by the death of someone near to him, or by a sceptical attack on religion, or by a sudden realization of the problems of pain or evil [10]. A rational consideration of such events seems to constrain man to a pessimistic view of the world. By temperament Browning reacted to them not by listless acquiescence but by an energetic attempt to establish from his total experience of life a picture of the world which should not be entirely hopeless.[1] To do this he used all the resources of his intellect, exploring possible solutions, and never expecting short answers to difficult problems. A favourite pattern is for this intellectual analysis to continue until, as it were mentally exhausted, the poet falls back on Montaigne's question, 'Que scais-je?' It is only when he has proved, or even enacted,

---

strictly logical the reasoning is in all its *parts*, the more irrational it is as a *whole.*' *Aids to Reflection*, ('Aphorisms on Spiritual Religion', Reflections Introductory to Aphorism X.) See also Robert Langbaum, 'Browning and the Question of Myth', *PMLA*, LXXI (1966), pp. 575–84, e.g.: 'He [Browning] is a poet of enduring interest – partly because his very faults show that he was turning analytic thought against itself, that he understood what had to be done.' (582)

[1] That is, he, like most of his contemporaries, accepts as an axiom that the world has a *raison d'être*. This is, of course, an optimistic assumption, but Browning's hopefulness is not of the same order as, for example, the retrospective satisfaction of Tennyson,

> Fifty years of ever-broadening Commerce!
> Fifty years of ever-brightening Science!
> Fifty years of ever-widening Empire!
> (*On the Jubilee of Queen Victoria*, IX)

or Gladstone's sanguine faith in the inevitability of progress: 'Above all things, men and women, believe me, the world grows better from century to century, because God reigns supreme from generation to generation. Let pessimism be absent from our minds, and let optimism throw its glory over all our lives henceforth and ever.' (Quoted in E. von Kuehnelt-Leddihn, *Liberty or Equality* (London, 1952), p. 12: I owe this reference to the kindness of Mr Brian Wormald.)

the inefficiency of the intellectual processes, that Browning decides to perform the crucial act of trust. Even then he is fully aware of what he is doing, as the last stanza of the *Epilogue* to *Ferishtah's Fancies* clearly shows.

This general pattern is of course varied enormously in the individual poems. In many of them there is a genuine sense that Browning is not ignoring but transcending the knowledge of the head: in others it is, I think, fair to complain that the resolution which Browning accepts is too easy. But in all of them the reader senses that Browning's starting-point is not a conviction but a question, that he has brought to it a mind unshackled by prejudice, and that his final position is held sincerely but undogmatically. It is characteristic of Browning that what he wants to maintain is not that everything is for the best in the best of all possible worlds, but that for himself personally there is still room, if not for certainty, at least for hope.

Jones, as I have shown, takes issue with this modest claim, accusing Browning simultaneously of pernicious scepticism and pernicious optimism. Once we have realized the incompleteness and inaccuracy of his argument, the way is open for a reconsideration of those poems in which Browning offers such resolutions as a poet may of the great paradoxes of human thought.

❦ 9 ❦

Browning's poems on Christianity and other ethical systems

No matter what paper they had before them, in the discussion they always got into Browning's optimistic theology.

G. B. SHAW, on the London Browning Society

Zion, like Rome, is Niebuhrized.

MELVILLE, *Clarel* Pt 1, sect. xxxiv

The real problems of art are always concrete moral problems.

ALLEN TATE

> Put by the curtains, look within my vail;
> Turn up my metaphors, and do not fail
> There, if thou seekest them, such things to find,
> As will be helpful to an honest mind.

BUNYAN, The Conclusion to the
First Part of *The Pilgrim's Progress*

Sir Henry Jones, who died in 1922, would be delighted to know that his work on Browning was not in vain. Echoes of his voice can be heard even in our own time. For example, in the course of an essay entitled 'Some Instances of Poetic Vulgarity'[1] Robert Graves writes, 'As the *Dictionary of National Biography* notes: "Browning's poems everywhere attested unflinching optimism".' No doubt most of Mr Graves's mind was occupied at the time by a natural concern to amuse his young audience, but it seems to me that to take a single sentence from an out-of-date work of reference and to treat it as a substitute for a serious reading of

---

[1] *Mammon and the Black Goddess* (London, 1965), pp. 55–68. The essay is a re-printing of a lecture given in Oxford at a time when Mr Graves was Professor of Poetry. He is better known as a novelist.

the poems in which for forty years Browning painfully examines his own grounds for hope, is as pat an example as one could find of vulgarity in criticism. It serves to show how an unthinking generalization can be perpetuated by those who are too complacent or too lazy to re-examine the particulars on which it is supposed to be based.

In the preceding chapter I have tried to rebut Jones by following the course of his argument, which moved indifferently between religion and philosophy. In this chapter I shall look at a number of poems and a number of topics which Jones ignored, and consider a question which he evades, that of whether the sort of general account of 'Browning's thought' which he offers has any critical status at all.

I

It is not possible to derive from Browning's works any coherent body of Christian doctrine which can be ascribed to the poet as a consistent statement of religious belief [1]. This is not surprising: he wrote about religion for over fifty years and was never in that time a committed subscriber to any fixed system of doctrine. Each of his poems moreover is a self-subsistent work, determined by its own nature and not by any requirement to harmonize with earlier or later poems.

It follows then that what is wanted is a study of each of Browning's poems about religious subjects, not a study of Browning as a religious teacher. The object is neither to use the poems to discover what Browning's personal religious life was like[1] nor to try to extract from the poems a body of teaching which can be compactly expressed in prose and used as a substitute for the poems, either to live by or to argue from or to demolish.

This last point is perhaps sufficiently obvious today. Indeed the assumption on which it rests is so general in modern theories

[1] This inquiry is impertinent in both senses. The details of Browning's relation to his subject are less important than the result of that relation. Browning publishes the simple work of art, and naturally provides no explanation of its part in a complex of emotions and objects. The poem itself is the thing he wants us to examine and take into our lives. Even if we had Shakespeare's lost essay 'How I Came to Write *Hamlet*' it would not alter the play. It is similarly beside the point to conjecture *why* Browning wrote, say, *Fifine at the Fair*.

of literature[1] that there is a danger of running to the other extreme and deliberately discussing the poems without reference to the ideas which constitute a vital part of them. It is clear that the ideal is to discuss all or most of the individual poems, trying to see each simultaneously as statement and as a formal organization of words. From a series of studies of this kind a pattern may emerge. If it does not, then there is no point in trying to impose one: but if it does it may have a limited value, especially for readers not well acquainted with the poetry, just as a map has some value for people before they learn their own way about. The generalizations that follow are of this kind – useful, I hope, but to be rejected as soon as possible in favour of the poems themselves.

Most of the important things that Browning has to say about the nature of belief and the claims of Christianity are to be understood from a careful reading of two poems, *Christmas-Eve and Easter-Day* (1850) and *A Death in the Desert* (1864). It is particularly instructive to notice the strategy of each poem and to see how far our assessment of the ideas which Browning examines is controlled by the way in which he presents them.

The twin poems *Christmas-Eve* and *Easter-Day* are closely connected in manner and theme. In the first the speaker enters a Dissenting chapel on Christmas Eve and finds the preacher and the congregation equally distasteful. He falls asleep there, and dreams first of a service in the Church of Rome and then of a lecture by a Higher Critic. These displease him as much as the Dissenters, but, when he reflects, he is able to see that there is some good in all three forms of worship. From this 'mild indifferentism' he is shaken to a realization that 'Needs must there be one way, our chief/Best way of worship.' (XX) At this he wakes and chooses as his own way of worship that of the chapel in which he finds himself. It is hard not to feel that in this poem Browning is writing about his own experience, especially as in Section XXII he identifies the speaker with the writer of the poem. While the choice of modes of worship is not of the first importance, except as marking out very broadly the kind of

---

[1] It is a point worth speculating on whether the predominantly linguistic or aesthetic tradition in modern criticism drew part of its force from a specific reaction against the Browning Societies and a deliberate repudiation of their treatment of Browning as a teacher whose poetry had value only as doctrine.

Christianity – lower than Catholicism, but certainly higher than deism – that appealed to Browning in 1850, the reflections to which the various religions give rise are of great interest [2].

For example, in Section V, after the speaker has rejected in disgust the preaching in the chapel, he talks of the origins of his own religious faith and relates that even in youth he was aware of the power of God made manifest in his Creation,

> Yet felt in my heart, amid all its sense
> Of that power, an equal evidence
> That His love, there too, was the nobler dower.
> For the loving worm within its clod,
> Were diviner than a loveless god
> Amid his worlds, I will dare to say.

This is a theme to which Browning recurs again and again, using part or whole of the following circle of ideas according to the needs of the poem. 'Love is the noblest human quality. God, if he exists, must, if he is God at all, be at least as capable of loving as his creatures. Therefore God is a God of Love. We can not only prove this intellectually, but establish it empirically, for God has shown us his love by sending Christ into the world. This we recognize as a supreme act of love. What is required of us in return is that we should also love God. When we love God or love our fellow-men we are ourselves closer to God. Therefore Love is the noblest human quality.' It is clear that a chain of reasoning of this kind can be used not only to lead from the premise that Christ died for our sins to the conclusion that love is the supreme human activity but also to lead from the premise that man is capable of loving to the conclusion that God loves man.[1]

A substantial part of this cycle of thought and feeling is to be found in Section V of *Christmas-Eve*, together with another idea which Browning often used elsewhere, the idea that man is

[1] In some later poems the idea of God is eliminated, and the sorites runs:

> Love is a certain thing, since we can be sure that it exists;
> Certain things are true things;
> Anything true partakes of absolute truth;
> Therefore by loving we can put ourselves outside the flux of time, and become acquainted with the eternal;
> Love is thus the noblest human quality.

created free to praise God or not: if he had not this freedom his praise would be of no value. This is the counterpart of the idea that certainty in matters of faith would *compel* belief and a belief so compelled would be worthless. Browning, of course, does not use this argument as an incitement to scepticism, as if doubt were *per se* good, but as a justification of God's ways in refusing to vouchsafe to man incontrovertible proofs of His existence.

In Sections XI and XII, in which the speaker rejects the form of worship of the Church of Rome, Browning is careful to emphasize that while the speaker is right to reject the extravagances of the Catholic services, 'the raree-show of Peter's successor', it is nevertheless important to remember what good the Church of Rome has done. 'I see the error; but above/The scope of error, see the love.' The bitter hostility of the early Church to the Classical intellect and even the destruction of Classical works of art can, with a charitable eye, be regarded as excesses caused by an overpowering love of God, and hence as venial. The complicated metaphor of the statue and the bust in Section XII emphasizes this point, since it implies that it is better for men to aim at the highest, even if their achievement will inevitably be incomplete, because at least this presents the world with an enlarged idea of *part* of human capacity. Thus Rome, for all its shortcomings, gave mankind, especially in its early days, some idea of the capacities of the human heart for love. The general argument implicit in the metaphor is, of course, one with which Browning often expressed his sympathy.

The next part of the poem, Sections XIII to XVII, is most difficult, and this for a reason not uncommon in Browning's religious verse. He is describing and rejecting the findings of the Higher Critics, but his own mistrust of dogma leads him to sympathize with many of the arguments put forward by the sceptics. Accordingly he has to make some rather close distinctions to define his own position. In Sections XVI and XVII he says that while organized religions may obscure the truth they are at least based on love and worship, whereas the Higher Criticism leaves us a vacuum. To say, as the Higher Critics allege, that Christ was merely man but still worthy of our respect leads to untold difficulties. For example, Christ did not say anything which had not been said already, and said by men who did not think that they were God. Moreover if Christ's goodness is no more than we should expect of a man, why is he to be revered? Had Christ invented right action and had everybody acquiesced in his definition of right and wrong, then you might worship him. But in fact right and wrong action is decided by the common conscience, and it would be just as absurd to worship Christ for having *originated* morality as it would be to worship Harvey for having *invented* the circulation of the blood. A 'human' Christ would of course rightly be respected for his unique achievement, which was to keep his mind pure, just as Shakespeare, for example, had his unique achievement. All human achievements are God's gifts, but no accumulation of faculties can bridge the gap between creature and creator. The only way in which we can aspire upwards is by spiritual growth. The section ends with the celebrated passage,

> What is left for us, save, in growth
> Of soul, to rise up, far past both,
> From the gift looking to the Giver,
> And from the cistern to the River,
> And from the finite to Infinity,
> And from man's dust to God's divinity?

In Section XVII Browning characteristically manipulates this idea, arguing that God depends on man as much as man on God. Man exists to do his Creator's will, of which there would be no evidence were it not for the 'inner sense' of man, a faculty so powerful that it could detect the will of God even if by some ill-chance the opposite had been proclaimed as God's law, for even the wickedest man has in his own conscience a powerful knowledge of right and wrong.

> And thence I conclude that the real God-function
> Is to furnish a motive and injunction
> For practising what we know already.

Christ provides this motive, and he does it by saying not 'Believe in abstract virtues' but 'Believe in me'. In short we are asked not to believe in Love but *to love*. This is as important to God as it is to man: as the love-cycle suggests, God and man are interdependent. 'Though he is so bright and we are so dim/We are made in his image to witness him.'

In Section XX Browning makes use of an idea which he ex-

plores again and again in his later poetry. Having recognized
that he must communicate the truth as he sees it to his fellows,
he consoles himself with the reflection that even if he fails in this
task God's care will nevertheless provide:

> I exult
> That God, by God's own ways occult,
> May – doth, I will believe – bring back
> All wanderers to a single track!
> Meantime, I can but testify
> God's care for me – no more, can I –
> It is but for myself I *know*.

This insistence on the personal nature of religious experience,
indeed of all experience, is scoffed at by Sir Henry Jones as a
shallow and fallacious subjectivism which need not be taken
seriously. To the student of nineteenth-century philosophy, however, such an insistence will be familiar through the great series
of Kierkegaard's works, notably the *Concluding Unscientific Postscript* of 1846.[1] Nor will Browning's conclusion seem strange to
readers of Kierkegaard:

> I, then, in ignorance and weakness,
> Taking God's help, have attained to think
> My heart does best to receive in meekness
> This mode of worship, as most to His mind,
> Where earthly aids being cast behind,
> His All in All appears serene,
> With the thinnest human veil between. (XXII)

Similarly when Browning turns at the end of *Christmas-Eve* from
a consideration of forms of worship to the examination in *Easter-
Day* of the vital question 'What does Christianity mean *to me*?'
he is treading in the footsteps of the Danish Socrates, and the
point from which he starts is one on which Kierkegaard continually insists – 'How very hard it is to be/A Christian!' (*Easter-
Day*, Section I, lines 1–2)

From this position Browning explores another idea (Sections

[1] The religious ideas and techniques of demonstration of Browning and Kierkegaard coincide so often that there is no room to comment on each instance. One or
two particularly interesting congruences will be specifically mentioned: otherwise
this general indication must suffice.

II and III), which is fundamental to all his religious speculations, that certainty of God's will would make a life of Christian
piety inevitable and therefore without value. He develops his
argument, as so often subsequently, by reasoning that God could
not possibly reward or blame us for doing something 'when we
can't but choose'. Therefore He puts before us a faith that has
some uncertainty in it and uses this as a touchstone of true belief.
Browning now wishes to establish from this theoretical position
some practical consequences, and sees that there are two possibilities. If God means us to grow strong through doubt we may
either shelve all religious difficulties on the grounds that God
does not intend them to be resolved, or we may accept constant
uncertainty and self-questioning as an essential part of the
Christian life. In effect the discussion in the first part of *Easter-
Day* turns on these two ways of Christian living, with neither
held to be utterly misguided. But Browning's interest naturally
inclines to the severer discipline, and the remainder of the poem
is taken up with a description of the meaning of Christianity to
the individual. The parallel with Kierkegaard's insistence on
Christianity as a personal affair (i.e. as an answer to the question
'How am *I* to become a Christian?') is too obvious to need
pointing. Similarly Kierkegaard's way of proceeding by argument between two pseudonyms (e.g. Climacus and anti-Clima-
cus) is very much in Browning's manner.[1] The question that

---

[1] For a study of *Easter-Day* it is of great importance to notice that the first twelve
sections are cast in the form of a dialogue between two characters, neither of whom,
as we see from Section XIV, is the same as the speaker of *Christmas-Eve*. One of
them (the Easy Christian) puts forward for the most part arguments for not allowing one's Christianity to become a burden – 'Here I live/In trusting ease'. (XI)
The other, whose monologue the poem is, finds it hard to be a Christian. It is
essential but extremely difficult to define Browning's attitude to the two of them,
since they both express opinions with which Browning has some sympathy and
both argue in a similar way. Indeed at one point the speaker comments, 'Did you
say this, or I? Oh, you!' (VIII) The point to remember is that the poem is formally a dramatic monologue and the poet is not obliged to identify himself with any
specific set of opinions. There are indeed faint suggestions, in Section XIII for
example, that the speaker is labouring under a delusion, that his opinions are considered by Browning to be extreme. Nevertheless they are in general views with
which Browning has considerable sympathy. One might say that the speaker
represents one side of Browning's mind, while the Easy Christian represents another.
The latter offers far too undemanding a solution, although he is not entirely wrong
(e.g. Section VII). He is simple, naïve, and trusting; these are all qualities which

the speaker of Browning's poem sets himself to answer is this

> 'How were my case, now, should I fall
> Dead here, this minute – do I lie
> Faithful or faithless?' (XIV)

His method is not the philosopher's but the dramatist's. The speaker talks facetiously of the last trump and the day of judgement,

>   And as I said
> This nonsense, throwing back my head
> With light complacent laugh, I found
> Suddenly all the midnight round
> One fire. The dome of Heaven had stood
> As made up of a multitude
> Of handbreadth cloudlets, one vast rack
> Of ripples infinite and black,
> From sky to sky. Sudden there went,
> Like horror and astonishment,
> A fierce vindictive scribble of red
> Quick flame across, as if one said
> (The angry scribe of Judgment) 'There –
> Burn it!' (XV)

It is the Day of Judgement and the speaker stands charged with having chosen the world rather than God. His attempt to excuse himself on the grounds that the world, being God's creation, was too beautiful to reject is met only by a solemn voice saying, 'Thou art judged for evermore!' (XVII)

The explanation of this stern decree is given in the next eleven sections. Once again Browning uses a favourite form, the debate, in this instance between the speaker and God himself, who appears in his majesty. The obvious hazards of such an enterprise are evidence of Browning's determination not to regard Christianity from outside, but to treat it as a direct relation between the individual man and God. The voice of God speaks:

Browning does not condemn out of hand. The speaker represents a different approach, austere, ascetic, extreme, dwelling in doubt rather than hope, but not in the end entirely contradicting his interlocutor. Mrs Orr's labelling of them as 'the man of faith' and 'the sceptic' wrongly implies that they take completely opposite sides in the argument. Neither, taken singly, speaks for Browning. Taken together they present the poles between which much of his religious thought turned.

> This world,
> This finite life, thou hast preferred,
> In disbelief of God's own word,
> To Heaven and to Infinity.
> Here, the probation was for thee,
> To show thy soul the earthly mixed
> With Heavenly, it must choose betwixt . . .
> Thy choice was earth: thou didst attest
> 'Twas fitter spirit should subserve
> The flesh, than flesh refine to nerve
> Beneath the spirit's play. (XX)

As the speaker has chosen earth, then all in the earth shall be his. The speaker foolishly rejoices at this gift of the world's 'vast exhaustless beauty', but 'the austere voice' rebukes him, explaining that the earth is merely the antechamber to Heaven. A wise man would know how much Heaven must exceed the earth in beauty. For man

> All partial beauty was a pledge
> Of beauty in its plenitude:
> But since the pledge sufficed thy mood,
> Retain it – plenitude be theirs
> Who looked above!   (XXIV)

Similarly the study of great works of sculpture and painting is ultimately unsatisfying, since, even though they transcend Nature, they are at best imperfect reflections of the ideal beauty in the artist's mind, as this world is itself an imperfect reflection of heaven. The world we know is adequate for the first stage of man's development, but compared with paradise it is seen to be as limiting and unsatisfying as a lizard's hole in the rock. Good men are content with the world, but always trust God to provide a more spiritually satisfying home for them.

This argument from the imperfections of earth to the perfection of Heaven is one which Browning uses frequently either as a proof of necessary existence of a better state or as an incentive to treat this world as a time of learning, probation and development. Similarly, the concept of Art as transcending Nature and as offering an earnest of the perfections to come is a very fertile one for Browning, both as evidence for a future life in which the artist's shadowing forth of the ideal shall become

reality and as a testimony to the powers of the artist, who appre-
hends, although at many removes, a complete world, and thus
shares and makes manifest some of the powers of the Creator.

The debate between the speaker and his God has by this time
settled into a familiar pattern, with the speaker trying to justify
his worldly life by a series of arguments, each of which his
opponent rebuts. The speaker's next despairing suggestion (Section XXVII) is that 'Mind is best – /I will seize mind, forego the
rest.' By studying the 'circling sciences,/Philosophies and his-
tories', and verse and music he hopes to liberate himself from
the chains of earth. Yet even as he speaks he knows that God will
reply that the operations of the intellect are earthbound; the
question, 'Whereto does Knowledge serve?' is sufficient to show
the limitations of mental activity. The suggestion that poetry
offers a means of transcending the human condition is rejected by
God at the end of Section XXVIII.[1] He says that even when a
poet is able to convey an insight into the nature of the infinite he
rightly claims only so much credit for his own craftsmanship as
you would give to the maker of an Aeolian harp. As it is the wind
that plays the harp, so it is God who inspires the poet. He does
this by vouchsafing him a fleeting glimpse of the world of the
spirit, fleeting because no man can experience it for long 'else
were permanent/Heaven upon earth'. The poet makes his vision
accessible to other men in his verse, which, however, can transmit
truth only by disguising it. Art is thus dependent on the world of
the spirit (which is the source of all that we find true or beautiful
in poetry) and a poor substitute for it, since it necessarily offers
an oblique presentation of reality.

His arguments successively dismissed, the speaker at last feels
that he has seen the conclusion to which God is compelling him,
and realizes that all that is left to him is love: he will, he says,
try to find a woman with whom he can live in affection. God,
however, scornfully replies that this choice is made rather late in
the day, since love has always been clearly manifest in the entire
Universe. In particular God had loved man so much that He had
died for him. How could anyone reject that story on the grounds
that there was 'too much love' in it? How presumptuous of man,
who is clearly better adapted for hatred, to suppose that he had

[1] As this passage is one which seems to give particular difficulty, I offer a fairly
full paraphrase of it.

himself invented the 'scheme of perfect love'. Thus at the climax of his poem Browning makes the whole debate centre on that article of Christian faith which was most compelling to him, that the Incarnation was a supreme act of God's love.

After this final rebuff from God, the speaker is left with nothing to say. All he can do is to ask that he shall at least be spared the knowledge that all is lost:

> Only let me go on, go on,
> Still hoping ever and anon
> To reach one eve the Better Land! (XXXI)

He receives a token of God's forgiveness (XXXII) and sees day dawn. In the crucial final section he asks himself, 'Was this a vision? False or true?' Was it perhaps caused by lack of sleep? Or by looking at the Northern Lights? So he goes on in doubt

> happy that I can
> Be crossed and thwarted as a man,
> Not left in God's contempt apart,
> With ghastly smooth life, dead at heart,
> Tame in earth's paddock as her prize.

He can even thank God that the world still tempts him, since this means that he is not yet ensnared by worldly things.

> Thank God, no paradise stands barred
> To entry, and I find it hard
> To be a Christian, as I said!

He thinks how dreadful it would be to be allowed complete ease of spirit like someone condemned to earth for ever.

> But Easter-Day breaks! But
> Christ rises! Mercy every way
> Is infinite, – and who can say?

The difficulties, rigours and anxieties of the Christian life are more emphatically stated and accepted than elsewhere in Browning. Indeed his wife was moved to write

I have complained of the *asceticism* in the second part, but he said it was 'one side of the question.' Don't think that he has taken to the cilix – indeed he has not – but it is his way to *see* things as passionately as other people *feel* them. [3]

Although Browning, as usual, maintained that he was writing dramatically, and this is technically correct, his own beliefs are allowed to emerge more clearly than from most of his later poems. Whether or not we are prepared to conclude that Browning was writing directly about his own religious experience, the importance of *Christmas-Eve and Easter-Day* is that it illustrates the sort of Christian Browning had to be if he was to be a Christian at all. No looser faith would be adequate. Therefore when he can no longer believe absolutely in Christ he cannot bring himself to accept the name of 'Christian' on easier terms.

It is particularly interesting to compare *Christmas-Eve and Easter-Day*, especially the latter, with *Bishop Blougram's Apology* (1855). The terrain of each poem is the same, and Browning's conclusions are substantially the same, but in the later poem Browning has almost completely externalized and inverted his presentation. Instead of being spoken by a man of intense faith earnestly arguing with an easy Christian, *Blougram* is spoken by a man happy in the world and confident that his casual analogies are adequate to justify his complacent acceptance of the rewards of his position. Instead of the austere voice of God solemnly condemning the vanities of this world we have the cultured voice of Blougram cynically defending them. Instead of the Day of Judgement made manifest in the heavens we have an obscure journalist sitting at a dinner table, listening to and judging his host. Artistically and dramatically *Blougram* is the finer work, but the version of true Christianity which lies behind it is very like that made explicit in *Easter-Day*.

DeVane suggests that the predominantly 'ascetic and austere tone' of *Easter-Day* is to be attributed to the effect on Browning of the death of his mother in 1849 [4]. This is probably true, but not, as DeVane implies, because sorrow for his mother's death led a remorseful Browning back to the Puritan Christianity in which she had instructed him and from which he had strayed. No doubt this played a part, but it seems likely that, as in *La Saisiaz*, a poem with which *Christmas-Eve and Easter-Day* has much in common, the death of someone near to him naturally set him wondering about immortality and the purpose of existence. Dissatisfied with the conventional answers of the churches he determined to base his faith, like the Puritans, on the witness of his own spirit. Accordingly he asked himself the question 'What do

I really think ?' The answer that he reached in *Easter-Day* was not a permanent one, but the arguments which he reviewed were to play their part in his religious poetry throughout his life. The last words of the poem – 'Who can say ?' – aptly convey his speculative inquiring approach to religion and show the inadequacy of regarding him as dedicated to a rigid conformity to an optimistic faith.

In *Men and Women* the principal poems on Christian subjects were *Bishop Blougram's Apology* and the revised version of *Saul*, which gave Browning's most powerful imaginative presentation of the love and humanity of Christ:

> O Saul, it shall be
> A Face like my face that receives thee; a Man like to me,
> Thou shalt love and be loved by, for ever! a Hand like this
> hand
> Shall throw open the gates of new life to thee! See the
> Christ stand!

In the same collection Browning published two poems, *Cleon* and *Karshish*, in each of which the crucial point is the spiritual barrenness of a world without Christ. Both poems are set in the first century A.D.: in each the speaker longs for some proof of God's love, yet rejects, however reluctantly, the rumours of Christianity which are already abroad. As I have suggested in Chapter 2, it is essential for the reader of these monologues to realize that the need of Cleon and Karshish is precisely filled by the acceptance of Christ. That is, the imaginative truth of Christianity, its correspondence to our deepest needs, is a powerful argument in its favour: the historical evidences are of less importance. If Christianity does not win assent in the heart, no intellectual assent is of value. If, on the other hand, the heart is sure of the central truths of Christianity it can resist all attempts to shake it by attacking the historical basis of its faith.

This was of course the main weapon of the Higher Critics of the nineteenth century. Browning's attitude to them is not simple. On the one hand he feels that their criticism is irrelevant, since it is concerned only with the accidents of Christian belief: on the other hand he is himself impatient of dogma and concerned to arrive at the central core of meaning in Christian teaching. The difficulty of his position is clearly seen in *A Death in the Desert*

(1864). The poem, which is spoken by John the Evangelist on his deathbed, presents us with an intricate, not to say confused, pattern of disputation. Two separate lines of argument are raised through the persons of two imaginary objectors:

A. The Love, Might, and Will of God are simply projections of human qualities.

A1. (John's answer) To reason like this is spiritual death.

B. Men might as well be told the truth in plain and certain terms, instead of being perplexed with doubts about miracles.

B1. (John's answer) Man's essence is development: therefore he must learn the truth gradually. Miracles were necessary once but are not now.

These arguments and counter-arguments occur in the following order in the poem: B1 – A – B1 – A1 – B – A1 – B1. In addition it will be noticed that A1 is not really a reply to A.

The various strands of the debate are held together only by the ingenious device of placing them all in the mouth of St John, the last person living to have known Christ. As he is dying he realizes that the testimony that he has left in his Gospel may be doubted. Men may even ask

> Was John at all, and did he say he saw?
> Assure us, ere we ask what he might see!

For him all the topics are of immediate and equal importance. He sees most clearly that the vital question is, 'Does God love,/And will ye hold that truth against the world?' but he foresees also the doubts which will perplex mankind. Objection B and its answer B1 are, as we shall see, commonplaces in Browning. Objection A is more distinctive.

It has been suggested that this line of argument was derived from Browning's reading of contemporary Biblical criticism, especially that of Strauss and Renan [5]. There is no doubt that the whole status of Holy Writ was under constant and expert scrutiny at the time, and it is, I think, a fair assumption that Strauss's *Das Leben Jesu* (which Browning had used in *Christmas-Eve and Easter-Day*) and Renan's *La Vie de Jésus* stimulated the poet to deal with the general question of the authenticity of the Gospels. Possibly too the poem was given its particular direction by Baur's attack on John's gospel. But Browning makes little attempt to supply specific answers to Strauss or Renan or Baur. Instead he makes his imaginary objector argue as follows:

> One listens quietly, nor scoffs but pleads
> 'Here is a tale of things done ages since;
> What truth was ever told the second day?
> Wonders, that would prove doctrine, go for nought.
> Remains the doctrine, love; well, we must love,
> And what we love most, power and love in one,
> Let us acknowledge on the record here,
> Accepting these in Christ: must Christ then be?
> Has He been? Did not we ourselves make Him?
> Our mind receives but what it holds, no more.
> First of the love, then; we acknowledge Christ –
> A proof we comprehend His love, a proof
> We had such love already in ourselves,
> Knew first what else we should not recognize.
> 'Tis mere projection from man's inmost mind,
> And, what he loves, thus falls reflected back,
> Becomes accounted somewhat out of him;
> He throws it up in air, it drops down earth's,
> With shape, name, story added, man's old way.
> How prove you Christ came otherwise at least? . . .
> Go back, far, farther, to the birth of things;
> Ever the will, the intelligence, the love,
> Man's! – which he gives, supposing he but finds . . .
> What proveth God is otherwise at least?
> All else, projection from the mind of man.'

Now this is an argument which John sees to be sincere and worth answering. It is also one which has a personal appeal to Browning, earlier in his life, as for example in Section XVII of *Christmas-Eve*, and later in his life, as in those poems which show him earnestly trying to separate the mythical accretions from the central core of Christian teaching. It seems to me probable that in this passage and elsewhere in *A Death in the Desert* he has in mind the work of another powerful German critic, Ludwig Feuerbach, whose *Wesen des Christentums*, was, like Strauss's *Life of Jesus*, translated by George Eliot.[1] Chapter IV, 'The

---

[1] Note that Feuerbach (Preface to the Second Edition, xiv–xv) expressly distinguishes between his own work and that of historical critics such as Daumer, Ghillany and Lützelberger. 'I . . . do not inquire what the real, natural Christ was or may have been . . .; on the contrary, I accept the Christ of religion, but I

Mystery of the Incarnation; or, God as love, as a being of the heart', has the following passage, which is very like the words which John puts into the mouth of his imaginary objector:

> God loves man for man's sake, *i.e.*, that he may make him good, happy, blessed. Does he not then love man, as the true man loves his fellow? Has love a plural? Is it not everywhere like itself? What then is the true unfalsified import of the Incarnation, but absolute pure love, without adjunct, without a distinction between divine and human love? For though there is also a self-interested love among men, still the true human love, which is alone worthy of this name, is that which impels the sacrifice of self to another. Who then is our Saviour and Redeemer? God or Love? Love; for God as God has not saved us, but Love, which transcends the difference between the divine and human personality. As God has renounced himself out of love, so we, out of love, should renounce God; for if we do not sacrifice God to love, we sacrifice love to God, and, in spite of the predicate of love, we have the God – the evil being – of religious fanaticism.
>
> While, however, we have laid open this nucleus of truth in the Incarnation, we have at the same time exhibited the dogma in its falsity, we have reduced the apparently supernatural and super-rational mystery to a simple truth inherent in human nature. [6]

Later in the same chapter Feuerbach writes, 'God is loved and loves again; the divine love is only human love made objective, affirming itself' [7].

This line of argument is extended to cover the whole body of Christian belief:

> I by no means say . . . God is nothing, the Trinity is nothing, the Word of God is nothing &c.; I only show that they are not *that* which the illusions of theology make them, not foreign, but native mysteries, the mysteries of human nature; I show that religion takes the apparent, the superficial in Nature and humanity, for the essential, and hence conceives their true essence as a separate, special exist-ence: that consequently, religion, in the definitions which it gives of

---

show that the superhuman being is nothing else than a product and reflex of the supernatural human mind.' He particularly stresses the difference between his work and that of Strauss and Bruno Bauer. 'Bauer takes for the object of his criticism the evangelical history . . .; Strauss, the System of Christian Doctrine and the Life of Jesus . . .; I, Christianity in general, *i.e.*, the Christian *religion*, and consequently, only Christian philosophy or theology.'

God, *e.g.*, of the Word of God, . . . only defines or makes objective the true nature of the human word. [8]

If 'consciousness of God is self-consciousness' man at first erroneously supposes God to have a real existence outside himself. So that what we mean by religious development is this, 'that what by an earlier religion was regarded as objective, is now regarded as subjective; that is, what was formerly contemplated and worshipped as God is now perceived to be something human.' Later he says, 'The divine being is nothing else than the human being, or rather the human nature purified, freed from the limits of the individual man, made objective – i.e. contemplated and revered as another, a distinct being. All the attributes of the divine nature are, therefore, attributes of the human nature.' Feuerbach goes on to argue for the illusory nature of religion, and thus, he insists, the greater glory of humanity.

It will be seen how closely Browning's imaginary sceptic follows the first part of Feuerbach's thesis, and how important it is for John to refute this if he is not to be forced to accept Feuerbach's conclusions. As I have said, he does not offer a direct defence. It is a singular feature of the structure of the poem that John, instead of replying immediately, puts forward his defence to a number of objections which have not yet been raised. Eventually he arrives at what may be called his rejoinder to the Feuerbachian sceptic. It is based essentially on putting forward as an axiom the proposition that

> the acknowledgement of God in Christ
> Accepted by thy reason, solves for thee
> All questions in the earth and out of it.

We must not spend our time in examining the origins of this knowledge, but recognize its truth and use it to advance. It would clearly be fatal if knowledge itself merely led us back to doubt. To allow this to happen is to suffer spiritual death. Similarly God manifested his love to satisfy man's craving for love. But if man, seeing love throughout the universe, presumptuously concludes that he is the sole origin of it, he again incurs spiritual death. Alone in a barren world he too suffers a death in the desert. It may seem that Browning provides John with a rather flimsy defence against Feuerbach's arguments: in fact it is a reasonably strong counter. Feuerbach offers the reader an account of the origin of God in the mind of man. This account appeals because it is economical and because it corresponds to one theory of the origin of the pagan deities. It does not rely on proof and cannot be rebutted logically, any more than you can prove by argument which way up a picture ought to be hung. Feuerbach acutely perceived that if you inverted the traditional picture of God and man it still made sense: John not unreasonably rejoins that it made perfectly good sense as it was and that there is nothing to be gained by questioning the traditional arrangements, since all that can result is a world where every statement can be contradicted and thus no certainty is possible.

Later, after a further interruption, John inverts Feuerbach's initial postulate. Where Feuerbach had said, 'Consciousness of God is self-consciousness', John says,

> Before the point was mooted, 'What is God?'
> No savage man inquired 'What am myself?'

In other words, self-consciousness depends on consciousness of God. Man must learn to recognize that *complete* knowledge of his own nature would be of no service to him. He has, however, the distinctively human gift of *progressive* knowledge of himself and of the world. This leads into Browning's familiar argument about the gradual development of man's faculties, and it is here that the relevance of the other wing of the poem becomes apparent.

Chapter XIII of Feuerbach's book deals in a similar fashion with faith and the miraculous. This suggests an explanation of the rather odd association of the arguments which I have called A and B, and the apparently arbitrary way in which John's defence moves from A1 to B1. If he is, as I think, answering Feuerbach, then he has continually to guard both flanks of his position. That is, he must meet the main argument that Christianity is merely a projection of human qualities and desires (i.e. that it has no supernatural element) and at the same time justify the fact that God no longer demonstrates his existence by means or miracles (i.e. that Christianity has now no supernatural element). Feuerbach makes the connection explicitly:

> The specific object of faith therefore is miracle; faith is the belief in miracle; faith and miracle are absolutely inseparable. (p. 125)

> Miracles are but a visible example of what faith can effect. (p. 125)

> The power of miracle is therefore nothing else than the power of the imagination.[1] (p. 129)

Feuerbach is, however, far from dismissing miracles on this account, and the final paragraph of the chapter begins as follows:

> The explanation of miracles by feeling and imagination is regarded by many in the present day as superficial. But let anyone transport himself to the time when living present miracles were believed in; when the reality of things without us was as yet no sacred article of faith; when men were so void of any theoretic interest in the world, that they from day to day looked forward to its destruction; when they lived only in the rapturous prospect and hope of heaven, that is, in the imagination of it (for whatever heaven may be, for them, so long as they were on earth, it existed only in the imagination); when this imagination was not a fiction but a truth, nay, the eternal, alone abiding truth, not an inert, idle source of consolation, but a practical moral principle determining actions, a principle to which men joyfully sacrificed real life, the real world with all its glories; – let him transport himself to those times and he must himself be very superficial to pronounce the psychological genesis of miracles superficial. (pp. 132–3)

The advice to the reader to 'transport himself' to the age of miracles reads almost as if it were the direct inspiration for the setting of *A Death in the Desert*.[2]

Browning takes up the challenge, and provides his imaginary first-century sceptic with the argument that the Gospels are deceptive: they are inevitably discovered not to be literally true, and man then naturally doubts even the truth which lies behind them. This is a poor way of giving knowledge. Why does John not give man certainty, instead of leaving him to distinguish between fable, myth and fact?

> Why breed in us perplexity, mistake,
> Nor tell the whole truth in the proper words?

The demand is not unlike that voiced by Philo in Hume's *Dialogues concerning Natural Religion*, Section XI, when he says

[1] Cf. 'Whether a change were wrought i' the shows o' the world,/Whether the change came from our minds which see/Of shows o' the world so much as and no more/Than God wills for his purpose . . . I know not.'

[2] The juggling with time and knowledge that it implies is reflected in the most unsatisfactory feature of the poem, the way in which realism in characterizing John is sacrificed to the desire to give him a prescient insight into nineteenth-century Biblical criticism.

that in the face of uncertain speculation the 'natural sentiment' of the mind is 'a longing desire and expectation, that heaven would be pleased to dissipate, at least to alleviate this profound ignorance, by affording some particular revelation to mankind, and making discoveries of the nature, attributes and operations of the divine object of our faith.'

John's reply to this demand is close to one of the arguments in *Biographia Literaria*: Coleridge writes, 'It [the existence of God] could not be intellectually more evident without becoming morally less effective; without counteracting its own end by sacrificing the *life* of faith to the cold mechanism of a worthless because compulsory assent' [9]. Browning puts it:

> Ye know there needs no second proof with good
> Gained for our flesh from any earthly source.

Fire, for instance, we recognize and value without any doubts at all.

> While were it so with the soul, – this gift of truth
> Once grasped, were this our soul's gain safe, and sure
> To prosper as the body's gain is wont, –
> Why, man's probation would conclude, his earth
> Crumble; for he both reasons and decides,
> Weighs first, then chooses: will he give up fire
> For gold or purple once he knows its worth?
> Could he give Christ up were His worth as plain?
> Therefore, I say, to test man, the proofs shift . . .

He deals with miracles in the familiar way. They were necessary at the time in order to make faith possible

> such was the effect,
> So faith grew, making void more miracles
> Because too much: they would compel, not help.

The argument, of course, is that man is a *developing* creature; the sort of revelation of God which was appropriate at an early stage of his evolution is replaced by one more in keeping with his later state. It is indeed in this progression that his distinctive nature as man consists. Thus this side of the debate leads ultimately to the same conclusion as the other, and John's final words serve as his summing-up of both sets of arguments.

It is sometimes objected that the language of the poem is as colourless and arid as the desert in which it is set: it is perhaps fairer to say that Browning is deliberately working in neutral tones. Rhetoric would be improper for a dying man carefully pondering the meaning of human life, and the arguments are too intricate to be settled by a passionate declaration of belief. In any case Browning has not at this point in his life any easy solution to offer. To distinguish his own position from that of the Higher Critics he has to make subtler and subtler discriminations, and his language is consequently circumspect and hesitant rather than bold and picturesque.

For example, with specific reference to Christianity Feuerbach writes as follows in Chapter XV:

> Christ alone is the personal God; he is the real God of Christians, a truth which cannot be too often repeated. In him alone is concentrated the Christian religion, the essence of religion in general. He alone meets the longing for a personal God; he alone is an existence identical with the nature of feeling; on him alone are heaped all the joys of the imagination, and all the sufferings of the heart; in him alone are feeling and imagination exhausted. Christ is the blending in one of feeling and imagination. (pp. 146–7)

This was, I suggest, the kind of argument against which Browning found it most difficult to defend his own form of Christianity. He was never particularly concerned to protect the outworks of Christian dogma or Christian evidences against the Higher Critics, and his insistence on discovering the essential kerygma of the Gospels brought him dangerously near to the position of an 'anthropological' critic like Feuerbach. In *A Death in the Desert* it is clear how little room he had left himself for manoeuvre.[1] So much of what Feuerbach has to say *almost* chimes with Browning's own opinions. Consider, for example, this passage from Feuerbach's Preface:

> This philosophy has for its principle, not the Substance of Spinoza, not the *ego* of Kant and Fichte, not the Absolute Identity of Schelling, not the Absolute Mind of Hegel, in short, no abstract, merely conceptional being, but a *real* being, the true *Ens realissimum* – man.[2]

[1] Compare, for instance, John's final definition of the nature of man and Feuerbach's first chapter. *Ixion* (1883) expresses a position very close to Feuerbach's, without any ironic distancing that I can detect.

[2] Preface, p. vii. It is interesting to note that Kierkegaard also had a considerable respect for Feuerbach. In the *Concluding Unscientific Postscript* he wrote, 'On the

Although this is a congenial foundation for Browning, he does not accept the construction that Feuerbach sets upon it. He meets Feuerbach by grounding John's arguments on the nature of man, but with a particular emphasis. The crucial step in the argument is the proposition that 'all things suffer change save God the truth'. Thus man has developed and it is his nature to develop.

We have seen how Browning argues from this position that man has now no longer any need of miracles. Similarly, basing his argument on the same premise that man's essence is that he develops, John meets the other wing of Feuerbach's attack. He reasons as follows. 'Life is a progression. Knowledge of God is a stage in Man's progress: it leads him, among other things, to a consideration of his own stature in the Universe. Now, however, he has rightly concluded that if he is the only existent thing in whom love, power and will combine he is himself the "first, last, and best of things", that is, God. If he reaches this conclusion nobody can prove to him that he is wrong, but "his life becomes impossible, which is death." ' This echoes a point that John has made a few lines earlier, answering Feuerbach's arguments directly:

> But when, beholding that love everywhere,
> [Man] reasons, 'Since such love is everywhere,
> And since ourselves can love and would be loved,
> We ourselves make the love, and Christ was not,' –
> How shall ye help this man who knows himself,
> That he must love and would be loved again,
> Yet, owning his own love that proveth Christ,
> Rejecteth Christ through very need of Him?
> The lamp o'erswims with oil, the stomach flags
> Loaded with nurture, and that man's soul dies.

But if, on the other hand, man will only admit in humility that he cannot *know* God's nature or his own with certainty, he will find his right place in the world. He develops,

> Finds progress, man's distinctive mark alone
> Not God's, and not the beasts': God is, they are,
> Man partly is and wholly hopes to be.

---

other hand, a scoffer [i.e. Feuerbach] attacks Christianity and at the same time expounds it so reliably that it is a pleasure to read him, and one who is in perplexity about finding it distinctly set forth may almost have recourse to him.'

This progress is possible only through man's ignorance and his desire for knowledge.

> He learns
> Because he lives, which is to be a man.

In a postscript to the poem Browning glances at some of his contemporaries' speculations about the nature of Christ, especially those who conjecture that he was a 'mere man'. He indicates obliquely that such theories are by no means new, having been voiced by the early heretic Cerinthus. Yet, he implies, it is not Christ who has passed into oblivion but Cerinthus himself. This is perhaps the only time that Browning offers the continuity of Christian tradition and the stability of the Christian churches as an argument for the truth of Christianity [10].

II

At this point it is useful to pause and to look backwards and forward in time from 1864. Backwards to Browning's nonconformist upbringing, his early Shelleyan defiance of religion, his marriage, the death of his mother, the Evangelical piety of *Christmas-Eve and Easter-Day*, the firm grasp of Gospel-truths in *Blougram*, and then the gradual questioning and elaborating of his original simple beliefs: forward to the remaining twenty-five years of his life, and his unremitting efforts to find a point of stability.

The process can be seen in little as early as 1850, for the framework of *Christmas-Eve* is a debate, recalling the disputations of the medieval schoolmen in which different religious beliefs are examined in the abstract with the idea of moving the argument by a process of elimination to an agreed conclusion: in *La Saisiaz* Fancy and Reason dissect the subject in a similar way. But such a debate cannot be limited to a consideration of ideas of the nature of God: sooner or later a sceptical or rigorous mind begins to demand evidence of God's existence, that is, of the reality of the subject under debate. The question of whether God's existence could be established from the natural world was one which exercised Browning considerably, and in his poems he resumes many of the arguments of the deists of the seventeenth and eighteenth centuries and of those who, like Hume, subjected the deists to scrutiny and criticism. But, again like Hume, Browning found that the intellectual processes themselves were not free from doubt. Thus instead of attempting to reason in the abstract from unknowable concepts such as the nature of the Universe, man must build on the only certainty he has – his own knowledge of his own existence.

Sir Henry Jones assumes that anyone who has been reduced to this degree of subjectivism must necessarily be a sceptic and therefore ought logically to be a pessimist. When he finds that Browning is not a pessimist he belittles the quality of Browning's optimism. But, as I have emphasized in the preceding chapter, Browning's faith was won only at great cost; this is clearly seen throughout *Easter-Day*, which describes a state of spiritual humiliation and abasement. Indeed it is only from his turbulence of spirit and his constant sense of his own imperfection that the speaker is able to derive even a provisional consolation and a qualified hope that mercy will be shown to him. He explicitly condemns a placid acceptance of the world and emphasizes the difficulties and the rigours of the Christian alternative.

Browning is, obviously, not one of the great original Christian thinkers, but he was prepared to travel himself the same difficult roads as the pioneers. Thus we meet in his poems echoes of many great men who tried successively to define afresh what is meant by 'understanding the nature of God', echoes of such independent thinkers as Erigena, as Scotus and Ockham, as Eckhart, as Hume and Hamann and Kierkegaard. This succession of active religious thought sometimes occurs in this order within a single poem, as medieval and eighteenth-century lines of thought are replaced by something more modern, more radical and less dogmatic. The arena of the argument contracts until it is centred inside the poet's own consciousness. The mode of the poem moves from hypothesis to induction and then to an affirmation, or rather to an expression of hope, tentative and grounded in a sense of the difficulty of maintaining an active Christian belief. The ideas are thus progressively more suited to the poet's gifts.

By 1864 this constant questioning and sifting of his faith had left Browning far from the safe harbour of any church. To say that he was as detached as Kierkegaard is hardly to exaggerate, although he was not animated by the philosopher's rancorous hatred of the Established Church. Like Kierkegaard he was isolated with his self-consciousness and the consciousness of God. In his mature poems he seldom shows much sympathy for pantheism or much confidence in the findings of so-called Natural Religion. One attractive reading of *Caliban upon Setebos* (see Chapter 7) is as a satire on those who suppose that it is possible to arrive at a proof of the nature of God by reasoning from His Universe. (The poem, which has the sub-title *Natural Theology in the Island*, may also be regarded as an oblique reply to Feuerbach, ironically indicating what sort of God one might expect if He were nothing but the objectifying of the characteristic qualities of man: on this view the poem would be a compacter and wittier reworking of some of the ideas of *A Death in the Desert*, the poem which it immediately follows in *Dramatis Personae*.)

When Browning contemplates Christianity he is in a dilemma, for while he sees the uselessness of dogma, and in his anxiety to be rid of it cuts back constantly to primitive Christianity, he realizes that much of the appeal of the New Testament is to the imagination. That is to say, it has power to move mankind because of its underlying significance, not because men suppose it to be literally true. After all these centuries the mere *fact* of Christ's ministry would be of no importance unless that ministry were still of imaginative force. Browning is thus continually fighting in his theological poems to avoid on the one hand the sterile doctrinal positions of rigid orthodox belief and on the other the spiritual death of utter scepticism. There is the added difficulty that from one point of view both unquestioning belief and outright disbelief seem more honest and more manly than the middle ground of compromise on which Browning must try to find a steady foothold.

Not surprisingly the poems on religious subjects in *Dramatis Personae* reflect this uneasiness. In *Gold Hair*, for example, it takes the form of a vigorous assertion of primitivist Christian belief in the last two stanzas which is hard to reconcile with what has gone before.[1] In *The Worst of It* there is the speaker's advice, surely ironic, to the woman he loves to

1 Browning seems here to be looking back almost with regret to the forthright Evangelical beliefs of his youth. He is writing very much in the spirit of William Wilberforce, who expressed his disgust with 'rational religion', with the idea that

strive and strain to be good again,
And a place in the other world ensure,
All glass and gold, with God for its sun.

Later in the volume the confident boom of Rabbi Ben Ezra
mingles with the hesitant whine of Sludge. That the contemporary questioning of Christian evidences played a crucial part
in inducing this unevenness of tone is well illustrated by the
Epilogue to *Dramatis Personae*, in which Browning speaks the
last stanzas in his own person. Here, if anywhere in the volume,
we can fairly claim to recognize an expression of his own religious state in 1864.

In the poem Browning contrasts three ways of looking for
God [11]. The first locates God in his Church. Kirkconnell
suggests very plausibly that Browning is here glancing at 'the
intense sacerdotalism of the Oxford Movement and the Church
of Rome', superlatively orthodox Christians, whose knowledge
of the Divine is gained through special revelation. To this first
speaker 'God's will is manifested in His church', and only in the
Lord's temple do we come into he actual presence of His glory.
In contrast to this exaltation the second speaker, whom Browning later specifically designated as Renan, expresses an extreme
pessimism, grounded on the belief that Christ, who once came
to earth and brought with him unimaginable bliss, has departed
for ever, leaving man desolate and doubting even God's existence, 'lone and left/Silent through centuries'.

The third speaker rejects both views of how God manifests
himself. After the long and complex image of the whirlpool
the speaker makes the application (Stanza X), 'If you grant,' he
says, 'that the world can provide an environment sufficiently
complex to differentiate all men into unique personalities (cf.
Stanza II) then you are already admitting the existence of an
extraordinarily powerful and subtle agency which is in fact
shaping man. Consequently there is no need to suppose that such

---

man is naturally good, and with the modern habit of regarding the devil 'as an
evanescent prejudice which it would now be to the discredit of any man of understanding to believe'.

The tenth Aphorism on Spiritual Religion in Coleridge's *Aids to Reflection* is
called 'On Original Sin': Coleridge's argument that anyone who wishes to insist on
the freedom of the will must also admit the existence of Original Sin perhaps explains
Browning's unlikely enthusiasm for the doctrine.

a power (which is equivalent to God) can appear only in one place or at only one time, for to do so is to limit His power. God is not limited by the walls of the Temple but is always present in His Universe, nor did He, as Renan suggests, appear once and then abandon mankind. To me the nature of God is not dependent on any actual historical revelation, either in the Temple or in the person of Christ. Thus my view of God does not fade but is continually developing. In a sense it is everything that I am. It is my Universe, considered not simply as the non-sentient Other, but as part of myself, as what for me constitutes the whole of *what is*.' In short the third speaker is contrasting two ways of looking for God *outside* the self (i.e. in the liturgies and sacraments of the Church, which leads to a misguided enthusiasm, and in the historical person of Christ, which leads to an equally misguided pessimism as soon as the critical intellect begins to scrutinize the evidence) with Browning's way, which is to look for and find God within himself [12].

The *Epilogue* records how far Browning had moved by 1864 from anything that might be called orthodox Christianity. Indeed even the idea of God's love of man being made manifest in the incarnation of Christ, which had animated so many of his poems, is found very rarely in his later work. We may, if we are interested in the personality of Browning, speculate about what he was thinking at this period in his life, and see his soul as a ground in which Feuerbach is battling with and proving stronger than the Reverend George Clayton of York Street Chapel. We may, if we are interested in Victorian religion, observe how representative Browning's shifting opinions are of the currents of *active* religious thought in the second half of the century, and either draw the obvious parallels with Newman and Arnold or lay stress on the common ground with Kierkegaard and honour Browning as the first existentialist poet.

Alternatively we may simply read each poem on its merits and ignore those before and after. While this is a perfectly practical approach, it is nevertheless interesting to see what lines of argument remain open to Browning and how these determine the strategies of developing a poem which are still available to him. To put the case crudely, he has really two possible ways of reconciling his loss of belief in fundamental revealed truth with his need for some stable principle in life. He can either demythologize Christianity and liberalize it until it no longer requires an act of faith to assent to it, or he can examine man's nature and hope to discover in it elements of the absolute. The difficulty is that Browning is always conscious that the first way may be hypocritical (cf. Blougram), while the alternative may result in the most blatant kind of self-projection (cf. Caliban). Browning has therefore to walk warily between the Bishop and the Beast.

III

The most celebrated example of the first approach is the Pope's monologue in *The Ring and the Book*. This is often quoted as Browning's final word on theological matters, but some caution is necessary. First of all, Browning is not speaking in his own person. Technically he is perfectly entitled to reject the ascription to himself of any of the sentiments expressed by the Pope. Against this, however, it is a valid point to observe that, like John in *A Death in the Desert*, the Pope indulges in speculation about a religious situation not existing in his own time but existing in the nineteenth century. If a poet is prepared to abandon dramatic realism so far as to endow his characters with foresight of this kind he may reasonably be said to have forfeited some of the impersonality of the dramatist. In other words we may well ask, 'If the opinions in Book X are not Browning's, whose are they, for it is hardly conceivable that they could belong to Pope Innocent XII?' Secondly, the monologue does occur in a dramatic context; it is therefore important to remember that even if the opinions are Browning's own what we read is not necessarily a *complete* version of Browning's thinking. He can use only those of his ideas which will accord with the part the Pope has to play in the action of the poem. Finally, Browning's religious thought was, as we have seen, not static: it changed in many important ways even after 1868. With these reservations we may observe four points where the Pope expresses in his soliloquy opinions which are useful for the understanding of Browning's religious poems.

First, even though the speaker is the Supreme Pontiff, there is no trace in his speech of respect for the Church or for Holy orders, but rather the reverse. For example, at the beginning of his monologue the Pope, seeking for assistance in his task of

judgement, consults the records of the Papacy only to find contradictions and evidences of fallibility. Clearly the past practice
of the Church offers no support to the earnest searcher after
truth (X, 1–161). Again when he asks himself, 'How do the
Christians here deport them?' (1451) the Pope has to recognize
that the Church has not shown up well in its dealings with
Pompilia; the 'Aretine archbishop', Abate Paul and Canon
Girolamo, 'the Monastery called of Convertites', have all,
although declared Christians, acted meanly and selfishly: 'The
mystic Spouse betrays the Bridegroom here.' (1490) Indeed the
whole argument of the monologue is that Guido himself, although technically able to claim protection as a minor priest, is
unworthy of his orders. Significantly the Pope judges the individual and sets aside the privileges of the Church.

Secondly, after the passage on the 'love-cycle' (1308–72),
there is an extremely interesting discussion of the relation
between faith and revelation. The Pope is certain of divine love,
and is even able to conjecture that there is a sufficient reason for
sin, pain, and sorrow in the world: perhaps they exist as a kind
of 'moral machinery' to develop man's qualities even closer to
the God-like. He then comments

>   this may be surmised,
> The other is revealed, – whether a fact,
> Absolute, abstract, independent truth,
> Historic, not reduced to suit man's mind, –
> Or only truth reverberate, changed, made pass
> A spectrum into mind, the narrow eye, – . . .
> What matter so the intelligence be filled? . . .
>   so our heart be struck,
> What care I, – by God's gloved hand or the bare?
> Nor do I much perplex me with aught hard,
> Dubious in the transmitting of the tale, –
> No, nor with certain riddles set to solve.

We can see here the prescient Pope threading his way through
two familiar problems which greatly agitated Victorian theo-
logians, the status of the Incarnation if the evidences for it could
be called in question and the perennial problem of pain. The
general lines of the answer which the Pope suggests are equally
familiar to readers of Browning: his position is broadly indicated by passages such as 'This life is training and a passage'

(1410), 'The moral sense grows but by exercise' (1414), and 'Life is probation and the earth no goal/But starting-point of man' (1435–36). If these positions are tenable then Browning can, like the Pope, safely say that neither problem constitutes an insurmountable obstacle to a belief in a just, powerful and loving God. But this line of argument places the burden of *sustaining* faith on the individual and on his own conviction that he is in fact developing and successfully completing his probation. He is thus, while well protected against assault from without, vulnerable to betrayal from within. Hence in Browning's divinity the antagonists are not so often truth and falsehood as hope and doubt, and the result of the struggle is always uncertain, however staunchly the poet asserts his confidence.

Thirdly, in lines 1570–1612, the Pope produces a similar argument which neatly combines the first two. He remarks on the minuteness with which diligent churchmen defend unimportant observances:

> So have I seen a potentate all fume
> For some infringement of his realm's just right,
> Some menace to a mud-built straw-thatched farm
> O' the frontier; while inside the mainland lie,
> Quite undisputed-for in solitude,
> Whole cities plague may waste or famine sap:
> What if the sun crumble, the sands encroach,
> While he looks on sublimely at his ease?
> How does their ruin touch the empire's bound?

The extraordinary accuracy and comprehensiveness of this simile, what an earlier age would have called its 'wit', should not distract our attention from the bitterness of the contrast which the Pope draws and which Browning had seen in his own century between 'the religious', who neglected the cardinal points of Christianity, and those who were prepared to make concessions of the outworks of their beliefs but were constantly attentive to the central bulwarks of their faith.

Finally in a bold and imaginative passage the Pope pictures Euripides scornfully contrasting the wisdom and insight and virtue of pagan Athens, which according to the Church was doomed to damnation, with the blindness of modern Christians. The Pope admits the justice of Euripides' charge and attempts to explain what has happened. Euripides, even in the darkness, managed to grope his way forward. Then came the dawn of Christianity: it was so bright after the blackness that had preceded it that the early Christians could hardly fail to see clearly. 'But that was in the day-spring; noon is now.' (1792)

> Was such a lighting-up of faith, in life,
> Only allowed initiate, set man's step
> In the true way by help of the great glow?
> (1813–15)

The Pope reflects how much easier it was to be certain of the true faith in the early days of the Church. Now even the faithful seem complacent and imperceptive. At this point he is visited, like John, with the power to see into the future. He reflects

> What if it be the mission of that age,
> My death will usher into life, to shake
> This torpor of assurance from our creed,
> Re-introduce the doubt discarded, bring
> The formidable danger back, we drove
> Long ago to the distance and the dark? . . .
> As we broke up that old faith of the world,
> Have we, next age, to break up this the new –
> Faith, in the thing, grown faith in the report –
> Whence need to bravely disbelieve report
> Through increased faith in thing reports belie?
> (1851–67)

The whole of this passage illuminates Browning's attitude to the Higher Critics. Far from condemning their work as blasphemous he saw that they might perform immensely valuable work for Christianity if they were able first of all to stimulate or provoke Christians to think about their religion, and secondly to direct Christian attention to the fundamentals of Christianity. If they could do this then they were not a menace but a challenge to an active religious faith. That his century could meet this challenge, as he was prepared to meet it himself, was perhaps the most optimistic of Browning's religious beliefs. His own answers to the hard questions posed by his time occupied much of his mature life: they may well be described, in the celebrated words of the Pope, as an enforced attempt to

> Correct the portrait by the living face,
> Man's God, by God's God in the mind of man.

In short, Browning, when his faith was challenged, was prepared to undertake almost a radical revision of his theology as Feuerbach, if this was the only way to reach solid ground on which to base his faith. In the process he moved very far from anything that might be called orthodox Christianity. He moved very far also from any poetic tradition that might help him. In many of his poems after 1864 his chief technical problem is to work out a strategy for developing a poem of exploration and discovery: his chief achievement is the creation of a large number of long poems which are based not on a story or a system of belief, but on a question.

IV

It should go without saying that when we abstract similar ideas from a number of poems and, because they do occur in a number of poems, ascribe them directly to the poet, we are not only making a number of assumptions about the poet's mind but also weakening the ideas themselves in the process. Handled in this way they are comparatively undistinguished and lifeless: they are most active in their individual context. For example, it has often been remarked that in his endeavour to discover some abiding principle Browning's favourite resource was the idea of development – that what is true and valuable at one stage of a man's life or of human history eventually gives way to what is needed at the next stage, but its truth and value were nevertheless real. We meet this in various colourings and adaptations, for example in *Easter-Day* XXI, in the Pope's monologue, and in the poem called *Development*. What matters is not simply the value of this idea in abstraction but what we learn fresh about it each time we encounter it actually operating in a poem. For example in *A Death in the Desert* John says,

> I say that man was made to grow, not stop;
> That help, he needed once, and needs no more,
> Having grown but an inch by, is withdrawn:
> For he hath new needs, and new helps to these.
> This imports solely, man should mount on each
> New height in view; the help whereby he mounts,
> The ladder-rung his foot has left, may fall,
> Since all things suffer change save God the Truth.
>   (424–431)

The idea that the Gospels themselves may in time be unnecessary takes on an added significance in the mouth of the dying Evangelist.

Similarly the Pope ends his monologue with the conviction not that he has made the right decision but that there is a right decision to make. That is the point of his anxious pondering of familiar arguments. It implies that there are better and worse answers to these questions, 'Life's business being just the terrible choice'. If this were not so he could simply toss a coin and Book X would be about 2,000 lines shorter. The entire structure of *The Ring and the Book* implies that there is an objective truth, variously refracted though its images may be. The poem is demonstrating, not simply asserting, the truth of these propositions.

These examples will serve to introduce Browning's other technique for providing a basis for human activity at a time when revealed religion seemed no longer adequate, that of attempting to derive absolutes from the simple conditions of human existence.

For example, in *La Saisiaz* (see Chapter 7) Browning accepts as a condition of the argument an almost Kantian isolation of the individual. He will start with nothing but the reality of ideas as they are given in experience and the necessary assumption that man is a freely willing agent. It is this search for first principles which shows most clearly Browning's relation to Fichte, different though their conclusions ultimately are.

La Saisiaz has been harshly criticized for its 'total subjectivism': it is important to see that this is posited by Browning as the essential condition of debate and demonstrates his utter independence in religious speculation. He is determined to discover whether it is possible to found a way of life on what can be known for certain, and he will not claim among the fundamental certainties of life the existence of an objective reality. Provided he can reach some solid ground, no sacrifice of doctrine is too painful, no flight of speculative reason too dangerous. It is a solitary struggle, and never easy, but in the end Browning survives as a man with something that may be called religious faith. To retain even this limited belief in the face of the pain and evil of the world, he has had to make a deliberate act of trust, and even when he has done so, he can still be plagued by mis-givings.

The struggle embodied in *La Saisiaz* is also evident in *Prince Hohenstiel-Schwangau* and *Fifine at the Fair* (see Chapter 11): indeed nobody could fail to observe it in these poems. But if we want to *experience* Browning's way of regarding the basic principles of human behaviour as opposed to *understanding* a prose abstract of them we find equally relevant material in poems which are not ostensibly about metaphysical ideas. *The Inn Album*, *Red Cotton Night-Cap Country* and the neglected but absorbing *Two Poets of Croisic* are all poems which proceed from an apparently trivial or sordid subject to explore the question of what standards a man ought to live by; lying under the poems is the further question of how those standards are to be given stability and authenticity.

If then it was Browning's main endeavour in his later years to understand how a world without Biblical certainties might nevertheless have sufficient certainties of its own and prove to be a place which a man might inhabit without distress or dis-honour, it is not surprising that he found himself compelled to consider the extent of human suffering and how it could be re-conciled with a just world.

This is most clearly seen in the late collection *Ferishtah's Fancies* (1884), which has been so widely criticized. I have men-tioned in the preceding chapter the way in which Sir Henry Jones used two of the poems, *A Pillar at Sebzevar* and *A Bean-Stripe*, as evidence of Browning's blind optimism. It would be more accurate to say that the poems offer complementary views of the possibility of hope [13]. In *A Pillar* Browning deplores the kind of pessimism which is the result of excessive intellec-tual scrutiny. Possibly, he suggests, the test of man is simply knowing what he loves and having the courage to say so truth-fully without looking before and after. Recognition of God's love is thus a duty of his creatures.

In *A Bean-Stripe* Ferishtah traverses a much wider expanse of argument and counter-argument. He begins with the question of whether good or evil predominates in life. Not unexpectedly he suggests that good and evil may be created by the individual:

> I am in motion, and all things beside
> That circle round my passage through their midst, –

> Motionless, these are, as regarding me:
> – Which means, myself I solely recognize . . .
>
> 　　　　　　　　　　(79–82)

The moon in her flight changes her surroundings by her motion.

> 　　　　　　　　So with me,
> Who move and make, – myself, – the black, the white,
> The good, the bad, of life's environment.
> Stand still! black stays black: start again! there's white
> Asserts supremacy: the motion's all
> That colours me my moment: seen as joy?
> I have escaped from sorrow, or that was
> Or might have been: as sorrow? – thence shall be
> Escape as certain: white preceded black,
> Black shall give way to white as duly, – so,
> Deepest in black means white most imminent.
> Stand still, – have no before, no after! – life
> Proves death, existence grows impossible
> To man like me.
>
> 　　　　　　　　　　(99–112)

The discussion then turns on the existence in the world of evil and pain, since Ferishtah himself sometimes suffers and is bound to admit that others are even more miserable. He is challenged to admit also that the plain truth, however dispiriting, is preferable to a fiction, however comforting. He replies, in a manner which is familiar to readers of Browning, that this plain truth which is called for is in fact unattainable: the most we can achieve is a paradox which by an effort of faith or the imagination we can comprehend. We cannot look for certain demonstrative knowledge even of the simplest thing, for example, of an atom.

> Yet, since to think and know fire through and through
> Exceeds man, is the warmth of fire unknown,
> Its uses – are they so unthinkable?[1]
>
> 　　　　　　　　　　(375–377)

In short one is left with no certainty except one's own experience of the world, and this is only relative to the observer. Yet one must give thanks, if one's experience happens to be compara-

---

[1] 'Since' here almost signifies 'although'. The sense would be clearer if the subordinate clause came after the main clause.

tively pleasant, and to whom should thanks be given but to God. Thus even from a consideration of the pain and evil in the world Browning shows that it is possible to derive a certain comfort.

The poem, of course, is unsatisfactory, and the argument, if that is what it is rightly called, disjointed. But at least it is an attempt, however unconvincing and over-clever, to examine the case for the existence of God who seems not to care that many of His creatures live a 'life/Splashed, splotched, dyed hell-deep now from end to end'. The consequences of the argument, which Ferishtah does not explore, would be that God is Himself subjective, existing or not according to whether the observer has or has not reason to postulate His existence.

It is hardly unfair to describe the poem, indeed the whole volume, as an attempt at rationalization, that is, the *a posteriori* intellectual justification of a position reached non-intellectually. We can easily relate this to Browning's personal history by supposing that because of the increasing independence and unorthodoxy of his religious speculations he had come to feel more and more strongly that somewhere in all his explorations of the nature of man he was compelled, if he wished to reach any positive conclusion, to take a step which a strict scepticism would not permit. Somewhere he had to perform an act of trust, a Kierkegaardian leap, which, however congenial to his temperament was nevertheless unsanctioned by the conditions under which he was arguing. We may see *Ferishtah's Fancies* as his attempt to justify this irregular proceeding to himself. He offers a series of analogies as a sop to intellectual doubt, for parallel instances, though unsatisfying to the logician, are often more sedative to an inquiring mind than a rigorous demonstration would be. But in the *Epilogue* to *Ferishtah's Fancies* it is clear that even if Browning's head was satisfied with the bland paralogisms of Ferishtah his heart was not always so readily stayed from misgiving.

After five stanzas of courageous affirmation of the glory of the creation comes the triumphant

> Then the cloud-rift broadens, spanning earth that's under,
>   Wide our world displays its worth, man's strife and
>   strife's success:
> All the good and beauty, wonder crowning wonder,
>   Till my heart and soul applaud perfection, nothing less.

There follows one more stanza. Its violent reversal of tone affects not only the earlier parts of the poem but all the other poems in the volume, and reverberates even further back into the poet's career. It reads:

> Only, at heart's utmost joy and triumph, terror
> Sudden turns the blood to ice: a chill wind disencharms
> All the late enchantment! What if all be error –
> If the halo irised round my head were, Love, thine arms?

The application is double. Browning wonders whether in fact his trust that life is a splendid battleground is perhaps a reflection of his own happy life, which was purely a result of fortunate accident and does not really argue a universally benevolent Creator. He also wonders how far the principle of love, on which his whole faith hangs, is similarly accidental: in other words, having consistently identified love between man and woman and the love of God to the enrichment of both, he is now paralysed by the dread that his whole picture of the world is a delusion caused by the very intensity of his love for his wife and hers for him.

This poem is a measure of the distance which Browning had travelled from any possible help from dogma, the Church, or philosophy, indeed from any source outside himself. His only resource now is that 'inner conviction' of which Sir Henry Jones spoke so disparagingly. If it fails him, nothing remains but the abyss. Mrs Miller makes great play with a quotation from a letter of Hardy's to Gosse, as follows:

> The longer I live the more does B[rowning]'s character seem *the* literary puzzle of the 19th. Century. How could smug Christian optimism worthy of a dissenting grocer find a place inside a man who was so vast a seer and feeler when on neutral ground? [14]

Perhaps the most charitable assumption is that neither Hardy nor Mrs Miller had read Browning's religious poetry with very close attention.[1]

---

[1] Mrs Miller might also have quoted the following account of Hardy on his death-bed: 'In the evening he asked that Robert Browning's poem *Rabbi Ben Ezra* should be read aloud to him. While reading it his wife glanced at his face to see whether he were tired, the poem being a long one of thirty-two stanzas, and she was struck by the look of wistful intentness with which Hardy was listening. He indicated that he wished to hear the poem to the end.' (Florence Hardy, *The Life of Thomas Hardy 1840–1928* (London, 1962), pp. 445–6.)

It has not been my purpose in this section of this chapter to present Browning's ideas on religion as a coherent or even a consistent body of doctrine, but rather to describe some of the ideas on religious matters which are most often present and active in his poems. As these poems have been treated in roughly chronological order a certain consecutiveness of opinion may be traced by those curious to know the history of the poet's mind. As a parallel to this activity it is interesting to consider a poem from his last volume, *Asolando* (1889).

It is called *Development*. Ostensibly it deals with the stages of Browning's own acquaintance with Greek literature. Speaking of his own childhood the poet remembers how, when he was only five years old, his father had explained the siege of Troy to him and how, with the help of furniture, domestic animals and the pageboy, they had enacted the story to the child's complete satisfaction. Later he was old enough to read Pope's *Iliad*, again with enjoyment, and later still to read Homer in Greek. By this time he was convinced that he had reached the summit of Homeric scholarship, but some years later he was introduced to the 'disintegrating' critics of Homer, critics who, like Wolf

> Proved there was never any Troy at all,
> Neither Besiegers nor Besieged, – nay, worse, –
> No actual Homer, no authentic text,
> No warrant for the fiction I, as fact,
> Had treasured in my heart and soul so long –
> Ay, mark you! and as fact held still, still hold,
> Spite of new knowledge, in my heart of hearts
> And soul of souls.

Yet Browning is on record as saying that waking knowledge is better than the delusions of dreams. Does this mean that he now blames his father for deceiving him into believing that Homer's stories were true and his text unquestioned? It might be said that his father should have told him the truth at once, or, if Browning was not yet old enough for this, kept silent, leaving his son to learn without the aid of fiction the values that Homer recommends. That is, Browning might have been set down at once to read Aristotle's *Ethics* instead of Homer. But even now that he is old Browning finds the *Ethics* hard to understand: however, having been well grounded in Homer, he is at least prepared to read it seriously.

The bearing of the poem on Browning's view of truth is easily seen: its implication is that the young are rightly encouraged to have a simple faith in, for example, the historical truth of Homer. Later they will learn that the truth is more complex, but to begin with they need a clear and vivid realization of ethical values. Like Browning they will find that the *essence* of Homer's teaching has become implanted in their hearts 'freed and fixed/From accidental fancy's guardian sheath', just as Browning outgrew his father's mimic version with cats and dogs. They will then be able to approach the *Ethics* with more respect and consider its arguments with more understanding. Browning is attempting to illuminate the paradox that while truth is never easy and is sometimes so difficult of access that it is sometimes only to be approached through fictions, it has nevertheless a value of its own which no fiction can ever have – 'Truth ever, truth only the excellent' [15]. (The similarity between this position and some of the arguments Blougram uses is no more than superficial. Blougram insists, for his own purposes, only on the first wing of the paradox, arguing that it shows the impossibility of ever attaining the truth and releases man from the responsibility of trying to do so: to Browning on the other hand Truth is an absolute good – the *Ethics* have to be studied at last – and a lifetime is not too much to devote to its attainment.)

But, as DeVane rightly observes, 'the higher criticism of Homer . . . was only a parallel to the higher criticism of the New Testament' [16]. The parallel is not exact, but a valid point remains, that the Higher Criticism of the Bible also affects only the accidentals of the story and leaves its essential trueness intact. So that even if we prove that the Gospels are only fables we can still say that God's device in putting them before man was justifiable, since, like Browning's father's mimic siege, they offered the closest approximation to the truth that was appropriate at that time. Browning can prefer 'waking' (i.e. knowing the truth about the Bible) to 'dreams' (i.e. believing it to be the Word of God and literally true) only because he has developed beyond the stage where 'dreams' are necessary, although they were an essential stage in that development.

Stanza VII of *Reverie*, the last poem but one in *Asolando*, gives us warrant for extending this allegory of Browning's development to that of the religious consciousness of mankind as a whole from the age of myth to the age of reason. Reason is admittedly better than myth, but it would not have served at an earlier stage.[1] This is borne out by lines 18–23 of *Development*:

> a huge delight it proved
> And still proves – thanks to that instructor sage
> My Father, who knew better than turn straight
> Learning's full flare on weak-eyed ignorance,
> Or, worse yet, leave weak eyes to grow sand-blind,
> Content with darkness and vacuity.

Development is a moving and entertaining poem, showing at its best Browning's power to promote convergent lines of inquiry at various levels in a poem whose surface gives little sign of the complexity and tension beneath.

Of Browning's own religious position it tells us little, unless we choose to understand him as writing specifically about his own beliefs concerning the Incarnation. It seems plain that the story of Christ, which moved him so deeply in his youth and early middle age, commanded less and less belief as he grew older, or rather that he saw less and less need to regard it as historically true, and it seems likely that after 1864 the figure of Christ himself no longer satisfied Browning's imaginative or emotional demands; presumably as a consequence of this, Christ and the doctrines of primitive Christianity seldom play any important part in his later poems. The Gospel story operates, if at all, at a remove. Because it amply and powerfully illustrated God's love it was essentially true, since God's love was real; in addition it occupied a vital place in the religious development both of mankind and of the individual, being more beneficial to the undeveloped than either immediate knowledge or continued ignorance.

We can note then three stages in his personal development. First his contempt for easy conformity and his insistence, especially in his early poems, that Christianity is an intensely *demanding* religion; secondly, his willingness to dispense with historical evidences of Christ's existence in favour of an imagina-

---

[1] Cf. Comte, who writes at the end of *The Catechism of Positive Religion*, 'Humanity definitively occupies the place of God but she does not forget the services which the idea of God provisionally rendered.'

tive conviction of the *truth* of his ministry; and finally his total lack of trust in dogma, doctrine and churches in general, a mistrust which naturally led him to lay more and more stress on the responsibility of the individual. These stages are not of course totally at odds – even when Browning was at his most Christian his emphasis was on the religious experience and duty of the individual – but the difficulties of Browning's position are plain. While his ideas often remind us of those of original Christian thinkers such as Kierkegaard they also approach dangerously close to the positions of sceptics such as Feuerbach and Hume.

Other features are more idiosyncratic – for example, his insistence that certainty is incompatible with faith and his corresponding refusal to condemn doubt and hesitation. As I have suggested, constant self-questioning was the motive force of those of Browning's later poems in which he attempts to establish, literally from internal evidence, a world governed by Christian values. Equally characteristic is his favourite argument that the soul must be immortal because earth is imperfect; thus many of his poems begin from an attempt to justify on these grounds a specific defect or inadequacy in the world.

These paths of religious perambulation it would be profitless to attempt to organize into a system of religious teaching, but three general points may be made. First, when we are discussing Browning's poems about religion it is particularly important to ensure that our consideration is not limited to an assessment of them purely as linguistic displays but includes a discussion of the ideas that Browning is putting before us. Secondly, the quality of these ideas considered in the abstract is not negligible. Especially when he writes about what Christianity really means Browning is talking in the same terms as the most advanced thinkers of his day. Indeed in so far as he seems often to be handling the idea that Christianity may be the most heroic attempt man has ever made to understand himself, his nature, and his destiny, Browning may claim to be moving in the same area as the religious thinkers of our own century. (The idea presents itself to Browning as one to be disproved rather than welcomed.) Finally the main tenor of his thought is not foolishly optimistic. He was able to assent to the idea that God is Love, but he recognized that his assent, in face of the woes of the world, was grounded on Faith, and that his faith was ultimately a matter of Hope. If to acknowledge this precarious inter-dependence of the three Christian virtues and yet not to lose heart is to be an optimist, then Browning was one indeed. But if the alternative was a poetry of despair I do not think that he would have rejected the title.

V

A useful aid to placing Browning's religious opinions in the context of Victorian religious thought is given by Mrs Humphry Ward's novel *Robert Elsmere*, which provides in its characters an almost complete spectrum of possible religious positions. Browning was never, of course, as fanatical as the Ritualist clergyman Newcome, or even as rigid as Catherine Elsmere, whose intolerant faith is continually emphasized. Possibly at its most orthodox Browning's belief was never more dogmatic than that of Bickerton and the general run of Church of England ministers, although his sense of the burden of Christianity was much more acute. For most of his life, especially after 1864, Browning's views could roughly be identified with those of Grey, especially in his advocacy of 'the claims and considerations of the higher life'. The words Mrs Ward uses of Grey might as properly be applied to Browning:

> He had broken with the popular Christianity; but for him, God, consciousness, duty were the only realities. None of the various forms of materialist thought escaped his challenge; no genuine utterance of the spiritual life of man but was sure of his sympathy.

We may even hear an echo of Browning's voice when Grey says, 'The thought of man, as it has shaped itself in institutions, in philosophies, in science, in patient critical work, or in the life of charity, is the one continuous revelation of God!'

As he grew older Browning, like Elsmere himself, began to move away even from Grey's extraordinarily liberal Christianity to a position, which, if it has a label at all, may be roughly classified as Unitarian. His was not, of course, a primitive Channing-style Unitarianism; much less did he approach the 'crude Jacobinisms' of Mr and Mrs Wardlaw, who believed in Comte and the religion of humanity. I have no doubt that in moving, as it were, 'left', Browning was deeply influenced by the demythologizing work of the Higher Critics, represented in *Robert Elsmere* at their most bitter in the character of Wendover, whose rancorous attacks undermine and finally destroy the hero's faith. Unlike Elsmere, Browning was able to stop short of leaving the Church and founding a new religion. The necessities of her plot hardly allowed Mrs Ward to acknowledge the existence of any intermediate position once criticism of the historical evidences of Christianity was admitted, but many of Browning's later poems are devoted to the quest for such a position, one in which a man may stand without sacrificing either his honour or his hope.

In *Asolando* he gives us the reflections of a man who does not claim to have found a final solution, but is content to remember that at least he never gave up the fight to discover one. This is perhaps the only sense in which Browning may fairly be said to have prized the quest for its own sake. The idea of *human* responsibility, of the need to keep trying to do what it is right for a man to do, is never long absent from Browning's poems about religion: when the framework of religion is stripped away the responsibility remains, and is even heavier. This is perhaps most compactly demonstrated by pointing to a poem from *Ferishtah's Fancies* called *The Family*. The wise Dervish Ferishtah is reproached by a bystander for praying, on the grounds that prayer seeks to set aside something ordained by God. Man ought to acquiesce joyfully in God's will 'since/That which seems worst to man to God is best,/So, because God ordains it, best to man.' Ferishtah denies this, and tells a story designed to show that to try to anticipate God's will is 'to discard humanity itself'. The poem concludes

> No, be man and nothing more –
> Man who, as man conceiving, hopes and fears,
> And craves and deprecates, and loves, and loathes,
> And bids God help him, till death touch his eyes
> And shows God granted most, denying all.

There follows one of the short intercalary lyrics, which are subject to no dramatic distancing. It begins

> Man I am and man would be, Love – merest man and nothing more.
> Bid me seem no other! Eagles boast of pinions – let them soar!
> I may put forth angel's plumage, once unmanned, but not before.

The phrase 'once unmanned' works in two ways. It means simply 'once I am dead' but also 'once you have taken my manhood away from me'. This is a quality which Browning prizes more than 'angel's plumage'.

In the last section of this chapter I examine briefly the standards by which Browning thinks men should live in so far as these are without a religious sanction, or, to put the matter more briefly, what Browning means by 'manhood'.

VI

As I know more of mankind I expect less of them, and am ready now to call a man a *good man*, upon easier terms than I was formerly.

JOHNSON, September 1783

Propria quae maribus. *The Eton Grammar*

To speak of Browning as a moral poet is not to imply that he set up as the vendor of any patent ethical system or offered a universal cure for the ills of Society: it is simply to observe that poem after poem is best understood as an exploration, now from one side, now from another, of the central question of what it means to be a man. If it is important to be 'man and nothing more', what qualities are integral to the poet's idea of manhood?

Once again the starting-point must be a warning that Browning's 'morality' is not to be regarded as an ingeniously detachable part of his poetry. If it is active at all it underlies the poetry and should inform every full discussion of a single poem. If it is taken sufficient account of in what has been said in this book about such diverse poems as *Blougram, Sludge, Fifine, The Inn Album, St. Martin's Summer, Rephan,* and *Popularity,* to take a random selection, this is, to my mind, all that is required. Obviously a pattern may be made to show itself by a suitable arrangement of individual critiques, but the pattern matters less than the poem. If, however, there are people who really feel that they need a pattern, or need help in coaxing one to emerge, or feel that they cannot hope to understand Browning unless they are warned in advance what to expect, a few leading ideas may be isolated and arranged in a relationship that may prove helpful.

We may ignore some of Browning's favourite paradoxical

punchballs, such as whether the end justifies the means, whether man is to be judged by intention or achievement and so on. It is enough to say that many of his works, major and minor, pivot on moral dilemmas of this kind, so that in a very obvious sense a discussion of his poetry involves a discussion of moral issues and points of view.

It is more important to make explicit some of the ideas that lie so deep within the poems that they really function not as propositions but as axioms, or as fundamental truths which the poet does not doubt that the reader will accept. What then are Browning's axioms, and do they stay constant? I number them for ease of reference.

1. The choice of religion is vitally important: it is equally important to *choose* unbelief. Even the sceptical Blougram does not deny this:

> In every man's career are certain points
> Whereon he dares not be indifferent;
> The world detects him clearly, if he dare,
> As baffled at the game, and losing life.
> He may care little or he may care much
> For riches, honour, pleasure, work, repose,
> Since various theories of life and life's
> Success are extant which might easily
> Comport with either estimate of these;
> And whoso chooses wealth or poverty,
> Labour or quiet, is not judged a fool
> Because his fellow would choose otherwise:
> We let him choose upon his own account
> So long as he's consistent with his choice.
> But certain points, left wholly to himself,
> When once a man has arbitrated on,
> We say he must succeed there or go hang.
> Thus, he should wed the woman he loves most
> Or needs most, whatsoe'er the love or need –
> For he can't wed twice. Then, he must avouch,
> Or follow, at the least, sufficiently,
> The form of faith his conscience holds the best,
> Whate'er the process of conviction was:
> For nothing can compensate his mistake
> On such a point, the man himself being judge:
> He cannot wed twice, nor twice lose his soul.
>
> (275–300)

Of course as he grew older Browning was progressively less able to believe in the Incarnation and was progressively less concerned with forms of worship, but he was never less insistent that one of man's prime duties was to think earnestly about his place in the Creation.

2 (*a*) Setting aside revelation, certain demonstrative knowledge of what man's life ought to be like is impossible.

2 (*b*) Since (from 2 (*a*)) knowing the right thing to do is impossible, man is confronted with a choice between doing nothing, and doing his best. Of these the second is the only manly course. This entails acting as if one were part of a just and beneficent creation, since there would otherwise be no motive for action at all.

2 (*c*) It follows from 2 (*a*) and 2 (*b*) that since no final goal can be attained the value of 'doing one's best' is terminal, not mediant.

> Though I do my best I shall scarce succeed –
> But what if I fail of my purpose here?
> It is but to keep the nerves at strain,
> To dry one's eyes and laugh at a fall,
> And baffled, get up to begin again, –
> So the chace takes up one's life, that's all.
> (*Life in a Love*, 10–15)

The simplest way to think of Browning is as a man who would like Absolutes, realizes that they are not to be attained, and makes do with Potentialities. He does this so wholeheartedly that Potential Good, the power to *become*, is almost elevated to the status of an Absolute, or at least an end in itself. (This trust that 'the prize is in the process' [17] is carried so far that Browning might almost be accused of saying that all certainties are bad, because they destroy man as a moral agent, and all unfulfilled aspirations are good, because they are the distinctive mark of the human condition.)[1] Hence the difficulty of being

---

[1] There is thus some basis for the taunt that Browning regarded the world as a kind of moral gymnasium. His reply would, I think, be to quote *La Saisiaz*, 'Were earth and all it holds . . . Only a machine for teaching love and hate and hope and fear/To myself . . . I must say . . . "Sorrow did and joy did nowise, – life well weighed, – preponderate." ' (319–334)

It is helpful to remember also that Browning's insistence on the value of exertion

sure whether Browning dissociates himself completely from his casuists, for casuistry thrives wherever contingent values can be given the status of absolutes.

2 (d) From 2 (a), 2 (b) and 2 (c) it follows that a man who is living as he should be living will be recognized by his activeness and energy. Thus anything that makes a man less active or less energetic is bad. (Old age may be an exception to this.)

3. To discriminate between beneficial and harmful kinds of human activity Browning's great touchstone is, of course, love, as one would expect from what we have already seen of his religious opinions. (It is also an Absolute – 'Love is victory, the prize itself' [18].) Characters who are in love or who act through love are almost always treated with affection and admiration. An exception is the faintly ridiculous speaker of *A Serenade at a Villa* [19]: the speaker of *Cristina* (1842), is, I think, presented extravagantly as a deliberate contrast to the lofty diction of *Rudel*, the poem with which it was originally linked under the title of *Queen-Worship*.

Otherwise love is the master passion, stronger than evil and stronger than death. ' "I end with – Love is all and Death is nought!" quoth She.'[1] As a corollary letting love slip is the greatest omission, especially through laziness or timidity. Poems such as *Too Late* and *Dîs Aliter Visum* illustrate Browning's general attitude to those who fail to grasp love when it offers. *The Statue and the Bust* is a more extreme example:

---

should be set against the Victorian insistence on the importance of *arriving*. Browning says in effect, 'Success isn't everything, as some people seem to think. But if it isn't, what is the alternative? Failure without effort? Unthinkable.' This leaves the effort itself as what matters. This line of argument is more likely to satisfy scoutmasters than metaphysicians, but it seems to me a fair account of the principles on which most people actually live. Cf. Pope, *Essay on Man*: 'In lazy Apathy let Stoics boast/Their Virtue fix'd; 'tis fix'd as in a frost,/Contracted all, retiring to the breast;/But strength of mind is Exercise, not Rest.' (II, 101–104)

[1] Epilogue to *Fifine at the Fair*, line 32. Cf. also *Parleying with Daniel Bartoli* XVI. One of Browning's most moving tributes to the qualities of human love occurs in Paracelsus' last long speech:

> Love which endures and doubts and is oppressed
> And cherished, suffering much and much sustained,
> A blind, oft-failing, yet believing love,
> A half-enlightened, often-chequered trust. (V, 703–706)

at the end of the poem Browning makes his own comment on
the faint-hearted lovers:

> Surely they see not God, I know,
> Nor all that chivalry of His,
> The soldier-saints who, row on row,
>
> Burn upward each to his point of bliss –
> . . . .
>
> Stake your counter as boldly every whit,
> Venture as truly, use the same skill,
> Do your best, whether winning or losing it,
>
> If you choose to play – is my principle!
> Let a man contend to the uttermost
> For his life's set prize, be it what it will!
>
> The counter our lovers staked was lost
> As surely as if it were lawful coin:
> And the sin I impute to each frustrate ghost
>
> Was, the unlit lamp and the ungirt loin,
> Though the end in sight was a crime, I say.
> You of the virtue, (we issue join)
> How strive you? *De te, fabula!*

Worsfold rightly observes that the spirit lying behind the poem
is precisely that of Luther's *Pecca fortiter* [20].

4. 'Doing one's best' involves choosing boldly and abiding by
one's choice. The mechanism that actually makes choices is a
non-intellectual one, as opposed to the mechanism that ranges
and classifies the issues between which a choice is to be made
and explores the implications of the various possible choices.
The head, that is, can tell you the best means to a given end, but
the choice of ends is a matter for the heart.[1] Taken with point
3 (above) this disposes Browning very much in favour of people
who act impulsively as the heart dictates. 'Let him rush straight,

---

[1] Another connection between heart and head is suggested when Paracelsus speaks
of one of the attributes of humanity as 'Knowledge – not intuition, but the slow/
Uncertain fruit of an enhancing toil,/Strengthened by love.' (V, 697–699)

and how shall he go wrong?'[1] Timidity and hesitation are condemned with more than usual emphasis. Browning shows dislike
and contempt for those who act cautiously and calculatingly, and
invariably contrasts them unfavourably with those who boldly
aim at a high mark. *Andrea del Sarto*, with its carefully subdued
tones of grey and silver, shows how little regard Browning had
for the man who undertook only what he was certain he could
achieve. In contrast the grammarian of *A Grammarian's Funeral*
sets his goal so high that it is perfectly plain that it cannot be
achieved in this world. Therefore he must rely on a life to come.
Thus his renunciation of the possibility of worldly success is in
itself an eloquent testimony of faith. He is 'still loftier than the
world suspects,/Living and dying' [21]. The Grammarian,
though he prefers books to the open air and puts his trust in the
life to come rather than trying to achieve worldly success, is
saved because of his perception that failure through attempting
too much may be heroic. Men's successes, by definition, can be
at best trivial compared with the works of God, but when he
fails man is doing what God himself cannot do. 'The incomplete,/
More than completion, matches the immense' [22].

5. Since choosing is of such crucial importance in Browning's
poetry it is plain that he assumes (though without saying it very
often) that the freedom of the individual to make his own choices
is a supreme good. Without this freedom man cannot define his
own manhood by his own actions.

6. It is also vitally important that man should, before making a
choice, have a clear knowledge of what he is doing and acknowledge honestly to himself the implications of the alternatives
before him. Thus 'truth' is to Browning more than just a term of
general approbation: it is an essential condition of man's understanding and realization of his manhood [23]. It is not hard to
see why Browning is so hostile to casuists and sophists, who
distort the truth (6), intellectualize their choices (4), and do
this as a device for avoiding energetic action (2 (*d*)).

This rather arid schematization can perhaps be understood
more readily by showing how Browning brings his moral ideas
to life in the characters of his poems. It is almost true to say that

[1] *The Ring and the Book* X, 1564. Cf. 'Ask thy lone soul what laws are plain to thee,/
Thee, and no other; stand or fall by them.' (*A Camel-Driver*, 54–55)

his fundamental moral insights are completely illustrated in three characters from *The Ring and the Book* – Pompilia, the Pope and Caponsacchi. Pompilia is presented as lovely and unmistakably good, but inexperienced and vulnerable. Her innocence is a sovereign human quality, but nobody can rely on preserving it. The Pope is the epitome of human experience, but nobody can count on attaining such wisdom. Between these two ideals is placed Caponsacchi, whose fine qualities are by no means so inaccessible. He is distinguished by his courage. The Pope says, in language whose rhythm and imagery alike bear witness to Browning's enthusiastic endorsement,

> Ay, such championship
> Of God at first blush, such prompt cheery thud
> Of glove on ground that answers ringingly
> The challenge of the false knight, – watch we long
> And wait we vainly for its gallant like
>
> . . . .
>
> Pray
> 'Lead us into no such temptations, Lord!'
> Yea, but, O Thou whose servants are the bold,
> Lead such temptations by the head and hair,
> Reluctant dragons, up to who dares fight,
> That so he may do battle and have praise!
>
> (X, 1156–60, 1187–92)

The Pope commends his ready sympathy (1138), his 'love and faith' (1114, 1548), and in particular his impulsiveness, his 'healthy rage', his 'chivalry/That dares the right and disregards alike/The yea and nay o' the world'. Caponsacchi may one day become wise: hence his potential value [24]. He may, as the Pope says, learn 'soldiership,/Self-abnegation, freedom from all fear,/Loyalty to the life's end!' These, unlike wisdom and innocence, are attainable qualities, which will enable man to live in the world as it is [25]. It is significant that the last words of the Pope's address to Caponsacchi are 'Work, be unhappy but bear life, my son!', where 'bear' means not just 'endure' but 'carry' and also 'give birth to'.

VII

Ultimately what tests Browning's 'philosophy' is whether his readers accept it as a true picture of what man is and what he can do. In this concluding section I offer a few points which carry some weight on one side or the other in the final balance.

First, the most obvious point to strike any reader about Browning's philosophy is its home-made nature. Although this naturally annoys the professional, who prefers the orthodox, 'houses are but built by men', however much architects may disapprove of the man who builds his own. Admittedly Browning sometimes seems to be devising *ad hoc* solutions to difficulties: it seems more charitable to regard this as a consequence of his lack of dogmatism. His strength is that he is prepared to proceed empirically, never trying to bend reality to fit a preconceived theory.

Secondly, it is perhaps unnecessary to repeat that Browning was not deluded by a foolish optimism, but it is significant that he has been almost universally assumed guilty of precisely this.[1] The reasons are fairly plain. The first is Sir Henry Jones's book, though this should not be considered coercive (see Chapter 8). Again, Browning does not demonstrate convincingly anywhere that he really comprehends points of view opposed to his own. He seems not to have understood anything of the values of the contemplative life: this is what gives Santayana's hostile criticism its point. He seems not to have had much sympathy for the depressed: he talks about 'sneaks' and 'aimless, hopeless, helpless' 'drivel', as if everyone who succumbed to despair did so on purpose or through lack of moral fibre. Finally he seems not to have realized what it is to be disillusioned, or why some people do not see evil as a foe to be challenged and vanquished in fair fight, but have simply learned from experience that impulsive positive emotions are not enough, that people who love wholeheartedly do not invariably find happiness, that the wicked flourish, and so on. This means that Browning's trust in energetic action annoys many people, as does his brisk way with those in low spirits. He appears unsubtle and insensitive; especially so if you compare him with, say, Clare, or Cowper, or even Hardy, less so perhaps if you think of him against Swinburne or James

---

[1] For example, an anonymous reviewer of a book on Arnold describes the author as 'an optimist of the Browning persuasion'. (*TLS*, 3 August 1962, p. 555) Similarly David Daiches can sum up Browning as 'an admired widower, successful and content with his lot, believing in life and love and work and immortality.' *A Critical History of English Literature*, II, p. 1007.

Thomson or Housman. 'Optimistic' is a convenient dismissive epithet.

I think that this point too must be conceded, but here too there is a positive side. Browning's heartiness at least saves him from inertia, from an indulged melancholy, and from cynicism. He does not, as his admirers once thought, offer a complete solution to human problems, but if we recognize that no philosopher will offer us more than a partial solution at best, then Browning might reasonably maintain that his was the right part to choose.

I shall end this chapter as I began, by recurring to the enormous importance for the critic of not disregarding a poet's moral ideas and the equally enormous difficulty of discussing them in isolation from their poetic or dramatic context. With Browning the problem is particularly acute, since as a dramatic writer he has a preference for depicting his characters in a moment of crisis, and this crisis is very often the moment of making a crucial ethical choice. Indeed, if today we ask not that a philosopher should 'solve' problems at all but that he should help us to understand more clearly what the problem is, then Browning is a very good philosopher indeed, since he has the vital gift of conveying a problem in terms of a complete human situation. As I have suggested, an abstract of Browning's favourite moral criteria gives the impression that an extremely naïve and rather clumsy, even barbarous, set of values is called into play. But when we read the poems themselves it is clear that Browning has realized the moral lives of his speakers in extraordinary fullness and complexity. He portrays his casuists, for example, with great sympathy and great insight, and endows them with great intellectual subtlety: this gives him the right to judge them, to weigh and condemn them by standards no less subtle than their own arguments. Behind all the equivocations the reader is made to feel the presence of moral values which, after all due allowances have been scrupulously made, will ultimately be used to assess the worth of the speaker, I do not think that Browning has anywhere expressed these values more straightforwardly than in his *Essay on Shelley* (1852), where he wrote

> I call Shelley a moral man, because he was true, simple-hearted and brave, and because what he acted corresponded to what he knew.

❖ 10 ❖

Browning's Diction

It is no verse, except enchanted groves
And sudden arbours shadow coarse-spunne lines?
Must purling streams refresh a lovers loves?
Must all be vail'd while he that reades, divines,
    Catching the sense at two removes? HERBERT, *Jordan*

We may say that the duty of the poet, as poet, is only indirectly to
his people: his direct duty is to his *language*, first to preserve, and
second to extend and improve.
T. S. ELIOT, *The Social Function of Poetry*

When you have said *shaggy urban virile* [in Dante's classification]
you have said all that needs to be said about Browning's diction.
H. C. DUFFIN, *Amphibian* (1956)

In Chapter 3 I examined Browning's reaction against the practices of the Romantic poets of the nineteenth century and his
rejection of what he considered their faulty use of worn-out
poetic machinery, especially that derived from Classical mythology. His objection to it was, in brief, that it served only to 'push
back reality', leaving the reader to 'catch the sense at two
removes'. That Browning in fact brought to his fresh and unconventional subject-matter a machinery equally modern and
unhackneyed is not in dispute, but it is not always conceded that
his diction also was notably direct and contemporary: few people
think of Browning as one of the masters of natural English verse.
    Indeed in the most extended recent study of Browning's lan-
guage, Professor Preyer goes so far as to say, 'The mean or
natural style is rare in Browning', and maintains that he 'belongs
with the dithyrambic or daemonic poets'[1]. He distinguishes
two principal modes of expression, 'simple' and 'difficult'. The
simple style, though it has a lot of surface buzz and clamour and

is busy, abrupt, energetic, exaggerated and dissonant, is not hard to understand; the basic syntax is so clear that the powerful verbs carry the reader rapidly along. The difficult style is what we find in any of Browning's verse which cannot be understood at a rapid reading, for example because of uncertain tenses or displaced syntax. It seems to me that what Professor Preyer is really discussing is the two different degrees of obscurity or difficulty which I have exemplified in Chapters 4–7: as I indicated there, an examination of them tells us much about the nature of Browning's poetry. But they should certainly not be allowed to distract our attention from the equally significant body of poems in which Browning uses a 'mean or natural style' precisely because he wishes not to write in a dithyrambic or daemonic vein but to deal with 'the daily and undignified'.

This extremely important side of Browning's diction cannot be adequately illustrated here, but the examples given may be supplemented by reference to Edward Lucie-Smith's excellent selection, which admirably illuminates this quality in the poet's work[2]. Mr Lucie-Smith's introductory remarks are especially interesting when he discusses the question of what the poets of today have learned from Browning. I wish to set this particular influence in a larger context, that of the whole tradition of the 'mean and natural style' in English verse.

I

In a celebrated passage Thomas Gray wrote, 'The language of the age is never the language of poetry'[3]. The most cursory glance at the body of European literature confirms the broad truth of the generalization that lies behind Gray's hyperbole. The Greek playwrights, even Aristophanes, had their own vocabularies and constructions, and anyone who has tried to compound a prose with the help of Lewis and Short will know how many useful Latin words and constructions are barred by the pervasive note 'poët'. The same holds good when we leave the Classical languages: the specialized and jealously preserved vocabulary and the 'kennings' of the Old English bards were equally remote from contemporary prose usage, and as far as we can judge, even more remote from the ordinary spoken language of the time.

Again if we consider Petrarch, or Camoens, or Spenser, or Milton and his imitators, it is easy to see why Gray made such a firm distinction between the language from which poets made their poems and the language used by smaller men for their smaller affairs. It is a distinction which can be readily allowed if its implication is that poets have a right to go beyond the limits of everyday conversation, that they are under no obligation to confine themselves to the rhythm, idiom and vocabulary of the man on the Clapham omnibus. But when the emphasis falls on the other side and we are invited to agree that poets have a positive duty to use, some or all of the time, words, phrases and constructions with a distinctively archaic or exotic colouring and that their work will be poetry only if it is so distinguished from common speech, then Gray must be resisted, first on the general grounds that no prior conditions are to be imposed on the poet, secondly on the grounds that many poets have in fact successfully employed 'the language of the age' to achieve effects obtainable in no other way.

We need not go back to the *sermo pedestris* of Horace for examples of this, for it is a strain of some antiquity in English verse. In general we find that it is, as we should expect, rare in epic and in formal poetry such as the Pindaric Ode; that it is, as we should again expect, most common when the writer is describing the life of his own times, as for example in satires, or in non-heroic narrative poems, or where, for dramatic reasons, the writer attempts to represent contemporary speech in verse; and that poetry of this kind still sounds modern, that is, even though it is by definition written in the idiom of a specific time and often describes events of particular topical interest, it is a way of speaking that has not dated.

In Chaucer's *Troilus and Criseyde*, although it is a poem of epic proportions set in the past, the language is simple and spontaneous. Pandare and Criseyde, as has often been remarked, converse in a light informal idiom, but it is notable that even where Chaucer writes as narrator there is no sense of a deliberate elevation in his language. (The invocations, the proems and the epilogue are more obviously 'poetic'.) The same pattern is seen in *The Canterbury Tales*. *The Knight's Tale* clearly exploits the advantages of the conventional diction of poetry, and the *Squire's Tale*, in a more sprightly way, does the same thing, but the

Miller's tale, the *Reeve's Tale*, and the *Nonne Priest's Tale* are distinguished by their swift racy colloquial language. This is perhaps to be explained as ventriloquism – Chaucer is simply reproducing for dramatic effect the speech of his characters – but this explanation clearly does not cover the links and the prologues, where Chaucer is speaking in his own person. In the *Wife of Bath's Prologue*, for example, his language suggests simple informal speech, yet who would deny that he is writing poetry? No doubt there will be some to do so, and to suggest that Light Verse is the proper category for Chaucer.

There is no need to contest the point, as there are many later examples. Wyat, to name the most obvious, has much of Chaucer's command over uninflated English, not only in his excellent *Satires*, but in his lyrics. The following stanza, which must be familiar to everyone, is only one of many which make the point:

> Thankt be Fortune, it hath been otherwise
> Twenty times better; but once, in special,
> In thin array, after a pleasant guise,
> When her loose gown from her shoulders did fall,
> And she me caught in her arms long and small,
> Therewith so sweetly did me kiss,
> And softly said, 'Dear heart, how like you this?'
>> ('They flee from me . . .', 8–14)

The world of the Elizabethan lyric is sometimes regarded solely as a 'garden with Pedantique weeds o'rspred', but even here convention and conventional diction were not seldom set aside in favour of natural contemporary words and figures. For example:

> The Andalusian merchant, that returns
>> Laden with cochineal and china dishes,
> Reports in Spain how strangely Fogo burns
>> Amidst an ocean full of flying fishes:
> These things seem wondrous, yet more wondrous I,
> Whose heart with fear doth freeze, with love doth fry. [4]

Although many other examples could be produced, such writing was not general at the end of the sixteenth century: for the most part the poets chose to distinguish their language from that of prose and of common speech. This situation could of course be exploited by any poet who was prepared to write more informally, and was so exploited by Sidney[1] and even more notably by John Donne. Carew in his *Elegy* puts the case thus:

> Whatsoever wrong
> By ours was done the Greek or Latin tongue
> Thou hast redeem'd, and open'd Us a Mine
> Of rich and pregnant Phansie, drawn a line
> Of masculine expression. (35–39)[2]

Certainly Donne has not in recent years lacked admirers to demonstrate the powerful poetic effects he achieves by the deliberate use of contemporary idiom; nor are examples necessary to convince a modern reader of the telling simplicity of Donne, Herbert and Vaughan, a simplicity which is far more characteristic of the best Metaphysical poetry than what Macaulay calls 'the quaint forms and gaudy colouring of such artists as Cowley and Gongora'[5]. Later in the century perhaps the most impressive examples of sustained poetry in contemporary language are to be found in Marvell:

> But now the *Salmon-Fishers* moist
> Their *Leathern Boats* begin to hoist;
> And, like Antipodes in Shoes,
> Have shod their *Heads* in their *Canoos*.
> How *Tortoise like*, but not so slow,
> These rational *Amphibii* go?
> Let's in: for the dark *Hemisphere*
> Does now like one of them appear.

This is the last stanza of *Upon Appleton House*, a poem which maintains throughout the accents of intelligent conversation.

It is a commonplace of criticism that the poets of the Augustan age found the speech of their contemporaries a not unsatisfactory basis for the diction of much of their verse, especially when they were writing on contemporary subjects[6]. At the end of *Religio Laici* Dryden writes candidly,

> And this unpolish'd, rugged Verse I chose;
> As fittest for Discourse, and nearest prose.

[1] See Sonnets I, VI, XV, XXVIII, and LXXIV: note that in each poem Sidney puts forward the simplicity of his language as an earnest of the sincerity of his love.
[2] But see Johnson, 'Allowance must be made for some degree of exaggerated praise. In lapidary inscriptions a man is not upon oath.' (Boswell, 5 December 1775)

Indeed it was a byword of the Romantic critics that Dryden and Pope were intolerably prosaic. Their simple, direct use of the vocabulary and idiom of polite conversation is naturally most obvious in their epistles: note particularly the *Epistle to Dr. Arbuthnot* and the *Epistle to Miss Blount* (on her leaving the Town after the Coronation):

> She went to plain-work, and to purling brooks,
> Old-fashion'd halls, dull aunts, and croaking rooks,
> She went from Op'ra, park, assembly, play,
> To morning walks, and pray'rs three hours a day;
> To part her time 'twixt reading and Bohea,
> To muse, and spill her solitary Tea,
> Or o'er cold coffee trifle with the spoon,
> Count the slow clock, and dine exact at noon;
> Divert her eyes with pictures in the fire,
> Hum half a tune, tell stories to the squire;
> Up to her godly garret after sev'n,
> There starve and pray, for that's the way to Heav'n.
>
> (11–22)

The effects that the Augustan poets obtained in this idiom are too obvious to require listing in detail. I would mention only three: first, a feeling of intimacy with the reader, and an intimacy on equal terms; secondly, a feeling of immediacy, that the poem is directly applicable to the contemporary situation and has not, as it were, to be 'translated' by the reader out of 'Poesie' into his own language; and finally, a feeling of naturalness, so that contemporary references can be introduced without affectation and without bathos. Gay, for example, can refer to an umbrella, or Pope to a door-knocker without resorting to periphrasis or destroying the tone of the poem. Nor does this confine the poet to the realm of everyday things and everyday emotions: it is notable that Pope in particular finds no difficulty in rising to the heights of heroic sentiment without disturbing the keeping of his satires. For example, in *Satire I Book II of Horace imitated* (To Mr Fortescue), he writes in plain terms

> Satire's my Weapon, but I'm too discreet
> To run a Muck, and tilt at all I meet;
> I only wear it in a Land of Hectors,
> Thieves, Supercargoes, Sharpers, and Directors. (69–73)

Within fifty lines he is able, without the slightest incongruity, to make his celebrated declaration of his purpose as a satirist:

> Yes, while I live, no rich or noble knave
> Shall walk the World, in credit, to his grave.
> TO VIRTUE ONLY and HER FRIENDS, A FRIEND:
> The World beside may murmur, or commend.
>
> (119–122)

One of the dangers of generalization about eighteenth-century poetry is that while some poets, in theory and practice, agreed with Gray that poetry required its particular diction, as many more wrote, without apparent consciousness of the problem, in language which was recognizably based on their own habits of speech. Even if we state the question in its simplest terms by setting aside the many others who wrote now in one idiom, now in the other, as they chose, we have still on the one hand the poets whose conscious search for a distinctively poetic style attracted the scorn and censure of Wordsworth: on the other, poets who used as the staple of their verse precisely the same register of English as they used for their letters or for social conversation.

The same division is found in the nineteenth century. There is no need to illustrate the diction usually associated with the Romantic poets, highly-coloured, admitting archaisms, rich in metaphor, and abounding in the devices such as alliteration and heavily marked metre which distinguish verse from prose, but in the same period it is not hard to find many poems written in a 'selection of the language really used by men'. Some of the *Lyrical Ballads* may be included among them, thought not nearly as many as one would expect from a reading of Wordsworth's *Preface*; Donald Davie has argued persuasively for Shelley's *Julian and Maddalo* [7]; but the most notable exponent is of course Byron.

Few modern critics of Byron find much to admire in the extravagant poems and poetic dramas, such as *Cain* and *Childe Harold*, which were so influential in Britain and in Europe during the nineteenth century. His reputation today rests on his later satirical poems, *Beppo*, *The Vision of Judgement* and especially *Don Juan*, which for all its casual diction and apparent lack of careful composition is now recognized as Byron's most satisfying and most serious poem. Of Byron's ability to catch the accents of informal speech there is no question.

> Where is Napoleon the Grand? God knows:
>   Where little Castlereagh? The devil can tell:
> Where Grattan, Curran, Sheridan, all those
>   Who bound the bar or senate in their spell?
> Where is the unhappy Queen, with all her woes?
>   And where the Daughter, whom the Isles loved well?
> Where are those martyr'd saints the Five per Cents?
> And where – oh, where the devil are the Rents?
>
> (*Don Juan*, XI, lxxvii)

This deliberately matter-of-fact tone was Byron's most effective instrument in the detection and destruction of pretentiousness and false sentiment.[1]

The Victorian poets in general eschewed any forms of language which suggested ordinary speech unless they were deliberately writing comic or light verse, which was extremely popular: the names of Hood, Barham, Lear, Carroll, Calverley, Arnold (*Poor Matthias*), and Tennyson (*Will Waterproof's Lyrical Monologue*) testify to the high quality of verse of this kind. No doubt the practice of writing and reading comic verse helped to prevent a total divorce between the language of men and that of the poet, but the gulf between light verse and poetry proved in practice to be nearly as deep and difficult to bridge.[2]

The examples which I have presented show something of the flexibility and diversity of this tradition in English verse, and something of its characteristic strength: yet in the reign of Victoria the strain almost died out. Of the major poets only Browning attempted to use consistently in serious verse the vocabulary and speech patterns of the ordinary middle-class Englishman, with what success I propose to examine in the remainder of this chapter.

[1] Cf. Byron's own comment, as recorded by Lady Blessington, 'Does the cant of Sentiment still continue in England? *Childe Harold* called it forth, but my *Juan* was well calculated to cast it into shade and had that merit if it had no other.' *Conversations*, p. 376 (1823)

[2] Hood, for instance, since he was labelled a comic poet, was consistently underestimated as a serious writer in the nineteenth century. Clough was perhaps the only poet to overcome the disability of being witty in verse.

II

Most studies of Browning's language reveal very little of this important element in his verse. Bernard Groom has an S.P.E. Tract [8], of which the middle section is devoted to an examination of Browning's diction. Mr Groom promises well when he observes, 'He [Browning] had no fastidious shyness of influences: his inner life was so robust that he delighted to rub shoulders with the outer world – the world of ideas and words, no less than the world of men and women. Hence his work reflects many aspects of the language of his time: it is a magazine of colloquial phrases . . .'. (p. 118) Later Mr Groom makes the point that many of the speakers of the monologues unburden their minds with the utmost freedom; 'To suit the frankness of these self-revelations, Browning cultivates the utmost informality of style.' Finally, 'Browning's most profitable example to later poets lay in his use of colloquial English for the impassioned lyric. As G. K. Chesterton excellently puts it, "He substituted the street with the green blind for the faded garden of Watteau, and 'the blue spirt of a lighted match' for the monotony of the evening star"'. But Mr Groom, it soon appears, is really proposing to discuss not style but vocabulary. Thus he gives slight and unsatisfactory treatment to Browning's use of everyday language, which by its nature cannot be demonstrated by citing individual words; instead he concentrates on Browning's singularities, his 'verbal freaks', archaisms and compound words, which can be more conveniently displayed.

In the same way Miss Josephine Miles takes the word as her unit and thus focusses attention simply on choice of vocabulary [9]. In addition her survey is based on a thousand lines only of Browning's work, and that not the most representative.[1] Nevertheless within these limits Miss Miles makes some interesting points about the words Browning uses. For example, her figures show that whereas the proportions of parts of speech in ten lines of Milton's verse are nouns sixteen, adjectives twelve, verbs eight, in ten lines of Browning the proportions are nouns

---

[1] Miss Miles uses the first 500 lines of *Pippa Passes* and the first 500 lines of *Dramatic Lyrics*: if I understand her references she has not used *Dramatic Lyrics* as first published in 1842 but taken the first 500 lines of the poems regrouped under that title in 1863 and later collected editions.

sixteen, adjectives eight, verbs twelve, a finding which corroborates what most sensitive readers will already have perceived
about the difference between the two poets.

In a more recent book devoted entirely to Browning [10]
Park Honan also makes one or two points about the poet's
vocabulary, especially in his dramatic monologues. In his seventh
chapter he notes key words in certain monologues (for example,
Blougram uses 'faith' and 'doubt'; the Bishop (St Praxed's) uses
'God'; and so on) and suggests that the proper nouns people
use are those you would expect. He reaches the perhaps not
altogether unpredictable conclusion that the words the speaker
uses may reveal his character and that on the whole Browning
chooses a vocabulary appropriate to the speaker.

On these studies I have two comments to make. First, that
what is of most interest to the reader of Browning is not what he
has in common with other poets of the 1840s (i.e. Miss Miles's
Primary poetic language) but what he does with the English
language in verse that nobody else does. Secondly that they
describe only a part of the topic. They tell us something about
Browning's vocabulary; similarly in Chapters 4 and 5 I have
offered an analysis of Browning's syntactical idiosyncrasies, but
neither vocabulary nor syntax gives a complete account of the
total idiom in which Browning is writing. I use the phrase 'total
idiom' to comprehend the whole area covered by the overlapping
expressions 'mood', 'tone', 'language', 'style', 'diction' and
'vocabulary'.

Ultimately what determines the total idiom of Browning's
poetry is the level of discourse which he chooses. This level is, of
course, partly dictated by dramatic propriety; thus, as many of
Browning's dramatic poems present a situation in which an
intelligent man is conversing with his equals, the level of discourse is that of informed conversation on a basis of equality.
Naturally in the dramatic monologues the consistent use of the
first person contributes to his effect.

But even when there is no question of dramatic appropriateness Browning tends to base his verse on the same level of discourse, or at least to give the impression of doing so. Miss Miles
and Mr Groom are right when they imply that this is contrived
in part by selection of individual words e.g. *pate* for *head*, or
popped instead of *exploded*, but even here it is not simply a matter

of choosing the more informal of two synonymous words. It is evident that Browning not only differs from Gray by rejecting the idea of an elevated super-English, which alone is suitable for poetry, but also differs from Wordsworth, since he refuses to limit his possible vocabulary to conform to any previously determined standards of poetic propriety. Thus he leaves himself free to choose any word he feels necessary for his poetic effects, even though it would have been too mean for Gray or too exotic for Wordsworth. He claims for himself in other words the rights of a man in ordinary conversation to use the *mot juste*, whether it happens to be vulgar (e.g. *pully-hauly*) or technical (e.g. *mono-stich* or *abductor*), newlycoined (e.g. *calotypist*) or oldfashioned (e.g. *quoth* or *terquisition*), familiar (e.g. *dirt-cheap*) or un-familiar (e.g. *acromia* 'shoulderblades'), prosaic (e.g. *bunghole* or *ginger-pop*) or fanciful (e.g. *rose-jacynth*). This freedom, by its nature, is not susceptible to statistical treatment. For example, Miss Miles's tables do not indicate that in the 1,000 lines she analyses Browning uses such strikingly 'unpoetical' nouns as *shrub-house, window-pane, silk-winding, flesh-bunch, weevil, gera-niums, slide-bolt, wittol, cut-throat, proof-mark, moustache, flap-hat, beer, tar, rocket-plant, rubbish, cheese, blister, slug, trousers, dry-rot, parsley*, and many others. Yet the unselfconscious use of these words simply because they are the normal way of referring to the things they name is one of the distinctive features of Browning's total idiom. Miss Miles's laborious totting up of the common words completely fails to take account of them, yet they constitute the really memorable elements of his vocabulary.

The forms Browning prefers are often conversational. Mr Groom draws attention to his fondness for 'compound adverbs of which the first element is the prepositional prefix *a-*, as in *adrift*' [11]. No doubt this is true, but it is not of the first importance. Far more important in establishing the idiom in which he writes are his colloquial contractions, not the clipped prepositions and articles which I have mentioned in Chapters 4 and 5, but the contractions which represent the normal elisions of informal speech. As we should expect, there are many examples of this in the dramatic monologues: e.g. in *Mr. Sludge, 'The Medium'*, we find 'He's the man for muck', 'I'd like to know', 'I'll try to answer you', 'I can't pretend to mind your smiling', and 'it don't hurt much', and also *you've, you're, it's, I've, 'tisn't*.

But they are equally frequent where Browning is not creating a specific imaginary speaker: e.g. in *Apparent Failure* we find 'No Briton's to be Baulked', 'their sin's atoned', 'You've gained', and also the forms *I'll*, *it's*, and *can't*. Similarly Browning omits the relative in the accusative case, as is common in familiar conversation, but uncommon in verse, e.g. 'I hunt the house through/We inhabit together' (*Love in a Life*), or in *Apparent Failure* 'A screen of glass we're thankful for', where the preposition at the end of the sentence would hardly be admitted in formal prose.

These colloquial licences are common everywhere in Browning except where he wishes to produce an effect of solemnity, for example when he is discussing his deepest intuitions about the nature of God and man in the *Epilogue* to *Dramatis Personae*. They are one of the more obvious ways in which Browning deliberately discards a rhetorical sentence structure in favour of a much less ceremonial and balanced way of putting his sentences together, full of loose qualifying phrases. The first two stanzas of *Christmas-Eve* yield a representative sample – 'Heaven knows how many sorts of hands', 'at least', 'perhaps', 'in part', 'somehow', 'a female something', 'plain as print', 'as I say', 'if you please', 'accordingly', 'as it were', 'there was no standing it much longer'. These help to prevent the use of metre from giving too much elevation to the verse and to disclaim any intention of rhetorical exaggeration on the part of the speaker. Note that Stanza II begins with a particle not uncommon in Browning – 'Well, from the road, the lanes or the common . . .' He uses it again very tellingly in the *Two Poets of Croisic*: Stanza LVIII ends

> 'Must a tear
> Needs fall for that?' you smile. 'How fortune fares
> With such a mediocrity, who cares?'

and Stanza LIX begins

> 'Well, I care – intimately care . . .'[1]

But the effect of these and other similar devices is more easily illustrated than isolated:

> This taught me who was who and what was what
> > (*Development*, 16)

---

[1] Note that *Time's Revenges ends* with 'Well'.

And the leaf-buds on the vine are woolly,
 I noticed that, to-day;
One day more bursts them open fully
 – You know the red turns grey.
    (*The Lost Mistress*, 5–8)

Wherever a fresco peels and drops,
 Wherever an outline weakens and wanes
Till the latest life in the painting stops,
 Stands One whom each fainter pulse-tick pains:
One, wishful each scrap should clutch the brick,
 Each tinge not wholly escape the plaster,
– A lion who dies of an ass's kick,
 The wronged great soul of an ancient Master.
    (*Old Pictures in Florence*, VI)

Sometimes this idiom functions as a local stylistic device: sometimes it establishes the whole level of the poem. For example, in *Too Late*, one of the poems in *Dramatis Personae* (1864), Browning contrives, while following a complicated stanza form, to give the illusion of informal conversation in the precise idiom of the day:

I liked that way you had with your curls
 Wound to a ball in a net behind:
Your cheek was chaste as a quaker-girl's,
 And your mouth – there was never, to my mind,
Such a funny mouth, for it would not shut;
 And the dented chin too – what a chin!
There were certain ways when you spoke, some words
 That you know you never could pronounce:
You were thin, however; like a bird's
 Your hand seemed – some would say, the pounce
Of a scaly-footed hawk – all but!
The world was right when it called you thin.

What is remarkable about this is that it is the last stanza but one of a poem spoken by a man who is bleeding to death, having stabbed himself in the heart from grief at hearing of the death of the woman he loved.[1] Browning has therefore to use the utmost skill to ensure that the realistic surface of the poem is not broken, or the result will be theatrical, and to ensure also that his speaker

[1] Cf. the similar situation in *Pauline*.

does not use a style too humdrum for his mood of passionate but resolute grief, or the result will be bathetic. In fact Browning preserves the tone in this poem with remarkable subtlety, giving the speaker the accents of a man of some sensibility and culture in intimate conversation, and placing all the indications that he is in fact on his death bed in images (e.g. lines 12, 48, 57, 71–72, 92–93, 98–100, 142–144.) or in phrases that sound like metaphors but are in fact literally true (e.g. lines 39, 94–95, 115–116, 120, 133). The extraordinary situation of the speaker, which holds such possibilities of melodrama, is made at once more credible and more pathetic by his deliberate reining in of his language, while it is this feeling of *controlled* language even behind such everyday phrases as 'On the whole, you were let alone, I think!' which makes it possible for him to move without a sense of incongruity from Stanza XI, which I have already quoted, to the more obviously expressive diction of the final stanza.

Another function of contemporary idiom and speech pattern is to suggest the topicality of a particular monologue. Thus Fra Lippo Lippi, in spite of a light scattering of *Zooks*, *God wot*, and Florentine local colour speaks recognizably in the language of nineteenth-century London:

> I was a baby when my mother died
> And father died and left me in the street.
> I starved there, God knows how, a year or two
> On fig-skins, melon-parings, rinds and shucks,
> Refuse and rubbish. One fine frosty day,
> My stomach being empty as your hat,
> The wind doubled me up and down I went. (81–87)

Sometimes Lippo's accents are close to those of Sludge:

> Well, sir, I found in time, you may be sure,
> 'Twas not for nothing – the good bellyful,
> The warm serge and the rope that goes all round,
> And day-long blessed idleness beside!
> 'Let's see what the urchin's fit for' – that came next.
> Not overmuch their way, I must confess.
> Such a to-do! They tried me with their books:
> Lord, they'd have taught me Latin in pure waste! (102–109)

This swift, slangy diction aptly suggests that Lippo is a man of his time, but also, I think, helps the reader to see that what Lippo has to say about the business of the artist is true of the nineteenth century as well as of the Quattrocento.[1]

Browning's ability to write verse in current English is put to many other uses: it is particularly effective as a touchstone of the heroic attitude. A good example is *Prince Hohenstiel-Schwangau*, a poem which takes much of its artistic point from the piquancy of its setting. The ex-ruler, inevitably identified with Napoleon III, at first appears to be conversing with what Mrs Orr calls 'a young lady of adventurous type' whom he has met in Leicester Square. She has, we gather, said that she would like to know him. In response he confesses that he cannot himself be completely certain who he is, and proceeds to explain at considerable length certain actions of his past, ostensibly to throw light on his own personality, in fact to offer a comprehensive examination of and apology for all his policies. We are to imagine all this directed to the young woman, who is drinking tea while the speaker smokes a cigar; the language of the poem is suitable to such an occasion, partly matter-of-fact and practical, partly abstract and hypothetical. But the constant reminders of the unsophisticated listener to the monologue serve to bring the Prince down continually from his flight of fancy. 'I'm no poet, and am stiff i' the back' he says. No heroics are possible before such an audience. The quality of the language is also a guarantee of truth, or if not of truth then of realism:

> Suppose my oedipus should lurk at last
> Under a pork-pie hat and crinoline,
> And, lateish, pounce on Sphynx in Leicester Square? . . .
> I don't drink tea: permit me the cigar!
> . . . .
> My rank – (if I must tell you simple truth–
> Telling were else not worth the whiff o' the weed
> I lose for the tale's sake) – dear, my rank i' the world
> Is hard to know and name precisely: err
> I may, but scarcely over-estimate
> My style and title. Do I class with men
> Most useful to their fellows? Possibly, –

---

[1] In contrast the speaker in *Pictor Ignotus* uses a solemn, formalized diction, which with its inversions, archaisms and laboured personifications aptly expresses the unknown painter's inability to sympathize with the artistic fashions of his time.

Therefore, in some sort, best; but, greatest mind
And rarest nature? Evidently no.
A conservator, call me, if you please,
Not a creator nor destroyer: one
Who keeps the world safe.

In the first part of the poem the Prince speaks thus in the first
person, but at the turning point of the poem he declares that he
will change his approach

God will estimate
Success one day; and, in the mean time – you!
I dare say there's some fancy of the sort
Frolicking round this final puff I send
To die up yonder in the ceiling-rose, –
Some consolation-stakes, we losers win!
A plague of the return to 'I–I–I
Did this, meant that, hoped, feared the other thing!'
Autobiography, adieu! The rest
Shall make amends, be pure blame, history
And falsehood: not the ineffective truth,
But Thiers-and-Victor-Hugo exercise.
Hear what I never was, but might have been
I' the better world where goes tobacco-smoke!
Here lie the dozen volumes of my life:
(Did I say 'lie'? the pregnant word will serve).
Cut on to the concluding chapter, though!
Because the little hours begin to strike.
Hurry Thiers-Hugo to the labour's end!

The second half of the poem does not show any marked change of
language at first, except that the speaker refers to himself in the
third person, and some of Sagacity's speeches assume a more
pompous style. When for example she urges the Head to marry
and found a dynasty she suggests the speech he should make to
his subjects if he marries an attractive commoner.

'Is it the other sort of rank? – bright eye,
Soft smile, and so forth, all her queenly boast?
Undaunted the exordium – "I, the man
O' the people, with the people mate myself:
So stand, so fall. Kings, keep your crowns and brides!
Our progeny (if Providence agree)
Shall live to tread the baubles underfoot

> And bid the scarecrows consort with their kin.
> For son, as for his sire, be the free wife
> In the free state!" '

This speech stands out as spurious partly by reason of the incongruity of its diction with the normally uninflated style of the Prince's conversation.

At the end of the poem there is one of Browning's more surprising reversals. We learn first that the whole of the second half of the poem is in fact, as had been suggested earlier, an exercise in fantasy undertaken by the 'Veracious and imaginary Thiers'. The Prince comments on this

> You see 'tis easy in heroics! Plain
> Pedestrian speech shall help me perorate.

In the last dozen lines of the poem the Prince reveals that the whole scene has been a reverie[12]. He is still in his Residenz. His only connection with Leicester Square is his memory of it from a previous time in exile. He has in fact been sitting alone through the night thinking about his career as ruler; it is a crucial moment in his career, because he has to decide whether or not to despatch a letter to a fellow-ruler. The letter is presumably an ultimatum, which may lead eventually to the Prince's losing his throne. No doubt Browning had Bismarck in mind here, and thought of the monologue as being spoken just before the Franco-Prussian war. Hence the motto from the *Heracles*:

> I slew the Hydra, and from labour pass'd
> To labour – tribes of labours! Till, at last,
> Attempting one more labour, in a trice,
> Alack, with ills I *crowned the edifice*.

The poem, then, is an illusion. There was no 'bud-mouthed arbitress', nor any of the everyday properties which helped to keep the discussion out of the realm of heroic history. But the fiction has served its purpose since it has made the Prince talk in prose terms rather than in the language of the rhetorician,

> Subordinating, – as decorum bids,
> Oh, never fear! but still decisively, –
> Claims from without that take too high a tone,
> – ('God wills this, man wants that, the dignity
> Prescribed a prince would wish the other thing').

The fact that he chooses 'plain pedestrian speech' is a pledge that he will offer honest self-examination instead of the inflated account which the historian will in time manufacture. Occasionally, however, Browning seems to forget the rather tenuous dramatic situation in which he has placed his speaker, and the result is hard to distinguish from a flat political speech manoeuvred into flat blank verse [13].

Elsewhere Browning usually remembers more consistently the imaginary *listener* to the monologue, and in consequence maintains the tone of the speaker more accurately. Thus the Englishman in Italy adapts his language to his young listener, talking quietly and easily. In contrast the Jew in *Holy-Cross Day* speaks in colloquial bursts:

> Aaron's asleep – shove hip to haunch,
> Or somebody deal him a dig in the paunch!
> Look at the purse with the tassel and knob,
> And the gown with the angel and thingum-bob!
> What's he at, quotha? reading his text!
> Now you've his curtsey – and what comes next? (V)

One is reminded of the language of Filippo Baldinucci:

> 'No, boy, we must not'– so began
> My Uncle (he's with God long since)
> A-petting me, the good old man!
> 'We must not' – and he seemed to wince,
> And lost that laugh whereto had grown
> His chuckle at my piece of news,
> How cleverly I aimed my stone –
> 'I fear we must not pelt the Jews!' (I)

Notice also the numerous poems of Browning's which are a conversation or half a conversation between a man and a woman talking about their relationship. I need only name *A Woman's Last Word, Love Among the Ruins, A Lovers' Quarrel, By the Fire-side, Two in the Campagna, Respectability, A Light Woman, James Lee's Wife, The Worst of it, Dîs Aliter Visum, Too Late, Youth and Art, A Serenade at the Villa, The Last Ride Together, St. Martin's Summer*, and many of the lyrics in *Asolando*.[1] These

---

[1] *Any Wife to any Husband* is one of Browning's most moving poems, but I have always felt a certain dissatisfaction at its archaic diction, especially the second person singulars. It is instructive to compare the first three and the last three lines of Stanza XIX.

are characteristic of Browning's love poetry: they all depend to a greater or lesser extent on recapturing the speaking voice, so that the emotion, whether of ardent love or of grief for love lost, is always tested against the language of the real world. Rodomontade is impossible, and so is the kind of love poetry which depends on substituting for a real woman an abstraction built up of conventionally charming clichés.

The end of *By the Fireside* is a good example of what I mean, when the speaker describes himself as one born

> . . . to watch you sink by the fire-side now
>> Back again, as you mutely sit
> Musing by fire-light, that great brow
>> And the spirit-small hand propping it,
> Yonder, my heart knows how!
>
> So, earth has gained by one man the more,
>> And the gain of earth must be heaven's gain too;
> And the whole is well worth thinking o'er
>> When autumn comes: which I mean to do
> One day, as I said before.

The falling rhythm is as important here as syntax in giving the feeling of quiet conversation at close quarters.

In *James Lee's Wife* Browning makes the contrast explicit. Section VI (Reading a Book, Under the Cliff) begins with Lee's wife quoting a poem by 'some young man'.[1] It opens:

> 'Still ailing, Wind? Wilt be appeased or no?
>> Which needs the other's office, thou or I?
> Dost want to be disburthened of a woe,
>> And can, in truth, my voice untie
> Its links, and let it go?'

Compare the language of this obviously highly-wrought stanza with, for instance, the beginning of Section IX (On Deck):

> There is nothing to remember in me,
>> Nothing I ever said with a grace,
> Nothing I did that you care to see,
>> Nothing I was that deserves a place
> In your mind, now I leave you, set you free.

[1] In fact we learn from Mrs Orr's *Handbook* that the verses were written by Browning himself when he was only 23. They were published in the *Monthly Repository* for May 1836 (DeVane, *Handbook*, p. 284).

The plainness of the expression here ensures that the speaker's sacrifice of her happiness for her husband's sake, which might appear a theatrical gesture, is accepted as an earnestly pondered resolution.

If further examples are wanted of Browning's deliberate use of the full range of the language, including, that is, colloquialisms and non-literary idioms, it will perhaps suffice to point to the obvious man-of-the-world slangy diction of *A Likeness*, or to the careful detail and quiet matter-of-fact compassion of *Apparent Failure*, or to one of Browning's most famous poems, *Confessions*, in which he shows plainly the advantages to be derived from using the phrases and rhythms of ordinary speech, and images drawn from everyday objects:

> What is he buzzing in my ears?
>   'Now that I come to die,
> Do I view the world as a vale of tears?'
>   Ah, reverend sir, not I!
>
> What I viewed there once, what I view again
>   Where the physic bottles stand
> On the table's edge, – is a suburb lane,
>   With a wall to my bedside hand.
>
> That lane sloped, much as the bottles do,
>   From a house you could descry
> O'er the garden-wall: is the curtain blue
>   Or green to a healthy eye?
>
> To mine, it serves for the old June weather
>   Blue above lane and wall;
> And that farthest bottle labelled 'Ether'
>   Is the house o'ertopping all.
>
> At a terrace, somewhere near the stopper,
>   There watched for me, one June,
> A girl: I know, sir, it's improper,
>   My poor mind's out of tune.[1]

It is the use of phrases like 'the old June weather' which brings vividly to life the dying man's picture of a suburban lane leading

---

[1] Cf. William Collins, the father of Wilkie Collins, who did a sketch on his deathbed of a scene suggested by objects at the foot of his bed.

to a house called 'The Lodge' and makes it possible for Browning
to present the remembered raptures of young love not as absurd
rhapsodizing but in the fullness of concrete detail.

As I have said, it is not surprising that Browning wrote in this
way when he was supplying words dramatically appropriate to
an imaginary character. It is, however, to be noted that even
when Browning is not specifically creating a dramatic situation he
very often speaks in the language of, say, his letters. This is true
equally of his early playful poems, such as *Sibrandus Schafna-
burgensis*, and of poems from *Asolando*, such as *Development* and
Inapprehensiveness, where the mood is essentially serious although
the language is casual. The last lines of the latter poem are
particularly striking:

> 'No, the book
> Which noticed how the wall-growths wave' said she
> 'Was not by Ruskin.'
>   I said 'Vernon Lee?'

I shall say more about *The Inn Album* in the next chapter.
Here I simply want to quote a passage from Browning's opening
description of the room which is the scene of the entire action
of the poem:

> Two personages occupy this room
> Shabby-genteel, that's parlour to the inn
> Perched on a view-commanding eminence;
> – Inn which may be a veritable house
> Where somebody once lived and pleased good taste
> Till tourists found his coign of vantage out,
> And fingered blunt the individual mark
> And vulgarized things comfortably smooth.
> On a sprig-pattern-papered wall there brays
> Complaint to sky Sir Edwin's dripping stag;
> His couchant coast-guard creature corresponds;
> They face the Huguenot and Light o' the World.
> Grim o'er the mirror on the mantelpiece,
> Varnished and coffined, Salmo ferox glares
> – Possibly at the List of Wines which, framed
> And glazed, hangs somewhat prominent on peg.

Clearly writing of this kind owes nothing to the conventional
diction of poetry – indeed the objection which is more likely to
be made is that it is not poetry at all but merely 'crippled prose'.

The point I want to establish is the obvious appropriateness of this way of narrating a poem of modern men engaged in modern transactions in modern times. The obvious contrast is with Tennyson, who attempts a similar effect in his *Idylls of the Hearth*. With *The Lord of Burleigh* he runs close to bathos, but even in a relatively successful poem such as *Enoch Arden* the diction is far from that of prose:

> Down to the pool and narrow wharf he went,
> Seeking a tavern which of old he knew,
> A front of timber-crost antiquity,
> So propt, worm-eaten, ruinously old,
> He thought it must have gone; but he was gone
> Who kept it; and his widow Miriam Lane
> With daily-dwindling profits held the house;
> A haunt of brawling seamen once, but now
> Stiller, with yet a bed for wandering men.
> There Enoch rested silent many days.

The distinctly elevated diction of the Tennyson effects a crucial difference in tone, a difference analogous to that between the novel and the novelette.[1]

The flexibility of the kind of idiom I have been describing is well illustrated in the poem *Shop*, which I have already mentioned (pp. 50–51) in connection with Browning's impersonality. The speaker (and there is, as I say, no reason to suppose that in this poem he is not Browning himself), speculates about the home of the owner of a grand shop:

> Some suburb-palace, parked about
>   And gated grandly, built last year:
> The four-mile walk to keep off gout;
>   Or big seat sold by bankrupt peer:
>   But then he takes the rail, that's clear. (VI)

> Nowise! Nor Mayfair residence
>   Fit to receive and entertain, –
> Nor Hampstead villa's kind defence
>   From noise and crowd, from dust and drain, –
>   Nor country-box was soul's domain! (VIII)

---

[1] Cf. Browning's use of 'moustache' (*Nationality in Drinks*) with Tennyson's periphrasis or euphemism in *The Passing of Arthur* – 'the knightly growth that fringed his lips'.

He then describes a shopkeeper of very different, much more casual ways:

> Howe'er your choice fell, straight you took
> Your purchase, prompt your money rang
> On counter, – scarce the man forsook
> His study of the 'Times', just swang
> Till-ward his hand that stopped the clang, –
>
> Then off made buyer with a prize,
> Then seller to his 'Times' returned;
> And so did day wear, wear, till eyes
> Brightened apace, for rest was earned:
> He locked door long ere candle burned. (XVII–XVIII)

At the end of the poem there is a good example of the ease with which Browning can alter his manner from the casual to the impassioned:

> Because a man has shop to mind
> In time and place, since flesh must live,
> Needs spirit lack all life behind,
> All stray thoughts, fancies fugitive,
> All loves except what trade can give?
>
> I want to know a butcher paints,
> A baker rhymes for his pursuit,
> Candlestick-maker much acquaints
> His soul with song, or, haply mute,
> Blows out his brains upon the flute!
>
> But – shop each day and all day long!
> Friend, your good angel slept, your star
> Suffered eclipse, fate did you wrong!
> From where these sorts of treasures are,
> There should our hearts be – Christ, how far! (XX–XXII)

In the same volume as *Shop* appeared *Of Pacchiarotto* etc., which gave its name to the book. It has been with reason compared to *Hudibras*; it carries to excess Browning's fondness for the rhythms of common speech brilliantly manipulated to accommodate apparently impossible rhymes. The effect is tedious. The rhymes determine the direction of the poem, the tone is coarse and violent, the subject is too petty to animate the prosaic vocabulary and rhythm, and the total effect is one almost of self-parody, like a man of high intellectual gifts writing with infinite labour a very long comic song which unfortunately proves to be neither tuneful nor amusing. We are left with nothing to admire but the writer's enormous energy.

The poem represents, so to speak, the *reductio ad absurdum* of Browning's catholic choice of word and phrase and consequently of tone. Because he wants to associate Alfred Austin with the vulgar melodies of 'saltbox and bones, tongs and bellows', *Pacchiarotto* is the work in which Browning can be seen most clearly choosing the commonplace word with the deliberate design of vulgarizing the tone of the poem. Normally, however, he chooses the ordinary word for a very different reason; he gives the impression that what he is saying is too important for him to treat it in 'poetic' language. Occasionally this abjuring of the poetic results in bathos,[1] but more often operates with wonderful precision.

III

I shall conclude with a short account of a poem which illustrates this, and shows the subtlety and delicacy of the effects Browning was able to achieve by the means I have been describing. *How It Strikes A Contemporary* was one of the few poems which appeared in the 1855 *Men and Women* and retained its place under that heading throughout the poet's subsequent reclassifications of his poems [14].

It is notable no less for its 'cleanness' of language than for the idea it gives of the poet's function in the world. The speaker is a young smart Spaniard, chatting to a friend [15]. He begins abruptly:

> I only knew one poet in my life:
> And this, or something like it, was his way.

He describes the poet in language that indicates an odd mixture of respect and contempt, recalling how he would walk about Valladolid 'scenting the world, looking it full in face':

> He stood and watched the cobbler at his trade,
> The man who slices lemons into drink,

---

[1] E.g. *La Saisiaz* 483–491, 501; or *Pippa Passes* 'Sebald, as we lay,/Rising and falling only with our pants . . .'

The coffee-roaster's brazier, and the boys
That volunteer to help him turn its winch.
He glanced o'er books on stalls with half an eye,
And fly-leaf ballads on the vendor's string,
And broad-edge bold-print posters by the wall.
He took such cognisance of men and things,
If any beat a horse, you felt he saw;
If any cursed a woman, he took note;

His observation of the daily life of the town was so acute that
people suspected him of being

The town's true master if the town but knew!
We merely kept a Governor for form,
While this man walked about and took account
Of all thought, said, and acted, then went home,
And wrote it fully to our Lord the King
Who has an itch to know things, He knows why,
And reads them in His bedroom of a night.

The young speaker wonders why the poet took such pains, since
he seemed to have no rewards for his work:

Our Lord the King has favourites manifold,
And shifts his ministry some once a month;
Our city gets new Governors at whiles, –
But never word or sign, that I could hear,
Notified to this man about the streets
The King's approval of those letters conned
The last thing duly at the dead of night.

The pattern of the poem so far is simple: a passage of low-keyed,
deliberately naturalistic description of the poet's humdrum daily
routine is followed by a passage of bored and ignorant speculation about his real power. The pattern is now repeated more
briefly. The speaker reflects that it is certainly not true that the
poet lived in luxury:

Poor man, he lived another kind of life
In that new, stuccoed, third house by the bridge,
Fresh-painted, rather smart than otherwise!
The whole street might o'erlook him as he sat,
Leg crossing leg, one foot on the dog's back,

> Playing a decent cribbage with his maid
> (Jacynth, you're sure her name was) o'er the cheese
> And fruit, three red halves of starved winter-pears,
> Or treat of radishes in April! nine,
> Ten, struck the church clock, straight to bed went he.

Yet in spite of this he was credited with untold powers:

> My father, like the man of sense he was,
> Would point him out to me a dozen times;
> 'St – St,' he'd whisper, 'the Corregidor!'
> I had been used to think that personage
> Was one with lacquered breeches, lustrous belt,
> And feathers like a forest in his hat,
> Who blew a trumpet and proclaimed the news,
> Announced the bull-fights, gave each church its turn,
> And memorized the miracle in vogue!
> He had a great observance from us boys; –
> We were in error; that was not the man.

Although neither father nor son has rightly identified the Corregidor, the father's guess is shrewder, and his error is more revealing, since it recognizes the impression of power given by the shabby figure of the poet.

The concluding section begins abruptly with the revelation that the poet is now dead:

> I'd like now, yet had haply been afraid,
> To have just looked, when this man came to die,
> And seen who lined the clean gay garret's sides
> And stood about the neat low truckle-bed,
> With the heavenly manner of relieving guard.
> Here had been, mark, the general-in-chief,
> Thro' a whole campaign of the world's life and death,
> Doing the King's work all the dim day long,
> In his old coat, and up to his knees in mud,
> Smoked like a herring, dining on a crust, –
> And now the day was won, relieved at once!
> No further show or need for that old coat,
> You are sure, for one thing!

Then the speaker abruptly breaks from the past to the present, notices himself and his companion and exclaims

> Bless us, all the while
> How sprucely we are dressed out, you and I!
> A second, and the angels alter that.
> Well, I could never write a verse, – could you?
> Let's to the Prado and make the most of time.

The point Browning makes about the true poet is obvious enough. As he observed at the end of his famous letter to Ruskin in 1855, 'A poet's affair is with God, to whom he is accountable, and of whom is his reward: look elsewhere and you find misery enough.' This poem explains what sort of reward the poet may look for. He need not expect to be considered by his fellows as anything better than a recording chief-inquisitor. He will have no glory – that is reserved for the flamboyant and ostentatious. There is a hint at the end of the poem that just as death can put an end to the smartness of the young speaker, so it may recompense the poet for the spareness of his life, but it is no more than a hint.

Lear V iii is cited by DeVane, for instance, in connection with this poem. It is clearly apposite, especially when Lear says '[We'll] take upon's the mystery of things/As if we were God's spies.'[1] It is to be noted that this passage, celebrated for its simplicity and directness, controls the diction of Browning's poem also. His poet is a man who lives among men, looking the world 'full in the face'. The deliberately unpoetic language of the poem emphasizes this and ties the poet down to the world of stucco, cribbage and radishes, lemons, coffee and bold-print posters. Similarly the imagery is kept in a low key; the poet's 'serviceable suit of black' and threadbare cloak, the spruce dress of the young speaker, the town crier's 'lacquered breeches, lustrous belt' are elementary devices for establishing relationships. The poet's dog 'bald and blindish', his exploration of

---

[1] In his edition of *Men and Women* (II, p. 271) Worsfold has a quotation from *Aurora Leigh* which is also very much to the point. Mrs Browning says that Poets are 'the only truth-tellers now left to God',

> The only speakers of essential truth,
> Opposed to relative, comparative,
> And temporal truths; the only holders by
> His sun-skirts, through conventional gray of looms,
> The only teachers who instruct mankind
> From just a shadow on a charnel-wall
> To find man's veritable stature out
> Erect, sublime, – the measure of a man.

the alley by the church 'that leads nowhither', his arrival on the main promenade 'just at the wrong time', all these add to the picture of the poet's life, drab, unfashionable, and above all not radically different from that of his fellow men.

The idiom in which he writes rather than the incidents he selects is what establishes so memorably in the poem Browning's conception of the Poet as Hero, unrecognized, unrewarded, living in a city and sharing in its life, 'trying a mortar's temper 'tween the chinks', 'doing the King's work all the dim day long'.

IV

In this chapter I have tried to describe the total idiom of Browning's best poetry, and to suggest that it is based on conversation between educated equals.

In a most interesting essay – 'Browning and the "Grotesque" Style' [16] – Isobel Armstrong looks at Browning's diction from a completely opposed point of view. Her position may be summarized by quoting her comment on Preyer's distinction between Browning's 'simple' and 'difficult' styles. She asks artlessly, 'Isn't the simple style just Browning at his worst anyway?' a question perhaps designed to prevent readers from considering too closely the reasons for her own concentration on the grotesque in Browning. Her description of the style is admirable, rightly emphasizing the essential element of theatricality. Browning is deliberately drawing attention to his own linguistic display: 'language has become a posture, a self-consciously exaggerated manner'. Mrs Armstrong comments acutely on what Browning can achieve by use of the grotesque, but she offers no evidence that this way of writing is particularly common in the poet, much less that the poems in this manner are of any special importance. She gives a few examples, some of which are debatable. In the absence of contrary evidence I think it fair to say that the element of grotesque, strictly defined, in Browning's diction is not great, and where it is found the excessive energy which it generates and which is its most annoying characteristic is often justifiable on dramatic grounds. To make her case Mrs Armstrong has to broaden her consideration of style to include the grotesque situation, as in *In A Gondola*, thus blurring a useful critical distinction.

An understanding of Browning's technique in, say, *How It Strikes A Contemporary*, is helpful in the reading of poems written in very different ways, revealing the colloquial basis of many poems which might otherwise seem merely eccentric. *Master Hugues of Saxe-Gotha*, for example, is grotesque in many obvious ways – it is about an organist alone at dusk in the organ-loft of a great medieval church, playing a fugue of Gothic complexity; one of the main images is the elaborately carved church roof; at another point the speaker imagines that he can see the dead composer's face made up of musical symbols – yet the language Browning uses is grotesque in Mrs Armstrong's sense only in Stanzas XII–XVIII, where Browning tries to create the verbal equivalent of a fugue. For the rest it is difficult only in the sense that Browning is so intent on carrying through the steps of his argument that he pays no attention to what Mrs Armstrong calls 'local uncertainties of style', while the last stanza ties the whole edifice of speculation firmly down to earth in a burst of simple energetic verse.

Browning often uses his 'neutral' style as a method of control in this way – either to ballast a vigorous physical poem such as *'How They Brought the Good News'*, or to establish familiar contact in a landscape of indefinable dread, as in *'Childe Roland'*, or to convey the reader, with the suppleness of conversation, into a world of rich objects and violent emotions, as in *The Bishop Orders His Tomb* or *My Last Duchess*. It is worth noting in particular how often Browning presents a powerful or macabre story or situation in matter-of-fact terms.

> For only last night, as they whispered, I brought
> My own eyes to bear on her so, that I thought
> Could I keep them one half minute fixed, she would fall
> Shrivelled; she fell not; yet this does it all!
>
> (*The Laboratory*, IX)

> The father's beard was long and white,
> With love and truth his brow seemed bright;
> I went back, all on fire with joy,
> And, that same evening, bade the boy
> Tell me, as lovers should, heart-free,
> Something to prove his love of me.
>
> (*The Confessional*, VIII)

It was roses, roses, all the way,
  With myrtle mixed in my path like mad:
The house-roofs seemed to heave and sway,
  The church-spires flamed, such flags they had,
A year ago on this very day.

(*The Patriot*, I)

The easy neutral colloquial idiom which I have illustrated in this chapter is sufficiently uncommon in the nineteenth century and the effects Browning achieves in it are sufficiently powerful to deserve better than Mrs Armstrong's summary dismissal.

It hardly needs to be observed that Browning's use of a vocabulary and syntax which might equally well be encountered in a novel or a newspaper does much to diminish the sharp distinction between poetry and the rest of literature which was such a prominent feature of nineteenth-century letters. The smaller this gap, the more readily a poet may expect to be judged simply by what he says and not by narrower standards of form or expression. It is reasonable to argue that such a way of judging poetry makes for a healthier relation between poetry and the other arts, and that one of the first signs of it will be a re-estating of Browning himself among the great English poets.

In the next chapter I shall suggest many ways in which Browning's poetry was different from that of his contemporaries, but perhaps none is so immediately noticeable and so perennially surprising as this determination to use as the staple of his poetry the common language of Victorian England, plain Queen's English.

❋ 11 ❋

Browning as a poet of
Victorian life

There is no such thing as a long poem.   POE

I honour both the rhythm and the rhyme, by which poetry first
becomes poetry; but what is really deeply and fundamentally effective – what is truly educative and inspiring, is what remains of the
poet when he is translated into prose.   GOETHE

As far as I can observe, it is a constant law, that the greatest men,
whether poets or historians, live entirely in their own age, and the
greatest fruits of their work are gathered out of their own age.
Dante paints Italy in the thirteenth century; Chaucer, England in the
fourteenth; Masaccio, Florence in the fifteenth; Tintoret, Venice in
the sixteenth; all of them utterly regardless of anachronism and minor
error of every kind, but getting always vital truth out of the vital
present.   RUSKIN, *Frondes Agrestes*

I have two objects in this chapter, first to demonstrate how consistently Browning found the matter of his verse not in the past
or in the world of myth but in the life of his own times, and
secondly to call attention to a substantial body of Browning's
works which has attracted little critical regard, the long poems
which followed *The Ring and the Book*, in particular *Prince
Hohenstiel-Schwangau* (1871), *Fifine at the Fair* (1872), *Red
Cotton Night-Cap Country* (1873), and *The Inn Album* (1875).
With this group *La Saisiaz* (1878) should perhaps be included.

I

I have already put forward some of the evidence for maintaining
that Browning's poetry stands in a singularly close relation to

Victorian life. In the previous chapter, for instance, I have shown how he found the pattern for his diction in the rhythms and phrases of ordinary nineteenth-century spoken English. Again in Chapters 7, 8 and 9 I have pointed to some of the many poems in which Browning grappled with the principal issues of his time. His religious poems pivot on the question of how far a man could reject the historical evidences for Christian belief and yet claim to remain a Christian. Similarly he gives the most exhaustive treatment in nineteenth-century verse of the familiar ethical quandary of ends and means, and of one of the great ontological problems, that of the status of the personality of the individual. All these were urgent questions to the thinking man of the last century and are with us in a more or less acute form today. They were, moreover, modern problems in the sense that it was only in that century that they became of primary importance. That is to say, it is broadly true that before 1800 the historical evidences for Christianity were publicly doubted only by those who were prepared to be known as sceptics or infidels. But during the nineteenth century it was clear that if Christian belief was not to degenerate into mere credulity it was the task of every Christian to examine the bases on which his faith rested. It is to this peculiarly Victorian labour that Browning addressed himself in his religious poems [1].

His ethical speculations are equally modern. He was writing at a time when absolutes, whether moral or social, were subject to continual question. In particular the violent change of Britain from an agricultural and rural community to an industrial and urban civilization, together with the growth of a political system which made power dependent ultimately on the favour of the people, had totally overthrown as a system commanding even nominal assent the old social structure of the country, although many of the institutions survived. To the foremost theorists of the day – Bentham, Mill, Disraeli, Carlyle, Ruskin, Arnold, Jefferies and Morris are only the most obvious names – the main question underlying all political issues was 'What are and what ought to be the ends of social organizations in general and of Great Britain in particular?'

Browning characteristically transposes this question into a personal key and discusses as a general rule the problem of how far a given individual can justify his conduct by reference to the ends for which he is working. Whereas Pope in the *Essay on Man* found in the structure of the Universe his model for the nature of man and human organizations, Browning dissects the motives of an individual in an endeavour to discover whether there are any universal laws of right conduct.

This increased concern with actions and their consequences distinguishes Browning's poetry from those earlier long poems which pivoted on the freedom of the will, most obviously the *Aeneid*, *Troilus and Criseyde*, Lydgate's *Falls of Princes*, *The Faerie Queene*, and *Paradise Lost*. Instead of presenting man wrestling with his destiny or acting under the influence of external powers or qualities, he presents man scrutinizing himself and discriminating between motives, trying to understand how a man ought to behave in the world by examining and assessing the value of the springs of action. God's will, in short, does not lie outside Browning's characters, compelling them to obedience or defiance: God's will for them is something that lies within the recesses of their own personality and can be ascertained only by the most rigorous self-analysis.

Since Browning treats the question of ends and means primarily from the point of view of their conflicting demands on a single person, he necessarily finds himself participating in the debate about the value and status of the individual personality which has been one of the chief preoccupations of post-Hegelian metaphysics and is a crucial assumption in the Romantic assertion of the autonomy of the individual. The argument, from whichever side it is approached, has been at the heart of philosophical, religious, aesthetic, political, psychological and economic speculation, particularly since 1800.

I have elaborated this point to show how close Browning's work was to the central problems of his time and, as it happens, of our own: this topicality is reflected in his choice of subject.

At first sight Browning's early poems *Pauline*, *Paracelsus* and *Sordello* seem far removed in subject and theme from the stresses of Victorian life. It is true that a reader of the eighteen-thirties would find in the incidents and the background very little which would be immediately familiar or which would relate directly to his own experience. But Lionel Stevenson is right to point out that in each of the poems we can see Browning at grips with the question of the proper business of the poet in the

modern world [2]. He is, as it were, debating with himself
what ought to be the direction of his own life's work. This finds
expression, for example, in Aprile's statement of his ideals in
poetry:

> common life, its wants
> And ways, would I set forth in beauteous hues:
> The lowest hind should not possess a hope,
> A fear, but I'd be by him, saying better
> Than he his own heart's language. (II, 556–560)

Paracelsus ultimately realizes that his great error has been the
exclusion of human sympathy and understanding, and neglect of
immediate practical service to men, while Sordello develops
similarly from egocentricity through utopianism to altruistic
tolerance. In *Sordello* Browning talks about his own writing of
the poem, and Professor Stevenson draws attention to the
significance of his revealing comment:

> Care-bit erased
> Broken-up beauties ever took my taste
> Supremely.

He concludes, 'The record of the three long poems, written
between 1832 and 1840, proves that Browning . . . trans-
formed the abstract Utopianism of Shelley into a very different
creed of practical, tolerant concern with commonplace human
affairs.'

The verse in Browning's next collections, *Dramatic Lyrics*
(1842) and *Dramatic Romances and Lyrics* (1845) is not
especially topical, and when it is topical does not always gain
much by it. *Through the Metidja to Abd-el-Kadr*, for example,
though it refers to a contemporary historical event which would
be perfectly familiar from the newspapers, is less immediate
than '*How they brought the Good News*', which has no such
reference. The most remarkable pieces in the 1845 volume were
the twin poems *Italy in England* and *England in Italy*, the first
because it had its origin in the intense interest that Browning
took in the fortunes of the Italian nation, an interest which
found frequent expression in his verse, at least until 1871: the
second because it finishes with a surprising direct reference to
the current controversy about the repeal of the Corn Laws:

And at night from the crest of Calvano
    Great bonfires will hang,
On the plain will the trumpets join chorus,
    And more poppers bang.
At all events, come – to the garden
    As far as the wall;
See me tap with a hoe on the plaster
    Till out there shall fall
A scorpion with wide angry nippers!

    – 'Such trifles!' you say?
Fortù, in my England at home,
    Men meet gravely today
And debate, if abolishing Corn-laws
    Be righteous and wise
    – If 'twere proper, Scirocco should vanish
    In black from the skies!

Perhaps this sudden introduction of politics is not altogether un-prepared for: the whole of the first part of the poem is written in a mood of determined objectivity, emphasising the speaker's concern with things as they are, with the rustling of the quail-nets, the horns and humps of the 'sea-fruit', the sheer hard work of the grape harvest, the 'slippery ropes' of lasagne and the great purple slices of fried gourd, the variations in whiteness of the flakes of the 'curd-white smooth cheese-ball', the weak wine in the thin green glass flask, and all the physical sensations of autumn near Sorrento. This abundance of concrete detail helps to establish a situation in which a practical man may reasonably comment scornfully on the solemn Parliamentarians who have to discuss the theoretical merits of a question instead of doing what is obviously necessary.

In the previous chapter I have mentioned *Waring* as a place where Browning demonstrates how easily he can make poetry out of colloquial speech; it is also the best example in this period of his writing on a contemporary native subject. Waring has moved in the normal London circle of 'indoor visits, outdoor greetings': he has lived in the literary world where 'our men scarce seem in earnest now'; the speculation about what has become of him takes place among his friends and acquaintances in the atmosphere of a club. The whole poem is like a brilliant sketch for a novel by Conrad.

Christmas-Eve and Easter-Day (1850), that most important product of Browning's early religious preoccupations, is notable for the remarkable sketch, in Sections I–III, of the nonconformist chapel, ' "Mount Zion" with Love-lane at the back of it', a piece of genre-painting of a sharpness and intimacy not common anywhere in Victorian literature and virtually unparalleled in Victorian verse. In the first half of the poem the symbols which denote the various choices open to the Christian at the mid-century – the chapel, the basilica, and the lecture-hall at Göttingen – are drawn from the world, not from myth. The problem, that is to say, is presented in terms of a choice between actual places of worship, not as a choice between abstractions, and the physical conditions of each place are realized as vividly and naturalistically as possible. Browning indeed fears that some readers may think that he has treated these high subjects in too 'low' a manner:

> I have done: and if any blames me,
> Thinking that merely to touch in brevity
>   The topics I dwell on, were unlawful, –
> Or worse, that I trench, with undue levity,
>   On the bounds of the holy and the awful, –
> I praise the heart, and pity the head of him,
> And refer myself to THEE, instead of him,
> Who head and heart alike discernest,
>   Looking below light speech we utter,
>   When frothy spume and frequent sputter
> Prove that the soul's depths boil in earnest!
> May truth shine out, stand ever before us!
> I put up pencil and join chorus
> To Hepzibah Tune, without further apology,
>   The last five verses of the third section
>   Of the seventeenth hymn of Whitfield's Collection,
> To conclude with the doxology. (*Christmas-Eve*, XXII)

The poems in *Men and Women* (1855) are poems with 'more music and painting' in them and draw their subjects from more exotic sources in space and time. Italy and the Renaissance, as ever, powerfully fire Browning's imagination.[1] But even in this

---

[1] Cf. the entry in a French guide-book to Venice:

Voici la Ca' Rezzonico, où mourut le poète Robert Browning en disant,
'Ouvrez mon coeur et vous y verrez ecrit "L'Italie".'

collection, the fruit of the many years he spent abroad with his wife, Browning does not neglect native subjects [3]. *Bishop Blougram's Apology* is a good example, and so, on a smaller scale, is *Evelyn Hope*, a poem which a single sharp detail rescues from sentimentality. The first line, 'Beautiful Evelyn Hope is dead', threatens the easy emotionalism of a drawing-room ballad, but Browning continues:

> Sit and watch by her side an hour.
> That is her book-shelf, this her bed;
> She plucked that piece of geranium-flower,
> Beginning to die too, in the glass;
> Little has yet been changed, I think.

The fact that he chooses a typically nineteenth-century flower,[1] with its suggestions of the ornamental garden or the conservatory, rather than a flower of conventional poetic significance, such as a rose or a violet, does much to establish the poem's tone of dry regret.

Browning's years abroad led him for a time to neglect native topics in favour of Italian, but even when he writes about Italy he does so in a way that emphasizes the immediacy of his subjects. He brings before the reader day to day life in nineteenth-century Italy, as in *Up at a Villa* and '*De Gustibus* –'. In particular he brings life to Italian politics, a subject in which he shared his wife's unfailing interest. When we remember what sustained and serious attention the Victorians gave to public affairs at home and abroad it is perhaps surprising that only the Brownings attempted to establish the poet's ability to deal with this vital area of human experience.[2]

In 1864 Browning published *Dramatis Personae*: perhaps because of his return from Italy to London after his wife's death in 1861 the poems reflected more closely the life of the time. DeVane puts it:

[1] He is obviously referring to the pelargonium (see line 30), and not to the native blue geranium.

[2] Exceptions might be made for Swinburne's *Songs before Sunrise* (1871), for some of Clough and John Davidson, and for a few Chartist poems, but these are insignificant compared with Browning's systematic exploration of the duties and motives of men in office: see especially *Prince Hohenstiel-Schwangau* and the *Parleying with Bubb Dodington*, also Mrs Browning's *Poems before Congress* (1860).

> It is generally true that Browning is much more interested in voic-
> ing his opinion upon some topic of vital contemporary interest than
> he is in . . . the nice delineation of character. The 'persons of the
> drama' have become, in larger measure, exponents of contemporary
> ideas. . . . The chief characteristic of *Dramatis Personae* is this:
> that in an age when the poets were mainly interested in escaping to
> the past – Tennyson to Arthur's medieval kingdom, Arnold to
> Greece, Rossetti and Morris to the Middle Ages, the young Swin-
> burne to Greece and Elizabethan England – Browning almost alone
> wrote of contemporary ideas and contemporary life, often in colloquial
> language and contemporary phrase. (*Handbook*, 280, 282)

DeVane's point can be illustrated on a simple level by observing
that one poem, *Apparent Failure*, was based on a newspaper item
about the threatened demolition of the Paris morgue, but the
more interesting signs of modernity are less obvious than this. I
have already mentioned Browning's love poems, which derive
their peculiar quality from the fact that Browning treats love
not as an ideal to be expressed in abstract language or conventional symbols, but as an emotion affecting the lives of ordinary
nineteenth-century men and women and most accurately expressed in terms of the real world. *Too Late, Dís Aliter Visum* and
Confessions are the most obvious examples, while *James Lee's
Wife* is the most comprehensive demonstration of Browning's
ability to present modern love without the least straining after
up-to-date detail or imagery.

Equally remarkable are the religious poems, in which Browning treats Christianity not as an idea to be discussed in transcendental terms but as a subject of immediate interest and
argument. For instance:

> The candid incline to surmise of late
>   That the Christian faith proves false, I find;
> For our Essays-and-Reviews' debate
>   Begins to tell on the public mind,
> And Colenso's words have weight. (*Gold Hair*, XXIX) [4]

I have explained in Chapter 9 that *A Death in the Desert*,
although set in the first century, is a direct contribution to
current theological controversy: similarly with *Caliban upon
Setebos*.

Perhaps the best example in this volume of Browning's way
of writing poetry in the present is *Mr. Sludge, 'The Medium'*,

in which setting and theme are equally topical. Its subject, that of spiritualism and the bogus medium, was one much in the public mind, while Home, who is usually taken to be the original of Sludge, was a notable, not to say a notorious, European figure at the time. But of course the topicality of the poem is not confined to its immediate occasion: it is especially contemporary in its imagery. This is evident alike in the casual references to Barnum, the Benicia Boy, 'Greeley's newspaper', or the 'nice stuffed chairs and sympathetic sideboards' and in sustained passages such as:

> The current o' common things, the daily life,
> This had their due contempt; no Name pursued
> Man from the mountain-top where fires abide,
> To his particular mouse-hole at its foot
> Where he ate, drank, digested, lived in short:
> Such was man's vulgar business, far too small
> To be worth thunder: 'small', folk kept on, 'small',
> With much complacency in those great days!
> A mote of sand, you know, a blade of grass –
> What was so despicable as mere grass,
> Except perhaps the life o' the worm or fly
> Which fed there? These were 'small' and men were great.
> Well, sir, the old way's altered somewhat since,
> And the world wears another aspect now:
> Somebody turns our spyglass round, or else
> Puts a new lens in it: grass, worm, fly grow big:
> We find great things are made of little things,
> And little things go lessening till at last
> Comes God behind them. Talk of mountains now?
> We talk of mould that heaps the mountain, mites
> That throng the mould, and God that makes the mites.
> The Name comes close behind a stomach-cyst,
> The simplest of creations, just a sac
> That's mouth, heart, legs and belly at once, yet lives
> And feels, and could do neither, we conclude,
> If simplified still further one degree:
> The small becomes the dreadful and immense!
> Lightning, forsooth? No word more upon that!
> A tin-foil bottle, a strip of greasy silk,
> With a bit of wire and knob of brass, and there's
> Your dollar's-worth of lightning! But the cyst –
> The life of the least of the little things?

This passage, with its ingenious and assured manoeuvring of the matter of biology and electrostatics, takes its place naturally in the argument and is dramatically suitable to Sludge. At the same time it is an acute comment on the sudden and violent shift of perspective imposed on the Western world by the discoveries of the scientist and the engineers: the microscope was challenging received ideas even more effectively than the telescope. Finally it provides, as it happens, an appropriate comment on Browning's own practice in verse and his continual sense of the enormous importance of 'the current o' common things, the daily life'.

The quotation from DeVane makes the most important point that it is in a comparison with the work of his contemporary poets that the actualness of Browning's poetry is most strongly felt. He does not draw a line between 'poetic' and 'non-poetic' subjects and he is seldom concerned to protect his poetry from contact with real things or manners or language or ideas, whereas in much of Tennyson, Arnold and Morris the reader has the sense that the least touch of the present has been deliberately excluded for fear it should destroy the entire poem simply by being more solid and substantial.

Browning's steadiness of purpose in this matter in the face of over thirty years of public neglect and misunderstanding is a remarkable feature of his poetic career. It is not surprising that in the poems of his maturity, when he had won a fair measure of recognition, he was still ready to handle in verse subjects of immediate, indeed of sensational interest.

II

Prince Hohenstiel-Schwangau (1871) is the first of a group of poems which have been little regarded by Browning's critics. DeVane, for example, says, 'The numerous volumes of the next years [after August 1871] add little to Browning's stature' (*Handbook*, p. 357). Similar verdicts are common:

> It is Browning's early Fourth Period books that have set so many folk unreazonably against him: *Schwangau, Fifine, Red Cotton, Inn Album*, and *Pacchiarotto*. [5]

> Like *Prince Hohenstiel-Schwangau* and other long poems of this period *Fifine* became unpopular at once. [6]

. . . The tedious word-spinning of the poet's last twenty years. [7]

These three long poems [*Prince Hohenstiel-Schwangau, Red Cotton Night-Cap Country* and *Fifine at the Fair*] are foredoomed to oblivion. [8]

As to content, it was in the period [1872–1875] that Browning fell into many metaphysical quagmires, and most readers have not cared to become bogged down with him. [9]

Now it is universally agreed by critics of all shades of opinion . . . that after *The Ring and the Book*, though his output of verse was vast, the poetic prerogative had faded before the demands of a more formally philosophic purpose . . . Inspiration gives way to dialectic; poetic creation becomes versified argumentation. [10]

Prince Hohenstiel-Schwangau, a product of Browning's intense interest in the cause of Italian liberty, shows his fascination with the intricacies of the human mind, intracacies nowhere more entertainingly displayed than in the professional apology of a man of politics. We know that Browning had Napoleon III in mind when he wrote the first version in 1860 and when he expanded the poem in 1871, and we know moreover that Browning's own opinions of Napoleon's career were extremely variable, concluding in 1871 in an attitude of pitying contempt. It is thus tempting to read the poem simply as a satire on the career of Napoleon III and to try to arrive at a viewpoint which allows us to see the fallacy of all the Prince's arguments. At once we notice that the poem resists any attempt at a naïve reversal of values such as would expose the speaker to our unqualified moral condemnation. Is the ambiguity then the consequence of Browning's own inability to decide whether or not Napoleon's career was defensible, or does it indicate that a more complex judgement is required of the reader than before?

In the previous chapter I have shown that by careful observation of changes in diction it is possible to establish certain broad movements of tone within the poem. At one point in particular the style and the speaker's approach to his subject alter abruptly, so that initially we may regard the poem as being divided into two contrasted parts, the first extending to p. 84 in the first edition, and the second covering the rest of the poem.

The first part has little direct reference to Napoleon III; it might apply to any ruler who is essentially a conservative, and on the whole makes out quite a strong case for conservatism, employing a favourite argument of Browning's that the world is so rich and diverse that it is worth preserving for its own sake (pp. 43–45). The problem to which he returns again and again is this:

> To save society was well: the means
> Whereby to save it, – there begins the doubt
> Permitted you, imperative on me;
> Were mine the best means? Did I work aright
> With powers appointed me? – since powers denied
> Concern me nothing.

In other words the first part of the poem is concerned with general theories of government, with little direct reference to actual political situations. The exception is at p. 57–59, where the Prince says that he once had an idealist cause at heart – that of the liberation of Italy. The diction rises to the level of his conception of a free Italy:

> Ay, still my fragments wander, music-fraught,
> Sighs of the soul, mine once, mine now, and mine
> For ever! Crumbled arch, crushed aqueduct,
> Alive with tremors in the shaggy growth
> Of wild-wood, crevice-sown, that triumphs there
> Imparting exultation to the hills!
> Sweep of the swathe when only the winds walk
> And waft my words above the grassy sea
> Under the blinding blue that basks o'er Rome, –
> Hear ye not still – 'Be Italy again'? (pp. 58–59)

From this position he proceeds to analyse the role of political ideals in practical government

> Once pedestalled on earth,
> To act not speak, I found earth was not air. (p. 63)

The defence that the Prince puts forward for abandoning the ideals with which he began government is the strongest one available, that his first duty was to keep his subjects alive. Many liberal measures had to be postponed.

> No, this should be, and shall; but when and how . . . (p. 63)
> 'Not bread alone' but bread before all else
> For these: the bodily want serve first, said I (p. 64)

This argument is clearly good if the circumstances are in fact such that a choice must be made between, say, keeping one's subjects alive and allowing them free speech. But when we transfer the general arguments to the specific situation implied in the poem it is hard not to suspect that they are deliberately exaggerated, that the two alternatives are not in fact mutually exclusive, and that the Prince is simply inventing a powerful reason for breaking his promise. Colour is given to this suspicion by the last words of the sentence, when the Prince speaks contemptuously of the culminating democratic ideal that

> '. . . divers hundred thousand fools may vote
> A vote untampered with by one wise man,
> And so elect Barabbas deputy
> In lieu of his concurrent.'

He argues that while idealism in politics is of supreme value –

> '. . . My brave thinkers, whom I recognize,
> Gladly, myself the first, as, in a sense.
> All that our world's worth, flower and fruit of man' (p. 76)

it functions best when resisted. In a typical series of figures he compares it successively with a drug that operates most effectively when it is dispersed and retarded by inert ingredients and with a river that falls sheer on to the rocks of ignorance and opposition only to rise the higher in a mist of spray. He agrees that the idealists must be protected from violence, and adds in lines in which it is possible, I think, to detect a trace of irony:

> But, justice seen to on this *little* point
> Answer me, *is it manly, is it sage*
> To stop and struggle with arrangements here
> It took so many lives, so much of toil,
> To *tinker up* into *efficiency*?
> Can't you *contrive to operate* at once . . .
> Without this *fractious* call on folks to crush
> The world together just to set you free,
> Admire the *capers you will cut* perchance,
> Nor mind the mischief to your neighbours? (pp. 79–80)

The words and phrases I have italicized indicate, for the first time, I think, in the poem, a certain obtuseness or disingenuousness in the Prince. But the last line is sound and unexceptionable.

With a final figure – that of Laocoön – designed to establish that stability implies not inertness but unceasing effort to maintain an equilibrium, the Prince concludes the first part of his defence. It is intended to emphasise that politics is the science of the practical and that the ideals of political theorists must take second place to the necessity of a stable government able to guarantee adequate material standards for its citizens. It has no particular reference to the politics of the 1860s and 1870s, although no doubt its original readers would make a number of applications to affairs of the day.

At this point the Prince says

> 'you have one half your wish,
> At least: you know the thing I tried to do!'

So far he has explained his political principles, that is the ends of government he had in view and the means he was prepared to adopt to secure those ends. He has made out a reasonable case for conservative measures in difficult times, and I can detect no trace of casuistry, except in the passages to which I have drawn attention where the tone suggests that possibly the Prince's belief in liberal institutions is more a matter of politic profession than of genuine enthusiasm.

In the second part he is describing in a mood of fantasy the different choices which were open to him on certain actual political issues while he was in power. He puts the alternative courses of action in the form of a dialogue between two parties – on the one side Sagacity, who advises always the course of low prudence and opportunism and comes almost to stand for popular political opinion, and on the other the Head Servant, an idealized ruler, who always acts from the highest motives and for the loftiest ends (see esp. pp. 119–31). The Prince warns his listener that what is to follow is 'pure blame, history/And falsehood: not the ineffective truth . . .' 'Hear,' he says, 'what I never was but might have been', and then claims always to have acted as the Head Servant. To be quite accurate he only implies that he was the Head Servant in question: we cannot even be sure that the Prince was in fact Napoleon III, but it seems fair to assume that there is only one political career in question, not three. Unless this last part of the poem is read with a knowledge of what choices Napoleon III actually made, it seems to me that it is meaningless. If we do compare it with the course of history it is plain that sometimes Napoleon III followed the advice of Sagacity, and sometimes acted as the high-principled Head of State. For example, the Head in the poem voluntarily laid down office and appealed to the people to appoint him 'master for the moment' with clearly limited powers (p. *96*): Napoleon III, when the Assembly refused to prolong his term of office, seized power in the *coup d'état* of 1851. After the people had returned him to power the Head, though prompt to put down opposition (pp. 98–99), pursued an egalitarian policy. This is partly true of Napoleon III. He introduced the *décrets-lois* against the Republic and gradually took all the reins of government into his own hands, but like the Head in the poem he tried to govern for 'the poor mean multitude, all mouths and eyes'.[1] On the central issue of Italian liberation the Head is advised by Sagacity to leave things as they are (pp. 106–7) but at once excises the canker with vigour. Once again Napoleon III's actions were more like those of the imaginary Head. He played his part in liberating Italy from 1856 to 1860, perhaps not as heroically as the Head, and certainly not for such elevated motives, but at least as a result of his actions Italy was 'free from the Adriatic to the Alps'. (p. 129) When this was done Sagacity hinted that some recompense would be acceptable to his subjects, while the Head indignantly rejected the suggestion. (p. 131) As is well known, Napoleon III obtained Nice and Savoy as his 'snug honorarium-fee'. Sagacity lastly advises the Head to establish a dynasty to continue his successful conservative rule: the Head replies that there is no certainty that a man's descendants will inherit his virtues, whereas an elected ruler is likely to have some merit. (134–42) Here again Napoleon's actions inclined rather to Sagacity than to the Head, since he attempted to secure the succession for his own family.

From this brief summary it can be seen that the choices of Napoleon III accorded with the opportunist advice of Sagacity at the beginning and end of his career, and with the admirable ideals of the Head only in the middle of his reign.

The difficulty in the second part of the poem lies precisely in

---

[1] That impartial witness *The Encyclopaedia Britannica* says, 'The idea of improving the lot of those who suffer and struggle against the difficulties of life was constantly present to his mind.'

this fact that Napoleon's actual career did not shape itself entirely by the low or by the high advice.[1] The poem, then, is a record as it were of Browning's own difficulty in assessing Napoleon III, whose part (itself not completely unequivocal) in the unification of Italy has clearly confused Browning's already complex feelings about him. If we could set aside the Italian episode and Napoleon's determination to relieve poverty we might deduce from the second part of the poem that Prince Hohenstiel-Schwangau realises that his real deficiency as a ruler has been his failure to follow the highest ideals, and I think that this is probaby what is intended. But this is in conflict with the first part of the poem in which the Prince advocates, without any casuistic arguments that I can identify, a government which holds fast to what is immediately practical. This inconsistency between the first part of the poem, in which we are told that what the Prince did was desirable, and the second part, where it is implied that the way he didn't act was right, is not resolved in the text of the poem. It remains as the central ambiguity, around which various subsidiary ironic effects are deployed.

I have mentioned in the last chapter the deft way in which variations of diction are used to control certain parts of the poem. The Prince in fact comments frequently on his own performance, notably at the very end of the poem, when he remarks on the difficulty of keeping alive in argument those motives which are so powerful when they are not expressed in words:

> 'Alack, one lies oneself
> Even in stating that one's end was truth,
> Truth only, if one states as much in words!
> Give me the inner chamber of the soul
> For obvious easy argument! 't is there
> One pits the silent truth against a lie . . .
> . . .   But, do your best,
> Words have to come: and somehow words deflect
> As the best cannon ever rifled will. (pp. 146–7)

The Prince's self-awareness is of an order quite exceptional among Browning's characters, and in the last dozen lines of the

[1] When Mrs Orr says (*Handbook*, p. 166) that 'practical wisdom, or SAGACITY, is made to suggest everything which he has really done' she is taking no account of Sagacity's advice not to meddle with Italian independence.

poem he increases his authority by revealing that the whole scene is imaginary, the entire poem is, as it were, his own creation. He occupies the same relative position to it as the poet himself, and throughout the poem has known more than the reader of the true circumstances of the monologue, with the extra irony that his fantasy anticipated the exile of Napoleon III. This makes it even more difficult for the reader to decide whether or not the poet is offering an indication of his own attitude to the arguments put forward by the main character. Normally this indication is given by leading the reader to ask 'Why does the speaker represent events in such an incomplete fashion?' Yet, as I say, Hohenstiel-Schwangau seems to have a remarkably full grasp of events, and of the tentative nature of his own arguments.

A possible approach is to observe that the monologue takes place at a crisis in the speaker's affairs very similar to those described in the second part of the poem. He has an ethico-political choice to make, in which he can be guided either by Sagacity or by the ideals of the Head. We leave him wondering whether to send a letter, possibly an ultimatum, to a cousin-Duke, presumably William I or Bismarck. The last line of the poem is

'Double or quits! The letter goes! Or stays?'

The Prince does not know what Browning's readers know, that Napoleon in fact by opposing the German candidate for the succession to the throne of Spain committed himself to the Franco-Prussian war, crowning the edifice with ills. He may see very clearly the path of ideal government, but his last crucial choice was the wrong one, entirely setting at naught the words of the Head about the criminal folly of war.

That is to say, the reader has the advantage of Prince Hohenstiel-Schwangau in only one respect, that he knows the subsequent history of the matters discussed (cf. *Cleon, Karshish*). Like Browning he knows that the war of 1870 'was unjustifiably determined on, imprudently begun, and foolishly carried on to its natural end at Sedan' [11]. Even the advantage of a larger historical perspective is not really decisive, however: it doesn't, for example, enable us to detect a consistent direction of ironic attack in the whole of the poem. The furthest, I think, that one can advance towards a unifying description of the poem is to suggest that the reader's knowledge of Napoleon III's final disastrous blunder warns him not to identify Prince Hohenstiel-Schwangau with the Head Servant in the second part of the poem and suggests that only when Napoleon acted from the highest motives did he succeed on the material level: as soon as he started to trim and compromise he sank. This in turn suggests that all that the Prince said in the first part of the poem about the necessity of prudence and the virtues of conservatism, though very reasonable in theory, is treacherous in practice, since, in the actual career of Napoleon all his carefully calculated plans to preserve the fabric of French society came to nothing. (There is more overt irony in the sub-title – 'The Saviour of Society' – than anywhere else in the poem.) In saying this I do not wish to be taken as agreeing with Professor W. O. Raymond when he writes that Browning 'leaves us in no doubt of Hohenstiel-Schwangau's casuistry' [12]. I think it is true, as Raymond suggests, that in the poem Browning ultimately supports, as usual, the cause of bold decisive action for an ideal against the counsels of prudence, but I cannot see that the arguments he uses in the first part of the poem are casuistical. The most I am pre-pared to say is that in the light of history it can be seen that even the limited ends proposed were not achieved, and this may lead the reader to reflect on the soundness of the arguments put forward.

Two general points arise from the poem. The first is the question of how far a poem is impaired by its dependence on the reader's knowledge of the relevant historical events. As I have tried to show, if *Prince Hohenstiel-Schwangau* were read by someone who had no notion that Napoleon III was glanced at it would be very puzzling indeed, for nothing is provided against which to check the Prince's arguments. This has to be supplied by the reader from his knowledge of Napoleon III's career. In a sense this is a weakness in the poem, since it depends for its full meaning on something outside itself. But the same might have been said two hundred years earlier about *Absalom and Achitophel*, or over 2,000 years earlier about *The Birds*. Political poetry has the quality of being especially relevant to one particular situation. This is its strength and its weakness. It seems to me that the only thing to do is to recognize this and, if we want to try to understand the poem, to equip ourselves with the necessary historical knowledge.

The second question is how far it is legitimate to use Browning's letters to decide his intention in the poem. Here we meet a more difficult problem. Most of the commentaries on *Prince Hohenstiel-Schwangau* quote the letters with some freedom. I have tried to give an account of it without recourse to our knowledge of Browning's private life. Had I wished to do so it would have been simple enough to show that my account of the Prince as at first unscrupulous, then rightly liberating Italy simply because it was just to do so, and finally compromising once more, is paralleled by Browning's own opinions of Napoleon III, from his unfavourable opinions early in 1852 [13] to his letter to Isa Blagden in 1870 – 'But there has been no knavery, only decline and fall of the faculties corporeal & mental: these came to their height ten years ago: since then he has been sinking into all the ordinary ways of the vulgar king, with "the dynasty" dangled before his nose by the verminous people about him' [14]. In addition it seems likely that when Browning wrote the poem he had in mind his wife's enthusiastic support of Napoleon, especially in the years just before her death. It is tempting also to find in the Prince's questions

> 'What's your want
> I' the son and heir? Sympathy, aptitude,
> Teachableness, the fuel for the flame?'

a reflection of the poet's own recent disappointment with his son's career at Oxford [15].

I cannot see that this adds anything to our understanding of the poem, however. I think the most that we can do, if we wish, is to establish that in 1871, when he wrote the poem, while he cannot conceal his contempt for the weakness and falseness of the Emperor's conduct in the Franco-Prussian conflict, Browning is not prepared to hold him completely responsible or to offer a completely unfavourable judgement on his whole career. As early as 1868 he had written to Isa Blagden 'I am profoundly disappointed in and sorry for the Emperor, who has lost, too certainly, splendid opportunities: he wants, as usual, to serve God & the Devil, and will succeed no better than anybody else' [16]. His letter to Isa Blagden during the war [17] is a notable example of the way in which the entire complex situation remained in his mind, unprecipitated. The tone is given by a sen-

tence from the first paragraph '. . . *morally*, everybody from
the highest to the lowest is as blamable as he.' Again, when the
war is over he writes to Isa Blagden '. . . no bitterness more
about the dear man who, if France likes, may try and do what he
can once more at the "edifice", with all the advantages of old age
and decayed faculty. The poor country seems properly to belong
to the devil, – and he is not, nor ever was, a devil, – only a
weaker mortal than one's respect for human nature thought conceivable when given such splendid opportunities for good' [18].
Finally he writes 'At his worst I prefer him to Thiers' best' [19].

I have given these extracts from the correspondence to show
that Browning was not *parti pris* in the matter, but that he
regarded the career of Napoleon as one on which it was extremely difficult to pronounce an unqualified judgement. When
he writes about his own poem he again disclaims a fixed point of
view 'It is just what I imagine the man might, if he pleased, say
for himself' [20], and 'I put forward what excuses I thought he
was likely to make for himself, if inclined to try.'[1]

In short the most that seems to me to emerge from the letters
is that it is not impossible that in writing the poem Browning
should for once have declined to indicate how the reader should
regard the arguments of the speaker. I think therefore that
DeVane puts the matter too strongly when he says (*Handbook*,
p. 363), 'Thanks to the letters we are in a better position than
his contemporaries were to see what Browning really meant'
and '[The poem] was a satire in effect because, as we now know,
Browning did not believe that any justification of the Emperor's
conduct was possible.' This obscures the fact that while the poem
considered in isolation is impossible to place, a knowledge of the
career of Napoleon III helps to focus it considerably, and virtually no further help is given by a study of the letters. The poem
depends on the contemporary situation, not on the poet's personal opinions. With this reservation I agree with DeVane's
judicious account of the poem.

[1] Hudson, p. 167. Browning continues, 'I never at any time thought much better
of him than now; and I don't think so much worse of the character as shown us in
the last few years, because I suppose there to be a physical and intellectual decline
of faculty, brought about by the man's own faults, no doubt – but I think he struggles
against these; and when that is the case, depend on it, in a soliloquy, a man makes
the most of his good intentions and sees great excuse in them – far beyond what our
optics discover!' (Letter of 1 January 1872)

One small interesting point that does emerge from the letters is that Browning spoke of the poem as 'what *I* can't help thinking a sample of my very best work'. This judgement has noticeably failed to find support, although the poem sold well enough when it first appeared. What is to be said then about the artistic value of the poem [21]?

I have already mentioned in the previous chapter the skill with which Browning deals with political matters in the normal speech of the educated Victorian, in lines such as

> And so the siege and slaughter and success
> Whereof we nothing doubt that Hohenstiel
> Will have to pay the price, in God's good time,
> Which does not always fall on Saturday
> When the world looks for wages. (p. 106)

and the ease with which he rises to such more elevated themes as the Prince's vision of Italy or the Head's denunciation of war as an instrument of policy. The poem does not disconcert by un-evennesses of diction or tone but by its weakness in the larger matters of structure and organization. One obvious failing is its lack either of a narrative line or, as an alternative, what is very common in Browning, a progressive revelation of the true character of the speaker. Prince Hohenstiel-Schwangau does not develop: one might say that his only function in the poem is to conduct visitors over it. Moreover the poem lacks Browning's usual powerful ironic grasp. Such irony as emerges is dramatic, in the technical sense, as if the poem were a soliloquy spoken by a tragic hero just before his downfall, looking back over his career, judging himself with some acuteness, realizing his fatal inability to act through principle rather than through expediency, but unaware that his doom is imminent through precisely this cause. But there are too many passages in which the drift of the poem is not detectable at all even to a reader acquainted with the politics of the time. It seems plain that the satirist can operate effectively only by taking a stand on one side of the question: fair-minded satire leaves the reader with no sense of direction. Since Browning seems to be offering us something of the sort it is hard to agree with his favourable verdict on his own poem.

It is possible that *Prince Hohenstiel-Schwangau* will be read more for its incidental interest than for its total effect, especially as it presents in an immediate form a problem which is recurrent in political thought, that of knowing how to judge a ruler of whose constitutional position one disapproves but whose actions have welcome effects, for example President de Gaulle's Algerian policy, or Russian opposition to Hitler. In addition the poem ranges over, as DeVane says, 'almost every conceivable topic of interest in 1871.' This must be qualified by pointing out that the topics are primarily political or politico-ethical topics, most of which would have been of even greater interest on the Continent than they were to British readers. In the first place the question of the liberation of Italy did not impinge directly on British party politics. Most Liberals were sympathetic, but there was not in England the same intense fervour as on the Continent for the ideas of national unity. Secondly the allied questions of the status of the President and the hereditary transmission of rule which the Prince discusses, were burning ones in Europe, in which every country in the nineteenth century had more than one constitution, yet had been effectively settled in England two hundred and more years before. 1649 had done for England what 1848 did for Europe. After the Protectorate the ultimate status of the Crown was never in doubt: 1688 merely recognized the *de facto* position. Consequently constitutional questions were limited to comparatively minor points such as the extension of the franchise. The political issues which divided the nation were social and economic: the poem deals with these only in the first part, that is in rather general terms. Nevertheless it is arguable that the national movements all over Europe were at least as important as the domestic concerns of British industrialism, and that in his poem Browning was discussing issues which in the next fifty years were to affect, directly or indirectly, every country in the world.

III

Prince Hohenstiel-Schwangau was published in December 1871. In June 1872 Browning put before his public an even longer and even thornier poem, *Fifine at the Fair*. Once again a major difficulty lies in determining the precise degree of sincerity in each of the speaker's arguments. The plan of the poem can be summarized easily enough. A philanderer, whom it is convenient to call Don Juan, on holiday with his wife at the little town of Pornic, notices one evening the arrival of a travelling fair. Next morning he has a bathe, observes that the circus tent is erected, returns home, smokes and thinks about the fair and the girls of the fair ground. He plays Schumann's 'Carnaval' on the piano, and as he is doing so falls asleep. He has a long and disquieting dream. That afternoon he walks with his wife Elvire to the fair, and back again to their villa: what he says to her on this walk constitutes the poem. He notices an attractive gipsy called Fifine and puts money in her tambourine. When his wife reproaches him he defends himself at length: the climax of his defence is a recital of his dream, which finishes when they reach an ancient monument at Pornic. They return to their villa, Don Juan protesting his devotion to Elvire, but at the end of the poem he leaves her on a transparent pretext and goes to see Fifine. The difficulty is that one would expect Don Juan's arguments to be sophistical, yet as far as one can tell they are for the most part perfectly good and put forward with sincerity: moreover they seem not to differ from similar arguments which Browning uses elsewhere when he is writing in his own person, notably in *La Saisiaz*.

There is the further complication that Browning was, as I have suggested was his habit at this time, writing about something which was a matter of current discussion. For example, it seems highly probable that the poet had in mind the feud between Dante Gabriel Rossetti and Robert Buchanan which Professor DeVane calls 'the literary sensation of the winter 1871–2' (*Handbook*, p. 365). This was the controversy in the course of which Buchanan used the phrase 'The Fleshly School of Poetry'. Rossetti certainly construed parts of *Fifine* as a personal attack, breaking off his friendship with Browning [22]. In a more recent article Professor Charlotte Watkins has argued very strongly that the relevance of the topics discussed is not limited to controversy about the merits of the aesthetic movement but includes also current speculation about a wide range of metaphysical subjects [23].

In particular she suggests that Browning had in mind the artistic and philosophical ideas of Walter Pater, who was prominent as a defender of the 'new' poetry: these can be succinctly represented by a few sentences from his review article on William Morris's *Earthly Paradise* etc., in the *Westminster Review* for October 1868:

> To regard all things and principles of things as inconstant modes or fashions has more and more become the tendency of modern thought.

If we exist in a completely 'relative' world, then,

> Experience, already reduced to a swarm of impressions, is ringed round for each one of us by that thick wall of personality through which no real voice has ever pierced on its way to us, or from us to that, which we can only conjecture to be without. Every one of those impressions is the impression of an individual in his isolation, each mind keeping as a solitary prisoner in its own dream of a world.

Professor Watkins makes the application to the poem in the following sentence:

> At a time when Buchanan's epithet 'the Fleshly School' had currency, Browning appears to have dramatized his judgement of the 'new' poetry of the 1870's by placing an argument analogous to the criticism which defended it in the mouth of a speaker for whose character he chose as an image the very prototype of the fleshly, Don Juan himself.

I do not quarrel with Professor Watkins when she suggests that current controversies were in Browning's mind when he wrote *Fifine*, nor when she indicates that relativism is the central theme of the poem. Where we part company is at the point when she tries to show from the poem Browning's own opinion in the debate. She writes

> The modifications which transform the symbolism of the prologue into the pervasive imagery of the poem serve also to identify the monologuist's philosophy of art with that which occurs in the early aesthetic criticism of Walter Pater. Browning dramatizes the speciousness of the aesthetic theory propounded by the monologuist by placing its exposition in the mouth of a casuist . . . whose idiom is a perverse development of the symbolic language of the prologue. (p. 427)

In short the only argument Professor Watkins offers for supposing Don Juan's arguments to be specious is that in putting them forward he uses symbols in a way in which they are not used in the Prologue to the poem. In the Prologue, she says, Browning is speaking in his own person, and describes in it how he has an imaginative vision of ideal truths: the noon sun is 'the essential symbol of truth in the prologue'. But the sun is mentioned only incidentally in the Prologue and ideal truth is nowhere mentioned. Indeed the whole point of the Prologue is the contrast between the dead, who have certain knowledge when they are in heaven, and the living writer, who makes his poetry a substitute for heaven:

> Whatever they are, we seem:
>   Imagine the thing they know;
> All deeds they do, we dream;
>   Can heaven be else but so? (p. 16)

That is to say, poetry offers a simulacrum of heaven just as swimming mimics flight ('Unable to fly, one swims!'), but the elements of air and water are utterly distinct, and the kind of knowledge available to the live poet is likewise utterly distinct from that available to his dead wife [24].

To use the Prologue then as a lever with which to turn the entire poem about is to place a weight on it which it will not bear, for the Prologue cannot be shown to give us an unambiguous statement of the poet's views from which we can extract the simple equation 'sun = truth', and then proceed to assume that this represents the poet's commitment to a doctrine of absolute values. When Professor Watkins tells us that

It is by contrast with Browning's presentation, in the prologue to *Fifine*, of the metaphysical, moral, and aesthetic convictions on which his new work continued to rest, that the subjective and relativistic philosophy of art and life set forth in the monologue is to be fully evaluated,

she appears to me to underestimate both the strength of Don Juan's arguments and the subtlety with which Browning presents them.

As I have suggested, one of the main objections to simply declaring that all Don Juan's arguments are specious is that we have no reason to suppose that Browning regarded them as fallacious and some reason to suppose that they were arguments

which he himself found troublesome to meet. *La Saisiaz* is a
good example of the difficulties Browning encountered whenever
he tried to clear his mind about questions of perception, subjective judgements and the existence of absolute values. The same
problem disturbs him in *Ferishtah's Fancies* and, as I have said,
was much in his mind when he wrote *Prince Hohenstiel-
Schwangau* less than a year earlier. When Browning felt himself
adrift in a world of unstable values his reassurance normally
came from a consideration of the reality and stability of love.
This alone can close the debate and give him peace. But in
Fifine at the Fair he poses the crucial question 'What sort of
terminus is possible to a man who does *not* find in love an abiding
power?' To answer this question he puts the debate in the mouth
of a man notorious for profligacy at the very time when he is
contemplating a fresh affair and contriving the opportunity for it.
I am suggesting that the dramatic element in the poem is not
very strong and that *Fifine* is a poem in which Browning is, as it
were, arguing out a hypothesis.

It is Don Juan's dream (Sections 93–125) which, as it were,
lays down the conditions of the debate. In the poem it comes very
late, but it is antecedent to the monologue in point of time. It is a
dream about the transience of all earthly institutions and hence
the relativism of all standards. Juan is watching a carnival in St
Mark's Square at which all the men and women wear masks instead of faces; his own judgement of them varies according to his
viewpoint, until he finds himself unable to judge at all (102); the
buildings of the square then change into the various buildings
with which he has been acquainted; these in turn appear to be
constantly changing their shapes and giving place to others –
Academies, churches, and the establishments of History,
Morality and Art all decay and pass; at last everything dissolves,
merging into the Druid monument at Pornic, the one object to
remain stable. It is the implications of this dream which Don
Juan discusses in the poem, notably the question which Pater
raises 'If all standards are relative and all perceptions subjective, what guarantee have we of the reality of anything but our
own perceptions? If none, then we live in a solipsistic universe,
and if that is so what certainly have we even of our own reality?'
Don Juan is trying in the poem to satisfy what he calls 'My
hunger both to be and know the thing I am.' (103) To do this he

searches for various sources of certainty, in a kind of fevered fear of emptiness.[1] He says to Elvire

> 'Are you unterrified?
> All false, all fleeting too! And nowhere things abide,
> And everywhere we strain that things should stay, – the one
> Truth, that ourselves are true!' (84)

The poem, as has often been observed, takes the form of a series of images, each worked out with a Metaphysical particularity, and each carefully designed to investigate the reality of a possible source of an absolute truth. For example, in Sections 2–13 Don Juan considers whether social values are permanent and universal. He takes the Fair as his image and shows that the actors despise what respectability holds most dear. Fifine appears in Section 15 and is hailed by Don Juan (it is perhaps worth remembering that he already knows her name) in the following terms,

> This way, this way, Fifine!
> Here's she, shall make my thoughts be surer what they mean.

This proves true: although Fifine plays a very small part in the action of the poem she suggests to Don Juan many of the images which he uses to explore his own mind. For example the lily which entices insects to their death (17), but which it would be irrelevant to *judge*, since like Fifine, it has made 'self-sustainment' into 'morality'. In general Fifine symbolizes everything that is fleeting and ephemeral: Elvire all that is stable and true.

Don Juan next explores the hypothesis that things simply are what they seem to be by the device of the procession before Louis XI (19–33). His method is to show that in each of four different women the 'outward sign' is to be distinguished from the 'inward grace'; but that what gives Fifine her attractiveness is precisely the fact that she is no more than she seems to be and makes no demands on him beyond expecting money.

---

[1] Cf. Bruno: 'The first step in the desire for the infinitely beautiful is but the beginning of an endless series; the heart goes out on an endless quest, while the intellect can but follow. The will cannot be satisfied with a finite good, but, if there is other good beyond, desires and seeks it.' Quoted in Sherwood, *Undercurrents*, p. 349.

'Does this much pleasure? Then, repay the pleasure, put
Its price i' the tambourine! Do you seek further? Tut!
I'm just my instrument, – sound hollow: mere smooth skin
Stretched o'er gilt framework, I: rub-dub, nought else within . . .
. . . All I plead is "Pay for just the sight you see,
And give no credit to another charm in me!" ' (32)

She *is* simply her appearance. That is part, perhaps the largest part, of her appeal to Don Juan. In Section 33, a complicated passage in which Browning suggests what Don Juan thinks Fifine would make Elvire say when reproaching him for his coldness, the terms of the main argument of the poem are stated. Elvire says that the passage of time only increases true love:

mature at noonday, love defied
Chance, the wind, change, the rain: love, strenuous all the more
For storm, struck deeper root and choicer fruitage bore,
Despite the rocking world; yet truth struck root in vain,
While tenderness bears fruit, you praise, not taste again.

The idea that constancy in love is a 'truth' is emphasized later in the same speech. Elvire points out Don Juan's folly in longing for love as a source of stability and, as soon as he has it, ignoring it in favour of a passing fancy.

Preposterous thought! to find no value fixed in things,
To covet all you see, hear, dream of, till fate brings
About that, what you want, you get; then comes a change.
Give you the sun to keep, forthwith must fancy range . . .

At the end of this image of the pageant before Louis XI Fifine virtually disappears from the poem except for Sections 80–84, 91, and her brief reappearance in the last section. It is worth noting that even when she is the topic of Juan's discourse his arguments are not unambiguously marked as specious. His direct references to her to Elvire are, we learn later, designed to deceive, but they are disingenuous rather than obviously false. This does not imply that his entire argument is an elaborate smoke-screen for his infidelity, much less does it imply that he is simply a cynic, for a cynic is someone who professes or denies belief in the real values of his society as seems most expedient and expects other people to do the same.

Don Juan on the other hand has a deep-seated belief that a

reality exists somewhere. 'So absolutely good is truth, truth never hurts the teller.' (32) But, confronted on all sides with evidence of the contingent nature of knowledge and of the transience of human systems and values he feels impelled to examine ruthlessly anything that claims to be the absolute for which he is seeking. Accordingly he subjects to his corrosive intellect various institutions which seem to have permanent validity. He is a sceptic in every way, a cynic in none.

As the poem unfolds he continues his quest. The three linked images of the painting by Rafael, the pictures scrawled in the sand and the mass of marble which may or may not be an elemental statue by Michelagnolo, lead him to question on the status of artistic truth. He admits the disinterested sincerity of the artist's quest for absolute truth, but observes that he must always begin that quest from a fleeting glimpse of a partial truth, must work, that is, towards what is entire and ultimate through that which is fragmentary and provisional.

> . . . Art, – which I may style the love of loving, rage
> Of knowing, seeing, feeling the absolute truth of things
> For truth's sake, whole and sole, nor any good, truth brings
> The knower, seer, feeler, beside, – instinctive Art
> Must fumble for the whole, once fixing on a part
> However poor, surpass the fragment, and aspire
> To reconstruct thereby the ultimate entire. (44)

But the products of the artist have value only in what the audience sees and remembers of them. For each man a work of art exists only in one place,

> Why, where but in the sense
> And soul of me, the judge of Art? Art-evidence,
> That thing was, is, might be; but no more thing itself,
> Than flame is fuel. Once the verse-book laid on shelf,
> The picture turned to wall, the music fled from ear, –
> Each beauty, born of each, grows clearer and more clear,
> Mine henceforth, ever mine! (41)

That is, art, though its aims are high and its pleasures exquisite, exists only in the soul of the 'judge of Art'. Its subjective character means that it cannot sustain the demands Juan makes for absolute truth. In the crucial Section 55 he relates his three artistic images to his own quest:

> I search but cannot see
> What purpose serves the soul that strives, or world it tries
> Conclusions with, unless the fruit of victories
> Stay, one and all, stored up and guaranteed its own
> For ever, by some mode whereby shall be made known
> The gain of every life. Death reads the title clear –
> What each soul for itself conquered from out things here:
> Since, in the seeing soul, all worth lies, I assert, –
> And nought i' the world, which, save for soul that sees, inert
> Was, is, and would be ever, – stuff for transmuting, – null
> And void until man's breath evoke the beautiful.

This summarizes Juan's philosophy and his discontent – if beauty exists only in the 'seeing soul', what becomes of beauty when the spectator dies? Is it too subject to mortality?

Considering this he is led to the other main wing of his argument: suppose we look at the problem from the opposite point of view and lay stress instead on this remarkable power in the individual, that he *can* create beauty, that the soul can create life from inert matter, may we not take pride in 'the challenged soul's response/To ugliness and death'. (55) In other words may we not find an enduring value in man's unceasing struggles to create the beautiful from the formless? This is to be seen not only in the world of Art but in personal relationships. In Section 44 he has already referred to

> . . . the fact that each soul, just as weak
> In its own way as its fellow, – departure from design
> As flagrant in the flesh, – goes striving to combine
> With what shall right the wrong, the under or above
> The standard: supplement unloveliness by love.

In Sections 50–54 he has developed this comparison between the artist, who brings out the hidden potentialities of his medium, and the lover, who penetrates through the accidents of appearance to the ideal essence.

> . . . Each soul lives, longs and works
> For itself, by itself, because a lodestar lurks,
> An other than itself . . .
> This, guessed at through the flesh, by parts which prove the whole,
> This constitutes the soul discernible by soul . . . (59)

When Elvire reproaches him with his unworthy dalliance with Fifine Don Juan is able to reply in effect that his conduct is justifiable because it is part of the process by which man tries to produce beauty out of ugliness, good out of evil, and truth out of falsehood. He continues to argue that the end justifies the means, not, I think, without a conscious tinge of sophistry at first. For example, in Sections 64–67 he puts forward the fact that a swimmer can keep only a small part of his body above the water, but this is enough to let him breathe. If he tries to raise himself further out of the water he will find that he sinks altogether. 'I liken to this play o' the body', he says, 'my spirit's life/'Twixt false, whence it would break, and true, where it would bide.' Although Juan is immersed in falsehood he can keep alive by snatching breaths of truth; if he tried to mount higher, his soul 'foiled by the very effort' would only sink deeper in the 'old briny bitterness'.

The worth of this analogy is hard to judge. It may be put forward in sincerity: it may be as disingenuous as the special pleadings of Guido. Two things, both slight, suggest that it is sophistical. First the argument is put forward to convince Elvire that Don Juan has no personal interest in Fifine, whereas the end of the poem shows this to be false. Secondly the argument is used by Juan to justify a minor intrigue, a dabbling in deceit, which is at variance with the profound scrutiny of man's place in the world which he undertakes in the rest of the poem. This shift from the absolute to the expedient suggests that the less elevated side of the speaker is being deliberately exhibited.

Later he speaks with a wider perspective and greater sincerity; in Section 80, for example, he says that Elvire and Fifine convince him

> That I am, anyhow, a truth, though all else seem
> And be not; if I dream, at least I know I dream.
> The falsity, beside, is fleeting: I can stand
> Still, and let truth come back, – your steadying touch of hand
> Assists me to remain self-centred, fixed amid
> All on the move. Believe in me, at once you bid
> Myself believe that, since one soul has disengaged
> Mine from the shows of things, so much is fact: I waged
> No foolish warfare, then, with shades, myself a shade,
> Here in the world – may hope my pains will be repaid!

How false things are, I judge: how changeable, I learn:
When, where and how it is I shall see truth return,
That I expect to know, because Fifine knows me!
How much more, if Elvire!

When Don Juan has reached this conclusion that a woman has
the unique power of convincing a man of the fact of his own
existence, his particular disabling weakness comes into play and
he tries to justify his preference for Fifine by arguing that she is
so much trickier and more difficult to manage than Elvire that
she assures him more rapidly of his own reality.

'Earth is not all one lie, this truth attests me true!
Thanks therefore to Fifine!'

Although Fifine is deceitful, this is part of her charm: she admits
that she is simply playing a part and thus evades a moral judgement on her deception.

That's the first o' the truths found: all things, slow
Or quick i' the passage come at last to that, you know!
Each has a false outside, whereby a truth is forced
To issue from within: truth, falsehood are divorced
By the excepted eye, at the rare season, for
The happy moment. Life means – learning to abhor
The false, and love the true, truth treasured snatch by snatch,
Waifs counted at their worth. (86)

This seems to me a fair summary of Juan's argument so far.
Truth and falsehood are hard to distinguish, in fact one has to
progress through successive falsehoods to an approximate truth,
but they are not the same. If one could feel that somewhere they
coalesced into a thing that was both and yet neither, there would
be nothing to worry about. But Juan cannot accept this easy
solution, any more than Browning himself could. Therefore
he must continue trying to progress by discarding what is
false or accidental until he is left only with what is true or
essential.

I do not think he is presented satirically here, nor is he
deceiving himself.[1] He foresees, as Browning foresaw, that the

---

[1] Don Juan is often classed as a casuist, with a certain justice, but it is to be noted
that casuistry is not necessarily an invalid method of proceeding: it becomes so
only if the object of the casuist is to present a series of hypothetical cases in such

difficulty is to know where to stop. Suppose we can find *nothing* that abides. To illustrate this he talks about artistic taste as a prelude to narrating the morning's dream.

He hoped for some kind of certainty in music, some 'truth that escapes prose, – nay, puts poetry to shame', since in playing music one is at least certain that one other person, the composer, has shared one's experience of the music and has contrived to record his experience. Yet even as he played Schumann,[1] he reflected on the mutability of artistic taste and how the palates of different ages required different flavours. His head full of this 'certainty of change,/Conviction we shall find the false, where'er we range,/In Art no less than nature' he began to dream the dream which he now describes to Elvire. We recognize in it several arguments which he has used earlier, e.g.

---

a way as to blur the distinction between morality and immorality and so justify immoral conduct. The opposite view of the matter is well put by George Eliot in Chapter II of the last book of *The Mill on the Floss*:

'The great problem of the shifting relation between passion and duty is clear to no man who is capable of apprehending it . . . we have no master key that will fit all cases. The casuists have become a byword of reproach; but their perverted spirit of minute discrimination was the shadow of a truth to which eyes and hearts are too often fatally sealed – the truth, that moral judgements must remain false and hollow, unless they are checked and enlightened by a perpetual reference to the special circumstances that mark the individual lot.'

The alternative, that is, to a subtle and painstaking discrimination in the application of moral standards (of which casuistry is an extreme form) is to be guided simply by maxims and formulas, 'thinking that these will lead . . . to justice by a ready-made patent method'. The difficulty confronting those who wish to represent Juan as a casuist is that of demonstrating precisely where he carries his discrimination of cases beyond the bounds of what is necessary.

[1] It seems certain to me that a fairly close connection could be demonstrated between *Carnaval* and Browning's poem. Some of the scenes have titles which are obviously relevant, such as 'Pierrot', 'Arlequin', 'Coquette', 'Masquerade', 'Reconnaissance', 'Aveu', and 'Promenade'. The title 'Sphinxes' calls attention to the cryptic element in *Carnaval* and to Schumann's delight in elaborate disguises and mystifications. 'Papillons' (cf. the butterfly in the Prologue to *Fifine*) alludes directly to an earlier work of Schumann's which is closely linked in many ways with *Carnaval*. The composer founded *Papillons* on a passage from *Flegeljahre*, the work of his early hero Jean Paul. The passage includes the following observation: 'A masked ball is perhaps the most perfect medium through which poetry can interpret life . . . The human being seeks in the masked ball to poetize both his very self and life as a whole.' One might also conjecture that Browning had in mind the tangled and distressing love affairs of Schumann at the time he wrote *Carnaval*.

'Are we not here to learn the good of peace through strife,
Of love through hate, and reach knowledge by ignorance.'

but their occurrence in this context touches them with a quality
of phantasmagoria, so that their ultimate implications yawn
beneath the feet like a bottomless chasm, and it is clear that Don
Juan is fighting against this vision of a world in which nothing,
literally nothing, is constant. He continues to narrate the events
of his nightmare until, as he reaches the end, he and Elvire find
themselves confronted with the very Druid monument into
which all the buildings of the dream had dissolved (121). It
seems to be a massive granite dolmen[1] with a doorway, and a
dark passage terminating in a Cross; the cross is not a sign of
Christian worship but something hateful [25]. Beside it in the
grass lies a huge stone menhir, perhaps once part of the other
building.[2] As Mrs Orr suggests [26] the first is consecrated to
death and is a kind of memento mori: the other is the object of
a spring cult, and sacred to life and love.

The monuments confront Don Juan with two certainties, love
and death. They assure him that 'truth is forced/To manifest
itself through falsehood' and thus, by falsely pretending to be
absolute truth leads men ever higher, but that at last men can
move through the 'fleeting' and find rest in the 'fixed'.

By hints which make the soul discernible by soul –
Let only soul look up, not down, not hate but love . . . (124)

The section concludes with an affirmation, which seems to me
free from all signs of sophistry, that ultimately 'the excepted
eye, at the rare season, for/The happy moment' can winnow
away the accidentals of 'speech, act, time, place' and see nakedly
the principle of things. It would require very strong evidence
indeed to establish that Browning is here presenting Juan's
arguments in such a way that the reader is intended to judge them
to be specious, especially as they represent a line of thought
which Browning himself found attractive.

[1] 'The dolmen, in all its varieties and modifications, was a sepulchre . . . The first
I examined consisted of a passage about ten yards long, formed of upright stones,
with flat ones laid on top of them.' J. M. Jephson, *Narrative of a Walking Tour in
Brittany*, (London, 1859), pp. 201–3.
[2] 'The moenhir, menhir, maensaâs, or peulvan, is a long single stone raised on one
end . . . They were analogous to the stone set up by Jacob as an altar on which he
poured oil.' Jephson, p. 199.

But in the next section Juan proceeds to apply his reasoning to his special case and to argue in effect that since we progress towards truth by a successive disengaging of veils he will be taking a step nearer truth by (metaphorically, one presumes) unveiling Fifine. Here, I think, one can detect a certain reservation on Browning's part about the language Juan uses. In Section 126 Juan realizes that he has not the quality of constant love which he has postulated as necessary for the ascent to the heights of absolute truth. He descends to 'homely earth', their circuit draws to a close, and Juan comments

> We end where we began: that consequence is clear.
> All peace and some fatigue, wherever we were nursed
> To life, we bosom us on death, find last is first
> And thenceforth final too. (127)

In the following sections (128 and 129) he rationalizes the significance of the monument's twin symbolism of love and death. These are the only abiding truths, and we know that they must have a real existence outside ourselves because they offer no inducement to man to project them on to the inside of his own mind. Normally we may suspect that pleasant experiences are purely subjective, but nobody would submit to death if it were purely a thing of his own imagination.[1] We must therefore recognize when we yield to 'time's pressure' and 'dark's approach' that we are confronted by something other than ourselves. Similarly love involves submission to something outside one's self.

> Such ending looks like law, because the natural man
> Inclines the other way, feels lordlier free than bound. (129)

It is, he confesses, wounding to his pride to find that breaking free from the bonds of love brings him no profit, simply the realization that constancy is essential. Don Juan thus brings his monologue to the same point of termination as his dream. Man

---

[1] Cf. Johnson, *Idler*, 52: 'When an opinion to which there is no temptation of interest spreads wide, and continues long, it may be reasonably presumed to have been infused by nature or dictated by reason. It has been often observed that the fictions of imposture, and illusions of fancy, soon give way to time and experience; and that nothing keeps its ground but truth, which gains every day new influence by new confirmation.'

can be sure of two things only outside himself – love and death, and if two people are constant in love, each can gradually enable the other to learn his or her true nature. Don Juan in a final flourish of the marine imagery which has pervaded the poem declares that he has determined to settle down as a land-locked householder, forgetting the 'fickle element' of the sea, that is, he will find a point of rest in a world of flux by binding himself constantly to one other person.

But he is reckoning without his own restless, insubmissive nature. In the last section of the poem he finds a note which Fifine has slipped into his glove and makes this an excuse for a further meeting with her. This does not invalidate his previous arguments or entitle us to dismiss them as 'the devil quoting Scripture for his purpose' [27]. It presents dramatically the central theme of the poem – that to abandon wilfully constancy in love is to leave oneself no certainty but death.

The Epilogue to the poem, subtitled 'The Householder', carries on the opposition of love and death. The householder, partly Juan and partly Browning himself, has just been reunited by death with his dead wife: they meet, complain, bicker and combine to write the notification of his death.

> 'What i' the way of final flourish? Prose, verse? Try!
> *Affliction sore, long time he bore,* or, what is it to be?
> *Till God did please to grant him ease.* Do end!' quoth I:
> 'I end with – Love is all and Death is nought!' quoth She.

Thus perfect love shows itself in the last line of the poem to be more powerful even than death. It alone endures and it alone can provide a firm basis for self-knowledge and the evaluation of the shifting shows of things.

This summary does little justice to the comprehensiveness of the argument or to the brilliant diversity of the imagery, but it shows that the poem was dealing with themes which were very close to the poet's heart, especially after 1861 – the difficulty of finding any stability in the world and the extent to which he was dependent on the memory of his dead wife in his quest for some permanent truth. He expresses this memorably in the *Epilogue* to *Ferishtah's Fancies* (see pp. 235–6), and even more strikingly in *Dubiety*, from *Asolando*, published on the day of his death. It finishes

Be life so, all things ever the same!
　　For, what has disarmed the world? Outside,
Quiet and peace: inside, nor blame
　　Nor want, nor wish whate'er betide.

What is it like that has happened before?
　　A dream? No dream, more real by much.
A vision? But fanciful days of yore
　　Brought many: mere musing seems not such.

Perhaps but a memory, after all!
　　– Of what came once when a woman leant
To feel for my brow where her kiss might fall.
　　Truth ever, truth only the excellent!

We have here precisely the same identification of perfect love
with the attainment of an enduring truth as we have in *Fifine*. I
find it a very strong argument for supposing that Browning's
presentation of Don Juan in the poem is satirical only in a very
few passages. If I may adopt the classification of J. T. Nettle-
ship [28] I should say that wherever Don Juan *applies* his
arguments to his own relationship to Fifine he is speaking dis-
ingenuously or with intent to deceive Elvire, but that elsewhere
he offers as powerful arguments as Browning is able to devise.
This is most evidently true where he is demonstrating the
mutability of human institutions, for there he is Browning's
probe. If he fails to discover a weak place or wrongly denies the
existence of a strong place then he is useless to Browning. As I
have tried to show, there is no reason to believe that Browning
provides him in the rest of the poem with arguments which the
poet knows to be false or feels to be inadequate. On the contrary
the closeness of Don Juan's position to Browning's own, which I
have described in earlier chapters, precludes any consistent presentation of Juan's arguments as patently unsound. It is moreover a position which was particularly in men's minds in the later
Victorian period. In *Prince Hohenstiel-Schwangau* Browning had
touched on the question of evolution (pp. 68–72): the Prince has
no qualms about accepting the theory and indeed welcoming it as
evidence of the coherent planning of the Universe. But to many
Victorian thinkers it posed the question, 'If man has evolved
gradually, and his moral standards have evolved with him, how
can we consider them as anything but purely accidental accom-

paniments?' Similarly the idea of the pettiness of human affairs in the immensity of the Universe made any attempt by man to govern his life by absolute values absurdly presumptuous. Tennyson spoke for his time when in *Parnassus* he wrote of

> Astronomy and Geology, terrible muses!

There was a natural tendency to look for comfort and reassurance in face of this threat to all established values, and, as Humphry House has observed, this comfort was commonly found in an intensification of personal relationships [29]. He instances *Dover Beach* and *In Memoriam*: *Fifine at the Fair* is concerned with the same fundamental question of the nature of man and his world, and of personal identity, with this refinement, that the speaker is by definition someone who cannot find permanent satisfaction in human relationships.

The poem was not a success. Browning's comment on its failure to win readers or even to be understood is best given in the words of DeVane:

> Browning wrote two passages in Greek upon the manuscript of *Fifine* before it was given to Balliol College. The first came from Aeschylus' *Choephoroe* (816–18); the second was from Aristophanes' *Thesmophoriazusae* (1128–31). They were both written, I think, several months after the publication of the poem. One may translate the first passage roughly thus:
>
> > And reading this doubtful word he has dark night before his eyes, and he is nothing clearer by day.
>
> And then Browning adds in English,
>
> > – if any of my critics had Greek enough in him to make the application!
>
> The second quotation is dated 'Nov.5,'72' [30] and may be translated roughly thus:
>
> > To what words are you turned, for a barbarian nature would not receive them. For bearing new words to the Scaeans you would spend them in vain. [31]

About the poem itself Browning wrote in a letter to Domett that it was 'the most metaphysical and boldest he had written since *Sordello*' [32]. I hope that I have shown the poem's metaphysical organization clearly enough for the first part of this claim to be accepted. Juan at one point states the central theme of the poem with some austerity as: 'From the given point evolve the infinite' (129). This exercise is conducted throughout in a spirit of intellectual and imaginative enquiry, with no introduction of revealed truth or *Christus ex machinâ* to close the debate. This is typical of Browning's later, freer thought on human nature and destiny. Of the poem's boldness I think there can be no question. It is not simply a matter of structure, though the central idea of a powerful mind stripping away the temporary to reveal the eternal is impressive enough. But the real boldness lies in Browning's initial assumption that it is possible that nothing whatsoever is outside the flux of time and in his willingness to examine the consequences of this for the nature of man. The choice of Don Juan as the *persona* of the poem is equally striking: the relevance of his personal situation, with its petty intrigue and furtive betrayal of love, to his profound speculations on mankind's ceaseless quest for stability is less obvious than, say, the appropriateness of John to the matter of *A Death in the Desert* or of Mr. Sludge to his reflections on truth and falsehood. But the way the personal and universal illuminate one another in *Fifine* is no less telling for being oblique [33].

As I have said, a concern with the implications of relativism touched one of the sensitive areas of the Victorian mind. It has been suggested that a sensitive place in Browning's own mind offered an even more immediate cause for the writing of *Fifine*, for it is known that he proposed marriage to Louisa, Lady Ashburton, probably in the autumn of 1869. He explained to her, with more candour than tact, that his heart was 'buried in Florence' (that is, with his first wife) and that 'the attractiveness of a marriage with her lay in its advantage to Pen' (that is, to his son). Lady Ashburton refused him, and there appears to have been some recriminatory correspondence. It seems likely that Browning had one final stormy meeting with Lady Ashburton in the autumn of 1871: thereafter he refers to her in tones of biting dislike. The facts are set out in an appendix to Hood/Wise.

It has been suggested that this experience constituted the 'leaven of bitterness' which Mrs Orr conjectured to have been working within Browning while he wrote *Fifine*, that is from December 1871 to May 1872. The case rests on certain similarities between Browning's own consciousness of his unfaithfulness to the memory of his dead wife and Don Juan's projected unfaithfulness to Elvire. I cannot see that such arguments can be proved or disproved, and I cannot see that they make the slightest difference either way to the poem. I agree that we cannot possibly *not* think of E.B.B. when we read the *Prologue* and the *Epilogue* to *Fifine*. Possibly too something is added to Section 130 of the poem if we superimpose on our picture of Don Juan addressing Elvire that of Browning talking to his wife:

> How pallidly you pause o' the threshold! Hardly night,
> Which drapes you, ought to make real flesh and blood so white!
> Touch me, and so appear alive to all intents!
> Will the saint vanish from the sinner that repents?
> Suppose you are a ghost! A memory, a hope,
> A fear, a conscience! Quick! Give back the hand I grope
> I' the dusk for!

Otherwise Mrs Browning's presence in *Fifine* is merely confusing, and since it is not necessary should not be assumed.

If we wish to use the episode to enhance any of Browning's poems the obvious candidate is *Any Wife to Any Husband*, which appeared immediately after *By the Fire-side* in *Men and Women* (1855). It is an uncannily accurate prefiguration of what was to occur fifteen years later: our knowledge of Lady Ashburton gives the poem an intense irony, especially if we take it as the wife's direct reply to the poet's own visions and protestations of constancy in *By the Fire-side*. Such irony is, of course, purely fortuitous: both poems, like *Fifine*, are intelligible as complete works of art without any additional illumination from Browning's private life.

IV

Browning's next productions in this astonishingly fruitful decade were *Red Cotton Night-Cap Country* (1873) and *The Inn Album* (1875), two long narrative poems which, as we shall see, had their origin in events of the day. While Browning was on holiday on the coast of Normandy in 1872 he learned that the owner of a house nearby had committed suicide two years previously. That very summer in the courts at Caen the validity of the dead man's will was upheld. The story took Browning's interest, and his friend Milsand furnished him with more particulars. It appeared that the man had been the son of a prosperous jeweller, that he had taken a married woman for his mistress, that he had tried to drown himself, that on another occasion he had thrust both his hands into the fire, and that at the end of his life he had shown an almost excessive interest in the Church. From this unpromising material, the very stock-in-trade of the sensational journalist, Browning made his poem [34]. He retained the actual names of the participants and made virtually no alteration in the circumstances of the story: indeed the whole affair was so readily recognizable that Browning felt it expedient to substitute fictitious names while the poem was in proof in order to avoid a possible action for libel.

The incidents themselves being given in this way, the main interest of the poem lies in Browning's narrative technique and in his probings for the motives of the characters involved. The comparison with *The Ring and The Book* is obvious, a comparison that extends beyond the similarity of subject. As Browning says

> You ought to sympathise –
> Not mock the sturdy effort to redeem
> My pledge, and wring you out some tragedy
> From even such a perfect common-place. (I, 742–745 p. 49)[35]

The whole poem may be seen as a further attempt to show that the great subject is not necessary for a tragic poem.

The first book is quietly but skilfully conducted. Miss Thackeray, who indirectly suggested the title of the poem to Browning, is used first as a pretext for writing the poem and then to represent the innocent trusting eye to whom Normandy appears like a fairy-tale landscape. She thus gives the superficial appearance of the *locale*. The poet moves in wide sweeps, describing the countryside at large and then gradually narrowing down to one village and one house. In lines 661–731 (pp. 43–48) Browning describes the house and park in terms that induce a vague uneasiness: the passage finishes with the explicit statement that

> something is amiss,
> Something is out of sorts in the display.

The house is right for Paris, but wrong for the countryside. The aesthetic judgement has moral overtones, which are explained in lines 919–1025 (pp. 60–67). Browning describes how a hard-working jeweller named Miranda made enough money for his son to shake off his connection with trade and retire to the country. It might be thought that the local aristocracy would not accept such a man, but Browning observes that lavish gifts to the Church would no doubt induce them to change their minds. It looks as though we had a common enough situation – the man whose money comes from the town but who lives as a country landowner, no uncommon situation, one may remark, in Victorian England. At the very end of the book, however, having used Miss Thackeray as his foil in his leisurely placing of the actors in their setting, Browning suddenly seats her as an audience, and like a Grand Guignol showman draws back the curtain with a shrieking of rings:

> Now comes my moment with the thrilling throw
> Of curtain from each side a shrouded case.
> Don't the rings shriek an ominous 'Ha! ha!
> *So* you take Human Nature upon trust?' . . .
> Sit on the little mound here, whence you seize
> The whole of the gay front sun-satisfied,
> One laugh of colour and embellishment!
> Because it was there, – past those laurustines,
> On that smooth gravel-sweep 'twixt flowers and sward, –
> There tragic death befell. (I, 1025–1038, pp. 67–68)

The poem is organized around two sets of contrasted metaphors – red and white, and turf, towers and tent. The first book has made it clear that white, not surprisingly, stands for innocence and serenity, red for guilt and sin. The second book introduces the more complex set of images:

> Keep this same
> Notion of outside mound and inside mash.
> Towers yet intact round turfy rottenness,
> Symbolic partial-ravage, – keep in mind!
> (II, 114–117, pp. 76–77)

The towers, the wall, the rock, the stone, or the ridge are a symbol for faith or moral living. Significantly they are normally spoken of as being in ruinous disrepair. The turf, or grass, or flowers are a symbol for youthful dalliance and self-indulgence. The young Miranda was born into a world strewn with ruins and was soon beguiled by a tempter who said

> Youth, strength, and lustihood can sleep on turf
> Yet pace the stony platform afterward. (II, 221–222, p. 83)

He embarked on a life of pleasure in Paris. He was always thinking that when the time came he would man the towers of faith. Meanwhile

> . . . fairly flat upon the turf sprawled he
> And let strange creatures make his mouth their home.
> (II, 334–335, p. 91)

This last fine line, with its literal and metaphorical meanings coalescing, characterizes the young man's way of life with great completeness.

The last element of the triple metaphor is the tent:

> Outside the turf, the towers: but, round the turf,
> A tent may rise, a temporary shroud,
> Mock-faith to suit a mimic dwelling-place. (II, 341–344, p. 91)

The tent is the temporary structure, based on turf, which serves to screen one's less reputable activities: its disadvantage is that it may prove difficult to lay flat when it has served its turn (II, 944, p. 131).

Having set up these points of reference Browning moves much more rapidly into his story. He tells how Léonce meets Clara, is deceived by her and then learns the truth; how she is divorced from her husband, and how the pair settle far from Paris in an old priory which they immediately rebuild. All this is done with great economy and yet Browning finds time for humour (e.g. II, 416–417, p. 96; 779, p. 120; 1119, p. 142), a sustained irony which at once delineates Miranda and makes available Browning's own view of his conduct, (575–586, p. 106), and casual reflections on the lot of the artist (1050–55, p. 138). What is especially notable is the easy way in which Browning moves from a vivid, essentially poetic simile to direct simple narrative without any jarring of tone (e.g. 611–627 and 628–678, pp. 109–13). Sustained and powerful images such as 714–724 (p. 116) or 1124–34 (p. 143) assort easily with the sordid details of Clara's career and the urbane accounts of Miranda's taste in art. The book is so full that one might well overlook the introduction of the most important element in Browning's reading of the episode – the church of La Ravissante (152 ff., p. 79).

The third book of the poem is a good example of Browning's way of handling incident and subordinating it to his interest in character. For example at the beginning of the book Léonce Miranda is summoned to Paris. His mother, whom he adores, reproaches him for his extravagance, especially his reconstruction of Clairvaux. She finishes

> '. . . what means this Belvedere?
> This Tower, stuck like a fools'-cap on the roof –
> Do you intend to soar to heaven from thence?
> Tower, truly! Better had you planted turf –
> More fitly would you dig yourself a hole
> Beneath it, for the final journey's help!
> O we poor parents – could we prophesy!' (64–70, p. 148)

Browning then analyses Miranda's state of mind. If he had been asked to choose either his mother or mistress at this point it would have been a difficult choice, but one that he might have been able to make. Instead he was instructed to retain both, but to make sure that neither harmed the other. Browning describes the tension this generated in Miranda and how he resented his mother's rebuking him from the refuge of a comfortable old age. The passage concludes

> In brief the man was angry with himself,
> With her, with all the world and much beside:
> And so the unseemly words were interchanged
> Which crystallize what else evaporates,
> And makes mere misty petulance grow hard
> And sharp inside each softness, heart and soul.

After this leisurely description of Miranda's feelings Browning narrates his actions in a series of rapid elliptical sentences:

> Monsieur Léonce Miranda flung at last
> Out of doors, fever-flushed: and there the Seine
> Rolled at his feet, obsequious remedy
> For fever, in a cold Autumnal flow.
> 'Go and be rid of memory in a bath!'
> Craftily whispered Who besets the ear
> On such occasions.
>   Done as soon as dreamed.
> Back shivers poor Léonce to bed – where else?
> And there he lies a month 'twixt life and death,
> Raving.   (III, 106–115, p. 151)

So Browning continues through the book, condensing the *action* for the most part – the main exception is the macabre account of Miranda's burning of his own hands, keeping the dialogue rapid and, as one would expect, dramatically varied (e.g. 165–189, pp. 155–6; 300–325, pp. 164–5), and introducing a new element, Miranda's relations. These are very cleverly handled. Browning wastes no time on individualizing them: he refers to them collectively as the Cousinry, and presents their actions obliquely. The whole passage in which they are introduced repays study (190–274, pp. 157–62). Browning describes their reasonings and the dress they put on their own motives. He contrives a substitute for the dramatic monologue by employing a pervasive irony, deliberately using the Cousins' own terms, which are designed to present their actions in the most favourable light, yet making his own reservations perfectly plain. The quite considerable weight of incident is conveyed without difficulty in under 1,100 lines, and Browning has still a fair amount of space for direct and indirect comment and pure digression. In this third book the distinction between these and the simpler narrative passages is rather more clearly marked. Two of the digressions, that on Milsand (727–783) and that on Luc de la Maison Rouge (889–919, pp. 203–4) are barely relevant to the main story at all: the digression on the soul and the body (490–508), though perfectly *à propos*, does not advance the action – it is more like Browning's signature: the digression on faith and its origins, (787–861, pp. 196–201) although its connection with the story is tenuous, throws some light on Browning's method in the poem. He argues that it is pointless to inquire into the origins of man's opinions, especially on religious topics, first because they will not thank you if you analyse their vague comfortable beliefs too minutely, secondly because it is too late for most men to do anything about the causes of their religious beliefs, thirdly because the important thing is not the causes of belief but its effects. That is, the only way you can really help a man in religious difficulties is to advise him about the consequences of his actions: conversely your judgement should be determined by what he does as a result of his beliefs, which are no concern of yours.

This lies behind Browning's presentation of Miranda. He is at great pains to describe his actions precisely and to invent appropriate speeches, but he offers no direct judgement or comment on

his motives. Even the imagery allows some doubt to remain about
Browning's own attitude. For instance when he describes how
abruptly and theatrically the Cousinry broke to Miranda the
news of his mother's death, for which they said he was responsible, Browning comments ambiguously:

> You hardly wonder if down fell at once
> The tawdry tent, pictorial, musical,
> Poetical, besprent with hearts and darts;
> Its cobweb-work, betinseled stitchery,
> Lay dust about our sleeper on the turf,
> And showed an outer wall distinct and dread. (269–274, p. 162)

He makes no remark on the passion of remorse that leads
Miranda to pension off Clara, or on the sudden change of heart
that leads him back to her, or on the attempted suicide or on the
burning of the hands. But when he describes the difficulties which
confronted Miranda, he allows it to be felt at one point that the
choice between 'turf' and 'towers' is becoming progressively less
simple. Miranda is at last understanding this and understanding
the seriousness of the choice. The implication is that this represents growth in maturity (see 657–681, pp. 187–9).

With his usual skill Browning has prepared for the climax of
the story. The repeated references to the tower of the house have
served to create an unease in the reader's mind. Book three ends
with Miranda's ascent of the tower, with five minutes to spare
while the grooms are saddling his horse.

The fourth book marks a change in Browning's method. He
says

> Who is a poet needs must apprehend
> Alike both speech and thoughts which prompt to speak.
>   (IV, 28–29, p. 219)

and with this excuse offers his own speculations about the
thoughts which passed through Miranda's mind as he stood in
the belvedere at the top of his high tower. This soliloquy, which
is the culmination of the poem, is over three hundred lines long.
It is in Browning's finest manner. It is conducted largely in
metaphors, of which the most important is that of the Virgin of
La Ravissante, the wonder-working statue of a nearby church,
of whose miraculous powers Miranda had been convinced from
childhood. In particular there was a legend that the statue had

been carried to its present position by angels. La Ravissante is personified, and symbolizes the Catholic church: opposed to her is 'the power' or 'the enchantress', who stands for the attractions of the world. All Miranda's ethical problems are stated allegorically in terms of relationships between persons. Browning sees as the crux of Miranda's dilemma his need for some unmistakable sign that his attempts to appease the Church have met with favour. The church has accepted his money, but in return has not given him peace of mind. Every day he hears of miracles of healing performed by La Ravissante: all he asks of her is to crown with success his hope

> Of managing to live on terms with both
> Opposing potentates, the Power and you. (207–208, p. 230)

But the Church maintains that Miranda is deficient in faith: in desperation he wonders how he can demonstrate his faith with sufficient power. 'Then his face grew one luminosity': he tells La Ravissante that to prove his indubitable faith he will ask her to bear him through the air to her feet.

> Thus, I bestride the railing, leg o'er leg,
> Thus, lo, I stand, a single inch away,
> At dizzy edge of death, – no touch of fear,
> As safe on tower above as turf below. (277–280, p. 235)

The miracle will usher in a new era in France and in Clairvaux. In particular Clara will be 'deodorized' (an unlucky word, perhaps tolerable in 1873, but impossible now). It is of Clara he is thinking, and of his perpetual conflict

> 'And may I worship you, and yet love her?
> Then!' –
> A sublime spring from the balustrade
> About the tower so often talked about,
> A flash in middle air, and stone-dead lay
> Monsieur Léonce Miranda on the turf. (337–341, p. 239)

This speech and the final decisive act are the dramatic centre of the poem. What follows is all very well done. Clara's soliloquy (410–467, pp. 244–8), the scene between her and the cousinry (468–735, pp. 248–65), and the Court's final judgement (894–955, pp. 275–9) are managed with great technical adroitness, but the effect is necessarily one of anti-climax: these incidents are included in the story not because they are required for its

artistic completeness but because they actually happened, because
the poem claims to be 'Truth and nothing else'. (982) Browning's own comments, designed to place the action, are very
interesting, though perhaps more relevant to a study of Browning than to a reading of his poem. They are of a complexity
which his drawing of the characters hardly warrants.

He begins with what are apparently rather heavy-handed
statements of his own opinions

> Of the masks
> That figure in this little history,
> She [Clara] only has a claim to my respect (740–742)

and

> Miranda hardly did his best with life.

but the tone of the school-report is soon dispelled as Browning
proceeds to explain the principles on which he apportions responsibility for Miranda's failure. Miranda is to blame for simply
not thinking hard enough about the nature of love and the nature
of religion. Thus he thought too highly both of Clara and of La
Ravissante:

> The heart was wise according to its lights
> And limits; but the head refused more sun,
> And shrank into its mew and craved less space.
> (757–759, p. 266)

This passage is seldom quoted by those who argue that Browning put all his trust in the heart and none in the head. It qualifies
rather surprisingly the approval which, as one would expect,
Browning extends to poor deluded Miranda's 'sublime spring',
his final unquestioning act of trust.

Clara is more difficult to place. Browning invokes two scales of
judgement, which he admits do not coincide. Aesthetically she
has the advantage over Miranda that she is a complete work of
art, he an incomplete attempt at a more ambitious subject

> Miranda, in my picture-gallery,
> Presents a Blake; be Clara – Meissonier. (771–772, p. 267)

so that on the level of a connoisseur he feels bound to respect the
sensible way in which Clara has organized her life. But beyond
that 'the incomplete,/More than completion, matches the immense', that is, in the sublimer regions of poetry and High Art,

'finish' is unimportant and an incomplete work (e.g. by Michelagnolo) can intimate most powerfully of all the ineffable complexities of the Universe. By these standards Clara's 'prettiness'
(I, 853) is found wanting. Morally also 'Success is nought, endeavour's all'. This sets the tone for Browning's long account of
his views of 'the finished little piece'. He admits that she re-
habilitated Miranda by humouring him, but, he says in the image
which dominates this part of the poem, she did so like a cater-
pillar which takes the tint of what it feeds on. While she was
suppressing her own feelings in order to fall in with Miranda's
moods, she was in fact eating him away. In Book I (865 ff.)
Browning has, with an echo of *Fifine at the Fair*, implied that
Clara's only value to Miranda was as a reflection of his own
personality, that she was merely a 'solace' to his 'conceit', never
a 'challenge' to him. Now he makes his final comment on her
negation of her own self:

> Friend, I do not praise her love!
> True love works never for the loved one so,
> Nor spares skin-surface, smoothening truth away.
> Love bids touch truth, endure truth, and embrace
> Truth, though, embracing truth, love crush itself.
> (IV, 861–865, p. 273) [36]

Ultimately then Browning's judgement of Clara is unfavourable – indeed his use of the caterpillar-image is almost
vindictive – but he qualifies it by setting her against the avari-
cious clergy and the dishonest cousinry. His final word on her
shows from how great a distance he views her faults. She is now
Chatelaine of Clairvaux:

> True,
> Such prize fades soon to insignificance.
> Though she have eaten her Miranda up,
> And spun a cradle-cone through which she pricks
> Her passage, and proves peacock-butterfly,
> This Autumn, – wait a little week of cold!
> Peacock and death's-head-moth end much the same.
> And could she still continue spinning, – sure
> Cradle would soon crave shroud for substitute,
> And o'er this life of hers distaste would drop
> Red-cotton-Night-cap-wise.   (966–976, p. 280)

Interesting and subtle as Browning's judgements are – the word 'distaste' in the preceding quotation is wonderfully precise – it is hard to feel that they are integrated with the rest of the poem. In the first three books he deliberately declines, with an almost Chaucerian disinterestedness, to offer an explicit opinion of the way his characters are behaving. In Book IV he not only attributes imaginary motives to them but judges their actions and motives with some minuteness.

The comparison with Conrad is illuminating. Like Conrad, Browning controls the reader's responses by using a series of dominant images: at the end of *Red Cotton Night-Cap Country* the characters are judged by a system of moral values at least the equal of Conrad's in complexity and fineness of discrimination. But Conrad at his best shows the distinctive power to integrate this evaluation with the action of his story so that the morality springs from the narrative: in *Red Cotton Night-Cap Country* it appears that Browning is first the puppet-master and then the external examiner, awarding marks to the characters in accordance with a predetermined schedule.

This is rather a harsh view of the poem, and should, I think, be modified to take account of the way Browning uses his master-images to give the poem unity and to prevent his different roles as narrator and adjudicator from becoming too widely separated. 'Turf' and 'towers' are first used as metaphors which allow the story to be narrated more vividly and economically. Then the action of the poem helps to define more closely the *meaning* of these metaphors, partly by making clearer the implied value-judgements which they embody, partly by the physical role played by actual turf and towers in the unfolding of the story. In this way moral judgements are constantly subject to qualification in the light of events and are thus kept fluid; Browning's poem mimics the situation in real life, where moral judgements determine our view of events at the same time as events are shaping our moral standards. The poem thus gives the impression of being a process, rather than two distinct and unrelated acts.

V

On the whole the public reception of *Red Cotton Night-Cap Country* was unfavourable, partly because the poem was thought

hard to read, partly on the grounds that the subject was intrinsically displeasing [37]. The same objections were made to his
next long poem on a domestic subject, *The Inn Album* (1875).
Like its predecessor this was based on a Victorian *cause célèbre*,
but one which existed, as far as I can gather, in the traditions of
London Clubland rather than in the records of the newspapers.
The central feature of the scandal of Lord de Ros was apparently
his offering of a woman whom he had ruined and discarded to a
young man in payment of a gambling debt, and her suicide in
horror at the proposal. Browning, of course, uses this incident,
but only as the main event in a poem whose chief interest is not
in event, but in character. Again it has been suggested that the
notorious Tichborne case, which had been the talk of London
from 1871 to 1874, was in Browning's mind when he wrote his
poem [38]. Finally it is worth noting that the first publication of
the *Inn Album* was in the columns of the *New York Times* on three
consecutive Sundays in November 1875. A desire for topicality
could hardly go further.

Just as *Fifine at the Fair* represents an advance in Browning's
art from the somewhat broken-backed *Prince Hohenstiel-
Schwangau*, so *The Inn Album* shows how quickly Browning had
learned to correct some of the deficiencies of *Red Cotton Night-
Cap Country*. He keeps the blank verse line of the earlier poem,
but to my ear at any rate, speeds it up a little, especially in the
earlier sections, to accommodate the rhythms of casual speech
between men of the world. He reduces his own comments on the
action until they are little more than stage-directions. The whole
shape of the poem suggests the drama that Browning originally
had in mind, even his final comment 'Let the curtain fall', but the
total effect is not in the least stagey.

One of the most striking features of the poem is the way in
which Browning observes the unities of time and place, accepts
the inevitable distortions of events, and makes these distortions
a source of strength and interest. A short analysis shows Browning's method clearly. The first part of the poem (Sections I–III)
is spent mainly in recapitulation. Once the scene has been set and
it is established that the Lord is heavily in debt to the Youth,
virtually nothing relates to the present. The whole object of the
sections is to dissolve out an unresolved incident from the past,
to which the events of the day are to be the conclusion. The

characters, like the reader, begin in ignorance of the chains which bind them together, and their suspicions grow as the reader's grow.

In the second part of the poem (Sections IV and V) the action of the poem moves into the present. Debate replaces recapitulation as the Lord tries first of all to win the Lady, then to entrap her. The whole of their lives in the preceding four years is sketched in obliquely.

In the last part of the poem (Sections VI to VIII) debate gives way to action. The Lord gambles for the last time, the Lady and the Youth prove invulnerable, his scheme recoils on himself, and the poem ends with the death of the Lord and the Lady.

It will be seen from this description that far from being hampered by the need to explain to the reader what happened four years ago Browning is able to make from the gradual enlightening of the characters themselves a continuous source of narrative interest. The Youth, the Lord and the Lady spend over half the poem discovering just how closely they are bound to each other. Only the Cousin remains in ignorance.

Of course a price must be paid for a situation where several characters simultaneously learn vital facts, previously unknown, about their relationships to each other. How high this price is depends on the audience's readiness to accept coincidence: *The Inn Album* would make severe demands even on readers who could accept *Martin Chuzzlewit* as a possible representation of real life. There is no coincidence in the facts that the Lord once knew the Lady, that the Lady also knew the Youth, and that the Youth had a Cousin, whom he proposed to marry, but we are also asked to believe that the Lord and the Youth have become intimate three years later. This would perhaps be just acceptable as a novelist's or dramatist's *donnée*, but it is totally incredible that the Youth's Cousin should also know the Lady and that all four should arrive at the Inn at the same time, even with the possible pretext of the approaching wedding. Equally hard to believe is that the Lord and the Youth have never mentioned the Lady's name to each other (partly, of course, because it would not be the done thing) and that the Cousin and the Lady never mention the name of the Youth. The situation is fashioned by coincidence and maintained by contrivance, for it is quite clear that if the characters had proper names the surprise of the successive discoveries would be imperilled.

Another feature of the poem suggests that the poem is not simply a naturalistic account of happenings in an inn parlour. Browning marries the rhythms of speech to those of blank verse so brilliantly that he almost persuades the reader to accept a dialogue carried on in a series of long speeches, some of over 200 lines, but any suggestion of naturalism must break down at the extended metaphors in those speeches. So that although the work has obvious affinities with the drama and with the Victorian novel, it has finally to be accepted on other terms.

The poem itself provides the clues which lead to Milton. In Section III the Lady describes her married life as being more like the *Inferno* than *Paradise Lost*, and in Section V she introduces the Eden imagery which works so powerfully in the rest of the poem:

> 'That reptile capture you? I conquered him:
> You saw him cower before me! Have no fear
> He shall offend you farther! Spare to spurn –
> Safe let him slink hence till some subtler Eve
> Than I, anticipate the snake – bruise head
> Ere he bruise heel – or, warier than the first,
> Some Adam purge earth's garden of its pest
> Before the slaver spoil the Tree of Life!' (2234–41, p. 153) [39]

The application is made at once to the Lord:

> 'Ah' – draws a long breath with a new strange look
> The man she interpellates – soul a-stir
> Under its covert, as, beneath the dust,
> A coppery sparkle all at once denotes
> The hid snake has conceived a purpose. (2249–53)

Thereafter the Lord is characterized by images of Satan, serpents, sin and so on, as at the beginning of Section VI:

> With a change
> Of his whole manner, opens out at once
> The Adversary,

where the Miltonic inversion is even more telling than the Miltonic noun. His temptation of the Youth culminates in an extended image (2621-33) of stripping a tree of fruit 'desirable to make one wise'. (See also 2660 ff., 2742 ff., 3014 ff., 3039.) A second hint of Milton comes in the debate between the Lord and the Lady: as she argues with a plausible seducer about vice and virtue the Lady recalls the heroine of *Comus*. Like *Comus*, the *Inn Album* is a Morality. The Youth stands in the position of the chooser: he is the Soul in need of guidance for whom the Lord and the Lady are both contending, the first with all the arguments of the world, the second with her virtue only. They both die, leaving the Youth thereafter to make his own decisions. The Lady's work is done. The Cousin is neutral: rightly married she is Innocence: wrongly married, as the Youth at first intends, she is simply one of the Prizes of Worldliness.

The interest of the *Inn Album* then, and the measure of Browning's success in the poem is this. That his characters perform what is almost a Masque of Vice and Virtue, enacting a basic ethical conflict, and yet the poem is not in the least abstract in effect. On the contrary, even with the non-naturalistic features that I have mentioned above, it gives the feeling of Victorian life that we find and value in the great novelists more convincingly, I think, than any other poem of the nineteenth century.

How this feeling is obtained would make the subject of an interesting study, but of a compass too great for the present volume. At present I would simply call attention first to the diction of the poem, which I have mentioned already in the previous chapter. One line must serve here to epitomize Browning's method. The Youth describes how he 'folded a cheque cigar-case-shape' (212). The compactness and concreteness of this detail are typical of Browning's rapid and incisive indication of the physical and social milieu of his poem, a milieu with which he had some personal acquaintance. The Inn Album itself is used for a similar purpose; it symbolizes the 'vulgar flat smooth respectability' of the 'stuffy little room', and aptly conveys the unpretentious nature of the inn. Browning describes the physical appearance of the parlour in the passage quoted in the previous chapter, sweeps out to give a rapid breath of the early morning landscape, then returns to focus on the scene inside – the burnt-out candles, the cards, the counters and the two gamblers. With equal speed Browning indicates their class and their relationship – the younger a 'polished snob', with a great deal of money but little knowledge of the world, the elder, well-born, experienced, 'refined', talked-about, and poor. He is a notorious gambler. His place in Society is somewhere between that of Mountjoy Scarborough and Captain Vignolles. He has spent the previous year teaching the Youth the ways of polite society, how to be happy although his father has made his money in trade. Under the Lord's direction the Youth is about to marry his Cousin for her money. The territory will be familiar enough to readers of the Victorian novel, in which differences of class, like differences of atmospheric pressure, generate the winds that blow the characters along, and in which preserving one's good name is an adequate motive for almost any action. But while the novelists almost as a convention set their action some years back into the past, Browning takes as his starting-point a scandal over thirty years old and deliberately moves it forward to the 1870s. The text is full of references to contemporary celebrities such as Landseer, Holman Hunt, Colenso [40], Corot, Ruskin, Rothschild, Gladstone, Carlyle, Tennyson, Disraeli, Trollope, Dickens, Brahms, Bismarck, Wagner and others.

Browning succeeds in solving the problem, which had defeated him in *Red Cotton Night-Cap Country*, of how to show unambiguously the moral bearing of his fable without formally dealing out judgement in his own person at the end. One can see fairly clearly in *Prince Hohenstiel-Schwangau*, *Fifine at the Fair*, *Red Cotton Night-Cap Country* and *The Inn Album* an increasing technical command. At the same time Browning offers less philosophizing, giving instead first an increase in dramatic action and later in objective description. In short, these four poems show a progressively greater affinity with the novels of the mid-century. Indeed DeVane quotes a letter of Swinburne's in which he refers to *The Inn Album* as 'a fine study in the later manner of Balzac, and I always think the great English analyst greatest as he comes nearest in matter and procedure to the still greater Frenchman' [41].

VI

Evidence that Browning enjoyed reading novels and had an intelligent acquaintance with what was being written is not hard to come by. His early letters to Elizabeth Barrett in 1845 and 1846 show that they were both familiar with the works of Lytton,

Dickens and Disraeli and for relaxation read Dumas or Soulié.
But even at that time Browning's favourite novelists were
George Sand and Balzac:

> Robert is a warm admirer of Balzac and has read most of his
> books . . . I put up Dumas' flag, or Soulié's, or Eugène Sue's (yet he
> [Browning] was properly possessed by the 'Mystères de Paris')
> and carry it till my arms ache. The plays and vaudevilles he knows
> far more of than I do, and always maintains they are the happiest
> growth of the French school – setting aside the *masters*, observe –
> for Balzac and George Sand hold all their honours . . . Then we
> read together the other day the 'Rouge et Noir', that powerful book
> of Stendhal's (Beyle), and he thought it very striking, and ob-
> served . . . that it was exactly like Balzac *in the raw*, in the
> material and undeveloped conception. [42]

It is clear that the Brownings were reading French novels fairly
regularly at this time. They enjoyed some English novelists also:
in 1860 Mrs Browning wrote to her brother George, 'I agree
with you in adhering to Anthony Trollope – & indeed Robert &
I both consider him first rate as a novelist – Framley Parsonage
is perfect it seems to me' [43]. Mrs Orr records that in his later
years Browning would read 'good works of French or Italian
fiction', and that 'his allegiance to Balzac remained un-
shaken' [44]. His ideas on the novel were clearly quite well-
formed, as we may see from a letter of his to Isa Blagden, giving
his verdict on her novel *Agnes Tremorne* [45]. The whole letter
is a good example of Browning's difficulty when confronted with
work to criticize. He does not wish to give offence, but is incapable of hiding his perceptions of deficiency. Most of the letter
is devoted to a detailed attempt to explain to Miss Blagden
exactly why *Agnes Tremorne* is so terrible, but three points of
general interest emerge. First he says 'I can however cordially
praise you for much observation of character and picking up of
"petits faits vrais".' As McAleer points out, this phrase is taken
from a letter of Stendhal's to Balzac (October 1840). Secondly
he refers in passing to Trollope and again praises the style of
Framley Parsonage. Finally, commenting on some absurdities in
Miss Blagden's book, he remarks 'There might have been made
a curious study, if worth while, of the case of a diseased som-
nambule, half-deceived, half suspecting deception, "checking"
perpetually her experiences, one sort by another, the sleeping

by the waking ones – but disease is best let alone.' Obviously
Browning's idea of the areas for a novelist to explore are closer
to those of Henry James than to those of Miss Blagden.

Browning refers again casually to Balzac [46] and with some
particularity to *Madame Bovary* [47]: his preference for the
French novelists is to be seen also in a letter giving literary
advice to Miss Blagden [48]. Once again he tactfully dismantles
one of her novels – *Nora and Archibald Lee* – and finishes 'I
advise you to go on, make your incidents as simple as you can,
put out your strength in the analysis of *character*, keeping in
mind the immeasurable superiority (to my mind) of French
models than English.' Perhaps the clearest indication of what the
French novelists meant to Browning is to be seen in the following most illuminating passage from yet another letter to Isa
Blagden:

> I dearly like this wild place [Le Croisic]: Guerande, where I was
> two days ago, is delightful – and a wilder place still, Piriac, where
> we all went, for the sake of the coast and caves. There was a great
> enterprise begun there and abandoned fourteen years ago, – the
> working a tin and silver mine: an English company built houses,
> sank wells, brought machinery, spent 'trois millions', then abandoned
> everything: there lie the boilers, pumps &c., exposed like rocks and
> sand. An old fellow . . . pointed to one and another 'That, now, is
> still worth 25,000 fcs – and that as much.' He said that all the
> money had been wasted in unnecessary expence, – house-building
> &c. – and that when the mines began to be worked, and give good
> metal, – in rushed the sea, – their funds were at an end, – there was
> no more to be done but go and leave all this ruin, 'these fourteen
> years now'! Depend on it, the imaginative men are not exclusively
> the poets and painters, as Balzac knew well enough. [49]

Although there are many other references to novels in the
letters [50] and although Browning helped to prepare Hawthorne's last novel *Septimus Felton* for publication, there is no
stronger evidence than this last quotation that he had not only
read reasonably widely in the novelists but had understood the
full implications of their treatment of everyday life. In the next
chapter I shall have something to say about the stand Browning
took in the critical debates of the century, especially about the
subjects of poetry.

Meanwhile the difficulty is to relate Browning's obvious

interest in the novel to *Red Cotton Night-Cap Country* and *The Inn Album*. The crucial point seems to me to be this. While it is true that these poems have a lot in common with the novel, and while it is natural and right that we should when we read them be reminded of Balzac or Trollope, nevertheless they are ultimately to be judged not as verse novels but as long poems. The history of the long poem in English is one of some antiquity, with few splendours and many disasters: the nineteenth century marks its final collapse.

The quality necessary for sustaining a long poem is invention – that is to say, the devising of an interesting and coherent succession of incidents. This normally but not essentially entails discovering and developing a narrative line: it is hard to think of any successful long poem written before 1800 that has not got a good story behind it, a story so good that it survives even in translation or prose paraphrase. Now, in spite of A. C. Bradley [51], it was not the case that the Romantics and their successors stopped trying to write long poems. On the contrary, every poet of note and many others attempted a poem of epic proportions. Unfortunately sustained invention is a quality in which Romantic poets are notably weak – indeed weakness of invention is the consequence of their exceptional powers in other directions – and in consequence the nineteenth-century is studded with gigantic relics, some never completed, of which Wordsworth's projected *Recluse* is the most ambitious and the most splendid in failure, some completed, but without the necessary intrinsic articulating power. *The Idylls of the King* is the greatest of these. The completed long poems of the century which can be called satisfactory are few indeed. *Prometheus Unbound*, which derives its basic plot from Greek legend, and certain elements of its structure from the Greek drama, is perhaps as close to success as the Romantic poets approach. Among the Victorians we can I think consider *Maud*, *The Ring and the Book* and the two poems I am discussing. It is notable that each of them has departed considerably from the idea of simple heroic narrative. *Maud* and *The Ring and the Book* use the dramatic monologue with striking originality, as is a commonplace of criticism; Browning's role in *Red Cotton Night-Cap Country* is very different from that of the conventional epic poet, especially in the last book: *The Inn Album* takes a novelist's subject and treats it with a dramatist's art. Observe for example how the murder of the Lord is huddled away from the audience:

> A tiger-flash – yell, spring, and scream: halloo!
> Death's out and on him, has and holds him – ugh!
> But *ne trucidet coram populo*
> *Juvenis senem!* Right the Horatian rule!
>
> There, see how soon a quiet comes to pass.

> (Section VII, 3024–28, p. 206)

This is a deliberate stroke – the *manner* of the Lord's death is of no consequence: Browning wishes to allow the Lady's death to be the climax of the poem. This once reached he has his own way of securing a dramatic ending without anti-climax. The Cousin returns and from outside (almost 'off-stage') addresses the Youth in tones of bubbling happiness as he stands motionless with the two dead bodies. When she begins to sing with sheer joy the echo of Pippa's voice is complete, and the poem ends.

Ultimately, as I say, these two long novel-poems must, like *Fifine* and *Schwangau*, be judged as poems. I do not think any of them can claim to be completely successful, but they all deserve a place among the best Victorian long poems. They are certainly a great deal better than they are generally admitted to be by those who have never read them. *Red Cotton Night-Cap Country* shows what a poet can do with a subject initially devoid of beauty, not just by using his imagination to reach into the participants' minds for nobility of motive, but by simply writing about it in verse, by subjecting every incident to the test of being refracted through a poet's language. The ability to stand the sort of scrutiny which Browning gives to his most casual utterances serves to discriminate between the characters with some accuracy. The final justification of Miranda is that he can speak, not incongruously, the final soliloquy which Browning has written for him. *The Inn Album*, of course, works in the same way, but here Browning's personal role is much smaller. Consequently much more depends on accuracy of language. It is some measure of Browning's success that a comparison of the Youth and the Lady to Caponsacchi and Pompilia comes naturally, and that the Lord not only recalls Guido but is explicitly compared with Iago, and this comparison seems by no means presumptuous.

In short, in all these long poems where he is using topical material Browning is writing not as journalist or a controversialist or even as a novelist, although this is nearer the truth, but as a poet building his poems from the 'petit faits vrais' of his experience.

VII

The *Pacchiarotto* volume (1876) is a heterogeneous collection. Some of the poems, though clearly written in irritable reaction to immediate annoyances, are more personal than social; of them *Shop* gives the best idea of Victorian life. But, as one would expect, short lyrics gave Browning little opportunity for relating his poetry explicitly to the familiar surroundings of his audience.

La Saisiaz (1878) has already been treated at length in Chapter 7. It will be remembered that the immediate occasion of the poem was the death of Miss Anne Egerton Smith. She had been staying with Browning and his sister near Geneva: in the opening section of the poem we have a charming picture of their life in the chalet – the walks, the climbs, the bathes,

> Then the meal, with talk and laughter, and the news of that
> rare nook
> Yet untroubled by the tourist, touched on by no travel-book . . .
> Last, the nothings that extinguish embers of a vivid day:
> 'What might be the Marshal's next move, what Gambetta's
> counter-play'
> Till the landing on the staircase saw escape the latest spark:
> 'Sleep you well!' 'Sleep but as well, you!' – lazy love quenched,
> all was dark.

The shock of Miss Smith's sudden death amid circumstances of such innocent enjoyment led Browning to write this peculiarly vivid elegy. His self-questionings are not abstract, but are simply the larger forms of the question that posed itself to him when he first knew of Miss Smith's death: 'Did the face, the form I lifted as it lay, reveal the loss/Not alone of life but soul?' (173–174) The form of the poem was undoubtedly influenced, as Browning tells us, by a series of articles in the *Nineteenth Century* on the subject of 'The Soul and Future Life', and so were some of the arguments. It is perhaps too strong to say, as DeVane does [52], that 'the conditions of the Symposium forbade Browning to draw comfort and faith from his strongest belief in the Christian revelation', for there appear to have been no such conditions laid down, and many of the contributors to the Symposium ultimately introduced Christian arguments [53]. But clearly even the most ardent Christian would not feel that he had made a contribution to the discussion if he simply asserted the truth of Christian revelation and refused to consider the question of whether future life could reasonably be assumed on other grounds. Room for debate would exist only if even the explicitly Christian contributors were prepared to set aside revealed truths for the sake of the argument. Browning is certainly prepared to do this, as he makes clear (146–160): he will try to answer a real question in human terms. Again, at the end of the poem, (545 ff.) Browning returns from the realms of abstract reasoning into which he has been led, and concludes by a brilliant evocation of the famous spirits who are associated with Geneva; he does this for a particular reason, in order to give humorous emphasis to the personal nature of his solution. Finally Browning writes of himself 'here in London's mid-November' reforging the chain of argument. As I have suggested in Chapter 7 the parts of the poem which appeal most immediately are the beginning and the end, where Browning uses all his powers to immortalize Miss Smith and the countryside in which she is buried.

In the last years of the poet's life he spent more time abroad and, perhaps as a consequence, wrote fewer poems about Victorian England. One may note a number – the poems about vivisection such as *Tray* and *Arcades Ambo*, or against cruelty to animals such as *The Lady and the Painter* and *Donald*, with its Clough-like picture of the scene in the bothie. In the *Asolando* volume, *Development* and *Inapprehensiveness*, as I have suggested, reflect the real world and the non-literary use of language as few other poets of the century were able to do, while *Bad Dreams*, especially *Bad Dreams IV*, is of a piece with the other poems in which Browning deals with modern love. Similarly *Gerousios Oinos*, designed for *Jocoseria* (1883) but not printed during the poet's life, renews his complaint against the insipidity of much late Victorian poetry.[1] The *Parleyings* are a more consistent

---

[1] Cf. his letter of 19 January 1870 to Isa Blagden (McAleer, *Dearest Isa*, pp. 327–9), where he writes, 'Well, I go with you a good way in the feeling about Tennyson's new book [*The Holy Grail and Other Poems*]: it is all out of my head already. We

attempt to bring contemporary affairs into focus through the medium of poetry.

Professor DeVane has clearly demonstrated that almost every one of them, although ostensibly directed at the auditor named in the title, is in fact one side of an argument with a notable figure of the 1880s [54]. He shows that in the *Parleying with Mandeville* Browning is obliquely addressing the shade of Thomas Carlyle (at that time six years dead), the subject being the familiar one of hope and despair in philosophy. In *Christopher Smart* he again opposes the doctrines of Rossetti, Morris, and Swinburne. In *George Bubb Dodington,* where the subject is politics, the real colloquant is not Dodington but Disraeli, who died in the same year as Carlyle, while *Francis Furini* is aimed at Victorian critics of painting the female nude, especially John Callcot Horsley, who was treasurer of the Royal Academy and had objected on moral grounds to paintings by the poet's son.[2] In *De Lairesse*, as I have said in Chapter 3, Browning joins issue with Matthew Arnold over the subjects proper to poetry, and in *Charles Avison* begins with a most agreeable sketch of a blackcap in a London garden, and then takes the opportunity to review the great musicians of his day, such as Brahms, Wagner, Dvorak and Liszt.

This lengthy survey has shown, I hope, that throughout his poetic career Browning was prepared to find in the life of his own times a fit *milieu* for poetry and subjects worthy of a poet's attention. This is most marked in the sixties and seventies and is more noticeable in his long poems than in his lyrics. I do not wish to exaggerate the contemporary element in his poetry: its extent is perhaps most accurately judged in a comparison with

---

look at the object of art in poetry so differently! Here is an Idyll about a knight being untrue to his friend and yielding to the temptation of that friend's mistress after having engaged to assist him in his suit. I should judge the conflict in the knight's soul the proper subject to describe: Tennyson thinks he should describe the castle, and the effect of the moon on its towers, and anything *but* the soul. The monotony, however, you must expect – if the new is to be of a piece with the old. Morris is sweet, pictorial, clever always – but a weariness to me by this time. The lyrics were the "first sprightly runnings" – this that follows [*The Earthly Paradise*] is a laboured brew with the old flavour but not *body*.'

[2] His strenuous objections to paintings of naked women earned him the nickname of 'Clothes' Horsley.

his fellow-poets. In the twenty years I have mentioned all the major Victorian poets produced at least one book of verse. A notable feature of many of them is that the poet has gone far afield in time or space for his subject. To name Landor's *Heroic Idylls*, R. W. Dixon's *Historical Odes*, Hawker's *Quest of the Sangraal*, Tennyson's *Idylls of the King*, Lytton's *Lost Tales of Miletus*, Arnold's *Saint Brandan*, Morris's *Life and Death of Jason*, *The Earthly Paradise*, and *Sigurd the Volsung*, Dobson's *Proverbs in Porcelain* and Edwin Arnold's *The Light of Asia* is to give in brief compass an indication of the exotic character of much of the most important productions in verse. Against these must be set the poets whose work had a closer connection with the age in which it was written – for example, Patmore's *Angel in the House*, Meredith's *Modern Love*, Tennyson's *Enoch Arden* volume, Arnold's *Thyrsis*, Swinburne's political poems and Thomson's *City of Dreadful Night*. It is plain that Browning has little in common with those poets in the first group who have deliberately chosen a subject of established heroic stature. It is, I think, equally plain that his affinities with the poets of the second group, though more evident, do not lie very deep.

Meredith and Patmore are closest to Browning, but they give the impression, which he never does, that they have as it were disinfected and refined Victorian life before admitting it to their verse; Browning's poems about Italian and French politics are far more closely directed than Swinburne's to the realities of the existing situation; the essential difference in approach between Browning and the Tennyson of *Enoch Arden* is well brought out in a letter to Julia Wedgwood [55]; least of all was Browning inclined to take his own society as his subject simply to find 'confirmation of the old despair' among the shadowy streets and ever-burning street-lamps of the sunless city, as Thomson did. On the contrary his attitude was one of acceptance. This does not mean that he approved of every element in Victorian England or that he considered himself a publicist for the nineteenth century, simply that when a subject presented itself he did not refuse to consider it on the grounds that it was too modern. Conversely when he had a story to tell he set it in the world he knew best unless there was a good reason for doing otherwise. Once again we observe the affinity between Browning and the great novel-

ists who were his contemporaries. Trollope, George Eliot and
Dickens all considered it perfectly natural for a novelist to offer
in his work a version of his own society. This is not to say that
they refused to write historical novels – in fact all of them did –
but simply that they did not feel that the Victorian world of
railway trains, elections, suburban villas, public houses, snob-
bery, violent crime, concert halls and art galleries was in some
way disqualified from artistic treatment. The burden of my
argument in this chapter has been that Browning, allowing for
the necessary differences between prose and verse, was of their
mind.

Now it is plain that the power to depict the living world is not
one which brings only rewards and no penalties. Victorian
painting, for example, is rich in representations of actual or
probable situations, executed with great technical skill and with
absolute fidelity to the common occasions of Victorian life. But,
even if we set aside their merits or demerits as compositions, it
is a common line of criticism that their very naturalism is a
debilitating quality.[1] Similarly the Victorian novelists have been
criticized for their parochial view of life, for giving too cosy
and 'Dutch' a picture of the world [56]. But on the whole the
great novelists of the nineteenth century gain immeasurably
from their contact with their audience. Not only did they find
readers in their life-time and firmly establish the novel as the
dominant literary form, but even today they attract a large
public, not least because of their faithfulness as recorders and
interpreters of Victorian life.

Browning shares with them the power to evoke the world for
which he was writing, partly by his choice of subject, partly, as
we have seen in the previous chapter, by his use of a diction
based on contemporary speech. This gives to *Mr. Sludge, 'The
Medium'*, say, or *The Inn Album*, a quality notably absent from
The Idylls of the King or *Sohrab and Rustum*. Browning further
distinguishes himself from his poetic contemporaries and aligns
himself with the novelists by his marked preference for writing
about men and women instead of about natural scenery, a pre-

[1] It is true that in the last few years such diverse painters of the Victorian scene as
Wilkie, Dyce, Frith, Hunt, Maclise, Madox Brown, Rossetti, Mulready and
Orchardson have attracted favourable critical opinion, but on the whole their close
connection to a specific place and period has told heavily against them.

ference I have described at more length in Chapter 3.[1] Finally
Browning alone of the poets is able to compete strongly with the
novelists in a field in which they were peculiarly strong, the
detailed portrayal of their characters in situations which could be
treated at length and with fullness. The amplitude of the Victorian
novel, its opportunities for leisurely description and careful
analysis of action and motive, its impression of a lavishness
which is closer to the prodigality of life than to the economy of
art, all these features, which distinguish the novel from the
short story, are denied to poetry except in the medium of the
long poem. As I have suggested, the successes of the nineteenth
century in this form were few, and mostly Browning's. It is a
nice point to decide how far Browning derived his narrative
technique from the novelists and how far they derived theirs
from his unremitting experiments with the form of his
poems [57]. One quotation from Henry James will perhaps
show how Browning's preoccupation with the art of telling a
story from the most effective point of view led him to explore
boldly much the same territory as the master-theoretician was
later to map with such subtlety and caution.

> I have already betrayed as an accepted habit . . . my preference for
> dealing with my subject matter, for 'seeing my story' through the
> opportunity and the sensibility of some . . . thoroughly interested
> and intelligent witness or reporter, some person who contributes
> to the case mainly a certain amount of criticism and interpretation
> of it . . . I have constantly inclined to the idea of the particular attach-
> ing case plus some near individual view of it . . . Anything in short
> seemed to me better than the mere muffled majesty of authorship.
> [58]

Had James required a demonstration of the possible ways of
avoiding such 'muffled majesty' he could have found many of
them illustrated in Browning: *The Flight of the Duchess*, *A Death
in the Desert*, *A Toccata of Galuppi's*, *Cleon* and *Karshish* come
at once to mind, but perhaps nothing else is quite so instructive
as a comparison of Books II, III, and IV of *The Ring and The
Book*, in which three different uninvolved narrators tell the
same story. 'The terms of [each] person's access to it and esti-

---

[1] Cf. letter of 19 August 1863 to Miss Blagden: 'But it's one thing to say pretty
things about swallows, roses, autumn etc., and another to look an inch into men's
hearts.' (McAleer, p. 173)

mate of it contribute by some fine little law to intensification of interest.'

Let me in conclusion make quite plain what I am trying to do in this section. I want to draw attention to the points Browning has in common with the novelists for a particular reason, because the novelists are generally seen to have achieved a body of literature of a very high order. I want to point out that many of the qualities which make this literature satisfying as serious entertainment – human interest, amplitude, psychological insight, fidelity to contemporary life, technical expertise – are also to be found in Browning, and I want to do this not in order to claim a place for Browning in the novelists' triumphal car but in order to make it easier to assess him fairly *as a poet*. Many of the wrong criticisms of Browning seem to me to spring from approaching him with the wrong expectations. Clearly to require him to please in the same way as Keats or Clare is to invite disappointment. He must be taken as a poet of his time.

It may be thought that at this point I am deliberately limiting Browning's stature. If the greatest poets are 'not of an age, but for all time', is it not consigning a poet to the second rank to admit that he accepts the limitations of his own period and country? Once again the example of the novelists will perhaps serve. If we think of *Tom Jones*, or *Sir Charles Grandison*, or *Tristram Shandy*, or *Emma*, or *La Cousine Bette*, or *Dombey and Son*, or *The Newcomes*, or *North and South*, or *Anna Karenina*, or *Moby-Dick*, or *The Bostonians*, or *Madame Bovary*, or *Crime and Punishment*, or *Virgin Soil*, or *The Prime Minister*, or *Germinal*, or *Jude the Obscure*, or *A Passage to India* or any of the great novels of our day, what comes back to us is not their general applicability to the human condition but their *specificness*, their ability to convey the reality of a particular existence. The reason why they have not dated is not that they are situated in some timeless void but that they have realized an actual period so thoroughly and completely that it has survived in them. They are for all time, because they were first of all true to their own age.

The same is true of poetry. We read the *Essay on Man* not just for its large general statements but equally for those qualities which are characteristic of the early eighteenth century. *Paradise Lost* is no longer regarded as a repository of theological truths: but as a seventeenth-century poem about the Creation it is of perennial interest. Similarly we do not expect to find, say, in *Julius Caesar* an eternally valid presentation of the problems of government: we know that the ideas are Shakespeare's own limited Elizabethan ideas and we value them none the less. The *Essay on Man*, and *Paradise Lost*, and *Julius Caesar* are not of course simply of historical interest: the relevant point is that what in them seemed to be purely an accident of the time in which they were written has proved an essential part of their enduring appeal.

In the course of time some particular presentations attain the status of myths – this explains the apparent exception of the Greek poets to my general rule – but in general it appears that while being of one's own time is not necessarily a handicap and may often, as we see from the novelists, be a positive source of strength, the deliberate *avoidance* of one's own time as a subject for poetry is fraught with dangers, dangers which in the course of the nineteenth and twentieth centuries have come close to reducing poetry from its once proud estate to that of a minority art form, with about the same number of genuine devotees as the ballet or handweaving.

If I claim Browning then as *par excellence* a Victorian poet I must not be understood to admit that he is in some vital way circumscribed. There is poetry in Browning and poetry in abundance, but it is neither Romantic poetry nor twentieth-century poetry. If we go to him expecting simply Victorian poetry we shall not come away unrewarded.

We shall at least be saved from the more obvious kinds of incomprehension, like this:

> Browning, unlike Tennyson, made no real attempt to come to terms with his age. He brushed aside its doubts and problems, to contemplate intriguing Renaissance figures in Italy. [59]

or this:

> The depths of his [Browning's] nature, however, were almost untouched by the anxieties and perplexities that weighed so oppressively upon his eminent contemporaries . . .
>
> He was essentially a man of the Renaissance who . . . had wandered into the wrong century and the wrong country, an error which he hastened to repair by emigrating and by concentrating his imagination upon a more congenial world. [60]

William Sharp, who proposed to bring out a volume of selections from Browning called *Transcripts from Life*, records the following anecdote:

> On another occasion I heard him smilingly add, to someone's vague assertion that in Italy only was there any romance left, 'Ah, well, I should like to include poor old Camberwell'. [61]

Browning's sympathies were wide enough to include the age of Dante and the age of Gladstone, without using one as a refuge from the other. On the contrary, more than any other nineteenth-century poet, more even than Wordsworth, he laboured to bring poetry

> Down to the level of our common life,
> Close to the beating of our common heart.
>   (*Aristophanes' Apology*)

Part Three

Part Three

Browning and his critics
before 1914

In this chapter I shall say something about criticism of Browning by his contemporaries and by the most influential writers in the quarter of a century following his death, partly to illustrate the way in which he struck the acutest literary intelligences of his day, partly to examine some of the critical works which have most powerfully influenced his reputation.

I hope that in doing this I shall not appear to be disinterring dead issues from a morbid love of disputation: my purpose is to avoid an irritating fault which is common in modern criticism, that of ignoring opposing points of view. It is of no help to the reader to state an opinion in flat contradiction of an earlier critic unless you are prepared to show not only that your own opinion is well-supported but that the opposite opinion can be proved wrong or incomplete. Unless this is done the reader is left with two incompatible manifestoes, each apparently true, and no means of knowing how the later critic would answer the earlier. Accordingly where there is a well-known hostile account of Browning's poetry I have thought it necessary to show why it does not invalidate my own generally favourable account.

It will, I think, also become apparent that although the critics are dead the issues they debated are very much alive.

Matthew Arnold (and H. B. Forman)

Schiller has the material Sublime; to produce an effect, he sets you a whole town on fire, and throws infants with their mothers into the

flames, or locks up a father in an old tower. But Shakespeare drops
a handkerchief, and the same or greater effects follow.

COLERIDGE, Ashe, p. 530

The subject of my first section does not fall into the category
of hostile critics, but, since he is by general consent the subtlest
and most widely-read Victorian man of letters, it is of particular
interest to trace, where we can, his opinions of a poet whose
practice was so different from his own.

In the first place we may note that personal relations between
the two poets were cordial. From published correspondence we
learn that Arnold frequently invited Browning to dinner, that
Browning regularly sent copies of his books to 'dear Mat
Arnold' (who told Browning that he proposed to keep one of the
volumes of *The Ring and The Book* to read while presiding at an
examination), that Arnold gave Browning his own copy of
Glanvill, in which he had first read the story of the Scholar Gipsy,
that Arnold would have voted for Browning if he had been a
candidate for Professor of Poetry at Oxford, and refused to stand
against him for the Rectorship of St Andrews, that Browning
approved of Arnold's letter to *The Pall Mall Gazette* about
Prussian tenant-right, and so on. In his letters to Browning
Arnold speaks with admiration of Browning's poetry, especially
of *Artemis Prologizes*, a significant choice. Acknowledging a copy
of *Aristophanes' Apology* he wrote to Browning on 20 May 1875:
'It is sure to leave me with the impression which your writings
from the first have given me and which the writings of so few
other living people give me – that the author is what the French
well call a *grand esprit.*'

To other friends, however, Arnold expressed himself in less
cordial terms. Two of his letters to Clough are distinctly unfavourable.

In one (1 May 1853), he is writing of the Scottish poet
Alexander Smith, and says 'This kind does not go far: it dies like
Keats or loses itself like Browning.' An earlier letter repeats the
conjunction of Keats and Browning, and begins to reveal the real
grounds of Arnold's disagreement with Browning, a theoretical
divergence as wide as any in the nineteenth century. He writes:

> As Browning is a man with a moderate gift passionately desiring
> movement and fulness, and obtaining but a confused multitudinous-

ness, so Keats with a very high gift, is yet also consumed by this desire: and cannot produce the truly living and moving, as his conscience keeps telling him. They will not be patient neither understand that they must begin with an Idea of the world in order not to be prevailed over by the world's multitudinousness: or if they cannot get that, at least with isolated ideas: and all other things shall (perhaps) be added unto them. [1]

There are three points of interest in this statement. First it was made some time after September 1848, perhaps during 1849. Arnold's knowledge of Browning was therefore limited to *Paracelsus* and *Sordello*, the *Dramatic Lyrics* (1842) and *Dramatic Romances and Lyrics* (1845), and possibly some of the plays. It seems likely that Arnold had *Paracelsus* and *Sordello* particularly in mind: if so his criticism, though severe, is not altogether unjustified. Secondly, one should note the characteristic largeness and vagueness of the prescription 'they must begin with an Idea of the world'. Perhaps twenty-seven is the greatest age at which such an injunction seems to have some useful meaning: considered after a reading of those poems in which Browning doggedly struggles to dissipate the confusion of appearances in order to reach some approximation to a stable Idea of the world, Arnold's advice appears simply a piece of condescension, which, however, is, like most youthful misjudgements, not altogether unpleasing. Finally, it points forward to the main area of disagreement between Arnold and Browning, the question of the choice of subjects for poetry. While they did not engage in public controversy, it is clear that Arnold's pronouncements, if they were generally true, must apply to Browning, and, as I shall show, it is certain that Browning was aware of this.

The discussion centres in an interesting way on Arnold's 'dramatic poem' *Empedocles on Etna*. This was first published in 1852, but omitted from the collected poems of 1853, for which Arnold wrote a long preface defending the exclusion of *Empedocles* and setting out his theories of the business of the poet [2].

At this point it is important to remember the extent of the common ground between Browning and Arnold. They agreed on a point which would not be generally conceded today – that the important thing about a poem is what it has to say, that poetry is important in the sense that it has implications beyond itself and beyond the action of the poem, and that it can affect the world. As Arnold put it in a letter to Clough, 'Modern poetry can only subsist by its *contents*: by becoming a complete *magister vitae* . . .' [3].

In the Preface Arnold uses the telling phrase 'pragmatic poetry', that is, poetry that is more than mere amusement and whose existence can therefore be justified in wide terms. The idea that there could be an 'abstract poetry' is not one that Arnold admits to his argument. If, like much modern verse, it was not 'pragmatic' it would be to Arnold merely recreational or pointless. He resists the idea that poetry should be directly didactic, but it must not be *trivial*. Arnold points to a corresponding defect in modern criticism, that it is not concerned with the poem as a whole, but only with parts of it; what he says is true of many critics of our own day:

> We can hardly at the present day understand what Menander meant, when he told a man who inquired as to the progress of his comedy that he had finished it, not having yet written a single line, because he had constructed the action of it in his mind. A modern critic would have assured him that the merit of his piece depended on the brilliant things which arose under his pen as he went along. We have poems which seem to exist merely for the sake of single lines and passages; not for the sake of producing any total impression. We have critics who seem to direct their attention merely to detached expressions, to the language about the action, not to the action itself. I verily think that the majority of them do not in their hearts believe that there is such a thing as a total impression to be derived from a poem at all, or to be demanded from a poet; they think the term a commonplace of metaphysical criticism. They will permit the poet to select any action he pleases, and to suffer that action to go as it will, provided he gratifies them with occasional bursts of fine writing, and with a shower of isolated thoughts and images. That is, they permit him to leave their poetical sense ungratified, provided that he gratifies their rhetorical sense and their curiosity.

So much is common ground between Arnold and Browning, and it is considerable; what they disagree about is first whether subject as such is of fundamental importance to the success of a poem, i.e. whether it is an essential condition of a great poem that the poet shall have selected an action which is itself of comparable stature, and secondly, whether modern subjects are

fit for poetry. Browning would not, I think, have gone on to put
the case even more strongly and argue that a modern subject is
positively necessary if a poem is to appeal to modern man.

It is in the Preface to his *Poems* of 1853 that Arnold most
clearly articulates his argument. He begins by saying that there
are certain situations from the representation of which no
poetical enjoyment can be derived, those 'in which the suffering
finds no vent in action . . . in which there is everything to be
endured, nothing to be done . . . When they occur in actual
life they are painful, not tragic . . . To this class of situations,
poetically faulty as it appears to me, that of Empedocles, as I
have endeavoured to represent him, belongs; and I have therefore excluded the poem from the present collection.' He says that
he has explained this at some length because he wants to make it
quite clear that the poem

> has not been excluded in deference to the opinion which many critics
> of the present day appear to entertain against subjects chosen from
> distant times and countries: against the choice, in short, of any
> subjects but modern ones. 'The poet,' it is said, and by an intelligent
> critic, 'the poet who would really fix the public attention must leave
> the exhausted past, and draw his subjects from matters of present
> import, and *therefore* both of interest and novelty.' Now this view I
> believe to be completely false.

The stage is thus set for a discussion of the principles which
should guide a Victorian poet. Arnold is ostensibly defending
the poet's right to choose his subjects from whatever country or
period he wishes, but in fact the Preface resolves itself into a
denial that poetry can be written about the present age and a
strong condemnation of those poets who offer to do so.

He begins by tacitly assuming that there are two main classes
of subject – 'excellent actions', about which alone a delightful
poem can be written, and those which are 'intrinsically inferior',
about which no poet, however skilled, can write anything but an
incurably defective poem. 'Excellent actions' are those which
'most powerfully appeal to the great primary human affections . . . These feelings are permanent and the same; *that
which interests them is permanent and the same also.* The modernness or antiquity of an action, therefore, has nothing to do
with its fitness for poetical representation; this depends on its

inherent qualities.' It is by arguments of this kind, based on a doubtful assumption and proceeding by doubtful assertions (see the sentence I have italicized), that Arnold is able, while still apparently defending the poet's freedom to draw his subjects from where he will, to make out a strong case against any poets who are so rash as to try to write about the world they live in.

He discusses the Greek drama and repeats his contention that its excellence is derived entirely from the excellence of its subjects, almost all drawn from mythic history. 'The Greeks felt, no doubt, with their exquisite sagacity of taste, that an action of present times was too near them, too much mixed up with what was accidental and passing, to form a sufficiently grand, detached, and self-subsistent object for a tragic poem: such objects belonged to the domain of the comic poet, and of the lighter kinds of poetry.' (He takes Shakespeare and Keats as illustrations of the importance of subject to an English poet, although his choice of *Isabella* is perhaps unfortunate, for if it has, as Arnold says, an excellent action but is nevertheless completely ineffective, it seems that something more is required of the poet than merely the choice of a suitable subject.) The defence of classical subjects once again turns into an attack on 'poetical works conceived in the spirit of the passing time, and which partake of its transitoriness'. The final direction of attack is made clear in a long paragraph in which Arnold describes the nature of those who constantly practise commerce with the ancients. It concludes:

> They do not talk of their mission, nor of interpreting their age, nor of the coming poet; all this, they know, is the mere delirium of vanity; their business is not to praise their age, but to afford to the men who live in it the highest pleasure which they are capable of feeling. If asked to afford this by means of subjects drawn from the age itself, they ask what special fitness the present age has for supplying them: they are told that it is an era of progress, an age commissioned to carry out the great ideas of industrial development and social amelioration. They reply that with all this they can do nothing; that the elements they need for the exercise of their art are great actions, calculated powerfully and delightfully to affect what is permanent in the human soul; that so far as the present age can supply such actions, they will gladly make use of them; but that an age wanting in moral

grandeur can with difficulty supply such, and an age of spiritual discomfort with difficulty be powerfully and delightfully affected by them.[1]

It is plain that Arnold is doing a number of different things in the Preface. Ostensibly its main subject is *Empedocles on Etna*, but this is soon lost from sight, and Arnold takes the opportunity to answer critics of his own early poems, especially Clough, and then to expose some of the excesses of the Romantic movement, especially as shown by Alexander Smith. This rapidly develops into a general condemnation of the poetry and the poetics of the previous fifty years. Naturally this implied an unfavourable judgement of Arnold's own contemporaries. The sixth paragraph of the Preface for instance is easily construed as an attack, perhaps deliberate, on *In Memoriam* [4].

Similarly if the age itself is intrinsically hostile to poetry, and poetry is absolutely dependent on the choice of subject, it follows that any poetry which draws its subjects from matters of present import is faulty *ab initio*. As I have illustrated in Chapter 11, many of Browning's most ambitious poems are about actions of the day, and actions moreover which are conspicuously lacking in grandeur. How did Browning meet or evade Arnold's implied criticism, which has an obvious relevance to *Christmas-Eve and Easter-Day*, published in 1850?

First, as has been widely recognized, he attacks a weakness of Arnold's theory in his dramatic monologue *Cleon*. Arnold's emphasis on the need for antiquity had led him to rely excessively on Greek authors. Browning's creation of a poet who is heir to all the riches of Hellenic culture, but who is in despair because of the apparent pointlessness of life, and is yet unable to understand the significance of Christianity for mankind, ingeniously draws attention to the underlying pessimism of Greek

[1] This is precisely in line with Arnold's celebrated remark in a letter to Clough in February 1849: 'Reflect too, as I cannot but do here more and more, in spite of all the nonsense some people talk, how deeply *unpoetical* the age and all one's surroundings are. Not unprofound, not ungrand, not unmoving: – but *unpoetical*.' (Lowry, p. 99; Arnold's italics.) Elsewhere he remarks on the 'damned times' in which he lived (ibid. p. 111). See also his letter to 'K' in January 1851, where he says that he is retiring 'more and more from the modern world and modern literature, which is all only what has been before and what will be again, and not bracing or edifying in the least.' (*Letters of Matthew Arnold 1848–1888* ed. G. W. E. Russell (London, 1895), I, p. 15).

philosophy, a pessimism which Arnold's own *Empedocles* embodied with striking power. At the same time *Cleon* suggests the inadequacy of pre-Christian antiquity as a source of subjects for the poets of a basically Christian civilization.

Browning made two more rejoinders to Arnold. In his prefatory note to his verse translation of the *Agamemnon* of Aeschylus, Browning, alluding to Arnold's Preface of 1853, writes:

> Fortunately, the poorest translation, provided only it be faithful . . . will not only suffice to display what an eloquent friend maintains to be the all-in-all of poetry – 'the action of the piece' – but may help to illustrate his assurance that 'the Greeks are the highest models of expression, the unapproached masters of the grand style: their expression is so excellent because it is so admirably kept in its right degree of prominence, because it is so simple and so well subordinated, because it draws its force directly from the pregnancy of the matter which it conveys . . . not a word wasted, not a sentiment capriciously thrown in, stroke on stroke.' So may all happen! [5]

In the translation which follows Browning is, as he says, 'literal at every cost save that of absolute violence to our language' and offers 'a mere strict bald version of thing by thing', deliberately eschewing all beauty of language and relying entirely on 'the action of the piece'. The result is barely readable [6].

It has often been suggested that the translation was intended by Browning as a practical demonstration of the fallacy of Arnold's arguments, especially of his contention that poetry resided entirely in the subject and was in no way dependent on the poet's treatment of that subject.

I find it very hard to believe that Browning indulged in such a laborious practical joke, but the ironic tone of the prefatory note suggests that the version is not being offered in complete seriousness. A comparison with Browning's other versions of Greek drama should prove conclusive, but does not. The version of the *Alcestis* in *Balaustion's Adventure* is written in a much freer, more flexible style, which seems to indicate that the contortions of the *Agamemnon* are deliberate. On the other hand the translation of the *Hercules Furens* in *Aristophanes' Apology*, which is designed to display 'the perfect piece' in all its perfection, has obvious affinities with his *Agamemnon*. The first lines spoken by the Chorus are enough to illustrate this point:

These domes that overroof,
This long-used couch, I come to, having made
A staff my prop, that song may put to proof
The swan-like power, age-whitened, – poet's aid
Of sobbed-forth dirges – words that stand aloof
From action now: such am I – just a shade
With night for all its face, a mere night-dream –
And words that tremble too: howe'er they seem,
Devoted words, I deem.

This would suggest that the manner was inseparable from Browning's attempts to give a straight translation of Greek drama. I hazard the conjecture that he discovered, when he was translating the *Hercules*, that the life and vigour of his *Alcestis* had depended on his freedom to treat the action in his own way, and that when he was debarred from interpreting the story for himself what remained was without any comparable vitality. Yet if Arnold's Preface was right, a retelling of the story which retained all the simplicity of the original should retain also its essential power. In what spirit Browning undertook the *Agamemnon* it is impossible to say, but it is clear from the tone of the prefatory note that by the time he had completed it he realized that it too could be used to refute Arnold. Whether we think that he deliberately set out to make an unreadable translation or think that he made opportune use of an artistic failure in order to score a point in debate it is clear that in 1877 he still had in his mind the arguments that Arnold had put forward a quarter of a century before [7].

Browning's last thrust was in his *Parleying with Gerard de Lairesse* (1887). As I have said in Chapter 3, this was in effect a prolongation of his argument with Arnold. In the *Parleying* Browning elaborates his objections to subjects and machinery drawn from Greek mythology. To go back to the ancient fables is 'plain retrogression': it is to abandon reality for 'feignings proper to the page'. Browning on the contrary speaks of himself as one who prefers fact to fable

I who myself contentedly abide
Awake, nor want the wings of dream, – who tramp
Earth's common surface, rough, smooth, dry or damp.

He is satisfied with 'the simply true' and therefore advises 'Let things be – not seem.' No genuine knowledge of the significance of the world as it is can come from myths, for 'the dead Greek lore lies buried in the urn/Where who seeks fire finds ashes'.

Browning is not disparaging the great Greek writers, as his constant devotion to Euripides should remind us, nor is he saying that modern writers cannot transform the myths of Greece into something that will illuminate modern life, as we may see from the end of *Balaustion's Adventure*. What he is denying is that the simple re-telling of a Greek legend, however heroic, is adequate to interest the mind of Western man two thousand years later and more.

At the same time he recognizes that his position by implication denies any *intrinsic* value to the subject. It happens to be true that men are more powerfully affected and influenced by literature that has a direct connection with their own experience, but the magnitude of the subject as such is of no importance whatsoever. Accordingly, almost it would seem as a matter of deliberate policy, Browning reinforced his direct rejoinders to Arnold by consistently choosing over a period of twenty years a series of subjects which were pointedly anti-heroic, and thus constituted an oblique and far more telling refutation. This was true not only of the long monologues, such as *Blougram*, *Caliban*, *Schwangau*, *Fifine* and *Sludge*, but equally of the narrative poems such as *Red Cotton Night-Cap Country* and *The Inn Album*. In each of these poems Browning began with a situation or action which was conspicuously deficient in all the qualities which Arnold claimed as essential.

The defiance, as it were, of Arnold's pronouncements was most striking in *The Ring and The Book*. G. K. Chesterton, whose chapter on that poem is the best in his book, puts the matter concisely:

> The supreme difference that divides *The Ring and the Book* from all the great poems of similar length and largeness of design is precisely the fact that all these are about affairs commonly called important, and *The Ring and the Book* is about an affair commonly called contemptible.

He points out that Homer, the author of the Book of Job, Virgil, Dante and Milton are all demonstrating 'the relations of man to heaven' and they all do so by choosing subjects of great magnitude. Browning, on the contrary, says,

'I will show you the relations of man to heaven by telling you a story out of a dirty Italian book of criminal trials out of which I select one of the meanest and most completely forgotten.' Until we have realised this fundamental idea in *The Ring and the Book* all criticism is misleading . . . It is the extreme of idle criticism to complain that the story is a current and sordid story . . .[8]

The choice of 'an episode in burgess-Life' is, of course, clean contrary to Arnold's advocacy of 'some noble action of a heroic time'. As the first step towards establishing that Browning, in spite of his rejection of Arnold's advice, succeeded in creating in *The Ring and the Book* 'a representation from which men can derive enjoyment', I should like to draw attention to much the most interesting contemporary review of the poem, that by Harry Buxton Forman in *The London Quarterly Review* of July 1869, subsequently reprinted as a pamphlet for private circulation under the title *Robert Browning and the Epic of Psychology*. It is interesting partly as a defence of Browning against criticism from Arnold's premises, partly in itself as an example of the thoroughness and acuteness of the best periodical criticism of the age. I have already mentioned in Chapter 2 Forman's sensible description of the nature and operation of the dramatic monologue, which originally appeared in the *Fortnightly Review* for January 1869, and which he repeats here in order to get the discussion on a firm basis.

He begins with a bibliography of Browning's published works up to 1869, the first to be devoted to the poet. He then offers a rapid survey of the state of English literature, which, he justly says, has entered upon 'an epoch of great splendour'. He divides the poets of the time into two main schools, a term whose use he justifies – the Idyllic School, centring on Tennyson and his imitators, and the Psychological School, of which Browning is the chief poet, although his originality has discouraged direct imitation. Forman grants that there are still writers of 'Renaissance' poetry, for example the pre-Raphaelite poets, but they are not 'in keeping with the contemporary aspect of things'. The writers of the Idyllic and Psychological schools, however, are, like the novelists, working on 'quite new principles in the technical procedures of literature' and they are, moreover, 'intimately connected with modern ideas'. The province of the Idyllic School, and here Forman is thinking of Tennyson's *Dora*,

Enoch Arden and so on, is to offer 'exquisite narrative pictures of our middle-class life in its more simple phases': the Psychological School, on the other hand, 'has a wide applicability to the idealization of the intellectual and emotional phases of being which, in modern city life, are so intensified as to preponderate immensely in importance over the life of physical activity'. Forman elaborates this description in a footnote in which he again quotes from his own article of January 1869 in the *Fortnightly Review*. He says that a great change has come over poetry in the previous thirty years: 'The entity "nature", which before the present era of poetry absorbed so large a proportion of our aesthetic energies, has in turn been absorbed by the real being, man; and the great bulk of poetic force is now brought to bear on the treatment of man, and of man alone . . . Under these auspices, the Psychological School of Poetry has been forming; and it is still forming, for a school of poetry does not spring up and become full-blown without ample time.'

Having explained his general position Forman moves to his particular occasion, and introduces Browning as a man 'whom we conceive to be a genius of a very high order – a claimant to a permanent and elevated place in our literature – and who has just put before the world a work of importance almost unprecedented in modern times'. As I have mentioned in Chapter 2 Forman has a very sound idea of the nature of the dramatic monologue and of the opportunities it offers for analysis and judgement. He approaches *The Ring and the Book* by considering the whole of Browning's poetic career in terms of his increasing mastery of the form, describing and assessing his early works briefly but with great perceptiveness.[1] He concludes that *The Ring and the Book* shows the method at its best and is 'also a great lesson on the adaptability of the strict monologue form for epic uses'. His consideration of the poem is thus primarily formal, but he sees clearly enough that its originality is not simply technical. He gives a detailed analysis of the story, pointing at its apparently unedifying nature, and is at some pains to show how Browning is constantly enlarging the action. His concluding paragraphs constitute the real interest of the review.

[1] Forman remarks at one point, 'Now that it has become heterodox to sneer openly at even these works . . .' He is referring to *Paracelsus* and *Sordello*; the comment shows clearly the increasing respect with which critics were treating Browning.

First he offers the hope that Browning may in this work appeal to a large audience, 'to the limitless circle for whom shilling Shakespeares are printed'. If Forman hoped that Browning would win back some of the immense public which the novelists had acquired, he was to be disappointed.

Secondly, he offers the following defence of Browning's choice of subject. To judge from the preciseness with which he meets the objections of the Preface of 1853 Forman had Arnold particularly in mind. 'The idea that epics have "died out with Agamemnon and the goat-nursed gods", is one which is so obviously absurd, even without practical evidence to the contrary, and has arisen from the false notion that "heroic" is a term applicable only to wars and large actions.' On the contrary, Forman argues, Whitman and Browning have shown that the epic is still possible:

> The day has long gone by when heroism meant pugilism, and the might of man was measured by magnitude of muscle. Breadth of mind and width of heart come first now, and the largest action is not that which covers the greatest area and deploys the largest aggregate of physical powers, but that which involves most disinterestedness, philanthropy, purity of heart, power of thought – in short, the maximum of intellectual and moral force. For such a display, one set of modern men and women serves as well as another for types; and the Roman murder case of 150 years ago, which has so strongly taken hold of Browning, was the germ of what is more essentially modern than any great poetic production of these latter centuries.

One must grant that Forman's style is a little long-winded and that his analysis of *The Ring and the Book* occasionally stops short just when it promises to become most interesting, but his review is in other respects a most creditable piece of work. His remarks on Browning's objectivity and on his early poetic career, though not new, are unexceptionable, while his survey of the literature of his own times shows great confidence and sureness of touch. It is interesting to note that he does not mention Arnold by name. He marshals a number of the most powerful arguments in defence of Browning against the criticisms which follow from Arnold's Preface, and suggests, but does not pursue, various other lines. For example he uses the phrase 'in modern city life' to distinguish the new kind of civilization into which Britain was leading the rest of the world. There is no space here to describe in detail the fundamental changes in the entire way of life of the country which took place with extraordinary speed between, say, 1750 and 1850 – the changes from a predominantly rural agricultural economy to a predominantly urban, industrial and mercantile economy, expanding so rapidly that it was almost exploding; the change, as the Victorians were fond of saying, from the Age of the Horse to the Age of Steam; the change from the Age of Gainsborough to the Age of Gladstone. It is enough to say that the watershed was crossed, irreversibly, in the lifetime of Browning and most of his readers, that most thinking Victorians were conscious that they were living in a new era, and were conscious also that this new era brought with it its own problems, economic, social and moral, and that these were now of an unprecedented size and consequence. The life of the urban worker, poised precariously above a pit of physical, moral and spiritual degradation was the most obvious of the ugly children of the Industrial Revolution to trouble the consciences of the more fortunate middle classes. When Ruskin wrote that he felt like a man in a great churchyard 'with people all round me clinging feebly to the edges of the open graves, and calling for help, as they fall back into them, out of sight', he was describing one of the spectres that haunted the Victorian of any sensibility and awareness.

A central issue of literary discussion in the century was the part that literature, especially poetry, should play in the new age. Apart from a minority, for whom aesthetic considerations were paramount and who consciously resisted social pressures, most writers felt that all authors, poets included, had some responsibility for ensuring that their work on the whole exerted a beneficial effect upon society. A. H. Warren jun. possibly puts the case a little strongly when he says 'The theory of poetry as one kind of panacea or another was almost universal in the period' [9], but there is no doubt that the role of the man of letters in society was under constant scrutiny, and, as we shall see, Arnold himself was not least among those who proclaimed the essential relevance of literature to life.

Another remark of Forman's may help to define more precisely the difference between Arnold's idea of how a poet's work affects his audience and Browning's. Forman expressly makes the point that the novel in the 1860s was a much more *serious* form than it used to be, and observes that poetry shares this tendency. In the previous chapter I have shown how closely Browning's practice approaches that of the great novelists of the mid-century, who are beyond question selecting subjects which have an obvious relevance to the world of their readers. Of course I am not thinking here of the many novels of overt social protest, such as *Mary Barton*, or *Yeast*, or *Sybil*, but of the general run of serious novels, treating as a thing of course of 'matters of present import'. There were historical novels and there were romances, but by and large the reader of a Victorian novel, English, French, or American, was moving in a version of the world he knew. Even though the author was not writing propaganda and was not attempting to state explicitly an attitude to his society, his readers would at least have the pleasure of seeing their world as it appeared to the eye of an artist, the pleasure of feeling that the author had been able to select from and discover an organization in the 'multitudinousness' of modern life, and the pleasure of observing with heightened perceptions the nature of certain real contemporary ethical and social problems.

It is these kinds of pleasure, to put it at its lowest, which are to be found in many of Browning's longer poems. If Arnold would condemn them as 'works conceived in the spirit of the passing time, and which partake of its transitoriness' he would, I suggest, simply be untrue to his own premises. For he has already argued that 'the date of an action signifies nothing'; it should follow therefore that no action can, simply by reason of its period, become 'dated', and thus modern actions are as eligible as any other. But Arnold goes on to argue, in what is really the heart of his disagreement with Browning, that the Victorian age is uniquely disqualified to provide material for the artist because of its lack of 'moral grandeur', its 'spiritual discomfort', and its 'bewildering confusion'. Browning, as I have suggested, is equally conscious of the confusion of the times and of the necessity to discover 'sure guidance' and 'solid footing': indeed many of his poems enact precisely this attempt to find in the dazzling shifts of subjective knowledge some abiding principle. But his method, again like that of the novelists, was to work from 'the particular attaching case', to seize on one particular, however small, in the multitudinousness of life, and to work through that towards some more widely applicable truth. Arnold, on the other hand, seems to demand the general truth first – 'they must begin with an Idea of the world'. This had never been the method of the great dramatists or of the great novelists, and Browning never practises it.

To the objection that the subjects Browning chose lack nobility the reply is much the same – that no subject is too trivial or too sordid to reveal fresh truths about the nature of man, and that the nature of man is the only subject which has and can have 'intense significance' for man. This is true at all times, and takes on special significance at a time when, as Arnold admits, it is particularly difficult to think clearly about the right relation of man to his fellows. At such a time the writer who offers to throw any light on the problem of social relations has a peculiar value.

The nineteenth century was a period in which, for various reasons, an intense interest developed not only in man's social relations but in his personality, especially in an examination of the springs of human action. This led, not surprisingly, to an exploration of the darker side of the human heart. Once again the novelists were among the leaders. Balzac, Dickens, Dostoevski, Flaubert and Zola – not to mention James, Wells, Bennett and Conrad – were finding the matter of their art in precisely the recesses of hidden motive which Browning knew so well. Like him they were accused of trading in the trivial and the sordid. Like him they have outlived their critics.

The story of Browning's relation to Arnold would not be complete without some brief account of Arnold's later views and his subsequent treatment of *Empedocles*. The account may be summarized by saying that Arnold's opinions from 1853 onwards represent an irregular but persistent moving away from the extreme position of the 1853 Preface to a point where he seems to entertain simultaneously two almost incompatible views on the importance of subject to the poet.

He had begun the Preface by saying that he had not withdrawn *Empedocles* because the subject was two or three thousand years old, 'although many persons would think this a sufficient reason'. There is no reason to disbelieve this, even though the Preface resolves itself into an attack on modern, and a defence of antique, subjects. It seems to me more probable that he felt the poem to be an artistic failure because it too accurately mirrored his own times and his own situation. The familiar passages from *Dover Beach* and *The Scholar-Gipsy* and the almost equally familiar passages from his letters to Clough, especially the one in which he speaks of being 'past thirty, and three parts iced over' [10], come at once to mind when we read the poem, and are painfully insistent during Empedocles' last despairing speech:

> And each succeeding age in which we are born
> Will have more peril for us than the last;
> Will goad our senses with a sharper spur,
> Will fret our minds to an intenser play,
> Will make ourselves harder to be discerned.
> And we shall struggle awhile, gasp and rebel –
> And we shall fly for refuge to past times,
> Their soul of unworn youth, their breath of greatness;
> And the reality will pluck us back,
> Knead us in its hot hand, and change our nature.
> And we shall feel our powers of effort flag,
> And rally them for one last fight, – and fail;
> And we shall sink in the impossible strife,
> And be astray for ever.

The knowledge that he had betrayed his own hopelessness would no doubt impart a keener edge to Arnold's criticism of his age as unpropitious to poetry. Whatever the reason, the 1853 Preface marks the most extreme form of Arnold's theories of the supremacy of antiquity. Indeed it would hardly be possible to adhere to them as they stand, much less make them more pronounced. Taken literally the Preface would leave virtually no field for the Victorian poet, except the unadorned retelling of heroic legends. By implication this is confined to Greek legends, and even then excludes such stories as that of Antigone, which turns on circumstances that are no longer of deep interest. Arnold did not state explicitly the principles on which the Victorian poet was to select from the great actions of the past: much less did he express clearly his idea of the positive values of a poetry which derives its qualities solely from the 'inherent excellences', the intrinsic 'poeticalness' of a previously-existing action or of the responsibilities of a poet writing such verse.[1] As

[1] The obvious objection to Arnold's position is that if he wishes to defend the importance of the subject he is committed to some such proposition as 'A good

far as his own poetry is concerned it is a singular fact that all his most celebrated poems are aptly described by his own strictures on *Empedocles*. *Balder Dead*, *Sohrab and Rustum*, and *Tristram and Iseult* all deal with situations in which man is forced to realize his own impotence – he must either wait in vain or act in vain: although the note of despair is less insistently sounded, *The Scholar-Gipsy* and *Thyrsis* deal with men cut off from their sources of power: many of the shorter poems, for example, *To Marguerite*, *To A Gipsy Child*, and *The Forsaken Merman*, take as their theme alienation and isolation: to all of them we may apply Arnold's own words: 'the suffering finds no vent in action; . . . a continuous state of mental distress is prolonged, unrelieved by incident, hope, or resistance; . . . there is everything to be endured, nothing to be done.' They are, as Arnold says, 'painful, not tragic'.

His poetry then is strong evidence that Arnold abandoned the beliefs he stated in the Preface, and his prose writings thereafter confirm this. Most striking of all, perhaps, because it was also written in 1853, is a letter to Clough, in which Arnold says:

> I am glad you like the Gipsy Scholar – but what does it *do* for you? Homer *animates* – Shakespeare *animates* – in its poor way I think Sohrab and Rustum *animates* – the Gipsy Scholar at best awakens a pleasing melancholy. But this is not what we want.
>
> > The complaining millions of men
> > Darken in labour and pain –
>
> What they want is something to *animate* and *ennoble* them – not merely to add zest to their melancholy or grace to their dreams. [11]

While this letter does not actually contradict the Preface, it is perceptibly removed from it in spirit. In the Advertisement to the second edition of the *Poems* (1854) Arnold makes certain concessions in reply to objections that had been raised in

---

subject makes a poem better', where, to be helpful, 'good' must mean something more than 'which makes a poem better', i.e. it must be definable in terms which lie outside the poem. Attempting to establish what these terms are seems to lead rapidly to a subordination of literary to social or moral or some other non-literary considerations. Arnold tries to evade this further objection by saying, when the dilemma becomes acute, that a 'good' subject is one that is *aesthetically* better than another, e.g. heroic actions are intrinsically more artistic than cowardly actions. It is clear that a definition of this kind, which is either tautological or purely empirical, is not what is needed to sustain the rest of his argument.

reviews [12]. The most important is that he now agrees 'that
the poetic faculty can and does manifest itself in treating the
most trifling action, the most hopeless subject', a partial retreat
from his earlier insistence that 'all depends upon the subject'.
But he still maintains that there is 'an immortal strength in the
stories of great actions'.

Arnold's next contribution to the subject was his inaugural
lecture as Professor of Poetry at Oxford, delivered in 1857, and
reprinted in 1869 in *Macmillan's Magazine* under the title 'On
The Modern Element in Literature'. Naturally one hopes to find
here Arnold's opinions of the literature of his own age, but he
disappoints expectation. Early in the lecture he makes it plain
that his main concern is to justify the literature of ancient Greece
as 'even for modern times, a mighty agent of intellectual deliverance; even for modern times, therefore, an object of indestruc-
tible interest.' Arnold explains that an intellectual deliverance
begins when the mind 'begins to enter into possession of the
general ideas which are the law' of the 'vast multitude of facts'
which constitute the 'copious and complex present', that 'immense, moving confused spectacle which, while it perpetually
excites our curiosity, perpetually baffles our comprehension'.

> This, then, is what distinguishes certain epochs in the history of the
> human race, and our own amongst the number; – on the one hand,
> the presence of a significant spectacle to contemplate; on the other
> hand, the desire to find the true point of view from which to con-
> template this spectacle. He who has found that point of view, he who
> adequately comprehends this spectacle, has risen to the comprehen-
> sion of his age: he who communicates that point of view to his age,
> he who interprets to it that spectacle, is one of his age's intellectual
> deliverers.

That is to say, while Arnold agrees that there is work for literature to do in interpreting the world he is still not prepared to
agree that this can be done by writing directly about it. His aim
is still the enunciation of 'general laws'.

The main argument of the lecture depends on an equivocation.
A highly-developed civilization with an adequate literature will
naturally interest the Victorian age, itself highly developed and
seeking to understand its own situation. 'Such an epoch and
such a literature are, in fact, *modern*, in the same sense in which
our own age and literature are modern.' Having set up this

dubious equivalence Arnold proceeds to show by its help that the
literature of Greece is more relevant than the literature of
Elizabethan England to the Victorian mind, that it is the product
of a more mature enlightened and tolerant society, that it is, in
a word, more modern.

Arnold turns next to Latin literature, and argues that while
Roman civilization was 'on the whole, the greatest . . . on
record' the literature of the Romans was inadequate. He takes
Lucretius as his first example. He admits that he is modern, but
asks 'How can a man adequately interpret the activity of his age
when he is not in sympathy with it?' Arnold's own case must, I
think, come to the mind of every reader when he reaches these
words, indeed throughout his discussion of Lucretius:

> He bids them [his disciples] to leave the business of the world, and
> to apply themselves '*naturam cognoscere rerum* – to learn the nature
> of things'; but there is no cheerfulness for him either in the world
> from which he comes, or in the solitude to which he goes. With stern
> effort, with gloomy despair, he seems to rivet his eyes on the ele-
> mentary reality, the naked framework of the world, because the world
> in its fulness and movement is too exciting a spectacle for his dis-
> composed brain. He seems to feel the spectacle of it at once terrifying
> and alluring; and to deliver himself from it he has to keep perpetually
> repeating his formula of disenchantment and annihilation.

In the same way he dismisses Virgil: 'Over the whole Aeneid
there rests an ineffable melancholy: not a rigid, a moody gloom,
like the melancholy of Lucretius; no, a sweet, a touching sadness, but still a sadness; a melancholy which is at once a source
of charm in the poem, and a testimony to its incompleteness.'
Horace is similarly described as 'exquisite', but not 'interpretative and fortifying', 'without faith, without enthusiasm, without energy'.

The object of the lecture is thus attained, to demonstrate, by
showing the deficiencies of the Romans and the Elizabethans, 'the
absolute, the enduring interest of Greek literature, and, above
all, of Greek poetry'. This is a position which few people would
feel inclined to deny. Dissatisfaction does not begin until we ask
precisely what Arnold had to say about the modern element in
literature, and realize how much has been left to be inferred of
his own opinions.

One point, however, seems clear: that if Latin literature failed through its lack of sympathy with 'the varied, the abundant' life of the day, with its 'fulness of occupation, its energy of effort', and through its failure to command a 'serious cheerfulness', then the Victorian poet can hope to succeed only by *accepting* the life of the day, by rejoicing with the children of the world 'in the variety, the movement of human life', and presumably by avoiding the morbid pessimism of the Romans. But although this seems to be the next step in the argument Arnold does not take it.

The next episode in this odd exchange is the publication in 1867 of Arnold's *New Poems*. This included *Empedocles*, once more in the leading position, and an announcement by Arnold that he had reprinted it 'at the request of a man of genius, whom it had the honour and the good fortune to interest, – Mr. Robert Browning.' We do not know what led to this paradoxical situation in which Arnold was prepared to reprint a poem whose tendencies to a despairing fatalism he had already recognized, and Browning was urging his friend to reprint a poem on the kind of subject which he thought obsolete.[1]

But if, as I have suggested, Arnold's real distaste for *Empedocles* came from his awareness that he had exposed too much of his own times and his own situation, it is possible that he felt by 1867 that such 'modernness' was not altogether reprehensible. Similarly Browning may be supposed to have perceived the way in which Arnold had related his antique subject to the nineteenth century. In any case Mrs Orr has recorded that he liked *The Scholar-Gipsy* in spite of its pessimism and was also an admirer of *Empedocles*: he was about to republish his own *Pauline* which he had allowed to remain out of print and unacknowledged for thirty-five years partly because he had been accused of exposing too much of himself in it: and he liked good poetry. No doubt Arnold also realized that the merits of *Empedocles* were too great to be hidden for ever.

The suggestion that he had grown gradually less averse to reflecting his own age in his verse is given support by a letter he wrote to his mother on 5 June 1869, after the publication of

[1] A letter from Arnold to his brother, 23 July 1867, casts a very faint light: '*Empedocles* takes up much room, but Browning's desire that I should reprint *Empedocles* was really the cause of the volume appearing at all.' (Russell, I, p. 371)

Poems (1869), that is, at the point in his life at which he virtually abandoned the writing of poetry:

> My poems represent, on the whole, the main movement of mind of
> the last quarter of a century, and thus they will probably have their
> day as people become conscious to themselves of what the movement
> of mind is, and interested in the literary productions which reflect it.
> It might be fairly urged that I have less poetical sentiment than
> Tennyson, and less intellectual vigour and abundance than Browning;
> yet, because I have perhaps more of a fusion of the two than either
> of them, and have more regularly applied that fusion to the main
> line of modern development, I am likely enough to have my turn, as
> they have had theirs. [13]

It is interesting to note that he is now priding himself on apply-
ing his talents to the main line of modern development and
praising Browning for his 'intellectual vigour and abundance',
whereas twenty years before he had described him as 'a man
with a moderate gift passionately desiring movement and
fulness.'

The main point at issue between them – the extent to which
the poet in a modern age was required to operate directly on the
abundance of life which surrounded him in order to arrive at
general principles – remained, and there are few signs of a
reconciliation. It is too large a topic to consider here how far
Arnold's *Culture and Anarchy* is a contribution to the debate [14].
Arnold is clearly still defending Hellenism, but with emphasis on
its superiority to the kind of individuality so strongly advocated
by Mill. It is tempting to see in the whole work a restatement
on a philosophical level of Arnold's dispute with Browning, to
perceive in Arnold's attacks on anarchy and disorder in the name
of culture a larger writing of his dislike of Browning's eccentricity, and in his search for the 'firm intelligible law of things' an
echo of his praise of the Greek dramatists, but here we cannot
follow him.

One last quotation, from his essay on Maurice de Guérin,
shows how far he had modified his earlier extreme position, and
may stand as a final word on the question of Browning's handling
of the contemporary world:

> The grand power of poetry is its interpretative power; by which I
> mean, not a power of drawing out in black and white an explanation
> of the mystery of the universe, but the power of so dealing with

things as to awaken in us a wonderfully full, new and intimate sense
of them, and of our relations with them. When this sense is awakened
in us, as to objects without us, we feel ourselves to be in contact with
the essential nature of those objects, to be no longer bewildered and
oppressed by them, but to have their secret, and to be in harmony
with them; and this feeling calms and satisfies us as no other can.

Joseph Milsand

At Dijon an episode occurred which illustrates Browning's deep
affection for Milsand; twice he went and stood before his friend's
house, 'to muse and bless the threshold'.

GRIFFIN AND MINCHIN, Life, p. 211

M. Milsand was one of the few readers of Browning with whom I
have talked about him, who had studied his work from the beginning,
and had realized the ambition of his first imaginative flights . . .
'Quel homme extraordinaire!' he once said to me; 'son centre n'est
pas au milieu.' . . . I remember that, at the moment in which the
words were spoken, they impressed me as full of penetration.

MRS ORR, Life and Letters

I turn now to a critic of a different kind, the Frenchman Joseph
Milsand, whose long and sympathetic reviews of Browning's
early poems are particularly striking illustrations of the rapidity
with which certain perceptive writers seized on the essential
qualities of Browning's verse.

The most convenient source of information about Milsand is
an article by his daughter, Mme Marie Blanc-Milsand, in *Scribner's Magazine* (1896)[15]. Writing under the name of 'Th.
Bentzon' she gives the most important facts of her father's life,
notably that he was born a Catholic but became a Protestant in
his middle years as a result of reading Ruskin and considering
the influence of religion on art. She devotes most of her article to
Milsand's intimacy with the Brownings, an intimacy which dated
from 1852, when Milsand approached Browning with an offer to
omit from an article he had written on Mrs Browning a passage
about her dead brother which he feared might give offence.
Thereafter, until Milsand's death in 1886, the two men were on
the friendliest terms.

The revised version of *Sordello* (1863) was dedicated to Milsand in a letter in which Browning speaks warmly of his affection for him. Milsand visited the Brownings in London regularly in the Spring, and they met also on the French coast. Their holidays together in Normandy were the occasion of the passage in *Red Cotton Night-Cap Country* (III, 704–783), in which Browning refers to Milsand as 'a man of men', says of him

> He knows more, and loves better, than the world
> That never heard his name, and never may,

and concludes with the celebrated apostrophe

> O friend, who makest warm my wintry world
> And wise my heaven, if there we consort too.

An important element in their association was that after his wife's death Browning sent copies of his poems to Milsand before they went to the printers, and Milsand, with some regularity it appears, would read them and make suggestions for their improvement. A letter of Browning's dated 13 May 1872 and quoted in 'Th. Bentzon's' article throws some light on this unusual practice. Browning is referring to Milsand's latest set of comments, presumably on *Fifine at the Fair*, and says 'There is not one point to which you called attention which I was not thereby enabled to improve – in some cases essentially benefit . . . The fact is, in the case of a writer with my peculiarities and habits, somebody quite ignorant of what I may have meant to write, and only occupied with what is really written – ought to supervise the thing produced. And I never hoped or dreamed I should find such an intelligence as yours at my service.' Browning seems also to have read Milsand's articles and given him advice about them.

Browning's affection for Milsand was clearly sustained by Milsand's own open, cheerful, positive temperament, but even before he knew him he had expressed approval of his writing. He wrote to his publisher Edward Chapman on 16 January 1852: 'I noticed the other day that you prefix to an advertisement of *Christmas Eve*, an opinion from a journal – if that is the best course (of which I have doubts) – why not take your extract from some real authority in the matter – such as the admirable critic in question?'[16] He is referring to the first of Milsand's two long reviews of Browning, that which appeared in the *Revue des Deux Mondes* on 15 August 1851 [17]. It was a review of *Poems* (1849) and *Christmas-Eve and Easter-Day*, which gave Milsand the opportunity to consider the whole of Browning's early career, since *Poems* (1849) included *Paracelsus*. The keynote of his survey is his emphasis on Browning's originality: as early as 1851 he had realized that Browning was not continuing the line of Wordsworth and Keats, but stood at the beginning of a new age of poetry.

What is characteristically modern about Browning, he says, is his development away from the old idea of a physical symbolism to a *moral* symbolism. Milsand aptly draws a parallel between the new poetry and a new wave of religious belief, as if the poets were seeking a new protestant poetry. Now, he says, like religion, poetry 'cherche le genre dans l'espèce, et l'universel dans le genre'. After a long and perceptive account of *Paracelsus* Milsand returns to this idea, and comments admiringly on Browning's ability to combine the most profound general ideas with an almost myopic particularity of observation:

> Bref, il a même la minutie d'un Flamand, et c'est là un précieux renseignement, car il nous apprend que M. Browning peut regarder ce qui se passe devant lui, quoiqu'il réfléchisse, ce qui est rare; il nous apprend aussi que c'est d'après ses propres observations qu'il généralise. Cela explique sans doute pourquoi ses généralisations, au lieu d'être des idéalités, sont des milliers de réalités dans une seule définition.

Milsand admits that Browning's plays are not successful, but argues with some plausibility that this is because of Browning's great impartiality, a phrase which here seems almost equivalent to Keats' 'negative capability'. It is sublime to detect grandeur in wickedness or elements of the grotesque in the most exalted, and to see the hand of the creator everywhere, but so even-handed a representation of life is not sufficiently definite for theatrical effect. Milsand therefore, while admitting the extent of Browning's dramatic powers, concludes that his writing for the stage represents a detour in his career, producing little of permanent value, but giving useful experience. In 1851 this was, I think, a perfectly reasonable judgement. Accordingly he sees *Christmas-Eve and Easter-Day* as representing a return by

Browning to his most powerful manner, combining his generalizing and dramatic strains, almost eliminating the distinctions
between particular and general, real and abstract, microscopic
observation and general law. Milsand's account of and comments
on *Christmas-Eve and Easter-Day* are sensible, but the real
interest of the article lies in its conclusion.

He looks forward into Browning's probable career and confidently expects that his next work will be even better – probably
an intellectual poem given additional strength by his training in
the theatre. Nor should he be surprised, he says, if Browning in
the end gravitated to epic poetry. 'Sa supériorité est intimement
liée à la force d'abstraction qui lui a été accordée, et, quoi qu'il
fasse, il paiera le prix de sa supériorité.' He will always be
liable to an overwhelming vision of the world:

> Son génie à lui, c'est de pouvoir ce que M. Tennyson ne peut pas;
> c'est de revoir dans chaque fait un abrégé de la création. Chacun
> son rôle: aux uns de centraliser toutes les émotions humaines, aux
> autres de centraliser toutes nos conceptions. Pour les uns, le lyrisme;
> pour M. Browning, la poésie épique. Avec lui, bien entendu, il ne
> serait plus question de batailles ni de Troyens; chaque chose a son
> temps, et les héros d'Homère, comme ses dieux, ne sont plus notre
> épopée.

Browning is the man who can clothe *our* truth in poetic form:

> De tous les poètes que je sache, il est le plus capable de résumer les
> conceptions de la religion, de la morale et de la science théorique de
> notre époque, en leur donnant un corps poétique.

Milsand foresees that one of Browning's difficulties will be to
discover a subject adequate for his universal themes and he fears
that the particular may at times become confused with the
general, but at least the general would be a true generalization,
'et l'âme de l'épopée ne manquerait pas', for Browning has
almost unbelievably subtle powers of discrimination.

The notable things about this review, apart altogether from
its generally assured style, its expert conduct and its numerous
striking aperçus, are three. First as I have said on pp. 5–6,
there is no suggestion in the review of the ideas that Browning
developed in his *Essay on Shelley*: Milsand is not concerned with
the uses of biographical material in the interpretation of a poet's

work, nor does he make any use of the broad division of poets into 'makers' and 'seers'. Secondly, in his discussion of the subject of modern epic Milsand avoids many of the snares which entrapped Arnold in 1853, and offers a sensible set of conclusions. Thirdly, the general picture of Browning which emerges is full of interest and shows clearly how the poet must have impressed his most acute readers at this stage in his career. Milsand admittedly attaches very little importance to Browning's dramatic gifts, considering his plays 'les régions où il n'était emporté que par la minorité de ses facultés' and scarcely mentioning the *Dramatic Lyrics* and the *Dramatic Romances and Lyrics*, but this is excusable at a time when *Paracelsus* and *Christmas-Eve and Easter-Day* were his longest and most ambitious poems. Certainly Milsand writes as one in no doubt whatsoever of Browning's stature and, what is more important, although he does not recognize what is to be the true bent of Browning's genius, he sees clearly that what he is doing is something new. Contrary to popular belief, Browning did not lack for favourable reviews before 1851, as a glance at the Browning Bibliography will show, and many writers praised him for his originality, but Milsand makes the central point of his review the complete freshness of Browning's approach. 'Ce n'est pas en continuant et en perfectionnant qu'il a montré ce qu'il pouvait et ce qu'il était; c'est en défrichant un coin de l'inconnu.' Milsand, in short, was one of the first to see that Browning was not continuing the tradition of the older Romantic poets but was beginning to write the poetry of his own time. It is this especial recognition, I think, that led Mrs Browning to write to Milsand in the following terms on 16 January 1853: 'For my own part, long before you had been kind to me, I was bound to you as the critic who of all others, in or out of England, had approached my husband's poetry in the most philosophical spirit and with the most ardent comprehension.'

Milsand's other considerable piece of writing on Browning is his review of *Men and Women* in the *Revue Contemporaine*[18]. It is also full of interest; if it seems less impressive than the earlier review, it is only because by 1856 other critics were writing almost as intelligently about Browning. Having said that the review approves of the state of English poetry in general and of Browning's new poems in particular and that it is conducted with the same skill and clarity as Milsand had shown in 1851, I need perhaps do no more than call attention to some of Milsand's acuter observations to show how thoroughly he had understood the nature of Browning's poetry. For example, after describing the characteristically empirical, factual genius of English writing he sums up the matter in brief compass by saying '. . . les Anglais ont le génie de l'anecdote. Ils se plaisent à exprimer leur opinion sur un homme en citant un épisode de sa vie', an observation which leads into the heart of his criticism of *Men and Women*, notably his point that Browning's imaginative preference 'serait pour les grands vérités qui se laissent apercevoir dans les petits épisodes.' He makes good use of Browning's *Essay on Shelley*, which he quotes, principally to establish that Browning represents a new departure in English poetry, which is now on a track 'qui . . . la conduit presque à l'antipode de Wordsworth et de son école' for it is 'à la fois plus intellectuelle et plus objective'. This, Milsand suggests later, is only one example of the changes taking place in England. Since 1800 the English have been engaged in the remarkable enterprise of appraising and if necessary discarding all the old normative critical standards. This had led to a fermentation, as it were, in which the whole nation has been discovering in itself a host of new qualities. Browning in particular is creating something new and astonishing. Milsand offers a translation of *Any Wife to Any Husband* and remarks on its unconventionality:

> En effet, ils [ces vers] ne sont pas loin d'être tout l'opposé de ce que, pendant deux siècles, on a entendu par poésie. Ce n'est plus l'art qui choisit et rectifie, qui calcule et dispose en vue d'agencer une composition parfaitement propre à produire un certain effet: c'est la nature même qui ne cherche qu'à se sentir et à s'articuler telle qu'elle est, et qui arrive à la poésie en entendant mieux et plus fortement les voix secrètes qui peuvent parler en elle.

The characteristic of Browning is that in his poetry intellectual concepts are almost tangible, and feelings and aspirations speak as clearly as physical needs. His work is always full of vivacity and first-hand emotion precisely because he is always aware of the connection between thoughts and things, of the power that things have to surprise and fascinate us, and of the lively panorama of life. 'En un mot, la poésie de M. Browning est celle des vitalités qui sont à l'œuvre dans ce monde.' The total effect of

Browning then is one not of charm, but of power and movement, incessant intelligence, and richness of impressions. Browning is always surprising and always exciting.

Such praise, anticipating, as we shall see, the comments of Henry James, coupled with the sympathetic perception Milsand shows, for example, in his analysis of Browning's use of the dramatic monologue, is valuable indeed, but perhaps the most valuable part of Milsand's essay is the third section, in which he considers the dangers of Browning's method, in particular his 'honesty', which is opposed to all kinds of affectation. He is trying to bend the language to his will, and his will is an unusual one. The danger he runs in his desire for freedom and accuracy of expression is of falling into 'the grotesque'. This quality Milsand exemplifies with great accuracy as being what we find in, for instance, a Gothic cathedral, when pure line is used together with significant line; the result is a mixture of modes, like a medieval picture with people saying things in speech bubbles. There is a confusion of the *active* principle, which causes an emotion, with the *figurative* or *linguistic* principle, which expresses an idea of the artist's.

Milsand rightly points to the combination of dogma and emotion as characterising the England of the 1850s. Browning, Milsand concludes, is no exception: he wants to push poetry as far as it will go, in both directions.

> Penser, connaître et sentir tout ce qui peut être connu, senti et conçu, retenir en soi toute cette expérience, et trouver moyen, par une sorte de pression continue, de la réduire en tableaux poétiques telle est, en quelque sorte, la tâche qu'il se donne.

Possibly, Milsand suggests, Browning's aims are too high, and in attempting too much he loses the music of poetry. But the important thing is to remember his high aim and his desire to give his readers 'un univers expliqué et compris, où les phénomènes raconteraient leur propre généalogie, et où l'œil de l'intelligence, au lieu de n'apercevoir que des effets dont la cause reste cachée, verrait directement les causes elles-mêmes accomplir leurs effets.'

Such a brief summary does less than justice to the breadth of Milsand's argument and to his detailed analyses of many of the poems, but it may serve to indicate his judiciousness, the high level of abstraction on which he moves without losing particularity, and the comprehensiveness of his terms of reference, which enable him to discuss Browning's poetry in terms of the whole pattern of English literature and the general movement of the nineteenth-century mind.

While one regrets that no British critics saw Browning's strengths and weaknesses with comparable clarity, it is pleasant to reflect that Browning met with such balanced appreciation in a country where he passed some of the happiest periods of his later life.

Walter Bagehot

In his *History of English Criticism* Saintsbury, referring to the paper 'Wordsworth, Tennyson and Browning' (1864)[19], observes that Bagehot was 'one of the earliest frankly to estate and recognise Tennyson – the earliest of importance perhaps to estate and recognise Browning – among the leaders of mid-nineteenth century poetry' [20]. This statement will ring a little oddly both to those who remember that Tennyson had been 'estated' as Poet Laureate as early as 1850, and those who are familiar with the essay and its treatment of Browning. My purpose in this section is first to defend Browning briefly against Bagehot's criticisms and secondly to set against the 1864 article another review written four years later, which shows a considerable change of approach.

Bagehot's strength as a literary critic lay not in his theoretical powers but in his sensible responses to individual works: in consequence the apparatus of aesthetic theory which he provides in his article of 1864 is not helpful, except to make clear the assumptions with which he approaches a poem. For example, a characteristic aphorism such as 'Poetry should be memorable and emphatic, intense and *soon over*' hardly portends a very receptive audience for a poet like Browning. Bagehot deals at some length with 'pure' literature, which describes the type in its simplicity, with just enough accessory circumstance and no more, that is, with the economy that is the keynote of Classical art: of this kind of writing, Milton and Wordsworth are the best examples in English. 'Ornate' art also wishes to give the typical idea in perfection, but 'wishes to surround the type with the greatest number or circumstances which it will *bear*. It works not by choice and selection but by accumulation and aggregation.' Its defect is that 'nothing is described as it is: everything has about it an atmosphere of *something else*.' Tennyson is chosen as the representative ornate writer.

Pure and ornate art thus, each in its way, try to depict the type as perfectly as possible. Bagehot's third category, 'grotesque' art, on the contrary prefers to depict the type *in difficulties*. 'It deals, to use the language of science, not with normal types, but with abnormal specimens, not with essences but with existences.' Of this way of writing Bagehot, of course, takes Browning for his example. It is important to note that Bagehot modifies his condemnation of grotesque poetry, since he concedes that it has its origins in a commendable attempt to depict the world as it really is. 'He [Browning] has applied a hard strong intellect to real life; he has applied the same intellect to the problems of his age. He has striven to know what *is*: he has endeavoured not to be cheated by counterfeits, not to be infatuated with illusions.' But his objection is to what Browning actually produces. As example he cites *Caliban*, which he suggests is typical of Browning's method, being disagreeable and hard to understand and requiring great 'staying power' of the reader:

> One of his greatest admirers once owned to us that he seldom or never began a new poem [of Browning's] without looking on in advance, and foreseeing with caution what length of intellectual adventure he was about to commence. Whoever will work hard at such poems will find much mind in them: they are a sort of quarry of ideas, but whoever goes there will find these ideas in such a jagged, ugly, useless shape that he can hardly bear them.

To show that *Caliban* is not 'an isolated error' Bagehot quotes extensively from *Holy-Cross Day*, which appeared in *Men and Women* (1855). After this he proceeds to generalize. 'An exceptional monstrosity of horrid ugliness cannot be made pleasing, except it be made to suggest – to recall – the perfection, the beauty, from which it is a deviation. Perhaps in extreme cases no art is equal to this; but then such self-imposed problems should not be worked by the artist: these out-of-the-way and detestable subjects should not be worked by him.' There follows a passage on Browning's religion which is too obviously wrong-headed to require answering, and then Bagehot, by way of reparation, quotes as a favourable specimen of the grotesque manner a large part of *The Pied Piper*, which appeared in *Dramatic Lyrics* (1842). He concludes by deploring the weakness of contemporary taste which leads so many readers to neglect pure art for 'showy art', that '*glaring* art which catches and arrests the eye for a moment, but which in the end fatigues it'.

The inadequacies of Bagehot's arguments in general are apparent. In particular he is shackled by his own arbitrary classification of art. Thus although he sees the weaknesses of Wordsworth and Milton as well as their strengths – Wordsworth has 'nothing of the stir of life'; *Paradise Lost* is 'radically tainted by a vicious principle'; about both poets 'there is a taint of duty; a vicious sense of the good man's task' – he does not admit that, if these represent pure art at its best in English, then pure art is not an ideal to which all artists must aspire but simply one of many possible ways of writing poetry, with its own qualities and its own dangers. On the contrary the pure style is set up as the essence of poetry and any deviation from it is by definition a falling off from perfection. Thus Bagehot is able to allow only an inferior merit to the kind of poetry which describes the individual rather than the type. Hence his unbalanced treatment of Browning, which is accentuated by his extraordinarily limited choice of examples. To take *Caliban* alone from *Dramatis Personae* and then to complain that Browning is trying to fashion a system of religious belief which will be popular with everyone, 'which stout men will heed, which nice women will adore', is not a critical procedure to inspire confidence. Similarly *Holy-Cross Day* and *The Pied Piper* – Forman calls it 'perhaps the best known but least worth knowing of all Browning's poems' – simply will not serve as typical examples of Browning's style. It is clear then that Bagehot is not wishing to offer an accurate description of Browning but to use a few of his poems as specimens in order to give some colour to a very dubious theory of art.[1]

---

[1] A recent biographer, Alastair Buchan, comments, 'His third classification – the grotesque – the universal type at odds, in embryo, or in combat, he centres around Browning. It is the least successful of the three for his comments reveal his one literary blind spot, his consistent equation of experiments on the boundaries of poetry with lapses of taste.' *The Spare Chancellor*, (London, 1959), p. 89.

When he is writing with his eye on the poetry and not on the theory, however, Bagehot is a much stronger critic. He reviewed *The Ring and The Book* in January 1869, probably having seen only the first volume (Books I–III), a circumstance which makes the quality of his appreciation all the more remarkable [21]. For example, he writes: 'Nothing can equal his [Browning's] suggestiveness in accounting for mental phenomena. No one obvious explanation of anything ever occurs to him. There is a recurrent "or" continually in his mind. He has always at command a dozen lines of rail tapering down to the same point on the horizon', a particularly happy comment on *The Ring and the Book* as a whole.

Again he pays tribute to Browning's dramatic skill, which he compares with Shakespeare's, and shows a clear understanding of Browning's dramatic method:

> Here, as elsewhere, the tragedy is related in an off-hand, matter-of-fact way by men who do not perceive the drift of what they are saying. The narrators are too near, are too much taken up with minute points of detail, to see or comprehend the majesty of suffering they are unconsciously revealing . . . In the very process of narration they are unconsciously exhibiting their own little failings, their odd notions of things, the particular range of their sympathies.

He concludes by welcoming 'a fresh work of genius . . . this powerful and elaborate work of art, written by one of the few strong men of our time.' The review as a whole is a penetrating piece of work, especially the speculations about the course the remaining books of the poem will take.

It is by no means certain that it was written by Bagehot, but I think that the attribution may be made with some confidence. In any case, whether Bagehot or some other critic wrote it, it shows how quickly and accurately an intelligent reader of 1869 was able to comprehend a major work of Browning's fresh from the press, and appreciate his powers justly in their most spacious exercise.

Henry James

I never found him anything but loud and liberal and cheerful, and I never heard him utter a paradox, or express a shade, or play with an idea . . . His opinions were sound and second-rate, and of his perceptions it was too mystifying to think. I envied him his magnificent health.

'[He] disappoints everyone who looks in him for the genius that created the pages they adore . . . He's always splendid, as your morning bath is splendid, or a sirloin of beef, or the railway service to Brighton. But he's never rare.'

'I've often wondered – now I know. There are two of them . . . One goes out, the other stays at home. One's the genius, the other's the bourgeois, and it's only the bourgeois whom we personally know.'

For personal relations this admirable genius thought his second-best good enough.

The narrator of *The Private Life* (1892) is talking about the celebrated man of letters, Clare Vawdrey. In a later preface James explains that the germ of the story came from his acquaintance with 'a highly distinguished man, constantly to be encountered, whose fortune and whose peculiarity it was to bear out personally as little as possible (at least to *my* wandering sense) the high denotements, the rich implications and rare associations, of the genius to which he owed his position and his renown.'

I have never ceased to ask myself, in this particular loud, sound, normal, hearty presence, all so assertive and so whole, all bristling with prompt responses and expected opinions and usual views, radiating all a broad daylight equality of emphasis and impartiality of address . . . what lodgement, on such premises, the rich proud genius one adored could ever have contrived, what domestic commerce the subtlety that was its prime ornament and the world's wonder have enjoyed, under what shelter the obscurity that was its luckless drawback and the world's despair have flourished. The whole aspect and *allure* of the fresh sane man, illustrious and undistinguished . . . was [*sic*] mystifying; they made the question of who then had written the immortal things such a puzzle.

This presence which James embodies with so exiguous a share of artistic transfiguration into his story is, he tells us, that of Browning. The whole episode, not least in the matter of *The Private Life's* total failure as a short story, is characteristic of the bewildered fascination which James was always to betray when confronted with the poet, or with his works. In his extra-ordinarily interesting memoir of his friend Story [22] he returns again and again to the figure of Browning. The following passage, celebrated though it is, must be quoted at length:

> The writer's London period was in fact to be rich and ample, was to be attended with felicities and prosperities of every sort, that cast the comparatively idyllic Italian time into the background and seemed, superficially, to build it out. But thus, really, was generated in the personal, social, intellectual way, the wonderful Browning we so largely were afterwards to know – the accomplished, saturated, sane, sound man of the London world and the world of 'culture' of whom it is impossible not to believe that he had arrived somehow, for his own deep purposes, at the enjoyment of a double identity. It was not easy to meet him and know him without some resort to the supposition that he had literally mastered the secret of dividing the personal consciousness into a pair of independent components . . . The poet and the 'member of society' were, in a word, dissociated in him as they can rarely elsewhere have been; . . . the wall that built out the idyll . . . of which memory and imagination were virtually composed for him stood there behind him solidly enough, but subject to his privilege of living almost equally on both sides of it. It contained an invisible door through which, working the lock at will, he could swiftly pass and of which he kept the golden key – carrying the same about with him even in the pocket of his dinner-waistcoat, yet even in his most splendid expansions showing it, happy man, to none . . . [In his letters of the 1860s we] see him without mystery or attitude, with his explicit sense and his clear, full, masculine tone, the tone, ever, of reason and cheer. He is always, to our conceit, on the hither side of the wall.

Just as the narrator in *The Private Life* convincingly presents Clare Vawdrey's commonplace exterior but thoroughly fails to convey the reality of Vawdrey's hidden life as a writer of genius, so James immediately persuades us of the truth of his picture of Browning 'the man of the London world' but is perceptibly less assured when he turns to Browning's poetry.

There is this minor exception, that with Browning as a lover of Italy James was completely in sympathy. He praises, almost without reserve, the poet's full and accurate picture of the Italian scene. 'A drive the other day with a friend to Villa Madama, on the side of Monte Mario; a place like a page out of one of Browning's richest evocations of this clime and civilization.

Wondrous in its haunting melancholy, it might have inspired half *The Ring and the Book* at a stroke' [23]. Again 'The Rome and Tuscany of the early 'fifties had become for him so at once a medium, a bath of the senses and perceptions, into which he could sink, in which he could unlimitedly soak, that whenever he might be touched afterwards he gave out some effect of that immersion' [24]. No doubt James intends the faintly comic suggestion of the white-haired, pink-cheeked poet exuding under pressure a perceptible smell of bathsalts; otherwise his tributes to Browning's evocation of Italy are frequent and generous.

The first open engagement between James and Browning's poetry has left as memorial James's review of *The Inn Album* [25]. 'This is a decidedly irritating and displeasing performance', James begins: the accents of annoyance and distress persist throughout the piece, as the following extracts will show:

> His wantonness, his wilfulness, his crudity, his inexplicable want of secondary thought, as we may call it, of the stage of reflection that follows upon the first outburst of the idea, and smooths, shapes, and adjusts it – all this alloy of his great genius is more sensible now than ever . . . There is not a line of comprehensible, consecutive statement in the two hundred and eleven pages of the volume . . . There is not a phrase which in any degree does the office of the poetry that comes lawfully into the world . . . The graceless and thankless and altogether unavailable character of the poem . . . We can as little imagine a reader . . . addressing himself more than once to the perusal of *The Inn Album*, as we can fancy cultivating for conversational purposes the society of a person afflicted with a grievous impediment of speech . . . He deals with human character as a chemist with his acids and alkalies, and while he mixes his colored fluids in a way that surprises the profane, knows perfectly well what he is about. But there is too apt to be in his style that hiss and sputter and evil aroma which characterize the proceedings of the laboratory. The idea, with Mr. Browning, always tumbles out into the world in some grotesque, hind-foremost manner . . . We frankly confess . . . that we have found this want of clearness of explanation, of continuity, of at least superficial verisimilitude, of the smooth, the easy, the agreeable, quite fatal to our enjoyment of *The Inn Album* . . . His book is only barely comprehensible.

The tone of vigorous but rather shrill indignation suggests at once Dickens chastising the Pre-Raphaelites, and an examination of the review confirms the opinion that James's accusations of incomprehensibility are violently exaggerated in order to disguise an inability to assess the poem accurately. For in the middle of his review James offers a summary of the plot, which, although ironically presented, is accurate enough to show that Browning has at least managed to convey his story. Moreover James concedes that the poem has dramatic situations and deep discriminations of character. One comment is most revealing. He says 'We are reading neither prose nor poetry; it is too real for the ideal, and too ideal for the real.' The implications of this remark are clear and do much to explain James's uneasiness. He implies that there is a certain sphere which is appropriate for poetry and another sphere appropriate for prose. Poetry 'that comes lawfully into the world' should deal only in the ideal: reality is reserved for the prose writer. Holding these opinions about the proper province of poetry he is naturally disconcerted to find a poem which offers to give something of the same kind of pleasure as a novel, which is set in the present and written in a vocabulary which is not obviously 'poetic'. Not knowing how to take such a work he excuses his own lack of comprehension by alleging incomprehensibility on the part of the author.

The same reluctance to accept the poem on the poet's terms is evident in a much more celebrated piece of writing – James's commemorative address 'The Novel in *The Ring and the Book*' [26]. The result is that James offers a basically unfavourable account of the poem, although he muffles his criticism in clouds of ironic praise and occasionally dazzles by the brilliance of his *aperçus*. James's general line of attack is soon made clear. Browning is 'one of the most copious of our poets' and the poem is 'the most voluminous of his works'.

> *The Ring and the Book* is so vast and so essentially Gothic a structure, spreading and soaring and branching at such a rate, covering such ground, putting forth such pinnacles and towers and brave excrescences, planting its transepts and chapels and porticoes, its clustered hugeness or inordinate muchness, that with any first approach we but walk vaguely and slowly, rather bewilderedly, round and round it, wondering at what point we had best attempt such entrance as will save our steps and light our uncertainty, most enable us to reach our personal chair, our indicated chapel or shrine, when once within.

James proposes in effect to make his quickest way through the poem to his 'own particular chair', from which he can see the part of the poem he prefers and ignore the rest. The implication is that the 'great loose and uncontrolled composition', the poem of 'a proportioned monstrous magnificence', represents little real improvement on the original documents, which offered Browning 'a subject stated to the last ounce of its weight'.

Browning's treatment of the crude facts of his story amounts to an expansion of them. His version of the story can be taken in only one way:

> We can only take it as tremendously interesting, interesting not only in itself, but with the great added interest, the dignity and authority and beauty, of Browning's general perception of it. We can't not accept this, and little enough, on the whole, do we want not to . . . Yet all the while we are in presence, not at all of an achieved form, but of a mere preparation for one, though on the hugest scale . . . He works over his vast material and we then work *him* over, though not availing ourselves, to this end, of a grain he himself doesn't somehow give us; and there we are.

James's chosen method of working through 'our poet's splendid hocus-pocus' is to look for the central point of view which Browning has neglected to provide. 'I find that centre in the embracing consciousness of Caponsacchi, which, coming to the rescue of our question of treatment, of our search for a point of control, practically saves everything, and shows itself, moreover, the only thing that *can* save.'

James concedes several virtues to Browning's handling of the theme, notably 'that, with whatever limitations, it gives us in the rarest manner three characters of the first importance'. Then James characteristically converts his praise to criticism by commenting 'I hold three a great many; I could have done with it almost, I think, if there had been but one or two . . . Deeply [Browning] felt that with the three – the three built up at us each with an equal genial rage of reiterative touches – there couldn't eventually not be something done (artistically done, I mean) if someone would only do it!'

He continues to describe the novel which he would hack out of the poem using 'the enveloping consciousness – or call it just the struggling, emerging, comparing, at last intensely living – conscience – of Caponsacchi as the isolated centre of our situation or determinant of our form.' He does not explain in much detail how he proposes to give his subject dignity 'by extracting its finest importance'. He talks of 'the tremendous little chapter' which would be 'devoted to the Franceschini interior as revealed to Comparini eyes', but does not disclose how this scene is to become available to his 'large lucid reflector'. Caponsacchi is to be 'turned on, with a brave ingenuity' from the very first, and shown as instinctively suspicious of Guido, who is in turn jealous and afraid of him. If we knew in detail Caponsacchi's reactions to Guido this would make him 'comparatively a modern man'. James would give us 'the Arezzo life and the Arezzo crisis with every "i" dotted and every circumstance presented.' The flight to Rome could be described in detail, and even the end could be done quite easily. Although Pompilia dies it is in Caponsacchi's consciousness that she flowers most intensely, 'so that *he* contains the whole.' There might even be a final scene in which he meets the Pope for a final confrontation, 'almost as august on the one part as on the other'.

Before I examine the relevance of James's address to Browning's poem I should like to call attention to some of the incidental observations which James makes and which show the extent of his insight into Browning's work. He repeats his praise of Browning's evocation of the Italian scene, and couples it with an interesting, if ambiguous, comparison of the poet with George Eliot. He precedes this by a paragraph in which he moves from a questionable premise to penetrating analysis of the characteristic experience of reading Browning:

> We feel ourselves in the world of Expression at any cost. That, essentially, is the world of poetry . . . Browning is 'upon' us, straighter upon us always, somehow, than anyone else of his race . . . as if he came up against us, each time, on the same side of the street and not on the other side, across the way, where we mostly see the poets elegantly walk, and where we greet them without danger of concussion. It is on this same side, as I call it, on *our* side, on the other hand that I rather see our encounter with the novelists taking place.

At the end of the address James makes a further general statement about Browning's art, when he says

> The thing for which we feel *The Ring and the Book* preponderantly done [is] the exhibition of the great constringent relation between

man and woman at once at its maximum and as the relation most worth while in life for either party; an exhibition forming quite the main substance of our author's message. He has dealt, in his immense variety and vivacity, with other relations, but on this he has thrown his most living weight; it remains the thing of which his own rich experience most convincingly spoke to him.

This last observation is typical of James's approach to *The Ring and The Book.* He sees it as existing primarily for the sake of the relation between Caponsacchi and Pompilia, and concludes that if this is so it would be improved by describing Caponsacchi's feelings at greater length, by using him as the central point of the story and by omitting everything that does not bear directly on the central relationship: although James does not say this in so many words, it must be assumed or what he says makes no sense. The suggestions he proffers have obvious merit, and, if Browning had wanted to write that kind of poem, would have been quite useful. It is plain, however, that James totally alters Browning's conception of the character of Caponsacchi, for it is central to Browning's interpretation of events that Caponsacchi should *not* have a long previous acquaintance with Pompilia, that his decision should involve the risk of acting wrongly through ignorance, and that its particular glory should reside in his 'good/Great undisguised leap over post and pale/Right into the mid-cirque, free fighting place.' His role is that of a knight rescuing an *unknown* lady not because he knows all the circumstances of her imprisonment but simply because she is in distress and it flashes on him in an instant that it is his task to rescue her.

More importantly James's notion of canalizing all the events through the consciousness of Caponsacchi destroys at a stroke the grand design of Browning's poem. Nobody understood better than Browning the advantages of presenting events as they appear to a single observer. But in his epic poem he decided, rightly I think, that a single internal point of consciousness would be too limiting. It would impose a kind of unity, but at the price of amplitude. In particular Browning does not wish to give us only Caponsacchi's idea of Pompilia, which might be false, but to present Pompilia herself. Similarly he gives us not a single cool appraisal of Guido by a fellow-Aretine who knows him thoroughly and is not deceived by his arguments, but Guido as he presents himself to the Roman world and finally as he appears to himself. As I have suggested, the multiplicity of narrators has an additional purpose. As well as providing variety and enabling Browning to present opposing views of the case in their fulness, this way of conducting the poem implies that, although each speaker describes the events from his own point of view and with his own personal distortion, there is, lying behind all their versions, however variously refracted, a genuine objective truth to which the reader can approximate more and more closely as he proceeds through the poem, until at last he is more fully aware of what really happened than any single speaker. With only one narrator Browning could scarcely have conveyed his over-riding vision of the truth as the one stable thing in a relativist world. The form Browning chose enables him to present the life of a particular time and place with a richness of detail almost unparalleled in literature. His success in this is shown by James's immediate desire to use the poem as a quarry, to treat it as if it were life, which has to be simplified drastically before it can be used by the artist. Browning is prepared to offer a much more complex picture of the situation than James can accept.

The main tenor therefore of James's article is to insinuate by carefully qualified praise that the poem is a grandiose failure because of Browning's extravagance, exuberance and lack of design and workmanship. James suggests also that we do not focus sharply enough on Caponsacchi's conflict to make him seem a 'modern man', although he proposes to make use in his own version of 'figures . . . reeking with the old-world character', and speaks of his own desire to shut out the whole of the modern 'spiritual sky'.

The charge that the poem is too large to be comprehended is, although obvious, a fair enough criticism, and one which might be the beginning of a profitable argument. But James does not produce evidence for his criticism: instead he describes an entirely different poem, the one Browning might have written but did not. Of course this discussion, even apart from its insights, is full of interest, but it is interesting not for what it tells us about Browning but for what it tells us about James. In a precisely similar way we learn little about Tennyson but a great deal about Browning from the celebrated passage in a letter to Julia

Wedgwood in which Browning explains at length exactly how he would have managed the end of *Enoch Arden* [27].

Nevertheless the whole article is distinctly more literate and more perceptive than most of the criticism Browning received in the years immediately after this death [28]. Although James was frequently disconcerted by Browning's poetry, his affection for the man and his conviction that somewhere in his writing lurked the spark of genius always led him to speak with warmth and generosity. His most moving tribute is 'Browning in Westminster Abbey', a valedictory address in which James praises Browning almost without reserve [29]. His most important qualification is made when he says:

> He [the patient critic] may finally even put his finger on some explanation of the great mystery, the imperfect conquest of the poetic form by a genius in which the poetic passion had such volume and range. He may successfully say how it was that a poet without a lyre – for that is practically Browning's deficiency: he had the scroll, but not often the sounding strings – was nevertheless, in his best hours, wonderfully rich in the magic of his art, a magnificent master of poetic emotion.

This is the most serious reservation of the piece; at least it withholds praise which Browning would have valued, whereas he would no doubt have enjoyed the careful hesitations and ironies of the following verdict:

> A good many oddities and a good many great writers have been entombed in the Abbey; but none of the odd ones have been so great and none of the great ones so odd. There are plenty of poets whose right to the title may be contested, but there is no poetic head of equal power – crowned and recrowned by almost importunate hands – from which so many people would withhold the distinctive wreath.

The two positive qualities on which James lays stress are Browning's Englishness and what he calls his 'bewildering modernness':

> It is as a tremendous and incomparable modern that the author of *Men and Women* takes his place in it [Westminster Abbey]. He introduces to his predecessors a kind of contemporary individualism which surely for many a year they had not been reminded of with any such force. The tradition of the poetic character as something high, detached and simple, which may be assumed to have prevailed among them for a good while, is one that Browning has broken at every turn.

Even here the ambiguity persists, for James deliberately does not say whether or not he prefers his poets to be 'high, detached and simple', but in his concluding paragraph he praises Browning with notable generosity as 'unmistakably in the great tradition . . . a magnificent example of the best and least dilettantish English spirit . . . a wonderful mixture of the universal and the alembicated.' He admires Browning because he spoke out clearly for 'the things that, as a race, we like best – the fascination of faith, the acceptance of life, the respect for its mysteries, the endurance of its charges, the vitality of the will, the validity of character, the beauty of action, the seriousness, above all, of the great human passion.' Browning gives 'a complete and splendid picture' of 'the special relation between man and woman', and 'somehow places it at the same time in the region of conduct and responsibility'. He concludes with the following sentences:

> With a sense of security, perhaps even a certain complacency, we leave our sophisticated modern conscience, and perhaps even our heterogeneous modern vocabulary, in his charge among the illustrious. There will possibly be moments in which these things will seem to us to have widened the allowance, made the high abode more comfortable, for some of those who are yet to enter it. [30]

If we set aside the ill-considered early review of *The Inn Album* we can see that James's feelings about Browning were fairly consistent. Browning the man of the London world baffled and teased James by his normality and healthiness, by his refusal to conform to James's ideas of what a poet should be like. He was not 'poetic' enough [31]. Similarly, James perceives many of the special qualities of Browning's verse, its modernness, for example, its Englishness, its exuberant immediacy, and its resemblance to the work of the novelists. 'The real is his quest, the very ideal of the real, the real most finely mixed with life, which *is*, in the last analysis, the ideal.' Yet all the while he is fretted by the feeling that, splendid though all this is, it cannot be poetry because it, like its author, is not 'poetic' enough. This explains his curious adaptation of *The Ring and The Book*. It cannot be poetry because it is not what James expects poetry to be: it cannot be a novel because a novel has to have a certain kind of unity which Browning has not provided: therefore it must be raw material still, and as such requires to be 'done', and 'done' with some thoroughness.

The history of James's baffled inability to reconcile the personality of the poet with his own ideas of the properly poetical lost its destined memorialist when Max Beerbohm died, but it is some consolation that James himself recorded it in *The Private Life*. So in a sense did Browning; he called his version *How It Strikes A Contemporary*.

George Santayana

The last critic I shall examine has been extraordinarily influential in the decline of Browning's reputation. His book *Interpretations of Poetry and Religion* was published in 1900 and contained an essay called 'The Poetry of Barbarism'. It was an examination of the poetry of Whitman and Browning and condemned them both.[1]

It has often been pointed out that Santayana proceeds from doubtful assumptions and gives an incomplete and inaccurate account of Browning's poetry. Helen Dryer Woodard in 1901 [32] and Margaret Sherwood in 1934 [33] deal carefully with many points in his essay. More recently K. L. Knickerbocker has suggested a reply on general grounds [34], yet DeVane in his *Handbook* still refers to Santayana's as 'the most devastating criticism which Browning has encountered' and the *Pelican Guide to English Literature* duly echoes 'devastating'.

I should like to explain how far I consider these three attempts at rebuttal successful, and then to suggest some further arguments which may be urged against Santayana.

Miss Woodard's rejoinder begins by taking the obvious point that Santayana is writing as an idealist to whom the 'real' world is of no genuine concern. He believes that the universe is 'alien' to man, who lives by contemplating his own ideal world, which can never become actual, and by acting as little as possible.

---

[1] Santayana's association of Browning with Whitman is reminiscent of Sir Henry Jones's trick of linking Browning with Carlyle. In each case the object is to attribute to Browning faults which are less characteristic of him than of the other writer in question.

Browning 'believing the universe to be of the same nature and constitution as ourselves, believes that it is possible and therefore morally obligatory to actualize our ideals.'

Similarly Santayana advocates 'completeness and finish' as our highest aims in life, whereas to Browning life is 'no goal but starting-point of men'. Perfection to Browning would be an undesirable quality since it would prove that man's capacity was limited, whereas it was an article of faith with him that development and not perfection was the primary attribute of mankind.

Miss Woodard has put her finger on a crucial difference of principle between the poet and his critic. However, although this may account for the impetuousness of Santayana's attack, it is still perfectly possible that his attack is justified. Miss Woodard goes on to argue that this is not so, because it is untrue to say, as Santayana does, that Browning advocates action for its own sake: on the contrary he advocates action which is an attempt to embody an ideal. She deals in particular with Browning's treatment of love and comments, with justifiable tartness. 'Professor Santayana says that Browning does not idealise love. It is hard to believe that a man who makes such a statement has ever read such poems as *By the Fireside*, *Dís Aliter Visum*, or *Two in the Campagna*.' She appositely quotes Paracelsus' last speech as a convenient epitome of Browning's constant idealization of love.

In the last part of her essay Miss Woodard concedes some of Santayana's criticisms, pointing to a tendency in Browning to allow deeply-felt ideals to take the place of thought. She concludes by adopting a central position between Browning and Santayana, suggesting that both thought and action are essential. We must, as Santayana suggests, be careful to make sure that we have instructed ourselves in the best course of action, but nevertheless we must act eventually and when we do there is still an element of risk. 'Whether we can take that risk hopefully or fearfully each must decide for himself.'

It is a temperate and sensible rejoinder, in which Miss Woodard's main concern is to reconcile Browning and Santayana by showing that while they are both idealists they differ in approach and emphasis. She demonstrates that Santayana has very little comprehension indeed of what Browning is doing, but the *rapport* she establishes between the two men depends on some inconsistency in her use of the word 'ideal'.

Professor Sherwood offers her defence of Browning as the last chapter of her valuable book on the Romantic movement as a whole, a book in which she has laid much stress on the essentially evolutionary colouring of much Romantic thought and on its reflection in Romantic poetry. Accordingly she, like Miss Woodard, begins by pointing to a central antipathy between Browning and Santayana, but she is more concerned to contrast Browning's progressive dynamic philosophy with Santayana's essentially limited inflexible views of development as 'the unfolding of a definite nature'. Santayana, she says, 'ignores the change from a static to a dynamic conception of the world order in the late eighteenth and early nineteenth centuries, and evidently disdains the prevailing wind of doctrine of his time in both science and the humanities . . . Mr. Santayana is like Lucretius, in that his only idea of change is of meaningless change.' However, it is again quite possible that 'the prevailing wind' may be blowing in the wrong direction: Santayana cannot be set aside simply because his point of view is no longer fashionable. Accordingly, Professor Sherwood undertakes to show not only that Santayana's demands are a hundred and fifty years out of date but that he has failed to realize what Browning is offering him instead.

Like Miss Woodard again, she criticizes his inadequate and unrepresentative choice of love poems, and goes on to make the important point that to Browning love is not simply physical passion but 'the force at work in all becoming'. She describes with clarity and perception Browning's great achievement of animating the abstract Deist idea of universal love and showing it at work in human hearts. This is simply the most prominent example of Browning's ability to present the ideal in real forms. 'Mr. Santayana's affirmation that Browning has no idea of the eternal shows that the critic fails to realize that Browning's lifelong effort was to reveal the infinite in the finite, the eternal making itself manifest in the experiences of time.' In the remainder of her chapter she amplifies this point with an unusually wide and helpful series of parallels between Browning and Plato, Plotinus, Boehme, Bruno and many other philosophers, all designed to establish the empirical nature of Browning's poetry and the part played in it by love. In the main then, Professor Sherwood takes the same tricks as Miss Woodard, but she lays rather more emphasis on the philosophical differences between the poet and his critic, and offers in addition a cogent defence of some of Browning's favourite speculative positions. In passing she makes the shrewd point that what Santayana seems to object to in Browning's poetry as such, quite apart from its pernicious doctrines, is simply the fact that it is often lyric or dramatic, that is poetry which depends on an effect of spontaneity rather than on an effect of matured reason. On this she comments succinctly 'Dramatic poetry, the result of effort to observe and understand the laws of life as manifested in individual experience, has, and will always have, its own validity, its own excuse for being.' Professor Sherwood's rebuttal is brisk and to the point; she has a nice cross style.

Professor Knickerbocker similarly offers two lines of defence. First that Santayana's 'expectations of a poet and of poetry . . . are unreasonable'; secondly that Santayana would not have found Browning so completely unable to fulfil these expectations if he had looked at the whole body of Browning's work instead of considering a few poems and ignoring the rest.

Knickerbocker points out that Santayana's definition of poetry, 'an ideal beyond human attainment', excludes Shakespeare from the first flight of poets, and ultimately rejects Lucretius, Goethe and even Dante, in spite of his 'spiritual mastery of . . . life, and a perfect knowledge of good and evil.' Next he takes the familiar point about Santayana's insistence on 'idealization', allowing that Santayana's opinions may be valid but denying that he has any right to expect Browning to conform with them or to dismiss him as a barbarian if he does not. Knickerbocker emphasizes that while Santayana makes a special point of the necessity of idealization in love poetry, the love poets he puts forward as 'the real masters of passion and imagination' are Dante, Guido Cavalcanti, Michael Angelo, and Lorenzo de' Medici. Knickerbocker contrasts their conventional monotonous abstraction with Browning's gallery of lovers, each a distinct, unique creation.

Finally he shows that on occasion Browning displays precisely those qualities whose total absence Santayana deplores, for example in *Abt Vogler*, where the poet demonstrates his understanding of the claims of mysticism. Professor Knickerbocker summarizes his argument, to whose wit and acuteness this brief summary has done little justice, by saying 'Santayana's views are exclusive, Browning's inclusive – even to the point of embracing some of Santayana's pet speculations.'

It will be seen that there is some agreement between these three writers about the weaknesses of Santayana's arguments; they all, I think, establish the points that they claim against him. Nevertheless a number of points remain, to which I propose to attempt an answer. It may be suggested that this is not necessary. When Santayana writes, in *Interpretations of Poetry and Religion*, 'the specific and the finite, I feel, are odious; let me therefore aspire to see, reason and judge in no specific or finite manner – that is, not to see, reason or judge at all. So I shall be like the Infinite, nay I shall become one with the Infinite and (marvellous thought!) one with the One' [35], or, 'Religion and poetry are identical in essence, and differ merely in the way in which they are attached to practical affairs. Poetry is called religion when it intervenes in life, and religion, when it merely supervenes upon life, is seen to be nothing but poetry' [36], it is tempting simply to conclude that the man who does not scruple to waste a skilled compositor's time on such vapidities is not worth powder and shot. But, as I say, his effect on Browning's reputation has been great, and in addition it is important to recognize that although his arguments are poor Santayana is directing them at a real weakness in Browning. He is a 'busy' poet: he is, as Santayana says, too much given to the 'confidential wink', the 'genial poke in the ribs', and the 'little interlarded sneer'; he does lack the quality of classical repose. Therefore what Santayana says must be answered: I shall argue that although these are weaknesses in Browning they are not indefensible, and that the arguments Santayana produces certainly do not justify him in dismissing Browning as 'a volcanic eruption that tosses itself quite blindly and ineffectually into the sky.'

Like the writers I have mentioned I offer two lines of defence – first, Santayana's failure to adopt a satisfactory general position, secondly, his failure to relate his remarks to Browning in particular. That is, I am denying the major and the minor premises of his argument. If therefore his conclusion is true, which I do not admit, it is true only by accident.

One of Santayana's most obvious weaknesses as a critic is his imperfect notion of what drama is and what it is proper for a dramatist to do. In the Browning essay he shows the same in-flexible lack of understanding as in his comments on the absence of religion in Shakespeare. In this essay he sees that a supporter of Shakespeare may argue that the dramatist worked 'by direct imaginative representation' instead of by abstraction and syn-thesis. Santayana replies by putting forward a general position:

> Suffice it to say that the human race hitherto, whenever it has reached a phase of comparatively high development and freedom, has formed a conception of its place in Nature, no less than of the contents of its life; and that this conception has been the occasion of religious senti-ments and practices; and further, that every art, whether literary or plastic, has drawn its favourite themes from this religious sphere.

Shakespeare however, was 'without a philosophy and without a religion'. Thus he presents simply 'the successive empirical appearance of things, without any faith in their rational con-tinuity or completeness . . . the successive description of various passions and events.' Santayana comments 'Those of us, however . . . who think that both human reason and human imagination require a certain totality in our views, and who feel that the most important thing in life is the lesson of it, and its relation to its own ideal, – we can hardly find in Shake-speare all that the highest poet could give. Fulness is not neces-sarily wholeness . . .' If Shakespeare had been a Christian, or a Pagan, or had offered a 'vague embodiment in some northern pantheon' of 'the material forces of Nature' then 'the various movements of events would have appeared as incidents in a larger drama to which they had at least some symbolic relation'.

Such traces of logical argument as can be glimpsed through the tangle of ideas are not hard to assess at their full value. San-tayana confuses the use of religious legends as themes in drama with the ability to offer 'a reasoned and unified rendering of life'. He suggests that an explicit declaration of general principles is an essential quality of the highest poetry, but offers nothing in support of this except assertion. When he says that any system is better than none, that however erroneous a poet's ideas of life as a whole they will, as long as they are sufficiently compre-hensive and sufficiently apparent in his work, confer the essential imaginative power which Shakespeare lacked, it is hard to believe that he is serious, or that he does not see that his arguments justify the deepest dulness and insipidity provided only that they are exercised on sufficiently large topics. Finally his conclusion that, since Shakespeare does not make any explicit statement about the nature of cosmic forces, the events of his plays are not related to anything larger than themselves indicates that Santayana had never seen Shakespeare acted or, if he had, had utterly failed to understand the nature of drama, more particularly of poetic drama [37].

I have dealt at length with this unhelpful essay because it brings out very clearly a primary defect in Santayana's approach to Browning – his inability to understand in the most elementary way Browning's use of the dramatic form. He says of the poet:

> When his heroes are blinded by passion and warped by circumstance, as they almost always are, he does not describe that fact from the vantage-ground of the intellect and invite us to look at it from that point of view. On the contrary, his art is all self-expression or satire. For the most part his hero . . . is himself; not appearing . . . *in puris naturalibus*, but masked in all sorts of historical and romantic finery . . . The impulsive utterances and the crudities of most of the speakers are passionately adopted by the poet as his own.

I cannot offer any explanation of the phrase 'self-expression or satire'. The rest of the argument, as far as I understand it, depends upon stating the facts wrongly. As I have shown in Chapter 2, there are some of Browning's poems in which he may be taken to be speaking in his own person, and there are some in which he is speaking dramatically: there are very few poems of the first kind and a very large number of the second. Santayana makes the fundamental critical error of supposing that all the poems are of the same kind. He thus erroneously concludes that Browning never takes a detached view of any of his creations. This is particularly confusing as he has complained earlier in the essay of Browning's 'didactic vein' and his 'habit of judging the spectacle he evoked'. We are told that Browning 'allowed his own temperament and opinions to vitiate his representation of life'.

This is a description of Browning which is rather more recognizable, but it is difficult to see why Santayana supposes that it constitutes a damning criticism. Having censured Shakespeare for not suggesting in his works his view of the world he now censures Browning for offering his own interpretation of events. What, we may ask, does Mr Santayana expect of the dramatist? The only answer he offers is implied rather than stated in another disparaging remark about Browning. 'He had not attained, in studying the beauty of things, that detachment of the phenomenon, that love of form for its own sake, which is the secret of contemplative satisfaction.' If this gelid precept is in fact Santayana's 'secret' it is not surprising that he finds deficiencies in Shakespeare and Browning, both of whom valued the dramatic form for what it could express and not for its own sake, thought more highly of truth than of the importance of subscribing to a generalized cosmic system regardless of its truth or falsity, and understood perfectly the dramatist's art of embodying the eternal in the phenomenal.

The same narrowness and frigidity which we have remarked in Santayana's views on the drama mark his ideas of what the poet should do. Once again they have to be inferred from a criticism of Browning, in whose work 'there is never anything largely composed in the spirit of pure beauty, nothing devotedly finished, nothing simple and truly just'. It is a nice point whether it is harder to think of any poets who have complied with this prescription or to think of anybody who would willingly read their poetry. Santayana, as we have seen, speaks respectfully of 'the real masters of passion and imagination', and says that 'they began with that crude emotion with which Browning ends; they lived it down, they exalted it by thought, they extracted the pure gold of it in a long purgation of discipline and suffering.' (It is difficult to repress the memory of that master of restraint, Wackford Squeers, and his equally austere advice, 'Subdue your appetites, my dears, and you've conquered human natur.')

Thus as a complement to his ideas of drama and poetry Santayana offers his notion of love. For a third time we must extract his own opinions from a negative criticism of Browning. As depicted by Browning love 'never rises into contemplation . . . it always remains a passion; it always remains a personal impulse, a hypnotization, with another person for its object or its cause.' We may comment on this that there is no reason to suppose that contemplation is necessarily more valuable than passion. One might speak with equal accuracy of love *declining* into contemplation. Moreover the criticism as a whole is absurdly inapposite to Browning. Generations of critics, Miss Sherwood among them, have examined the extraordinary way in which Browning has used love, the mundane kind of love 'with another person for its object' which earns Santayana's prim reprimand, as the foundation of an imaginative picture of man's nature and his place in the Universe.

However it is not to be denied that in a few poems Browning expresses, with apparent approval, the emotions of people in a state of violent passion, and that there is no suggestion that these emotions have a value beyond themselves. The minute kernel of useful criticism to be extracted from Santayana's essay is the observation that from one point of view these are the least satisfactory of Browning's love poems. Santayana offers five quotations in support of this point. The second is a composite of two stanzas of *Love Among the Ruins*, a poem which requires no defence from me [38]. The third and fourth are from *In A Gondola*, and effectively constitute Santayana's case. One must admit that if all Browning were like that, instead of only one poem, then much of what Santayana says about his love poetry would be justified. The first and fifth quotations are both from the same speech near the beginning of *In a Balcony*, where Norbert is describing the first feelings of his love for Constance and then his motives for serving the queen. Santayana declares, 'Browning unmistakably adopts them as expressing his own highest intuitions.' Setting aside the dramatic nature of *In A Balcony*, which one would suppose obvious enough to strike even Santayana, if only typographically, we need look no further than Norbert's next speech to see that Browning does not leave him at the initial stage of simple passionate desire:

> Set free my love, and see what love can do
> Shown in my life – what work will spring from that!
> The world is used to have its business done
> On other grounds, find great effects produced
> For power's sake, fame's sake, motives in man's mouth.
> So, good: but let my low ground shame their high!
> Truth is the strong thing. Let man's life be true!
> And love's the truth of mine.

The piece is, of course, essentially theatrical: its justification is its climax, when Norbert says

> You and I –
> Why care by what meanders we are here
> I' the centre of the labyrinth? Men have died
> Trying to find this place, which we have found. [39]

Santayana is right, I think, to speak of this as 'intense, voluminous emotion' and 'sudden over-whelming self-surrender'. Even
when it finds its most splendid expression in the works of
Webster and Ford it is not perhaps a very lofty ideal of life, but
it becomes warmly attractive when Santayana compares it unfavourably with a 'a life of rational worship, of an austere and
impersonal religion, by which the fire of love kindled for a
moment by the sight of some creature, was put, as it were, into a
censer, to burn incense before every image of the Highest Good.'
Love of this kind, in which emotion is converted to a kind of anti-
septic pastille, is not, one must admit, to be found in Browning.

The final judgement on Santayana's account of Browning's
love poems can be passed only by someone who bears in mind
not merely *In A Gondola* and *In A Balcony* but the whole range
of his work from *Pippa Passes* and *Two in the Campagna* through
Andrea del Sarto, *One Word More*, *James Lee's Wife*, *The Ring
and the Book*, and the long poems of the 1870s, to the glowing
lyrics of *Asolando*.[1] A reader who has these poems in his mind
and heart will know whether to accept Santayana's verdict that
'the love he describes has no wings; it issues in nothing', or
James's conclusion that Browning's 'treatment of the special
relation between man and woman' is 'a complete and splendid
picture of the matter, which somehow places it at the same time
in the region of conduct and responsibility'.

Whenever we confront Santayana's vague generalizations
with what Browning actually wrote they lose their lofty im-
pressiveness and appear simply untrue.[2] For example, he says
'Browning's philosophy of life and habit of imagination do not
require the support of any metaphysical theory', a statement
whose hollowness is at once evident when we recall Browning's
patient attempts to discover whether 'metaphysical theory' as

---

[1] Santayana needed to look no further than *Time's Revenges* to see that Browning
was perfectly well aware that passion could be over-indulged and that such over-
indulgence was destructive of the personality.

[2] It is not, I think, possible to decide from the essay whether these false statements
are deliberate or due to incompetence, but see *Bishop Blougram's Apology*, 404–406.

such had any significance, attempts which spanned the last thirty years of his life and produced poems such as *Fifine at the Fair* and *La Saisiaz*. Ignoring these poems and, for instance, *Christmas-Eve and Easter-Day*, Santayana can write that Browning's faith is 'a matter of pure lustiness and inebriation'. It is plain that he has either not read or not understood the many poems in which Browning debates his faith with himself, showing incidentally that he understands the *nature* of belief a good deal more clearly than Santayana. Again when we read that to Browning 'the exercise of energy is the absolute good, irrespective of motives or consequences' we naturally ask where we are to find the evidence for this remarkable generalization, but we shall not be given the answer in Santayana's essay. Santayana speaks of Browning's concept of the 'Soul' as an impulse conscious of 'a certain vague sympathy with wind and cloud', a phrase which will mystify those who have read his poetry. Possibly Santayana had some other writer in mind here; possibly he just felt that anyone as uncouth as Browning was probably a sort of pantheist as well.

Again Santayana says that Browning's conception of con-tinued life is 'that we are all to live indefinitely, that all our faults can be turned to good, all our unfinished business settled, and that therefore there is time for anything we like in this world and for all we need in the other . . . He gave, as he would probably have said, a filling to the empty Christian immortality by making every man busy in it about many things.' If we challenge this large statement and ask Santayana how he recon-ciles it with, for example, the speech of the Fisc (*The Ring and the Book*, IX, 1160–67)[1] or with the following stanzas from *Old Pictures in Florence*:

[1] The Fisc imagines how agreeable it would be if all men took every quarrel to Law:

> No foolish brawling murders any more!
> Peace for the household, practice for the Fisc,
> And plenty for the exchequer of my lords!
> Too much to hope, in this world: in the next,
> Who knows? Since, why should sit the Twelve enthroned
> To judge the tribes, unless the tribes be judged?
> And 't is impossible but offences come:
> So, all 's one lawsuit, all one long leet-day!

Browning, of course, rejects this self-centred idea of the after-life.

There's a fancy some lean to and others hate –
　　That, when this life is ended, begins
New work for the soul in another state,
　　Where it strives and gets weary, loses and wins:
Where the strong and the weak, this world's congeries,
　　Repeat in large what they practised in small,
Through life after life in unlimited series;
　　Only the scale's to be changed, that's all.

Yet I hardly know. When a soul has seen
　　By the means of Evil that Good is best,
And, through earth and its noise, what is heaven's serene, –
　　When our faith in the same has stood the test –
Why, the child grown man, you burn the rod,
　　The uses of labour are surely done;
There remaineth a rest for the people of God:
　　And I have had troubles enough, for one. (XXI–XXII)

all that is given by way of reply is, 'It is the temperament . . .
that speaks; we may brush aside as unsubstantial, and even as
distorting, the web of arguments and theories which it has spun
out of itself.' In other words, Santayana is really saying, 'Please
do not worry about what Browning actually wrote: we know
what sort of vulgarian he must have been, so let us pay attention
to what he must have wanted to say but didn't.' What worries
here is not the critic's looseness of intellect, but the way in which,
to use a phrase of Santayana's own, he 'cloaks irrationality in
sanctimony', and reproaches Browning in the name of a high-
minded asceticism while unscrupulously distorting the evidence.

One might continue multiplying examples, especially from the
last few pitiful pages of Santayana's jerry-building. He mentions
or quotes with fair accuracy nine poems, mostly short, and two
plays, and gives no indication at any point that his acquaintance
with Browning extends beyond this meagre body, though it
seems not unlikely that he had read Sir Henry Jones's book on
Browning. Yet he does not hesitate to make the widest possible
general statements about the whole compass of Browning's
work: seldom has so pompous a mausoleum been erected on such
inadequate foundations.

This is the basic fallacy of Santayana's procedure: the basic
fallacy of his approach to literature in general is well brought out
by one of his most recent editors, Mr. Irving Singer. He writes:

The trouble with Santayana's theory of idealisation is that it seems to minimise the importance of truth. Idealisations do not tell us how things are, but how they ought to be, or how the 'heart's desire' would like them to be. If aesthetic excellence is primarily determined by idealisation, art is treated as wish fulfillment more than anything else. As long as we concern ourselves with the artist's idealisation, we are not especially interested in what he tells us about the world: what matters most is his dream of perfection, his prophetic blueprint . . . Santayana never faces up to the possibility that *a priori* there is no reason to favor idealisation over realism; and he fails to see how this preferred kind of harmonization distorts much of what is generally considered to be essential in both poetry and religion. [40]

Ultimately Santayana is led not only to renounce the real in favour of the ideal but to reject every manifestation of life.[1] This he does in the name of 'traditional culture, aesthetic and moral', of 'the habits of a cultivated mind', of 'purity and distinction', and his most powerful instruments are the words 'crude' and 'vulgar'. There is a certain class of mind which is satisfied that it has said all that is necessary about a work of art when it has once affixed the label 'vulgarity'. This is the real burden of Santayana's complaint against Browning, and it is not hard to see why he makes it. There is something about Browning which is pulsing with crude energy, an animal vigour which appears at once if we turn to, say, *Sludge* after reading, say, *Empedocles*. The quality which disconcerts Santayana is there without doubt, but he is in error to suppose that its presence reduces Browning's poetry to the level of a volcanic eruption. His error arises from his inability to understand the simple propositions that poetry is multiform, that every poet, however eccentric, has his own contribution to make, and that barbarism is not the only alternative to idealization.

Conclusion

It is clear that Santayana was continuing, though at a far remove and on an infinitely lower level, the line of criticism initiated by

[1] In Browning's heaven there would be an infinity of different drinks, each with a distinctive taste; in Santayana's heaven there would be only one drink, called 'Beverage', which would have all the virtues of cocoa, burgundy, ginger-beer and Guinness without any of their characteristics.

Matthew Arnold. They both appealed ultimately to the authority of the literature of Classical Greece, they both spoke in the name of 'culture', they both condemned the Philistine pragmatism of the Victorian age, and they both deplored Browning's failure to reject 'the world's multitudinousness' in favour of 'an Idea of the world'. Bagehot similarly censured Browning for confronting his readers with 'a sort of quarry of ideas' instead of offering 'pure poetry', which presents an ideal perfection. James in turn accepts and elaborates the criticism that Browning offered only 'the raw materials of truth, the unthreshed harvest of reality', but he was at least aware of what Browning was trying to do in his dramatic presentations of the world. When he draws attention to what he considers Browning's artistic failures in his longer poems his criticism is more specific than Santayana's and Bagehot's and thus more damaging.

When it is remembered that Sir Henry Jones's book appeared in 1891, it will be seen that a remarkable number of the most celebrated critics of Browning before 1914 were hostile. The favourable critics were on the whole less influential. Percy Lubbock's extended review of the Centenary edition in 1912 is the most notable exception: Milsand appeared only in French, Buxton Forman wrote only one article, which did not apparently attract much attention, and G. K. Chesterton's *Robert Browning*, published in 1903 in the English Men of Letters series, though full of clever arguments, ingenious paradoxes, and perspicacious analysis, was unable to halt the decline in Browning's reputation, perhaps because it was felt to be brilliant and therefore unsound.

Although the London Browning Society met for the last time in 1892, the faithful continued to worship in the provinces and in America. But it soon became plain that Browning's claims to immortality as a *guru* were not to last long: indeed it is fair to say that those who treated him simply as a prophet did much to submerge him as a poet. Now the task of interpreting Browning has passed into other hands, more skilled perhaps, but certainly less sympathetic.

In my final chapter I review briefly some of the tasks which still await the world of Browning scholarship.

❖ 13 ❖

After the Browning Society – What?
or Landmarks in the Vacuum

We understand that Mr Browning was not consulted in the Foundation of the Society in London which bears his name, and that it does
not in any way meet with his approval. *The Critic*, 22 October 1881

> There's a Me Society down at Cambridge,
> Where my works, *cum notis variorum*,
> Are talked about . . . J. K. STEPHEN, *Of R.B.*

. . . There lay before me an array of literary material, about which
a question had arisen. The material was that of a critical anthology,
setting out some typical comments upon the chief Romantic poets,
and the two most prominent Victorians, Tennyson and Browning.
The critiques on each poet were to be displayed in chronological
order, from the contemporary reviews up to the present day . . .
This general plan, which had sufficed for the production of an earlier
volume of the same kind, proved to be more or less extendible to this
later period, save that no criticism upon Browning later than 1912
had been found – none, at least, that seemed to my serious editorial
eye to merit inclusion. . . . There was a kind of vacuum in criticism
here.   HUGH SYKES DAVIES, *Browning and the Modern Novel*[1]

I

Browning's own feelings about the Browning Society were
mixed. He wrote to Miss E. Dickinson West on 12 November,
1881:

> I will tell you how I feel about the Society. It was instituted without
> my knowledge, and when knowledge was, I do not think that ac-

[1] The St John's College Cambridge Lecture 1961–2 delivered at the University of
Hull, 16 February 1962 (University of Hull Publications, 1962, p. 3).

quiescence had need of being asked for. I write poems that they may be read, and – fifty years now – people said they were unintelligible. If other people, in the fulness of days, reply 'we understand them, and will show that you may, if you will be at the pains,' I should think it ungracious indeed to open my mouth for the first time on the matter with 'Pray let the other people alone in their protested ignorance' . . . As for Dr. Furnivall, I am altogether astonished at his caring about me at all. I suspect it is a late discovery with him, like that of Fontenelle when, chancing upon some out-of-the-way literature, he went about asking everybody 'Do you know Habbakuk? He's a genius!' [1]

In his letters to Furnivall he answers with patience the manifold detailed inquiries, and expresses with apparent sincerity his appreciation of the work of the Society. It is perhaps not wrong to detect that he is more gratified by the honour which the members are paying him than convinced that their labours are necessary or beneficial.

His opinions are probably most clearly expressed in his letter to Edmund Yates, written not long after the Society was founded:

The Browning Society, I need not say, as well as Browning himself, are fair game for criticism. I had no more to do with the founding it than the babe unborn; and as Wilkes was no Wilkeite, I am quite other than a Browningite. But I cannot wish harm to a society . . . busied about my books so disinterestedly . . . That there is a grotesque side to the thing is certain; but I have been surprised and touched by what cannot but have been well intentioned, I think. [2]

Once the London Browning Society and the numerous provincial societies were established the poet appears to have treated them with courteous reserve, declining for example to look through uncorrected proofs of the proceedings of the London Society [3], but occasionally visiting the smaller societies.

Max Beerbohm's celebrated caricature *Robert Browning, taking tea with the Browning Society* captures exactly this mixture of enjoyment and amusement. John Rothenstein, in his introduction to the King Penguin edition of *The Poets' Corner* (1943) observes that 'no contrast recurs so frequently in Max's work as that between the full-blooded, sagacious and realistic person on the one hand, and on the other the desiccated, predominantly cerebral person', and rightly cites as an example the contrast in this drawing 'between the abounding vitality of Browning and the twittering pedantry of his disciples.'[1] The same point is brought out in one of the best Browning stories. E. F. Benson records how Browning took tea at Newnham with some members of the Cambridge Browning Society and was solemnly crowned with a wreath of roses.

> So there he sat, bland and ruddy, and slightly buttery from the muffins, with the crown of pink roses laid upon his white locks, and looking like a lamb decked for sacrifice . . . When tea was done he was asked to fulfil his gracious promise and read . . . What he chose was *A Serenade at the Villa*, and the young ladies (since there were not enough chairs) grouped themselves gracefully on the floor round those revered feet. He began reading from the book, but he found he knew the poem by heart and closed it.
>
> > When the firefly hides its spot (said Mr Browning)
> > And the garden voices fail,
> > In the darkness thick and hot –
>
> And just then he raised his eyes and saw in the mirror the image of himself crowned with pink roses. He broke into a peal of the most jovial laughter. 'My dear young ladies,' he said, 'Shall I not read *The Patriot* instead? "It was roses, roses all the way".'[2]

While Browning, according to Mrs Orr [4], did not read with much critical interest the Society's studies of his poetry, the general public, again according to Mrs Orr [5], derived considerable benefit from them.

This is not the place to describe the proliferation of the Browning societies in Britain and America or to offer an account of their contribution to the understanding of Browning's poems. The weaknesses of the most famous, the London Browning Society, were obvious: many of its members in its brief career commented on its lack of balance. Bernard Shaw, who was a member for six years, a member of the executive committee for two, and a regular contributor to the debates, seems to have taken a strongly critical line. Some of his criticism was specific, as when he attacked with some bitterness Oldham's paper on Browning,

---

[1] See Frontispiece. For some reason Mrs Miller did not reproduce the drawing in her book, *Robert Browning: A Portrait*.

[2] E. F. Benson, *As We Were* (1930), Ch. VII. Mrs Miller quoted this story, but omitted Browning's last remark. This has the effect of making him appear to accept uncritically the adulation of his disciples.

concluding with the soothing observation that 'he was sorry if his remarks had been almost uniformly abusive, and could only say that the writer of the paper richly deserved it.' Sometimes his comments were more generally pertinent, as when he observed that the Society seldom dealt with art in Browning, or philosophy, or history, or alchemy. 'Mr Gonner was perfectly right in saying that no matter what paper they had before them, in the discussion they always got into Browning's optimistic theology . . . if they could not get papers on any other subjects it showed that the Society had done its work' [6].

Shaw here expresses one of the most frequent objections to the London Society. Ever since the Rev. J. Kirkman in his Introductory Address to the first meeting of the Society declared that just as Shakespeare was humanity so was Browning religion, the temptation to discuss Browning as seer instead of as maker was strong. The prospectus of the Society, July 1881, contained the following significant sentence: 'Browning's themes are the development of Souls, the analysis of Minds. Art, Religion, Love, the relation of Man and Nature to God, of Man to Man and Woman, the Life past, present, and to come.' The capital letters are especially ominous.

It is my impression, based on no very profound study of the material, that the American societies on the whole avoided this particular hazard. Certainly, when the news of the imminent closing of the London Society reached America the comments in *Poet-Lore* were acute.[1] The editors observed that there are three successive phases of Browning study. First, the elucidation of obscurities. Secondly, the discovery that Browning is a philosopher, which leads to a spate of papers either on Browning as a religious teacher, or on Browning's relation to Science. Finally the student discovers the rareness of Browning's dramatic qualities. The editors comment tartly 'The London Society has

[1] In a most interesting passage written earlier in 1891 the editors, Charlotte Porter and Helen A. Clarke, had suggested that one important feature of the Browning Societies was that they ushered in an intellectual democracy, where all were free to contribute to the discussion, as opposed to intellectual domination by critics, who lectured down to a passive audience. The implication is that only Browning could effect this change, since he wrote 'a new kind of song', which the ordinary man could approach on equal terms with the critic, and since his poems dealt with the 'ethical, religious and philosophical problems which enter so deeply into modern society'. See *Poet-Lore*, III (1891), pp. 43–44.

hardly got beyond the second stage, and its outlook has in consequence been somewhat circumscribed' [7].

The London Browning Society was dissolved in 1892.[1] By some this was taken as an admission of failure, but even before the society was founded, it had been clearly envisaged that its initial purposes might be accomplished in a fairly short time. The American societies, notably in Philadelphia and Boston, continued to flourish,[2] but the London Society, short-lived though it was, remains in the public mind as *the* Browning Society, and by its performance and by its publications alone Browning Societies are estimated in the popular mind. In assessing its value to Browning studies it is, I think, important not to lay too much stress on the published papers of the society. By and large they are no longer of value; but when we say this, however, we must remember that they are now eighty or ninety years out of date, and very little critical writing can reasonably be expected to survive as long as that. Further, a careful study of the papers shows that a fair proportion were not concerned with Browning's Christian optimism; perhaps less than a third of the principal papers dealt with this as a major topic. No doubt the discussions, as Shaw said, tended to gravitate towards Browning's theology, but the papers themselves took a reasonably wide field, ranging from 'The Moorish front to the Duomo in *Luria*' to 'How Browning Strikes a Scandinavian'. Among them one may find papers which are still useful and interesting, notably J. B. Bury's paper on Browning's Philosophy: in addition there is a certain amount of useful, if rather low-geared, expository criticism of which the Rev. J. H. Bulkeley on *James Lee's Wife* is a good example [8].

[1] The Girton Browning Society was wound up in 1886 and the funds (2s. 2d.) spent on chocolate creams, an incident which gave rise to the best of Browning parodies *A Girtonian Funeral*. See *Journal of Education*, 1 May 1886 (n.s. VIII), pp. 207–8; also in *A Century of Parody*, ed. W. Jerrold and R. M. Leonard (London, 1913). According to Robert Sidney (*Saturday Review*, CXIII, 11 May 1912) Browning commented, 'I'm perfectly sure that if the chocolates were good, they would be much better for them than my sour stuff.'

[2] There was also a Browning Club at Meadville called 'Women and Roses' 'because the members were all women, and because roses almost invariably grace the presence of their meetings', *Poet-Lore*, III (1891), p. 539. According to Edward J. McAleer in *Learned Lady* (Harvard U.P., 1966), p. 122, there were fourteen Browning Societies still active in the United States at the time he wrote, that is presumably in 1964.

Although the members of the Browning Society very sensibly devoted a large part of their energies to the elucidation of the major poems and did this as well as they could, one must, I think, accept the popular view that most of their published proceedings are no longer of interest. Perhaps the major advance in criticism of the last seventy years is the development in critical techniques and vocabulary which gives the modern critic, if he wishes to use it, so much more power than his predecessors to discuss a complex and vital work of art without having to reduce it first to a flat, lifeless simplification; again and again in the Browning Society's papers the overwhelming impression is one of sheer immaturity, as the distinguished contributors parade their pallid simulacra of the poems they are discussing, like schoolchildren whose essays on *Romeo and Juliet* seem adequate, but only until you compare them with the play itself. I don't think I am here expressing the habitual contempt of the professional for the amateur – a particularly silly contempt, since if the professional's work is to have any tangible product at all it must be the creation of a large body of enthusiastic non-professionals – but rather pointing to a wide-spread weakness in Victorian criticism, which we are right to describe as 'old-fashioned'.

I should like, however, to draw attention to one side of the Browning Society's work which is far from contemptible. Dr Berdoe in his Introduction to *Browning Studies* makes the following claim for the achievements of the London Browning Society in its twelve years of active life.

> We accomplished however all we set out to do. We had acted all the really actable plays, had published thirteen volumes of papers and discussions, with many beautiful photographs of pictures referred to in the poems. Mrs. Sutherland Orr had published her useful Handbook to the works of the poet; Mr. Nettleship had written his invaluable Essays; Miss Hickey had contributed her 'Notes on Strafford'; Mr. Arthur Symons had given us his 'Introduction to the Study of Browning'; Miss Wilson and Miss Defries had each published her *Primer of Browning* and the present writer his *Browning Cyclopædia*, and written the 'Biographical and Historical Notes' to the poet's complete works; all this was the direct outcome of the Society's activity. But beyond this, as due chiefly to the interest awakened in Browning's works by our efforts, an enormously increased demand arose for the poems themselves. Many volumes of essays and other explanatory works had helped to spread the light

and set thousands studying a poet now no longer neglected nor unloved by English people. All this would have come in time, Society or no Society; but it is certain that the time was greatly hastened in the twelve years of its existence. [9]

All this and more [10] was accomplished by 1900. I want, in the rest of this chapter, to compare with this the efforts of the present century to supply the necessary materials for the understanding and appreciation of Browning.

II

I should make it plain that I do not intend to provide in this section a *catalogue raisonné* of Browning literature since 1900. Those who want this should go to Professor Raymond's 'Browning Studies in England and America, 1910–1949' [11] or to the relevant part of *The Victorian Poets: a Guide to Research* [12]. The books and articles which I have found to be of especial value I have already mentioned in their place in the text. My main emphasis now is on what is still to be done and on the *lacunae* of Browning scholarship.

These can be most easily shown by quoting once more from the Introductory Address by the Rev. J. Kirkman to which reference has already been made. He suggests as among the future labours of the society: 'a separate treatment of special poems which need a key', 'treatises on his humour: his attitude towards science: the poems of *a class*, as *Music, Painting, Art*:', 'short introductions to such poems as hardly require a separate treatment, giving the "Argument" as it is called', 'a Lexicon of names, remote allusions, learned things fetched from somewhere in the universe where he has been, and other mortal foot hath ne'er or rarely been', and 'a *digest of Reviews*' in order to trace the course of Browning's popularity. These would all, Kirkman says, be 'real helps'.

It will be seen that some of these were furnished in the last century, while others are still to do. Berdoe's own *Cyclopaedia* and Mrs Orr's *Handbook* did something to provide the Lexicon and the arguments, though neither is especially thorough or helpful, and the work requires to be done again. Professor DeVane's *Handbook* (1935, 2nd ed. 1955) is of course the indispensable tool of every Browning scholar, consulted daily, and constantly to be trusted. As a guide to the circumstances of publication of each poem, its background, and its after-history it cannot be faulted: perhaps no other English poet is so well served. But it does not pretend to offer more than a minimum of explanatory comment. What is needed as a complement to DeVane is a revised and enlarged work of the kind of Mrs Orr's *Handbook*, in which the primary object is exposition [13].

More recent scholars can point also with some satisfaction to two extraordinarily useful compilations – the *Concordance* of 1924 [14] and the *Bibliography* of 1953 [15]. But the *Concordance* has been unobtainable for many years. Unless there is a re-issue, students of Browning can only hope to catch the eye of the editors of the admirable Cornell concordances. The *Bibliography* is invaluable: if it is regularly revised and brought up to date, as it has been in Litzinger and Knickerbocker's *The Browning Critics* (1965), it will do much to facilitate every kind of work on Browning.

These then are the indisputable achievements of the century, of a kind which the Browning Society would recognize. But apart from these the product is scanty indeed and, it is my impression, becoming scantier.

Perhaps the most obvious task is to present Browning's correspondence to the public in some coherent form. The 'Calendar of Letters' at the back of the *Bibliography* lists over 2,000 items, most of which have been published in some form or another. Apart from the large number scattered in books and magazines there are two main collections (one edited by T. L. Hood, the other by DeVane and Knickerbocker) of the poet's letters to various correspondents at different periods of his life. There are also several collections of Browning's letters to particular correspondents, such as Alfred Domett (letters dating from 1840 to 1846), Elizabeth Barrett (1845–6), her brother George (1861–89), W. W. Story and J. R. Lowell (1853–89), Isa Blagden (1857–72), Julia Wedgwood (1864–70), and Mrs Fitzgerald (1876–89).

In the introduction to their edition DeVane and Knickerbocker commented 'Perhaps the next step toward making accessible Browning's complete correspondence is the collecting and editing of all his letters printed separately in books and magazines. . . . It is obvious that the time is approaching, though it has not yet

arrived, when a complete and thoroughly edited collection of the
poet's letters can be made.' Perhaps they are right to say that the
time has not yet come, in the sense that there is always a reasonable chance that as the years pass a few fresh letters will come to
light. It seems to me, however, that a much stronger case can be
made out for acting now. It is true that simply to reprint and
annotate the items in the 'Calendar of Letters' might, as DeVane
and Knickerbocker imply, be premature, and it is true also that
many of the letters are of little or no intrinsic interest, but they
would at least provide a coherent and orderly body of biographical material and bring advantages greater than those to be obtained by delay. For to defer a full publication of the letters in
the hope of ultimately producing a definitive collection untouch-
able by the hand of time is, as DeVane and Knickerbocker admit,
to defer 'another desideratum of Browning scholarship: a full
and proportioned biography of the poet'. As they say, 'Until the
correspondence is fairly complete this latter task cannot be undertaken with assurance.'[1]

Griffin and Minchin's *Life* (1910, revised 1938) is at present
the standard biography, but, as has often been remarked, it is no
longer satisfactory. I am no very great believer in the value of
biographical studies of poets – they seem to me the province of
the historian rather than of the literary critic or man of letters –
but we have some letters of Browning and we have some facts
about his life, and it is plainly better to have a comprehensive
edition of the letters and a completely reliable *Life* than not to
have them. When they appear I do not think that they will change
the general critical opinion about Browning, or affect his unpopularity with the reading public. The one thing that might win
him new admirers would be a short selection from his letters.
Most people who have dipped into his correspondence have found
it extremely dull – either incomprehensible love-letters, or tart
reminders to his publisher or evasive notes declining to visit
Mrs Charles Skirrow. But occasionally Browning succeeds in

---

[1] There is news that Philip Kelley and Ronald Hudson have undertaken a definitive
edition of the Brownings' correspondence which may run to as many as thirty-two
volumes and is not expected to be complete before 1980. Presumably therefore the
definitive biography lies even further in the future: meanwhile Maisie Ward's
sympathetic study – *Robert Browning and His World* – will be read with pleasure
and satisfaction.

writing letters of general interest, notably when he is discussing literature. There his epistolary haste is subdued and his social affectations drop from him. Whether he is discussing his own poems or Miss Blagden's novels, *Enoch Arden* or the poems of the wretched John Baldwin Fosbroke he writes with the interest and directness of the professional. A small volume of these literary letters might do much to win Browning the respect of competent judges.

So far my survey of Browning studies has shown some deficiences but no actual *lacunae*. But when one turns to the literary, as opposed to the historical side of Browning scholarship there is a marked change. The most notable gap is the lack of a really sound edition of the poems. Work on a variorum edition has started in America, but at present the best that we can offer are Birrell (1915), Kenyon (1912), and the Florentine edition (1898).[1] None of them provides a textual apparatus, and though the Florentine edition has many annotations they seem invariably to leave the darker passages unilluminated. As I have suggested repeatedly in earlier chapters much of the 'difficulty' of Browning would vanish if editors explained concisely every allusion in the text, and the inexperienced reader could refer to the notes for guidance whenever the syntax became in the least involved. It is regarded as self-evident that Shakespeare, or Milton, or Wordsworth demands for full understanding careful study in an edition as helpful as modern scholarship can make it: it is a mistake to suppose that because Browning died only some eighty years ago his verse can be read precisely as if he had written in contemporary English for a modern audience.

III

My final point is the one indicated in the quotation from Hugh Sykes Davies which stands at the head of the chapter. Mr Davies deliberately overstates his case in order to emphasize his most startling conclusion, but in his anthology *The Poets and Their Critics* (2nd volume) he in fact offers no quotations from critics of Browning later than James and Lubbock, both in 1912. If this eloquent omission were left without comment one would

[1] 'Called the Florentine Edition in full levant, the Camberwell Edition in flexible leather on buckram' (*Bibliography*, p. 40).

suppose that it meant quite simply that for the last fifty years nobody had taken Browning seriously enough to bother to write about him, either to praise or blame, that Browning was in the same case as say, Montgomery or Tupper, a bestseller who had had his day and now interested no one. But of course there has been a steady volume of Browning criticism from 1912 onwards, as a glance at the *Bibliography* will show [16]. Mr Davies' complaint is, by implication, that it is all worthless, or at least that it does not provide the convenient compact estimation of the value of a poet (considered as a body of work) which he finds particularly significant. It will be clear that I do not find myself in entire agreement here. In the course of the book I have incurred (and, I hope, acknowledged) debts to many Browning scholars. Hardly a chapter could have been written without frequent recourse to previous work on the subject. The lack that I am conscious of, however, is not that of judgements on Browning's stature or on his total achievement so much as that of detailed studies of single poems.

In spite of the work of such acute critics as R. D. Altick, Isobel Armstrong, William Cadbury, Roma King, Robert Langbaum, R. E. Palmer, F. E. L. Priestley, W. O. Raymond, and Charlotte Watkins [17], to name only those to whom I feel particularly indebted, it is still true that Browning is least adequately served in precisely this matter of providing rational attempts to suggest the essential quality of specific poems, and true also that the general neglect of and indifference to Browning which this shows go far to confirm Mr Sykes Davies' dismal picture of Browning's reputation among the leaders of modern literary opinion.

Neglect and indifference are by their nature difficult to illustrate, but they may be inferred from an off-hand and unengaged treatment. For example, the admirable Penguin Books published in 1958 the sixth volume of the *Pelican Guide to English Literature* [18]. Different scholars contribute a chapter on the major figures. Browning, one is surprised and relieved to see, still has a chapter to himself – ten pages. It would be unkind to quote out of their context some of the general judgements on Browning which the author produces as if they were daring revaluations. In fact his observations on particular poems are virtually confined to the shorter early pieces, including a useful account of *Two in the Campagna*, which, however, takes up almost two pages. Not surprisingly he has to condense his account of Browning's larger works into sentences such as 'It was only a short step from *The Ring and The Book* to the tedious word-spinning of the poet's last twenty years', and to rely for his personal judgements on Mrs Miller and his critical judgements on James and Santayana. The volume also contains a general introduction to 'the literary scene' by G. D. Klingopoulos. In the three pages which can be spared for Browning this offers us Bagehot and Sir Henry Jones, a description of Browning as 'a Victorian Hemingway', a long quotation from *Amphibian* (silently omitting one stanza), the astonishing statement that 'Browning has few doubts about the sea of "passion" and "thought" in his monologues', and five stanzas from *Two in the Campagna*, a poem that many people must now consider to be of quite extraordinary importance. To complete the impression that neither the contributors nor the editor had the slightest interest in Browning, the chapter on the Pre-Raphaelites, by one of the white hopes of English criticism, W. W. Robson, quotes four lines from *The Statue and the Bust* and attributes them to *The Flight of the Duchess*.

Possibly the most severe blow to Browning's chances of serious critical attention in this century was the publication of F. R. Leavis's *New Bearings in English Poetry* [19], a book whose many glaring failures of judgement have not lessened the influence it deservedly exerts on the assessment of poetry since 1800. In the first chapter Dr Leavis offers a brisk knock-'em-down-and-drag-'em-out survey of the poets of the nineteenth century. 'Poetry, it was assumed, must be the direct expression of simple emotions, and these of a limited class: the tender, the exalted, the poignant, and, in general, the sympathetic.' (p. 9) 'Nineteenth-century poetry, we realize, was characteristically preoccupied with the creation of a dream-world.' (p. 10) 'Victorian poetry admits implicitly that the actual world is alien, recalcitrant and unpoetical, and that no protest is worth making except the protest of withdrawal.' (p. 15) Having thus analysed the poetry of seventy years, Leavis has to deal with Browning. He does so in a paragraph. It begins 'Where, it might be asked, does Browning come into these generalizations? His can hardly be described as a poetry of withdrawal. It belongs to the world he lives in, and he lives happily in the Victorian world with no sense of disharmony.' The last five words may make the thoughtful reader pause. But, accepting this for the moment, one is tempted to suppose that Browning is about to be admitted to the Pantheon, since he possesses the quality – living in the world – whose absence has damned all his contemporaries. Browning however fails on other counts:

> . . . It is too plain that Browning would have been less robust if he had been more sensitive and intelligent. He did indeed bring his living interests into his poetry but it is too plain that they are not the interests of an adult sensitive mind . . . He was a naïve romantic of love and action on the waking plane . . . [He was] unaware of disharmonies because for him there were none or, rather, only such as were enough to exhilarate, to give him a joyous sense of physical vitality. It is possible to consider him as a philosophical or psychological poet only by confusing intelligence with delight in the exercise of certain grosser cerebral muscles. When he is a poet he is concerned merely with simple emotions and sentiments . . . So inferior a mind and spirit as Browning's could not provide the impulse needed to bring back into poetry the adult intelligence.
> (pp. 19–20)

One point in this evaluation seems to me to be worth serious consideration – the suggestion that Browning writes poetry only when he is at his simplest. I do not think that is is true, but I can imagine a plausible case being made for it, although perhaps only at the cost of conceding that *all* great poetry is essentially simple. The rest of what Leavis has to say is of two kinds. Part of it is mere error. To say that Browning was 'unaware of disharmonies' is to disclose that one has never in any sense read *La Saisiaz* or *Fifine at the Fair*, to name only the most obvious refuting cases. To call Browning 'a naïve romantic of love and action' is to disclose that one has never in any real sense read his love poems, or even considered what it means to call a poet a 'romantic'. It is to allow a recollection of that distinguished contributor to *Scrutiny*, George Santayana, to serve instead of a reading of Browning. To say that Browning's interests are not the interests of 'the adult sensitive mind' suggests that 'the adult sensitive mind' must be remarkably empty.[1]

---

[1] The whole passage calls to mind a letter of Browning's to Furnivall, which begins: 'I am beginning to enjoy the results of the institution of the "Society" . . .

The remainder of Leavis's dismissal of Browning hinges on his use of the word 'intelligence', especially as qualified by its association with 'sensitive' or 'sensibility'. Leavis is noted for the exactness of his discriminations, and it is worth some effort to discover what he means here. Obviously 'intelligence' is a virtue in a poet. But what precisely does it denote? Clearly it cannot mean mere 'cleverness', since in the next paragraph Meredith's 'cleverness' is not enough to protect him from a side-swipe into oblivion. There is a possible clue earlier in the chapter (p. 9), when Leavis commends 'Wit, play of intellect, stress of cerebral muscle.' If we compare this passage, where 'stress of cerebral muscle' is put forward as a good in itself, with the paragraph on Browning, where 'intelligence' is carefully distinguished from 'delight in the exercise of certain grosser cerebral muscles', it appears that the crucial point is the word 'grosser'. This in turn suggests that 'intelligence' for Leavis is of two kinds; one of a lower order, such as is useful only for algebra, metaphysics, logical thought, consecutive reasoning and such crude processes; the other operating in a rarer atmosphere. Browning may be granted the first, but, lacking the second, cannot be considered a poet of any importance. To assess this statement we must see whether the first part is true of Browning and whether the second part means anything at all.

It is not easy to understand what Dr Leavis means by 'a philosophical or psychological poet' if he denies the title to Browning. For the 1950 edition of the book Leavis wrote a concluding chapter in which he offers an account of the importance of T. S. Eliot, who is, he says,

> a much greater and more significant poet than his Anglo-Catholic admirers make him. He is also more disturbing. His religious poetry, read for what it is, disturbs radically, by the depth and subtlety of its analysis: it explores the nature of believing, and the nature of conceptual thought; in relation, especially, to religious dogma. Its extreme continence (defeating the 'lethargy of habit') in the use of conceptual currency goes with an extreme continence of affirmation.

in the evident annoyance it is giving my dear old critics who have gone on gibing and gibbering at me time out of mind. If these worthies could point to a single performance in which they had themselves "read and studied" anything of mine, far less induced others to do so, there might be a reason for their wrath . . .'
Letter of 12 January 1882 (Hood/Wise 1882:1, p. 207).

I cannot attach any meaning to the last sentence I have quoted, but include it in case others find it helpful. The same applies to the phrase 'read for what it is'.

However difficult it is to decide what Leavis means, one thing is plain – the note of awe with which he records that Eliot's poetry 'explores the nature of believing, and the nature of conceptual thought; in relation, especially, to religious dogma'. Yet, as I have shown in earlier chapters, a major if not the dominant theme of Browning's poetry from *Christmas-Eve and Easter-Day* in 1850 to the day of his death was precisely this relation between knowing, thinking and believing. I intend no dispraise of Eliot's poetry when I say that to me Browning's exploration of this territory seems the more penetrating and the more comprehensive.

If Dr Leavis still maintains that Browning is lacking in 'intelligence', he can only defend his position, as far as I can see, by attaching to 'intelligence' a meaning quite distinct from 'intellectual power or capacity', a meaning in fact so general that the term becomes a kind of imprecise honorific synonym for 'literary excellence'. That the word has some such vague approbatory associations seems likely if we observe its use elsewhere in Leavis's criticism.

Probably the most celebrated *locus* is the last paragraph of his essay, 'The Irony of Swift'. After an essay devoted to an account of Swift Leavis concludes, 'We shall not find Swift remarkable for intelligence if we think of Blake.' It seems then that we shall be able to determine fairly easily what Leavis means by 'intelligence' if we discover the quality in which Swift was most notably excelled by Blake, a difficult task, but well worth the effort when we are dealing with so meticulous a critic.

Unfortunately we meet with a check when we examine the essay on Swift, of which the central feature is an analysis of Section IX of *A Tale of A Tub*. This is, by general consent, the vital section of the book: to fail to grasp its drift is to fail to understand Swift's entire strategy. Yet Leavis's account takes at its face value Swift's ironic praise of credulity, that 'peaceful possession of the mind': hence Leavis can say, 'That Swift feels the strongest animus against "curiosity" is now beyond all doubt.' Leavis proceeds in tranquil innocence of the operation of

Swift's satire, and when he reaches the last sentence of the paragraph – 'This is the sublime and refined point of felicity called
the possession of being well-deceived, the serene peaceful state
of being a fool among knaves' – he is understandably astonished
and annoyed at what he takes to be a sudden reversal of Swift's
attitude and can only comment 'What is left? . . . The positives
disappear.' Assuming as he does that Swift has nothing to say in
this passage, or rather that he says two things which cancel each
other out, Leavis can write without misgiving such sentences as
'In his use of negative materials – negative emotions and attitudes – . . . the aim is always destructive', or 'Swift's way of
demonstrating his superiority is to destroy . . .' or 'We have,
then, in his writings probably the most remarkable expression
of negative feelings and attitudes that literature can offer – the
spectacle of creative powers (the paradoxical description seems
right) exhibited consistently in negation and rejection.' or '. . .
He shared the shallowest complacencies of Augustan common
sense: his irony might destroy these, but there is no conscious
criticism.'

It is perhaps uncharitable to press too hard for the definition
of 'intelligence' which emerges from this essay: but presumably
the quality in which Leavis, after his reading of *A Tale of A Tub*,
finds Swift deficient is curiosity, the *need* to exercise the reason,
however disagreeable its discoveries. But when we go to Leavis's
account of Blake to find the quality which is to be set against this,
the difficulty is still not completely resolved. The clearest statement of what Leavis particularly admires in Blake is on p. 186
in the essay on 'Literature and Society'. The passage runs, 'Blake
in his successful work says implicitly "It is I who see and feel.
I see only what I see and feel only what I feel. My experience is
mine, and in its specific quality lies its significance." ' If we
assume that Leavis is here referring to an expression in the previous paragraph in which he speaks of 'the deeper sources of
originality, the creative springs in the individually experiencing
mind' we can come, I think, as near as the evidence will take us
to understanding what Leavis means by 'intelligence'. The
quality in which Leavis finds Swift deficient and Blake strong
is reliance on the evidence of the senses. Swift takes refuge
in 'the shallowest complacencies of Augustan common sense':
Blake on the other hand insists on the uniqueness of individual

experience as the primary material of all knowledge and all poetry.[1]

If we take the trouble to weigh Leavis's terminology and to address ourselves earnestly to elucidating his meaning we can only arrive, I think, at a definition of 'intelligence' which is clearly distinguished from the normal use of the word in the way in which I have suggested. We find some confirmation of this, for if the definition is applied to the paragraph of Browning which prompted the inquiry, it can be connected at once with a sentence which I did not quote earlier – 'If he [Browning] lived in the Victorian world, it was only as *l'homme moyen sensuel* might live there.' Browning, presumably, like Swift, is primarily found wanting as 'an individually experiencing mind'. But just as Dr Leavis's account of Swift is based on an eccentric, if not simply erroneous, interpretation of the evidence, so his account of Browning proves extremely difficult to accommodate to the poet's actual works. I have laboured the point in this book, and it is in any case a commonplace of criticism, that Browning, foremost among our poets, is perpetually conscious of the nature of individual experience and, I may add, of its limitations. This is true of his major works and equally true of comparatively unimportant books like *Ferishtah's Fancies*. I do not think that anybody who has read Browning's poems can be unaware of this. It is not hard therefore for a reader reasonably well acquainted with Browning to reject as groundless the main part of Leavis's criticism.

Many others however, trusting in Dr Leavis's well-founded

---

[1] Even when Leavis addresses himself directly to this point he is not easy to follow. 'When I mentioned [the affinities between Lawrence and Blake], I was thinking of the vital intelligence, unthwarted by emotional disorders and divisions in the psyche, that makes [Blake] (as I have suggested in an analysis of Swift's irony) the antithesis of Swift.' *D. H. Lawrence: Novelist* (London, 1955), p. 12. The idea of intelligence as the quality which makes for a healthy psychic life is repeated later in the book, 'Lawrence makes plain that without proper use of intelligence there can be no solution of the problems of mental, emotional and spiritual health. . . . The power of recognizing justly the relation of idea and will to spontaneous life, of using the conscious mind for the attainment of "spontaneous-creative fulness of being" is intelligence.' (p. 310.) When we notice that in *Two Cultures?* (p. 26) 'vital intelligence' is described as being a characteristic of the Bushman and the Indian peasant, we must, I think, conclude that Leavis uses the word in various private senses as convenient, and that collecting further examples of these will not help to clarify his criticism of Browning's poetry.

reputation for acute and discriminating indexical[1] criticism, have accepted what he says as the final verdict on Browning.[2] The result is that Browning is not attacked but ignored, like a prescribed text which the lecturer has indicated will not be the subject of an examination. One practical consequence of this is that in *Scrutiny*, a journal of which it has been said 'Its judgments have invariably turned out to be right' [20], Browning was never the subject of a major article and his very existence hardly admitted. Indeed the only reference of any substance at all that I have been able to trace is in Vol. XVIII, where R. G. Cox, perhaps with Dr Leavis's comments beneath his eye as he wrote, concluded a brief, and strangely familiar, characterization of Victorian poetry as follows:

. . . The Victorian poets attain their most characteristic successes where they turn away from their problems and difficulties to an ideal world of romantic beauty and glamour. The one obvious exception to all this is clearly Browning, who did at least break to a considerable extent with conventionally poetic style, though his example had little general effect upon the main stream of poetic development. He certainly brings into poetry the energetic and active side of his age, but to many to-day he seems too much at ease in his time – representative, no doubt, but hardly of its finer consciousness. This view has perhaps been most adequately stated by Santayana in his *Poetry and Religion*, but it had been anticipated by Arnold's severer judgment: 'Browning is a man with a modern gift, passionately desiring movement and fulness, and obtaining but a confused multitudinousness.' [21]

The 'sustained creative work of positive valuation and revaluation over the whole range of English literature' [22] produces only this insipid brew, compounded of twenty-year-old Leavis, fifty-year-old Santayana, and century-old Arnold. The secret is in the blending, no doubt.

[1] A word of Professor Wimsatt's.
[2] E.g. G. Ingli James in 'Browning, Grammar and Christianity', *Blackfriars*, XLII (1961), pp. 312–19 has a footnote: 'Dr. Leavis devotes little more than one page to Browning, but his brief comments constitute a juster estimate of the poet than any other I know of, save Santayana's.' Even Cleanth Brooks repeats and endorses Leavis's dismissal of Browning in *Modern Poetry and the Tradition*, (London, 1948), p. 234.

IV

My points then may be briefly summarized as follows. First, the general quality of writing by English scholars about Browning is not high, and this is the measure of the low esteem in which he is held. Secondly, what is most necessary for an appreciation of Browning's stature is a series of detailed studies of individual poems. In this field almost all that has been done is the work of American scholars. It is Americans also in the main who are to be thanked for the gradual accumulation of useful aids to study, bibliographical and biographical; much has been done, but, as I have said, we have even yet not completed the programme which the Browning Society set itself over eighty years ago. My final point is one so large that I can do no more than indicate its scope. I suggest that nothing will do more to reveal the true stature of Browning than the dispersal of some of the fogs of prejudice and ignorance which billow still around the age in which he lived. Lewis Namier spoke advisedly when he called the nineteenth century 'the unknown century'. The materials are there in daunting abundance, and it is now surely time to abandon the affectation that the Victorians are too dull, or too old-fashioned, or too complacent, or too stupid, or too stuffy, or too material to have any relevance to our own exciting, intelligent, anxious, ideal lives. More and more, I think, we are coming to see that the Victorians were confronted, as we are, with the problems of an urban industrial society, and tried, as we are no doubt trying, to evolve the values by which man can live in such a society. As we learn more about them we shall understand more clearly their crucial resemblances to ourselves and the significance of their equally crucial differences. It is my conviction that the more we know about the nineteenth century the greater Browning will be seen to be. The corollary to this is that as interest in the century grows, the works of Browning will be found ever more valuable for the interpretation of his age.

I shall not resolve the apparent paradox. If anyone finds it hard to comprehend how a reading of Browning helps us to understand the England of Victoria, while a knowledge of Victoria's England is likely to increase our respect for Browning, I would simply recommend a study of the quotation which concludes the chapter. It has a curiously modern ring, but it is from *Poet-Lore* (1891).

> It strikes us, in short, that the study of letters is a vital part of sociological inquiry which it is unscientific for the student of humanity to exclude. The essential relation of Literature to Ethics is even more apparent. Nowhere have we a more continuous series of phenomena for the examination of the moral status of different periods, for tracing the growth and explaining the generation of spiritual energy than in Literature. [23]

Conclusion

There are two things which I am confident I can do very well: one is an introduction to any literary work, stating what it is to contain, and how it should be executed in the most perfect manner; the other is a conclusion, shewing from various causes why the execution has not been equal to what the authour promised to himself and to the publick.   JOHNSON

A year or two ago I met two friends of mine at different times on the same day. They were both, as it happened, in the same line as myself, lecturers in English Literature at a University. Each of them asked, as such people do, what I was working on. When I replied that I was writing a book about Browning each of them looked faintly embarrassed and then said, 'Oh, I see. *Rehabilitating* him.'

Although I protested on both occasions that this was by no means my intention, what I really meant was that in a well-ordered world no such rehabilitation would be necessary. Yet in fact, as I have worked among Browning's poems and particularly as I have explored modern critical opinion, written and verbal, of Browning, it has become steadily plainer to me that something very like a rehabilitation is what is needed. The implied metaphor, however, is wrong: Browning is not a forgotten wax-work who needs to be re-attired in a new and modish dress to attract the customers. He is more like one of the great city buildings of his own lifetime – the admiration of all when new, then taken for granted, the stonework dirty, the ornament crusted with grime, the proportions obscured by newer, shoddier buildings, and at last ignored or pointed out as a dreadful warning to the young. It is my hope that just as we are rediscovering that Victorian architecture is not without its virtues, especially when it is cleaned, so the qualities of Browning will be recognized. Browning needs not rehabilitation but cleaning, so that his poetry can be seen clearly for what it is. One of my objects in writing this book has been to show where the soot lies thickest.

In particular I have tried to combat what I take to be the false ideas of Browning which are current, whether they show themselves as popular superstition or academic prejudice. Possibly this has led to an excessive amount of wrangling, but I cannot feel that it was to be avoided: at present any book about Browning which is to be useful must be polemical. I hope however that in Chapters 10 and 11 I have traversed less contentious ground. A number of critics have drawn attention to Browning's use of the language of conversation and to his interest in the technique of the novel. In discussing Browning's poetry the names which conveyed its quality most illuminatingly were, I found, those of novelists rather than those of poets – Stendhal and Trollope, Flaubert and Hawthorne, above all Balzac and James. That Browning fits naturally into such a company shows more clearly than anything else his originality and his singular sense of what was alive and what dying in the Romantic tradition.

I have not been able to avoid the habit which Bernard Shaw deplored in the London Browning Society, that of discussing Browning's optimism and his attitudes to Christian belief. The point which seems to me to need stressing here, however, is not the conventional but the unconventional nature of Browning's religious speculations. It has not, of course, been my object to resituate Browning in that high place among the philosophers of the world to which the Victorians elevated him. Such an attempt would be absurd. But it is equally absurd to shuffle the metaphysical themes of Browning's poetry out of sight, as if they were not altogether respectable and as if the poetry could only be enjoyed by a tactful agreement not to pay any attention to the poet's profoundest insights into the nature of human experience. In the study of his metaphysics I found once more that the comparisons which suggested themselves were not with the received figures of the Victorian age, but with minds, earlier or later, which were open to new and exciting ideas, with Law, Butler, Hume, Berkeley, Coleridge, Mill, Feuerbach, George Eliot, with Lotze even, with Sartre, and above all, in his insistence on the reality of selfhood, and the consequent insistence on the importance of human choice, human freedom, and human love, with

Kierkegaard. I am not putting these people forward as influencing Browning or as being influenced by him, but simply to illustrate the areas of metaphysical thought in which he was interested at various periods in his life and the kind of minds that were moving parallel to his. Doubtless they were sounder philosophers than Browning, but in such territory the poet may have something to contribute which cannot be formulated in the terms of the philosopher, for

> Art, wherein man nowise speaks to men,
> Only to mankind, – Art may tell a truth
> Obliquely, do the thing shall breed the thought,
> Nor wrong the thought, missing the mediate word.

The notion that a poet has some responsibility to tell the truth will certainly seem to many readers a peculiarly Victorian idea, and I should not deny that Browning is a distinctively Victorian poet. What I do want to suggest is first that the Victorian age stands in a peculiarly significant relationship to our own, which gives its literature an immediate interest and relevance, and secondly that Browning is preeminently the poet in the Victorian age whose face is turned towards us. He is our man in the nineteenth century. Like Johnson a hundred years before he is essentially of his own time and in many ways typifies it; yet, like Johnson, he transcends it. With these deliberate qualifications I call him also a modern poet because he speaks from his age to our own.

There will not be wanting those who are ready at this point to retort to Browning in his own words, ' 'Tis you speak, that's your error. Song's our art.' As I have been at some pains to point out in the last two chapters, a central reason for the general critical neglect of or hostility to Browning is the feeling that he directed his main energies to speaking rather than to singing, to communicating rather than to fashioning, and is therefore not to be taken seriously as a poet. If the modern poet accepts Wyndham Lewis's dictum that 'the primary pigment of poetry is the IMAGE', then he must, I think, see the end of poetry as an exploration of the possibilities of language, as painting is an exploration of the possibilities of paint. Browning never sees language like this. For him language is always a means of expression. 'Look through the sign to the thing signified.'

If this disqualifies Browning from being numbered among the poets according to the current definition of what a poet is, then it is time to change the definition. As soon as it is recognized that poetry is a special way of telling the truth, that this truth is a truth of correspondence to a world outside the poem and not simply a truth of coherence, and that the critic's is therefore not a purely aesthetic concern, so soon will Browning, the phrase cannot be evaded, come into his own. For any study of his poetry must confirm the earnestness with which he tried, throughout his life, to communicate with his readers through the medium of his art, and must compel respect for his

> love of loving, rage
> Of knowing, seeing, feeling the absolute truth of things
> For truth's sake, whole and sole.

APPENDIX A

Men and Women (1855)

The fifty-one poems published in 1855 as *Men and Women* are dispersed in collected editions after 1863, and appear under the following headings:

Dramatic Lyrics (30)

Love Among the Ruins
A Lovers' Quarrel
Evelyn Hope
Up at a Villa – Down in the City
A Woman's Last Word
A Toccata of Galuppi's
By the Fire-side
Any Wife to Any Husband
A Serenade at the Villa
My Star
A Pretty Woman
Respectability
Love in a Life
Life in a Love
Master Hugues of Saxe-Gotha

Memorabilia
Before
After
In Three Days
In a Year
Old Pictures in Florence
Saul
'De Gustibus – '
Women and Roses
The Guardian-Angel
Popularity
Two in the Campagna
One Way of Love
Another Way of Love
Misconceptions

Dramatic Romances (12)

Mesmerism
Instans Tyrannus
'Childe Roland to the Dark
   Tower Came'
A Light Woman
The Statue and the Bust
The Last Ride Together

The Patriot
Protus
Holy-Cross Day
The Twins
The Heretic's Tragedy
A Grammarian's Funeral

Men and Women (8)

Fra Lippo Lippi	Andrea del Sarto
An Epistle . . . of Karshish	Cleon
How It Strikes a Contemporary	'Transcendentalism'
Bishop Blougram's Apology	One Word More

'In a Balcony' was placed among *Tragedies and Other Plays* in 1863. Since 1868 it has stood in an independent position before *Dramatis Personae*.

APPENDIX B

The principal events of Browning's life

1812 Born in Camberwell, south-east London, on 7 May

1828 Briefly attended London University

1833 *Pauline* (L) published

1835 *Paracelsus* (L) published

1837 *Strafford* (D) published

1840 *Sordello* (L) published

1841 *Pippa Passes* (D) published

1842 *King Victor and King Charles* (D), *Dramatic Lyrics* (C), and *Essay on Tasso and Chatterton* (P) published

1843 *The Return of the Druses* (D) and *A Blot in the 'Scutcheon* (D) published

1844 *Colombe's Birthday* (D) published

1845 *Dramatic Romances and Lyrics* (C) published

1846 *Luria* (D) and *A Soul's Tragedy* (D) published in one volume. On 12 September Browning married Elizabeth Barrett. They went to Pisa and made their home in Italy until Mrs Browning's death.

1849 Robert Barrett 'Pen' Browning born

1850 *Christmas-Eve and Easter-Day* (L) published

1852 *Essay on Shelley* (P) published

1855 *Men and Women* (C) published: for details see Appendix A

1861 Mrs Browning died in Florence on 29 June. Thereafter Browning lived in London.

1864 *Dramatis Personae* (C) published

1868–69 *The Ring and the Book* (L) published

1871 *Balaustion's Adventure* (L) and *Prince Hohenstiel-Schwangau* (L) published

1872 *Fifine at the Fair* (L) published

1873   *Red Cotton Night-Cap Country* (L) published
1875   *Aristophanes' Apology* (L) and *The Inn Album* (L) published
1876   *Pacchiarotto* (C) published
1877   *The Agamemnon of Aeschylus* (T) published
1878   *La Saisiaz* (L) and *The Two Poets of Croisic* (L) published in one volume
1879   *Dramatic Idyls* (C) published
1880   *Dramatic Idyls (Second Series)* (C) published
1881   London Browning Society founded
1833   *Jocoseria* (C) published
1884   *Ferishtah's Fancies* (C) published
1887   *Parleyings with Certain People* (C) published
1889   Browning died in Venice on 12 December. He was buried in Westminster Abbey.
1890   *Asolando* (C) published

(L) Long poem   (C) Collection of poems
(D) Drama   (T) Translation   (P) Prose work

NOTES

Chapter 1

1. Perhaps most conveniently in M. H. Abrams' *The Mirror and the Lamp* (New York, 1953), especially Ch. IX. It is in this chapter that Abrams remarks, in terms which precisely characterize the concerns of my present inquiry:

   > That fecund but disorderly thinker, Friedrich Schlegel, who introduced the distinction between classic and romantic which has turned out to be equally indispensable and unmanageable to literary critics and historians, helped also to popularize other contraries which are scarcely less attractive, or less equivocal. (p. 237)

   Abrams is referring to the 'set of cross-distinctions revolving about the terms "subjective" and "objective".'
2. But not by Ruskin. See Abrams, *op. cit.* p. 242.
3. *Handbook* p. 579. W. K. Wimsatt and Cleanth Brooks (*Literary Criticism: A Short History* (1957) pp. 536–7) similarly misinterpret the *Essay on Shelley*.
4. 'La Poésie Expressive et Dramatique en Angleterre', *Revue Contemporaine*, XXVII (1856), pp. 511–46. For a more detailed study of Misland's articles see Ch. 12, pp. 375–82.
5. *Portrait*, p. 162.
6. For a rather different reading of the *Essay* see Thomas J. Collins, *Robert Browning's Moral-Aesthetic Theory 1833–1855* (Lincoln: U. of Nebraska Press, 1967). See also correspondence in *TLS* (February and March 1966), pp. 167, 205, 314.

Chapter 2

1. 'Robert Browning and the Epic of Psychology', p. 11 (reprinted from the *London Quarterly Review*, XXXII (July 1869)).
2. *Select Poems of Robert Browning*, ed. W. J. Rolfe and H. E. Hersey (New York, 1886) p. 195.
3. In his review of *Graffiti d'Italia*, by W. W. Story, the friend of Browning and Henry James.

4. 'The Dramatic Monologue', *PMLA*, LXII (1947), pp. 503–16.

5. Cf. M. K. Starkman, 'The Manichee in the Cloister', *MLN*, LXXV (1960), pp. 399–405; David Sonstroem, 'Animal and Vegetable in the Spanish Cloister', *VP*, VI (1968), pp. 70–73.

6. The full dramatic effect of this lyric is well brought out by H. B. Charlton, 'Browning as Dramatist', *Bulletin of the John Rylands Library*, XXIII (1939), pp. 57–67.

7. See Ch. 11.

8. 'Religious Implications in Browning's Poetry', *PQ*, XXXVI (1957), p. 448.

9. 'La Poésie Expressive et Dramatique en Angleterre', *Revue Contemporaine* XXVII (1856), pp. 511–46. See also Ch. 12, Joseph Milsand.

10. For further examples of differing judgements see *Bishop Blougram* (Ch. 6), *Caliban* (Ch. 7), *Rabbi Ben Ezra* (Ch. 8), *Fifine* and *Prince Hohenstiel-Schwangau* (Ch. 11).

11. It has twice as many entries in the index as any other poem of Browning's.

12. Although I have quoted and paraphrased Langbaum at length it is not possible to do justice in a summary to the book's wealth of interesting quotation and perceptive critical insights. I hope, however, that I have fairly represented the argument of the relevant chapters. There are signs in a more recent article – 'Browning and the Question of Myth', *PMLA*, LXXXI (1966), 575–84 – that Langbaum has modified his earlier position. He says, for example, 'It is because the speaker is not trying to tell the truth about himself, but is trying to accomplish something or make an impression, that he actually does reveal himself truly' (576–7) and speaking of the psychological movement of the best dramatic monologues' he says, 'It is after the speaker has told all his lies, that inadvertently, and as if of its own accord, the truth rises to the surface.' (583–4)

13. The personal note in these Prologues and Epilogues is strongly reminiscent of Milton's inductions to Books III, VII and IX of *Paradise Lost*.

14. See Ch. 7.

15. An unobtrusive example of this is to be found in the early poem *Incident of The French Camp*. The first line reads 'You know, we French stormed Ratisbon.' The use of 'we' instead of 'the' here has two important effects. It adds to the immediacy and credibility of the piece by placing the story in the mouth of a survivor of the action, and also relieves Browning of any direct personal responsibility for the sentiments of the poem.

16. For an extended examination of Browning's satirical use of the dramatic monologue and a further comment on Langbaum's position see 'A Note on the Lawyers in *The Ring and the Book*', *VP*, VI (1968), pp. 297–307. It is tempting to speculate on the connection between Browning's ironic uses of obliquity and the fact, noted by Maisie Ward (*Robert Browning and his World*, I, pp. 18–19), that 'in an early eighteenth-century edition of Dryden's translation of Juvenal, Browning wrote, "My father read the whole of the Dedicatory Preface aloud to me as we took a walk together up Nunhead Hill, Surrey, when I was a boy." '

Chapter 3

1. *Handbook*, p. 73. For *Pauline*, *Paracelsus* and *Sordello* and their place in Browning's development as a poet see Robert Preyer, 'Robert Browning: A Reading of the Early Narratives', *ELH*, XXVI (1959), pp. 531–48. 'The obsessive subject matter of [Browning's] youth had become the self and its prehensions seen as other than or opposed to society and reason. But it was no easy problem (as Goethe had discovered before him) to drive beyond this "subjectivity" and replace, at the centre of his art, the relations and interconnections between the self and society. That he did so is evident in the masterpieces of his maturity; but the effort cost him almost ten years of sustained effort and defeat.'

2. Browning's letter to Ruskin of 1 February 1856 (printed in the Baylor University *Interests* in 1958) is full of interest, especially when he discusses *Sordello*. See also M. Mason, 'The Importance of *Sordello*', in Armstrong, *Reconsiderations*, pp. 125–51. This essay has particular relevance to the questions under discussion.

3. See R. D. Altick, 'Memo to the Next Annotator of Browning', *VP* I (1963), pp. 65–66.

4. In the notes to his useful edition of *Men and Women*, Vol. II, p. 313.

5. *Browning* (Longmans Green & Co., 1959), p. 9.

6. Whether Browning had any particular 'poem in twelve books' in mind when he wrote it is impossible to say. However, *The Prelude* (in fourteen books) had been published in 1850, and Browning's poem is sufficiently *à propos* to make one wonder a little. For another view of the poem see R. D. Altick 'Browning's "Transcendentalism" ', *JEGP*, LVIII (1959), pp. 24–28.

7. The line 'Dumb to Homer, dumb to Keats – him, even!' does not mean that Browning thought Keats a greater poet than Homer and therefore even more worthy to see the new side of the moon. Keats is singled out, of course, as the author of *Endymion*.

8. For Hugo see McAleer, *Dearest Isa* pp. 48–49; Swinburne ib. p. 333; Rossetti ib. p. 336.

9. *RB/EBB* II, pp. 455–6.

10. *Childe Harold* IV, clxxix–clxxxiii. This passage seems to have irritated Browning for many years, if we may judge from *Sordello* (vi, 1–7).

11. This passage is to be found on pp. 36–39 of the first edition of the poem (London, 1871).

12. My punctuation.

13. DeVane (*Handbook*, pp. 400–1) has the interesting suggestion that Rossetti's *The House of Life* was the immediate occasion of the poem. See also R. D. Altick, *VP*, I (1963), pp. 67–68.

14. For the history of this poem see DeVane, *Handbook*, pp. 565–6.

15. DeVane, *Parleyings*. See also Robert Langbaum, 'Browning and the Question of Myth', *PMLA*, LXXXI (1966), pp. 575–84.

16. Arnold's poem *Epilogue to Lessing's Laocoön* is an invaluable compendium of Victorian attitudes to the relation of painting, music and literature.

17. See ' "Real Vision" and "Right Language" ', *The Listener*, LXXVII (1967), pp. 854–6.

18. Cf. *Bernard de Mandeville* VII.

19. *Handbook*, p. 528. With the Prologue cf. Yeats – 'The Woods of Arcady are dead/And over is their antique joy,/Of old the world on dreaming fed,/Grey truth is now her painted toy.'

20. *Avison* XIII.

21. *Handbook*, p. 483.

22. See the discussion of *Rabbi Ben Ezra* in Ch. 8.

23. Readers of Mark Abrams' invaluable *catalogue raisonné* of Romantic criticism, *The Mirror and the Lamp*, will recognize by how much this position differs from general Romantic theory, if there was such a thing.

Chapter 4

1. For a good discussion of some elements in Browning's diction see William M. Ryan, 'The Classification of Browning's "Difficult" Vocabulary', *SP*, LX (1963), pp. 542–8. Ryan's lists draw attention to many obscure words, but also include words which are fairly common in poetic use (especially in Shakespeare) or in British dialects. His general conclusion is that Browning's archaisms occur chiefly in poems where they are reasonably appropriate, while his coinages, though puzzling at first sight, are usually justifiable. For

the actual size of Browning's vocabulary see A. J. Armstrong, *Baylor Monthly* (April, 1926). Browning used 38,957 words (including 3,413 names), Shakespeare 19,957, and Tennyson 19,729.

2. A river in the North Island of New Zealand *(The Guardian-Angel)*.
3. India *(Waring)*.
4. John Guillim (1565–1621), English writer on heraldry: he became Rouge Croix Pursuivant in 1619 *(The Inn Album)*.
5. An opera by Handel (1711) *(Parleying with Charles Avison)*: *Radaminta*, which is mentioned two lines earlier, is perhaps a conflation of *Radamisto* (1720) and *Rodelinda* (1725).
6. A kind of marble *(Christmas-Eve and Easter-Day)*.
7. The Ebionites ('poor men') were an early sect of Jewish Christians who denied the divinity of Christ and rejected the Pauline epistles. Hippolytus invented a founder called Ebion, and is followed in this by Tertullian, Epiphanius and Browning *(A Death in the Desert)*.
8. St Benedict's sister *(Parleying with Daniel Bartoli)*.
9. Jacob Boehme (1575–1624) German mystic *('Transcendentalism')*.
10. Antonio Escobar y Mendoza (1589–1669), Spanish Jesuit and celebrated casuist. His arguments were attacked by Pascal *(Master Hugues)*. Cf. the French verb 'escobarder'.
11. 'Prince of nativity-casters' *(Paracelsus*, Act Two).
12. The Rocky Ones were the Athenians: a famous bronze statue of Athene Promachos stood in Athens *(Aristophanes' Apology)*.
13. A digest of authoritative decisions on points of Roman Law, compiled by the orders of Justinian *(The Ring and the Book*, V).
14. *Handbook* (1896), pp. 10–11, under the heading 'General Characteristics'.
15. Orr, *Handbook*, p. 35.
16. *Browning* (E.M.L.), Ch. VI. With all its faults of over-emphasis and over-simplification this is still the most helpful general introduction to Browning's poetry.
17. *SP*, XXXII (1935), pp. 120–5.
18. See Geoffrey Tillotson, 'A Word for Browning', *Sewanee Review*, LXXII (1964), pp. 389–97; reprinted in Geoffrey and Kathleen Tillotson, *Mid-Victorian Studies* (London, 1965), pp. 110–17.
19. Basil Worsfold, in the notes to his extremely useful small edition of the 1855 text of *Men and Women*.
20. For a detailed discussion of the style of *By the Fire-side* see Armstrong, *Reconsiderations*, pp. 105-111.

Chapter 5

1. This course is followed by, for example, George Williamson in his *A Reader's Guide to T. S. Eliot* (London, 1955), p. 93. Grover

Smith Jr., *Eliot's Poetry and Plays: A Study in Sources and Meaning* (Chicago, 1956) actually quotes the line as 'Superfetation of τὸ ἕν', but still concludes that the poem is 'obscure, precious and bombastic'.

2. F. Mary Wilson *A Primer on Browning* (London, 1891), p. 36. A. J. Whyte comments in his Introduction to his edition of *Sordello* (London and Toronto, 1913), 'The reader [of this edition] will probably notice the number of references made to *Johnson's Dictionary*, the reason of which is that Browning made a close study of that work when he first determined to adopt poetry as his profession in life.' Whyte glosses several words by reference to Johnson.

3. Typical examples are 'phalanges' *(Red Cotton Night-cap Country)* and 'asymptote' *(Fust and his Friends)*.

4. Among the most useful are Margaret Lee and Katharine Locock's edition of *Paracelsus* (London, 1909); A. J. Whyte's *Sordello* (see note 2 above); Basil Worsfold's *Men and Women* [1855]; Joseph E. Baker's *Pippa Passes and Shorter Poems* (New York, 1947), [including *The Flight of the Duchess, Christmas-Eve and Easter-Day*, many poems from *Dramatis Personae*, and *Apollo and the Fates*]; A. K. Cook's *Commentary* on *The Ring and the Book*.

   There is also some helpful information in *Pauline* ed. N. Hardy Wallis (1931); *Strafford* ed. Emily Hickey (1884); *Christmas-Eve and Easter-Day* ed. Oliver Smeaton (*c.* 1918); *A Death in the Desert* ed. G. U. Pope (1897, 1904).

5. The most generally useful is Mrs Sutherland Orr's *Handbook*, to which Browning gave his approval and contributed a few notes. Mary Wilson's *Primer* (see note 2 above) has some shrewd comments, and E. Berdoe's *Browning Cyclopaedia* (London and New York, 1892) is occasionally helpful, although it more often calls to mind T. R. Lounsbury's observation, 'Commentaries on Browning generally bear a close resemblance to foghorns. They proclaim the existence of fog; but they do not disperse it.' (*The Early Literary Career of Robert Browning*, p. 196). W. C. DeVane's invaluable *Handbook* is consistently helpful on details of the publication, genesis, source, text and after-history of each poem, and often has illuminating interpretative comments.

6. E.g. Helen J. Ormerod, 'Some Notes on Browning's Poems referring to Music', *Browning Society Papers*, II (1888), pp. 180–95; Herbert E. Greene, 'Browning's Knowledge of Music', *PMLA*, LXII (1947), pp. 1095–99; R. W. S. Mendl, 'Robert Browning, the Poet-Musician', *Music and Letters*, XLII (1961), pp. 142–50; George M. Ridenour, 'Browning's Music Poems: Fancy and

Fact', *PMLA*, LXXVIII (1963), pp. 369–77; W. Stacy Johnson, 'Browning's Music', *Journal of Aesthetics and Art Criticism*, XXII (1963), pp. 203–7.

7. F. E. L. Priestley, 'The Ironic Pattern of Browning's *Paracelsus*', *UTQ*, XXXIV (1964), pp. 68–81, will be found helpful. The *Biographie Universelle* (Paris, 1822) was used by Browning in writing *Paracelsus* and *Sordello*. For *Paracelsus* (and many other poems) he used Nathaniel Wanley's *The Wonders of The Little World* (1677): see Griffin and Minchin, *Life*, pp. 20–25.

8. Some of these poems are discussed in Ch. 11, pp. 282–349.

9. See also D. W. Smalley, 'A Parleying with Aristophanes', *PMLA*, LV (1940), pp. 823–38.

10. E.g. Jeanie Morison (Campbell), '*Sordello': an Outline Analysis* (1889); W. O. Raymond, 'Browning's *The Statue and the Bust*', *UTQ*, XXVIII(1959), pp. 233–49; F. E. L. Priestley, 'A Reading of *La Saisiaz*', *UTQ*, XXV (1955) pp. 47–59, also on *Paracelsus* see note 7 above; Isobel Armstrong's careful study of *Mr. Sludge*, '*The Medium*', *VP*, II (1964), pp. 1–9; C.C. Clarke, 'Humor and Wit in *Childe Roland*', *MLQ*, XXIII (1962), pp. 323–36; Roma A. King Jr., *The Bow and the Lyre* [*Andrea del Sarto, Fra Lippo Lippi, The Bishop Orders his Tomb, Bishop Blougram's Apology, Saul*] (Ann Arbor, Michigan, 1957), also 'Browning: "Mage" and "Maker" – a Study in Poetic Purpose and Method' [*Cleon*], *Victorian Newsletter* No. 20 (Fall 1961), pp. 22–25; R. D. Altick, '*A Grammarian's Funeral*: Browning's Praise of Folly?', *SEL*, III (1963), pp. 449–60, also 'The Symbolism of Browning's *Master Hugues of Saxe-Gotha*', *VP*, III (1965), pp. 1–7, also 'Lovers' Finiteness: Browning's *Two in the Campagna*', *Papers on Language and Literature*, III (1966), pp. 75–80; Eugene R. Kintgen. 'Childe Roland and the Perversity of the Mind', *VP*, IV (1966), pp. 253–8.

There are also a number of illuminating controversies about specific poems, e.g. on *Count Gismond* see J. V. Hagopian (*PQ*, XL (1961), pp. 153–5), J. W. Tilton and R. D. Tuttle (*SP*, LIX (1962), pp. 83–95), and Sister Marcella M. Holloway (*SP*, LX (1963), pp. 549–53); on *My Last Duchess* see B. R. Jerman (*PMLA*, LXXII (1957), pp. 488–93), and L. Perrine (*PMLA*, LXXIV (1959), pp. 157–9); on *Bishop Blougram's Apology* see F. E. L. Priestley (*UTQ*, XV (1946), pp. 139–47), H. N. Fairchild (*UTQ*, XVIII (1949), pp. 234–40), and R. E. Palmer Jr. (*MP*, LVIII (1960), pp. 108–18); on *Caliban upon Setebos* see J. Howard (*VP*, I (1963), pp. 249–57) and L. Perrine (*VP*, II (1964), pp. 124–7.)

11. See Ch. 7, pp. 157–166.

12. 'Browning: Semantic Stutterer', *PMLA*, LX (1945), pp. 231–55. See also his 'Browning's *Sordello* and Jung: Browning's *Sordello* in the light of Jung's Theory of Types', *PMLA*, LVI (1941), pp. 758–96.

13. See 'The Two-Headed Symbol' [Melville's Later Novels], *The Listener*, LXXIV (1965), 300–301, 313. Cf., also 'He [Plato] leads you to see, that propositions involving in themselves contradictory conceptions, are nevertheless true.' Coleridge, *Table Talk* (30 April 1830).

14. Letter to A. W. M. Baillie, 10 September 1864.

15. See Browning's letter to his publisher, Edward Chapman, 17 December 1855 (DeVane and Knickerbocker, p. 85).

16. Letter of 10 December 1855, in W. G. Collingwood, *Life and Work of Ruskin* (1893), I, pp. 193–202, and *The Works of John Ruskin*, ed. E. T. Cook and Alexander Wedderburn (1909), XXXVI, xxxiv. Cf. Browning's letter to Ruskin of 1 February 1856 (Baylor *Interests*, 1958).

17. Letter of 27 November 1868 (Hood/Wise, pp. 128–9). Cf. also Robert Sidney, 'Some Browning Memories', *Saturday Review*, CXIII (1912), pp. 584–5, where Browning is reported as saying, 'I do hope that if, and when, you can make yourself heard, you will tell people that I have never wanted to bother them. I have always done my best, and if I'm not always clear, I suppose it's some sort of kink in my brain. I have too much respect for my trade to be wilfully careless about anything I write.'

18. Letters of 17 and 24 March 1883 (McAleer, *Learned Lady*, pp. 155–8).

19. Letter of 21 April 1856 to Edward Chapman (DeVane and Knickerbocker, p. 92).

Chapter 6

1. See R. D. Altick, 'Memo to the Next Annotator of Browning', *VP* I (1963), p. 64.

2. Priestley, *UTQ*, XV (1946), pp. 139–47; Fairchild, *UTQ*, XVIII (1949), pp. 234–40.

3. *Browning* (EML), Ch. VIII, p. 196.

4. ib. p. 201.

5. Rupert E. Palmer Jr., 'The Uses of Character in *Bishop Blougram's Apology*', *MP*, LVIII (1960), pp. 108–18.

6. It is accepted for example by DeVane in his *Handbook* (2nd ed.), by Roma A. King Jr. in *The Bow and the Lyre*, and by C. E. Tanzy,

'Browning, Emerson and Bishop Blougram', *VS*, I (1958), pp. 255–6.

7. *Handbook*, p. 174.

8. Robert Langbaum in *The Poetry of Experience* (1957), pp. 100–1, offers an elaborate paraphrase, in which he takes the line to mean 'Blougram is right with the wrong reasons', or 'Blougram makes his case, even if on inappropriate grounds'. I do not see how this can be taken from the line. In any case it is clear from Mr Langbaum's analysis of the poem that the Bishop can be said to 'make his case' only if we accept his own definition of 'belief'. But when Blougram tries to establish the value of his own opportunist faith he is nowhere provided by Browning with a valid argument. Indeed it is the 'inappropriateness' of Blougram's 'grounds' which ultimately undermines his whole position.

9. But the imagery here (lines 1000–4) is odd, cf. *The Ring and the Book X*, 1888–92.

10. *Infinite Moment*, Ch. VIII, p. 143.

11. Cf. Isobel Armstrong, 'Browning's *Mr. Sludge, "The Medium"*,' *VP*, II (1964), pp. 1–9.

Chapter 7

1. E.g. John Howard, 'Caliban's Mind', *VP*, I (1963), pp. 249–57; Laurence Perrine, 'Browning's *Caliban upon Setebos*: A Reply', *VP*, II (1964), pp. 124–7. Cf. also Park Honan, 'Belial upon Setebos', *Tennessee Studies in Literature*, IX (1964), pp. 87–98; Michael Timko, 'Browning upon Butler; or, Natural Theology in the English Isle', *Criticism*, VII (1965), pp. 141–50.

2. Letter of 25 April 1884, (Hood/Wise, p. 228). The evidence from the poem is plain enough, but two points may be emphasized. (*a*) The language suggests serious reservations on Browning's part: in particular the constant shift between the first and third person indicates that Caliban is not offered as a speaker with a stable view of the world or of his own personality. Cf. E. K. Brown, 'The First Person in *Caliban upon Setebos*', *MLN, LXVI* (1951), pp. 392–5.

   (*b*) The poem ends with the sudden onset of a storm: it is tempting to take this as the storm which is raging at the beginning of *The Tempest*. If this is so then Caliban soliloquizes while Prospero and Miranda think that he is drudging for them, presumably chopping wood. Then the storm breaks, and in a few hours Caliban is saying to Stephano, 'I'll show thee every fertile inch o' the island; and I will kiss thy foot: I prithee be my god.' The shallowness of Caliban's religious feelings needs no comment.

3. This poem is of great importance in the history of Browning's developing beliefs about Christianity (see Ch. 9). In this chapter I am concerned to mention only some of the obstacles with which it presents the reader.

4. *Handbook*, p. 422. Hoxie N. Fairchild ('*La Saisiaz* and *The Nineteenth Century*', *MP*, XLVIII (1950), pp. 104–11) qualifies DeVane's account, principally by pointing out that in fact all the Christian contributors wrote as committed Christians. But even they agree not to cut the argument short by pleading Divine revelation at the outset.

5. Note here the theme of *The Two Poets of Croisic*, the other poem in the volume.

6. F. E. L. Priestley, 'A Reading of *La Saisiaz*', *UTQ*, XXV (1955), pp. 47–59.

7. *Lectures and Notes on Shakespeare and other English Poets*, ed. T. Ashe (Bohn's Popular Library, London, 1914). Appendix IV, p. 529.

Introduction to Part Two

1. The use of terms of this kind must not be taken to imply that there is a clear line of definition between them or that every feature of a poem can be completely classified under one heading or the other. But it is a fallacy to suppose that if there is an area where two things cannot be clearly differentiated it is therefore legitimate to treat them as if they were both the same thing. 'No man can say when day ends and night begins, but every man knows the difference between light and darkness.'

2. An exception should be made in favour of David Lodge's *Language of Fiction: Essays in Criticism and Verbal Analysis of the English Novel* (London, 1966).

3. See '*Aylmer's Field*: a Problem for Criticis', *The Listener*, LXXI (1964), pp. 553–7.

Chapter 8

1. *Time's Revenges: Browning's Reputation as a Thinker, 1889–1962* (Knoxville, Tennessee, 1964).

2. René Wellek and Austin Warren, *Theory of Literature* (London, 1949), p. 107, footnote on p. 317.

3. For an alternative reading of the poem see Robert Langbaum, *The Poetry of Experience*, p. 140.

4. Page references are to the second edition (Glasgow, 1892).

5. See 'Henry Jones on Browning's Optimism', *VP* II (1964), pp. 29–41, where the evidence against Jones is presented in rather greater detail. Attention is drawn particularly to his handling of the *Parleying with Francis Furini, A Bean-Stripe*, and *La Saisiaz*.
6. Cf. pp. 9, 241, 248, 262.
7. Note that Jones has earlier relied on Kant to refute Berkeley.
8. E.g. 'After Puritanism came Charles the Second and the rights of the flesh . . .' (p. 52).
9. There is an obvious convergence here between Browning's thought and Hume's, and of course between Hume's and contemporary analytic philosophy. Cf. also Hume, *Dialogues concerning Natural Religion*, Section XII: 'To be a philosophical sceptic is, in a man of letters, the first and most essential step towards being a sound, believing Christian.' It is important not to exaggerate the resemblances, however. Browning was always prepared to adopt arguments similar to Hume's, but only as the first positions in a debate designed to establish that man is not constrained by his intellect to a pessimistic view of the world. Like William Law, Berkeley, and Bishop Butler, Browning turned his scepticism not against religion but against rationalism. Like them also he was able thereafter to affirm his religious faith, although not in the same terms throughout his life, for while his scepticism about the cogency of intellectual processes persists he slowly changes the form of his suprarational beliefs. His religious development may be very roughly represented by saying that in 1850 he was prepared to assert a strongly Christian, almost Evangelical, faith, but that his emphasis on Christianity grew gradually weaker until, towards the end of his life, he was prepared to affirm very little more than a general trust in God's existence. For a fuller discussion see Ch. 9.
10. See, for example, the first stanza of the *Epilogue* to *Ferishtah's Fancies*.

Chapter 9

1. Those who want to know what can be done in this way should consult Hugh Martin, *The Faith of Robert Browning* (London: S.C.M. Press, 1963). See also Kingsbury Badger, ' "See the Christ stand!" : Browning's Religion', *Boston University Studies in English*, I (1955–6), pp. 53–75, a useful article with suggestions for further reading in the footnotes.
2. For some comments on the style of *Christmas-Eve* see Ch. 11, p. 287. For a different view of the poem see Phyllis J. Guskin, 'Ambiguities in the Structure and Meaning of Browning's *Christmas-Eve*', *VP*, IV (1966), pp. 21–28.

3. 4 May 1850; *Letters of Elizabeth Barrett Browning*, ed. F. G. Kenyon, I, p. 449.

4. *Handbook*, p. 197, p. 204.

5. E.g. by DeVane, *Handbook*, pp. 295–8; see also DeVane's concluding paragraph.

6. Ludwig Feuerbach, *The Essence of Christianity* tr. Marian Evans (1854), Ch. IV, pp. 52–53.

7. id. ib. p. 55.

8. Preface pp. x–xi, cf. also Ch. I, pp. 12–31.

9. *Biographia Literaria* ed. Shawcross, I, pp. 135–6.

10. For Browning's general view of the Church, especially that of Rome, see, for example, *The Confessional, The Heretic's Tragedy, Holy-Cross Day, Soliloquy of the Spanish Cloister, Bishop Blougram's Apology*, and *Red Cotton Night-Cap Country*. Cf. also occasional references in the letters, e.g. McAleer *Dearest Isa*, p. 348.

11. There is a helpful short article on the *Epilogue* by Watson Kirkconnell, *MLN*, XLI (1926), pp. 213–19). I make considerable use of it here, differing from it only in conclusion.

12. Note that 'Face' in Stanza XII is not the face of Christ, as Mrs Orr suggests. There is a good account of the last section of the *Epilogue* in J. Hillis Miller *Disappearance*, pp. 153–6.

13. *In Ferishtah's Fancies* the speaker, Ferishtah, is a professional exponent of dialectic. The poems are essentially a series of homely analogies or conceits reducing theological difficulties to everyday terms, with a touch of conscious humour and a scholastic interest in propounding an ingenious argument. The character of the resultant discourses is so much in accord with Browning's own temper that there is little pretence at dramatic distancing of poet and speaker, cf. Donne's *Eclogues*, especially Eclogue VIII. It is worth noting that *Ferishtah's Fancies* is formally a kind of *Satira Menippea*.

14. Miller, *Portrait*, p. 173.

15. *Dubiety*, line 24. D. Smalley, 'Browning's View of Fact in *The Ring and the Book*', *VNL*, XVI (1959), pp. 1–9, draws attention to a similar expression in *Two Poets* CLII, 'But truth, truth, that's the gold!' Cf. 'Well, now; there's nothing in nor out o' the world/ Good except truth.' (*The Ring and the Book*, I, 698–699.)

16. *Handbook*, p. 548.

17. *A Pillar at Sebzevar*, line 22.

18. *Ibid.*, line 25.

19. For the rather ambiguous ethical position of the speaker of *Fifine at the Fair* see Ch. 11, pp. 303–21.

20. Introduction to *Men and Women*, xxxiv. See also W. O. Raymond,

'Browning's *The Statue and the Bust*', *UTQ*, XXVIII (1959), pp. 233–49.

21. G. Ingli James ('Browning, Grammar and Christianity', *Blackfriars*, XLIII (1961), pp. 312–19) has an odd footnote: 'It is amusing to note that, thanks to the imagery, the grammarian is not in fact, as so many readers seem to think, a failure by the world's standards. Missing his million by a unit, he scores 999,999 to the low man's 100. A successful failure, indeed.' Mr James appears not to have understood that 'misses an unit' means 'does not even score one'.

22. For different views of *A Grammarian's Funeral* see Richard D. Altick, '*A Grammarian's Funeral*: Browning's Praise of Folly?' *SEL*, III (1963), pp. 449–60; Martin Svaglic, 'Browning's Grammarian: Apparent Failure or Real?' *VP*, V (1967), pp. 93–104; Robert Kelly, 'Dactyls and Curlews: Satire in *A Grammarian's Funeral*', ib. pp. 105–12.

23. In addition to the passages mentioned in note 15, see *La Saisiaz*, 139–146.

24. Cf. VI, 2081–96, where Caponsacchi ponders whether it is possible
    > To have to do with nothing but the true,
    > The good, the eternal – and these, not alone
    > In the main current of the general life,
    > But small experiences of every day,
    > Concerns of the particular hearth and home.

25. Cf. *Two Poets*, LXII–LXIII, especially lines 503–504, where Browning says that the real crown of life is to 'Be warranted as promising to wield/Weapons, no sham, in a true battle-field.'

Chapter 10

1. 'Two Styles in the Verse of Robert Browning', *ELH*, XXXII (1965), pp. 62–84.

2. *A Choice of Browning's Verse* (London, 1967).

3. Letter to West, April 1742.

4. Anonymous, published in T. Weelkes's *Madrigals of 6 Parts* (1600).

5. Preface to *Lays of Ancient Rome*.

6. Donald Davie, *Purity of Diction in English Verse* (London, 1952), puts with great cogency the arguments in favour of a diction of this kind.

7. *Purity of Diction*, pp. 141–4.

8. *On the Diction of Tennyson, Browning and Arnold*, S.P.E. Tract, LIII (Oxford, 1939).

9. *The Primary Language of Poetry in the 1740s and 1840s*, University of California Publications in English, Vol. 19, No. 2, (1950).

10. *Browning's Characters: a study in poetic technique* (Yale U.P., 1961).

11. S.P.E. Tract LIII, p. 119.

12. From DeVane, *Handbook*, p. 358, it might appear that these vital lines were an afterthought. This is not so. The lines which Browning added later were 2126–34, inserted to correct a verbal slip.

13. For a fuller treatment of *Prince Hohenstiel-Schwangau* see Ch. 11, pp. 291–303.

14. See Appendix A.

15. See Charline R. Kvapil, '*How It Strikes a Contemporary*: A Dramatic Monologue', *VP*, IV (1966), pp. 279–83.

16. Armstrong, *Reconsiderations*, pp. 93–123.

Chapter 11

1. The influence of the Unitarians on Browning is sometimes mentioned in this connection (e.g. by C. R. Tracy, 'Browning's Heresies', *SP*, XXXIII (1936), pp. 610–25). No doubt the Unitarians must bear some responsibility for making Browning dissatisfied with any religious opinions imposed from without, whether by the Bible, by a church, or by dogmatic instruction, with the result that his life's work was a labour to found his own faith on his own human experience. But when he had succeeded in doing this he found a further task in defending his newly-established beliefs, such as that in the immortality of the soul, from the attacks of the Unitarians and similar schools.

2. 'Tennyson, Browning and a Romantic Fallacy', *UTQ*, XIII (1943–4), pp. 175–95. On *Pauline* see also Robert Preyer's interesting article 'Robert Browning: A Reading of the Early Narratives', *ELH*, XXVI (1959), pp. 531–48.

3. William Irvine, 'Four Monologues in Browning's *Men and Women*', [*Fra Lippo Lippi, Bishop Blougram's Apology, Karshish*, and *Cleon*] *VP*, II (1964), pp. 155–64, argues that all four poems are designed to comment on matters of immediate interest in 1855.

4. A. O. J. Cockshut's *Anglican Attitudes* (London, 1959) has clear, brief accounts of the 'Essays-and Reviews debate' (pp. 62–87) and Colenso (pp. 88–120).

5. *A Bibliography of Robert Browning from 1833 to 1881*, compiled by F. J. Furnivall (London, 1881), p. 157.

6. L. N. Broughton, C. S. Northup, and R. Pearsall (compilers), *Robert Browning: A Bibliography 1830–1950* (Cornell Studies in English XXXIX) (Ithaca, New York, 1953), p. 17.

7. L. G. Salingar, 'Robert Browning', in *The Pelican Guide to English Literature* (ed. Boris Ford), Vol. 6 (Harmondsworth, 1958), p. 254.

8. Sharp, *Life*, p. 183.

9. John M. Hitner, 'Browning's Grotesque Period', *VP*, IV (1965), pp. 1–13.

10. H. B. Charlton, 'Browning's Ethical Poetry', *Bulletin of the John Rylands Library*, XXVII (1942), pp. 36–69.

11. McAleer, *Dearest Isa*, p. 347.

12. *Infinite Moment*, p. 150.

13. Landis and Freeman, p. 169.

14. McAleer, *Dearest Isa*, pp. 347–8, see also p. 371. Cf. Hudson p. 129: 'Oh, Napoleon! Do we really differ so thoroughly about him after all? No understanding comes out of talk on such questions, because one presses to the support of the weaker points, – not necessarily untenable, but weak – and the end is, *these* seem the argument. But I never answer for what any man *may* do, if I try and appreciate what he *has* done: my opinion of the solid good rendered years ago is unchanged. The subsequent deference to the clerical party in France, and support of brigandage, is poor work – but it surely is doing little harm to the general good.' (Letter of 5 September 1863.)

15. See the letters to George Barrett in 1870 (Landis and Freeman, pp. 292–8, especially p. 295).

16. McAleer, *Dearest Isa*, p. 302, letter of 19 October 1868.

17. ib., pp. 342–4, letter of 19 August 1870.

18. ib., p. 357, letter of 25 April 1871.

19. ib., p. 371, letter of 29 December 1871.

20. ib., p. 372, letter of 19/25 January 1872.

21. H. C. Duffin in his stimulating book *Amphibian: A Reconsideration of Browning* (Cambridge, England, 1956), says uncompromisingly, 'The poem has not virtue enough to sustain its ponderous bulk, and occupies the lowest place among its author's productions' (pp. 167–8)

22. See W. C. DeVane, 'The Harlot and the Thoughtful Young Man: A Study of the Relations between Rossetti's *Jenny* and Browning's *Fifine at the Fair*', *SP*, XXIX (1932). pp. 463–84.

23. 'The "Abstruser Themes" of Browning's *Fifine at the Fair*', *PMLA*, LXXIV (1959), pp. 426–37.

24. For corroboration of this point of view see the review of *Fifine* in *Temple Bar*, XXXVII (Feb. 1873), pp. 315–28.

25. For the Cross as a hateful object see Steven Runciman, *The Medieval Manichee* (Cambridge, England, 1947), p. 22.

26. Orr, *Handbook*, p. 159.

27. Raymond, *Infinite Moment*, p. 111.

28. Paper read at the 14th meeting of the Browning Society, 24 February 1882.

29. *All in Due Time* (London, 1955), pp. 122–40.

30. I.e. about five months after publication. (My note.)

31. *Handbook*, p. 370.

32. Quoted in Griffin and Minchin, *Life*, pp. 248–9.

33. For another view of *Fifine* see Barbara Melchiori, 'Browning's Don Juan', *Essays in Criticism*, XVI (1966), pp. 416–40. There is a rejoinder to Mrs Melchiori's article in *Essays in Criticism*, XVII (1967), pp. 244–55.

34. The details of the case are to be found in DeVane, *Handbook*, pp. 371–3.

35. References are to the first edition by line-number and page.

36. Cf. Bk. II, 455–461, p. 99.

37. This criticism persisted, and still persists. E.g. F. Mary Wilson, *A Primer on Browning* (London, 1891): 'More especially in *Red Cotton Night-Cap Country* Browning's passion for strange backwaters of character takes him among that which is morally ugly and even worthless.' (p. 48); Griffin and Minchin, *Life*: 'The sketch of Milsand is . . . the sole relief in a desert of moral ugliness.' (p. 252); S. C. Chew in *A Literary History of England* ed. A. C. Baugh (London, 1950): 'The uncouth title is as repellent as the sordid narrative.' (p. 1396); DeVane, *Handbook*: '[The poem] is built upon an ugly and sordid piece of history . . . No great characters emerge, and we are left with the vulgar, contemporary story and the figures of a diseased man and a most ordinary woman for hero and heroine.' (p. 374); John M. Hitner, 'Browning's Grotesque Period', *VP*, IV (1965), pp. 1–13: 'Only a confirmed Browningite could find pleasure in his next poem, *Red Cotton Night-Cap Country*.'

38. The connection seems to me so tenuous as to be almost invisible, but see DeVane, *Handbook*, pp. 389–90: Browning uses the name 'Orton' in the poem (809).

39. References are to the first edition by line-number and page.

40. Here (108) invoked not as a theologian but as the author of a number of mathematical textbooks.

41. *Letters of A. C. Swinburne*, ed. Gosse and Wise (1918), I, pp. 246–7. Cook (*Commentary*, pp. 236–7) points out that Swinburne wrote of Book XI ('Guido') of *The Ring and the Book* as a 'model of intense and punctilious realism . . . so triumphant a thing that on its own ground it can be matched by no poet; to match it we

must look back to Balzac.' ('Notes on the Text of Shelley', *Fortnightly Review*, 1 May 1869.)

42. Letter of 8 February 1847 to Miss Mitford (*Letters of E. B. Browning*, ed. Kenyon (London, 1897) I, pp. 318–19.)
43. Landis and Freeman, p. 248.
44. *Life and Letters*, p. 363.
45. Letter of 13 May 1861, McAleer, *Dearest Isa*, pp. 76–78.
46. ib., p. 244.
47. ib., p. 295. In 1863 Browning had written to Miss Blagden about his 'continuing passion' for *Madame Bovary* and his 'immense disappointment' with *Salammbô*. (ib., p. 173.)
48. ib. p. 266.
49. Letter of 19 August 1867 to Miss Blagden, ib. pp. 281–2.
50. E.g. Hood/Wise, p. 91, where Browning prefers Trollope's unpretentious realism to the sensationalism of Miss Braddon.
51. Cf. 'The Long Poem in the Age of Wordsworth' in *Oxford Lectures on Poetry* (1909).
52. *Handbook*, p. 422.
53. See Hoxie N. Fairchild, '*La Saisiaz* and *The Nineteenth Century*', *MP*, XLVIII (1950), pp. 104–11.
54. DeVane, *Parleyings*.
55. Letters of 2 September 1864 to Julia Wedgwood, (Curle, pp. 75–77); the passage is of great interest.
56. Notably by Mario Praz, *The Hero in Eclipse in Victorian Fiction* (London, 1956).
57. See Hugh Sykes Davies, *Browning and the Modern Novel* (The St John's College Cambridge Lecture, 1961–2, University of Hull Publications, 1962).
58. Preface to the New York edition of *The Golden Bowl* (1909).
59. David Daiches, *A Critical History of English Literature*, II, p. 1007.
60. John Press, *The Chequer'd Shade* (Oxford, 1958), p. 115.
61. *Life*, p. 129 and p. 105.

Chapter 12

1. *Letters to Clough* ed. H. F. Lowry (1932), p. 156, p. 97.
2. For a full discussion of this important document see Sidney M. B. Coulling, 'Matthew Arnold's 1853 Preface', *VS*, VII (1964), pp. 233–63. The Preface is reprinted with extremely helpful annotations in *Complete Prose Works of Matthew Arnold* ed. R. H. Super (1960), I, pp. 1–15, and in *Poems of Matthew Arnold* ed. Kenneth Allott, Longmans Annotated English Poets (1965), pp. 589–607.
3. 28 October 1852.

4. Cf. *The Scholar-Gipsy*, lines 182–191.

5. Browning not only makes minor changes in punctuation but stops his quotation in mid-sentence. The original runs: '. . . not a sentiment capriciously thrown in: stroke upon stroke, the drama proceeded . . .'

6. It is worth noting that the play is described on the title page as 'Transcribed by Robert Browning'.

7. If Browning had read Arnold's various lectures on the translation of Homer (1861–2) he might have remembered that Arnold had already made it quite clear in his remarks on Francis Newman that he did not expect *every* literal translation to recapture the full quality of the original. As he says, the question is not whether we get full change for our Greek, but whether we get it in gold or in copper.

8. *Browning* (EML), Ch. VII, pp. 163–4, p. 167.

9. *English Poetic Theory 1825–1865* (Princeton, 1950), p. 169.

10. 12 February 1853 (Lowry, p. 128).

11. 30 November 1853 (Lowry, p. 146).

12. For details see *Prose Works* ed. R. H. Super, I, pp. 224–5. Arnold was possibly influenced also by Clough's review of the *Poems* in the *North American Review* of July 1853, especially perhaps by the following sentence: 'Not by turning and twisting his eyes, in the hope of seeing things as Homer, Sophocles, Virgil, or Milton saw them; but by seeing them, by accepting them as he sees them, and faithfully depicting accordingly, will he attain the object he desires.' See also S. M. B. Coulling, *VS*, VII (1964), pp. 254–6.

13. Russell, II, p. 9.

14. Arnold refers to it in his prefatory remarks to the printed version of 'On the Modern Element in Literature'.

15. 'A French Friend of Browning's – Joseph Milsand', *Scribner's*, XX (1896), pp. 108–20.

16. DeVane and Knickerbocker, p. 54.

17. 'La Poésie Anglaise depuis Byron: II – Browning', *Revue des Deux Mondes*, n.s. XI (1851), pp. 661–89. The first article of the series had been on Tennyson: the third dealt with Mrs Browning among others.

18. 'La Poésie Expressive et Dramatique en Angleterre', *Revue Contemporaine*, XXVII (1856), pp. 511–46.

19. 'Wordsworth, Tennyson, and Browning; or Pure, Ornate, and Grotesque Art in English Poetry', *National Review*, XIX (n.s. I) 1864, pp. 27–67. The article is an extended review of *Dramatis Personae* and Tennyson's *Enoch Arden* volume.

20. Edinburgh (1904), III, p. 543.

21. 'Mr Browning's New Poem', *Tinsley's Magazine*, III (1869), pp. 665–74. The review is signed 'W.B.': although some of the opinions expressed in the review do not sit very happily with critical ideas which Bagehot has expressed elsewhere I agree with the tentative attribution to Bagehot in the Cornell *Bibliography*. Consistency is not a characteristic of Bagehot in literary matters.

22. *William Wetmore Story and his Friends*, 2 vols., Boston, 1903.

23. Letter of 30 January 1873; reprinted in *Italian Hours* (1909), p. 207.

24. 'The Novel in *The Ring and the Book*', *Quarterly*, p. 79. See note 26.

25. 'On a Drama of Mr Browning', *The Nation* (New York), XXII (1876), pp. 49–50.

26. Originally delivered before the Academic Committee of the Royal Society of Literature in commemoration of the centenary of Robert Browning 7 May 1912. Reprinted in *Transactions of the R.S.L.*, 2nd series XXXI, Pt. IV (1912). Revised text in *Quarterly Review*, CCXVII (1912), pp. 68–87. The later text is given in *Notes on Novelists*. I quote from the *Quarterly*.

27. Curle, pp. 75–77.

28. An exception should be made for Percy Lubbock's article in the *Quarterly Review*, CCXVII (1912), pp. 437–57, which is a mine of intelligent and perceptive judgements.

29. First published unsigned in *The Speaker*, I (1890), pp. 10–12; reprinted in *Essays in London and Elsewhere* (1893) and *English Hours* (1905).

30. Hugh Sykes Davies in *Browning and the Modern Novel* (The St John's College, Cambridge, Lecture, 1961–2, University of Hull Publications, 1962) observes, 'He [James] might, indeed, not ineptly have adapted Wordsworth's notable phrase to the occasion, and said that Browning had done something to create the taste by which the modern novel could be enjoyed.' (p. 11)

31. It will be remembered that James objected to Tennyson as being 'unTennysonian'.

32. 'Santayana on Robert Browning: A Pessimist Criticism', *Poet-Lore*, XIII (1901), pp. 97–111.

33. *Undercurrents of Influence in English Romantic Poetry* (Cambridge, Mass., 1934), pp. 323–50.

34. 'Robert Browning: A Modern Appraisal', *Tennessee Studies in Literature*, IV (1959), pp. 1–12.

35. 'Understanding, Imagination, and Mysticism'; *Interpretations* (New York, 1900), p. 14.

36. *Interpretations*, Preface p. v.

37. For criticism on similar lines of Santayana's ideas of Shakespearean tragedy see F. R. Leavis, *The Common Pursuit* (London, 1952) at the beginning of the essay called 'Tragedy and the "Medium" '.

38. Note that the quotation is wrongly punctuated and contains a verbal error – 'follies' for 'glories'.

39. See Elmer Edgar Stoll, 'Browning's *In a Balcony*', in *From Shakespeare to Joyce* (1944), pp. 328–38.

40. *Essays in Literary Criticism of George Santayana*, edited by Irving Singer (New York, 1956), pp. xxiv–xxv.

Chapter 13

1. Hood/Wise, 1881:11, p. 202. I can find no confirmation elsewhere of Fontenelle's interest in Habbakuk: perhaps Browning had in mind La Fontaine's remark, 'Avez-vous lu Baruch?'

2. Hood/Wise, 1882:9, p. 212. Cf. Browning's remark to Robert Sidney, 'It's really very kind of them to bother about me, and I wouldn't have you suppose that I'm not grateful to all these strangers who want to explain me – but really I'm not sure that I'm worth all this trouble.' ('Some Browning Memories', *Saturday Review*, CXIII (1912), pp. 584–5.)

3. See letters to J. Dykes Campbell, the secretary, 15 and 18 March 1884, Hood/Wise, 1884:2 and 3, pp. 227–8.

4. *Life and Letters*, Ch. XIX, p. 329, p. 331.

5. *Op. cit.*, p. 332.

6. For all my information about Shaw and the Browning Society I am indebted to Donald Smalley's entertaining article 'Mephistopheles at the Conventicle', *The Saturday Review of Literature*, XXVII (No. 30, 22 July 1944), pp. 13–15. More information about the Browning Society is to be found in William S. Peterson, 'Outram *v* Furnivall'. *Bulletin of New York Public Library*, LXXI (1967), pp. 93–104. See also Mr. Peterson's forthcoming book, *Interrogating the Oracle*.

7. *Op. cit.*, p. 590.

8. Paper read 25 May 1883. Reprinted in *Browning Society Papers* IV; also in *Browning Studies*, edited by E. Berdoe (London, 1895), pp. 130–42.

9. Introduction, p. xi.

10. The sort of thing I have in mind is the helpful little volume of *Notes* (1897) edited by Alex Hill for the National Home-Reading Union.

11. In *The Infinite Moment*.

12. Second edition, edited by F. E. Faverty (Harvard U.P. 1968). The chapter on Browning is contributed by Park Honan.

13. *Browning: How to Know Him* (1915, enlarged ed. 1932) by William Lyon Phelps shows something of what might be done in this direction.

14. L. N. Broughton and B. F. Stelter, *A Concordance to the Poems of Robert Browning* (New York, 1924).

15. L. N. Broughton, C. S. Northup, and R. Pearsall, *Robert Browning: A Bibliography, 1830–1950* (Cornell U.P., 1953).

16. There are two collections of critical essays on Browning, which provide a convenient way of sampling the best work in the field – *The Browning Critics*, edited by Boyd Litzinger and K. L. Knickerbocker (U. of Kentucky Press, 1965), and *Robert Browning: A Collection of Critical Essays*, edited by Philip Drew (Methuen, 1966). Each has an introduction in which the questions here considered are discussed in some detail.

17. E.g. R. D. Altick on *A Grammarian's Funeral* (*SEL*, III (1963), pp. 449–60), on *Master Hugues* (*VP*, III (1964), pp. 1–7), on *Two in the Campagna* (*Papers in Language and Literature*, III (1966), pp. 75–80); Isobel Armstrong on *Mr Sludge* (*VP*, II (1964), pp. 1–9); William Cadbury on *Love Among the Ruins* (*UTQ*, XXXIV (1964), pp. 49–67); Roma A. King on *Cleon* (*Victorian Newsletter* No. 20 (Fall 1961), pp. 22–25); Robert Langbaum on the *Parleyings* and *Balaustion* (*PMLA*, LXXXI (1966), pp. 575–84); R. E. Palmer on *Bishop Blougram* (*MP*, LVIII (1960), pp. 108–18; F. E. L. Priestley on *La Saisiaz* (*UTQ*, XXV (1955), pp. 47–59), on *Paracelsus* (*UTQ*, XXXIV (1964), pp. 68–81); W. O. Raymond on *The Statue and the Bust* (*UTQ*, XXVIII (1959), pp. 233–49); C. C. Watkins on *Fifine* (*PMLA*, LXXIV (1959), pp. 426–37). See also Ch. 5, note 10, p. 444.

18. *From Dickens to Hardy*, ed. Boris Ford (Harmondsworth, 1958).

19. First published in 1932; new edition in 1950.

20. F. R. Leavis, 'The Responsible Critic', *Scrutiny*, XIX (1953), p. 181.

21. R. G. Cox, 'Victorian Criticism of Poetry: The Minority Tradition', *Scrutiny*, XVIII (1951), p. 3. Those who are puzzled that Santayana's unconsidered observations on Browning are so widely accepted as authoritative and who are interested in charting the channels by which they have spread will find some relevant material in 'The Critical Writings of George Santayana' (*Scrutiny*, IV (1936), pp. 278–95) by Q. D. Leavis. In the course of an adulatory survey of Santayana's criticism Mrs Leavis singles out the essay on 'The Poetry of Barbarism' and refers to it in the following

terms: 'We have the best possible instance of the inter-relation this critic's work exhibits between criticism of the "philosophy" and criticism of the "poetry" '; '. . . admirable and closely-argued . . .'; 'It must evidently be a rarely talented mind that can be as fine, sure and original a critic in a foreign language'; '. . . the justice of the case presented there cannot but be admitted when once made.'

22. F. R. Leavis, 'Valedictory', *Scrutiny*, XIX (1953), p. 256.
23. The Editors, *Poet-Lore*, III (1891), p. 647.

INDEX

(Numerals in bold type indicate the more important entries)